# Merchants and Society in Modern China

T0298690

In ancient China, as the lowermost class in the social hierarchy, merchants were viewed as greedy and immoral, commanding little respect. But since the sixteenth century, when China entered modern times with the sprout of capitalism, merchants have become a strong force to transform the ancient society.

By absorbing methods of anthropology, psychology, geography, and economics, as well as cultural and genealogical studies, this book explores the development and rise of the merchant in modern China. To start with, it examines the golden times of the merchant and the dilemmas facing them in the two-millennia-long traditional society where the "pro-agriculture and anti-commerce" policy was implemented. With the economic development, merchant groups gradually came into being and formed a vibrant social class in the modern era. Major merchant groups, their psychological integration, and the interaction between merchants and capitalism in China are specifically studied. Also, merchants' role in the communal life is analyzed, including their contribution to the making and expansion of modern communities, which led to China's social transformation.

With a multifaceted description of Chinese merchants whose development interweaves with the transformation of the ancient country, this book will appeal to scholars and students in economics, history, sociology, and cultural studies. Readers interested in Chinese culture and social history will also be attracted by it.

**Tang Lixing** is professor in the College of Humanities and Communications, Shanghai Normal University. His research focuses on Chinese social and business history.

# China Perspectives

For more information, please visit www.routledge.com/series/CPH

The *China Perspectives* series focuses on translating and publishing works by leading Chinese scholars, writing about both global topics and China-related themes. It covers Humanities & Social Sciences, Education, Media and Psychology, as well as many interdisciplinary themes.

This is the first time any of these books have been published in English for international readers. The series aims to put forward a Chinese perspective, give insights into cutting-edge academic thinking in China, and inspire researchers globally.

# Merchants and Society in Modern China

Rise of Merchant Groups

**Tang Lixing**

Routledge
Taylor & Francis Group

LONDON AND NEW YORK

This book is published with financial support from the Chinese Fund for the Humanities and Social Sciences

First published 2018 by Routledge

2 Park Square, Milton Park, Abingdon, Oxfordshire OX14 4RN
52 Vanderbilt Avenue, New York, NY 10017

*Routledge is an imprint of the Taylor & Francis Group, an informa business*

First issued in paperback 2020

*British Library Cataloguing-in-Publication Data*
A catalogue record for this book is available from the British Library

*Library of Congress Cataloging-in-Publication Data*
A catalog record for this title has been requested

ISBN: 978-1-138-08912-9 (hbk)
ISBN: 978-0-367-53680-0 (pbk)

Typeset in Times New Roman
by Apex CoVantage, LLC

# Contents

# Illustrations

**Figure**

**Tables**

# Preface

In the early 1980s, I began to work on a project of collecting, organizing, and studying archival materials about Huizhou merchants. It took me ten years before I completed this book in the early 1990s. My choice of this topic was directly related to China's ongoing social transformation. After the policy of opening and reform was implemented to bring order out of chaos, the government ruled that even in socialism, market economy was desired. Thus, how could we position the merchant, the protagonist of market economy? How could the merchant, the lowest of the four classes, keep themselves away from predicaments they suffered during the traditional times? How could the merchant maintain independent subjectivity without being dependent on or being incorporated into the bureaucracy? My exploration of the interactions between the merchant and China's modern society testifies to Benedetto Croce's argument, "All history is contemporary history."

My study on the merchant in China's modern society was also intimately related to my own thinking, personal interests, and experiences. The 1980s is a decade to remember, as people in China were brought out of the shadows of the Cultural Revolution, removed fetters from the mind, and entered into an era of enlightenment. The circle of historians engaged in profound discussions about topics such as the long duration of China's feudal society, the mechanism of historical development, and the basic pattern of development in modern Chinese society. Their magnitude and profundity were unprecedented since 1949. The circle of historians collectively reflected upon whether the calamitous Cultural Revolution that befell China took place accidentally or was structurally inevitable in China. Is class struggle the only mechanism of historical development? Could the three high tides of revolution, all of which centered on class struggle, cover every aspect of the development of modern society? The raising of such questions itself was of great significance in enlightenment. I was particularly interested in them. Therefore, I wrote articles such as "On Causes of the Slow Development of the Sprout of Capitalism in Ming and Qing" (*Lun Ming Qing ziben zhuyi mengya huanman fazhan de yuanyin*), "On Surplus Labor in China's Feudal Society – Also on the Long Duration of China's Feudal Society" (*Shilun Zhongguo fengjian shehui de shengyu laodong – jianlun Zhongguo fengjian shehui changqi yanxu de yuanyin*), "A Humble Opinion of Social and Economic Reforms in Late

Qing" (*Qingji shehui jingji gaige chuyi*), and "On the Impact of Feudal Rulers' Economic Policies on Social Development" (*Lun fengjian tongzhizhe de jingji zhengci dui shehui fazhan de yingxiang*) to propose my macroscopical thinking on social transformations in China. I have been particularly impressed by the second National Symposium of Historical Theories whose emphasis was methodology of historical study. In the meeting, most participants reached a consensus on the necessity of having shared theories and methodologies for historians. That is, dialectical materialism and historical materialism were common theories and methodologies of all social scientists, and the study of history should also be under their guidance. However, historical materialism and dialectical materialism were not supposed to replace theories and methodologies unique to history. As a sophisticated discipline, history deserved its own theories and methodologies. This argument opened up a new territory and helped to clarify confusions for the further development of history in the following three decades. After that, Western historical theories and methodologies were massively introduced to greatly internationalize and modernize historical studies in China. The symposium concluded that the significance of this meeting did not lay in how many new methodologies had been discussed but a confirmation of a transition from unitary to multiple theories and methodologies of historical studies, and such a significance would be verified in the future. During the meeting, I gave a talk, "A New Exploration of Some Issues of Historical Theories from the Angle of System Theory" (*Cong xitonglun de jiaodu chongxin tantao jige shixue lilun wenti*), to systematically elaborate on my views on some issues of theory. This essay was included in the conference proceeding, which turned out to be the first *Essays on Theories and Methodologies of Historical Studies* (*Lishi yanjiu fangfa lunji*) (Shijiazhuang: Hebei renmin chubanshe, 1987) in China. Since 1988, I became involved in activities of the Society of Chinese Social History. Its second annual meeting held by Nanjing University focused on the issue of the intellectual. A heated debate was conducted regarding the inherent quality of the intellectual. Most scholars reached a consensus that aside from being knowledgeable, intellectuals must be ahead of the times and assume the role as the guide in their thinking and scholarship, which meant that they would have to conflict with the realities. Therefore, intellectuals always kept moving forward in an environment where the ideal and the reality painfully entangled. After that, I have attended many academic conference meetings but could rarely see a scholarly atmosphere like that. It was during that meeting that Professor Cai Shaoqing, the editor of the "Series of Chinese Social History," invited me to write a book about the merchant class in Chinese history. The 1980s is a decade when my scholarship began to take off. As I was conducting studies on merchants, I enhanced the depth and breadth of my research and improve my awareness and visions to allow me to look forward. Theories and mythologies, especially those of social history, helped me construct a research platform to study the macro history. On such a platform, I was able to engage in historical studies at the micro- and meso-levels. That was the uniqueness of my research and embodied my interests and experiences, all of which left a deep imprint on my maiden work.

History is an endless dialog between the present and the past. The merchant class permeates in every corner of social life. In the trend of social reform, the story of the merchant keeps unfolding, reflecting the maturity of civilization and the change of time. After many years, I am still staying in the territory of research that this book opened up to engage in dialogs with the merchant class. Those dialogs have been included in works such as *Society of the Patriarchal Clan in Huizhou (Huizhou zongzu shehui)* (Heifei: Anhui renmin chubanshe, 2005), *Suzhou and Huizhou: A Comparative Study on the Interactions and Transformations of the Two Regions between the Sixteenth and Twentieth Centuries (Suzhou yu Huizhou: 16 zhi 20 shiji liangdi hudong yu bianqian de bijiao yanjiu)* (Beijing: Shangwu yinshuguan, 2007), and *Continuation and Breaking: the Hyperstable Structure in Rural Huizhou and Social Transformations (Yanxu yu Duanlie: Huizhou xiangcun de chaowending jiegou yu shehui bianqian)* (Beijing: Shangwu yinshuguan, 2015).

With the development of a commodified economy, peasant-workers massively migrate to cities. Issues of agriculture, the countryside, and the peasant grow more severe. *Society of the Patriarchal Clan in Huizhou* focuses on issues of the merchant and self-government in the countryside. Rural society in Huizhou has long gained a reputation as a place where "the Wuling creek seemed to be here." A profound cultural foundation, a strong merchant group, and organizations of patriarchal clan that lasted for a millennium constituted the three factors of a system of social life in a specific region. Among them, Huizhou merchants provided material conditions for clans to live together and for clansmen to receive education and take the Civil Service Exam; organizations of patriarchal clan and the robust inner cohesion were the internal mechanism of a sturdy and competitive Huizhou merchant group. The elevated educational level made the majority of Huizhou merchants Confucian merchants with relative high quality as businessmen. Wealth that Huizhou merchants consistently infused in and the gentry class's cultural power ensured the autonomy, stability, and prosperity of a society of patriarchal clan in rural Huizhou.

The development of a commodified economy leads to a wide difference between the coastal areas and the hinterland. *Suzhou and Huizhou* is a study on the developments and complementarity and difference from the sixteenth to the twentieth centuries between Suzhou, which is situated in the low land in the coastal area, and Huizhou in the mountainous hinterland. Suzhou boasted as the economic center of both the Yangzi Delta and the whole country. The enormously wealthy Huizhou merchants were particularly active in Suzhou and reaped huge profits. Objectively, Huizhou merchants' commercial activities caused social transformations in Suzhou and other places. Yet, merchants' injection of commercial profits into Huizhou consolidated the old order in Huizhou. The interactions between Suzhou and Huizhou proceeded constantly to permeate every aspect of social production and life. They reached even to the core levels of social culture and the ethos of the general population. Communications led to interactions, competitions, and mutual recognition, which was a process that endlessly repeated itself but gradually moved upward. It was because of such a historical process that the two small regions in the Yangzi Delta prospered but maintained their respective directions of social development which demonstrated the pluralism in society of the Yangzi Delta.

When a commodified economy develops, the binary opposition between the city and the countryside grows more intense. There exists a positive correlation between the prosperity of the city and the decline of the countryside. *Breaking and Continuation* indicates the virtuous cycle of three factors in Huizhou, economy, culture, and society. Aside from an internal cycle domestically in Huizhou, there was an external cycle that transcended individual regions. Huizhou merchants prevailed across the country. This was particularly true in the Yangzi Delta, where there was a saying: "a town could not prosper without Huizhou merchants." The internal and external cycles was mutually supported. During the Taiping Rebellion, the internal cycle of Huizhou died, while during the Anti-Japanese War, the external cycle broke. However, once wars ended, the disrupted cycle could soon be restored because of the support of the other cycle, and therefore stability and prosperity could re-emerge in the countryside. This was the hyper-stable structure in rural Huizhou. In the most difficult times during the Anti-Japanese War, self-government in Huizhou was practically unsustainable. However, bolstered by the urban self-government organizations – native-place associations of various Huizhou counties in Shanghai – self-government in the countryside declined but did not perish, showing a tenacious vitality. Based on existing materials, after World War II, a network of culture power dominated by the gentry continued to prevail in rural Huizhou. Traditional self-government in the city ended in the 1950s, after which a new chapter of history unfolded.

Since the publication of the first edition of this book, it has been over two decades. In the process, Chinese society has undergone dramatic transformations, but the dilemma of the merchant remains the same. My dialog with the merchant class will certainly continue. For readers of the English edition of this book, it could be a window through which China's history and reality can be understood. Raymond Aron said, "History is the living people's reconstruction of the lives of the dead for the living people." That makes great sense.

September 30, 2016

# 1 The merchant in traditional society

China's traditional society structurally privileged the peasant and discriminated against the merchant, who was dismissed as the lowest of the four classes. The merchant dwelled on a dilemma of wealth and social standings. Based on different criteria, traditional merchants could be classified into ten categories. In addition, based on their wealth, reputations, and power, they could also be hierarchized into four strata.

## Section one: the merchant and the social structure

### 1 The golden times of the merchant

Commercial activities emerged in China very early. The "Commentary on the Appended Judgments" (*Xici*) of the *Book of Changes* (*Yijing*) stated,

> When Paoxi's clan was gone, the clan of the Devine Farmer appeared. He installed stores in the city and opened markets in the morning to reach people and gather goods under the heaven. After exchanging goods, [people] withdrew [from the markets] and returned to their appropriate places.

In the "Great Treatise" (*Dazhuan*) of the *Book of Documents* (*Shangshu*), it was recorded that Shun once "sold goods in Dunqiu and went now and then to Fuxia" before Yao resigned the throne to him. Thus, Shun was the most famous merchant in the Chinese mythology. Although such tales were created in the distant past and therefore became unverifiable, the fact that "people of the Yin Dynasty valued commerce" is verified because of the excavation of a large number of relics and oracle inscriptions. China boasts of one of the earliest commercial activities in the world, second only to Egypt.

The golden times of the merchant in Chinese history was the era of the Spring and Autumn. The social structure of Western Zhou, which bore resemblance to that of medieval western Europe, heralded this epoch. The feudal system of Western Zhou was conducive to political pluralism in the times of the Spring and Autumn and the Warring States. The nationalization of lands in Western Zhou precluded the rulers from implementing policies to suppress and discriminate against the merchant. Since sales of lands were not permitted, issues such as merchants' seizure of lands and peasants' "quitting agriculture and engaging in trading" did not arise. Based on the social stratification specified in the *Rites of Zhou* (*Zhouli*), the merchant enjoyed a higher status than the peasant. It was stated in the *Rites of Zhou* that

> kings and dukes sit and pontificate; literati rise and take action; artisans examine the curvature and straightness of five materials to process them and enable the people to know how to use them; merchants keep valuable goods from all directions circulating for people to purchase; farmers use physical force to increase the value of lands; female workers weave silk and hemp to make [clothing].

However, the self-sufficiency nature of the "well-field" system (*jintianzhi*) significantly limited the demands for goods in society, while the system of government and business, which was derived from the feudal system, adversely affected the development of free merchants.

When King Ping of Zhou relocated eastward to Luoyi and the Zhou Dynasty was in decline, the system that "all artisans and merchants supplied the government" (*gongshang shiguan*) came to an end. The new political pluralism compelled the Zhou government and rulers of various feudal states to understand the connection between national strength and commerce. They realized, "Society obviously must have farmers before it can eat; foresters, fishermen, miners, etc., before it can make use of natural resources; craftsmen before it can have manufactured goods; and merchants before they can be distributed."

> These four classes are the source of the people's clothing and food. When the source is large, there will be plenty for everyone, but when the source is small, there will be scarcity. On the one hand, the state will be enriched, and on the other hand, powerful families will be enriched.

"If the merchants do not produce, then the three precious things will not circulate."[1] Therefore, all states implemented pro-commerce policies to recruit merchants. The first hegemon in the Spring and Autumn period, Duke Huan of Qi, relied on commerce to make the state affluent and "allied with various feudal lords for nine times to dominate [the area] under the heaven." Duke Huan appointed Guan Zhong, who was initially a merchant, as the prime minister. In his 40-year tenure, Guan Zhong promoted aggressive trades between Qi and other feudal states. He once enacted a regulation to "check but not to levy [taxes on goods] in strategic passes and markets." He thereby adopted the measure of tax exemption to encourage foreign merchants to ship materials of military supplies, such as animal skins, bones, strings, horns, bamboo arrows, feather, ivory, and leather, which the Qi State needed, to Qi. Meanwhile, fish, salt, and manufactured goods that Qi produced were shipped to other states. Guan Zhong also gave merchants favorable treatment. Not only was a station set up every 30*li* to supply food to itinerant merchants, "guesthouses were also established for merchants from other feudal states" in Linzi, Qi's capital, to offer food so that "merchants under heaven streamed into Qi like flowing water."[2] In his meetings with allies, Duke Huan of Qi did not fail to maintain his pro-merchant stance by urging various feudal states "not to forget traveling merchants" and demanding lowered tariffs.[3] The proposal certainly served Qi's commercial interests. During the Spring and Autumn era, rulers of the Zheng State also placed a great emphasis on commerce. Zheng, as a small state, was situated in a traffic hub and among numerous great feudal states. In the west, there was the Qin State, while in the east there was the Qi State. It was thus an area of strategic importance for states such as Jin, Chu, Qi, and Qin for their entry into the Central Plain (*Zhongyuan*) and a must-go place for merchants. The Zheng State made use of its special geographic location to deal with various feudal states in order to intensify the exchange of commodities among different states to protect itself. A balance was thus achieved to create a situation that no one could dominate it exclusively. Based on the story of "Xian Gao's rewarding Qin's troops with material gifts," we understand Zheng merchants' activism in various states. Commodities from all states needed to be transshipped and redistributed through Zheng so that Zheng, though sandwiched between great states, enjoyed a special status as a thriving place. Meanwhile, the passing of commodities and the resultant tax revenues strengthened the Zheng State. Because the fortunes of the state and the merchant were closely tied to each other, the Zheng State placed great emphasis on protecting the merchant's interests. In 522 BC, the envoy from the Jin State, Han Qi, implored the king of the Zheng State to solicit from a Zheng merchant a jade bracelet in order match his own. Zichan, regent of the Zheng State, told Han Qi,

> Our late Duke Huan and merchants were all from Zhou in the past. [They] worked together to clear the lands with moxa to eliminate crown daisy chrysanthemum, pigweed, and bean leaves, allowing them to co-exist with each other. We have an oath of alliance for generations so that we can trust each other. [The oath] states, "You don't betray me, and I don't do business with you by coercion. I don't solicit [goods] by force, and you don't have to inform me of lucrative businesses and treasury goods."[We] rely on the oath so that we maintain our security until today. Now, your highness kindly visit my country, but ask me to snatch [the bracelet] away from the merchant. You are instructing me to breach the oath. I beg to disagree.[4]

Zichan highlighted an agreement reached by the Zheng State and merchants two centuries before. As long as merchants did not betray the state, the state would not purchase or grab merchants' goods by force or interfere with merchants' commercial activities. Therefore, Zichan made it clear that he would not violate the oath to solicit the jade bracelet from the merchant. Although it was a minor incident, it indicated Zheng's seriousness in protecting merchants' interests.

In the late Spring and Autumn and Warring States, iron tools were more extensively used in farming, while the "well-field system" collapsed. The rising feudal landlord economy gradually replaced the slavery one. The rapid growth of social productivity paved the way for the development of a commodified economy. Under landlord economy, the basic of productive unit was small peasant households. Small households, which usually featured five members, could not achieve self-sufficiency. They had to depend on commodity exchange to acquire goods they could not produce by themselves, such as salt, iron, liquor, and copper. Peasants exchanged for goods they needed, and therefore had to sell some of their own products. They not only sold surplus goods but also goods of daily necessity. Products used for exchange were in small amount for individual households. Yet, the amount was enormous in aggregation. That set a stage for a number of great merchants who "had huge amounts of money, excellent abilities to trade, and great social skills." The most famous merchants during the Spring and Autumn period were Fan Li, Zi Gong, Yi Dun, Guo Zong, and Bai Gui. Fan Li was a native of the Chu State in the late Spring and Autumn times. After he assisted Gou Jian, king of Yue, in overthrowing the Wu State and restore the Yue State, Fan Li gave up office and engaged in business. He settled down in Taoyi (today's Dingtao of Shandong Province), then a transportation center. He called himself as "Lord Zhu" (*Zhu gong*). "[He] stored away goods, looking for a profitable time to sell, and not making demands upon others." "In the course of nineteen years, [Lord Zhu] three times accumulated fortunes of a thousand catties of gold."[5]Later, "Lord Taozhu" (*Taozhu gong*) became an alternative term to the rich merchant. Zi Gong's surname was Duanmu and given name Ci. Hailing from the State of Wei in the late Spring and Autumn times, he was Confucius's student. After graduation, he was unwilling to take office in the government but chose to engage in trade. His decision gained support from Confucius. "Zi Gong did not follow orders [from the government], but went on to do business. [He was able to] guess correctly every time."[6]When Confucius toured various states, Zi Gong gave him full financial support. As Sima Qian commented, "It was due to Zi Gong's efforts that Confucius's fame was spread over the empire. Is this not what we mean when we say that a man who wields power may win greater and greater eminence?"[7] In addition, Zi Gong

> rode about with a team of four horses attended by a mounted retinue, bearing gifts of bundles of silk to be presented to the feudal lords, and whatever state he visited the ruler never failed to descend into the courtyard and greet him as an equal.[8]

Yi Dun was originally "a poor person in the Lu State" during the Warring States period. At an early stage, he "raised cattle massively in the area south of Yishi. After a decade, [he earned] countless revenues. [Therefore,] his wealth was comparable with that of kings and dukes, making him well known under the heaven."[9] Later, he engaged in the production and marketing of lake salt in Hedong and thereby became extremely rich. Guo Zong, a great entrepreneur engaging in iron smelting in Handan of the Zhao State during the Warring States times. "[He] made a business of smelting iron, and their wealth equaled that of the ruler of a kingdom."[10]Bai Gui, hailing from the Zhou State, once served as the prime minister of the Wei State but later took office in the Qin State. In the process, he engaged in the trade of agricultural products. He was a great merchant excelling in business skills.

All those merchants were specialized in forecasting price fluctuations and making profits from price differences between supply and demand of goods. The wide circulation of metal currencies during the Warring States period allowed merchants to manipulate commodity prices more easily. Their experiences in commercial activities enabled them to create a "learning of economics" (*zhisheng zhixue*). Fan Li and Ji Ran proposed a business strategy of hoarding goods awaiting the time when goods was in short supply – namely, "Understanding what people use in order to know the [circulation] of commodities, and understanding the battle in order to prepare for war materials." They also proposed "[As the goods were] extremely expensive, the price would go down to reach the lowest; while the price was extremely low, [the goods would revalue and become] as precious as pearls and jades."[11] Bai Gui paid attention to the forecasting of market situation. He stressed "observing the change of time" and "reacting quickly in the right time" to take the initiative of transactions. He emphasized the dialectical relationship between "taking" and "giving" by proposing a principle of business: "[When] others abandon, I take; when others take, I give away."[12] He also put a premium on elevating merchants' qualities by arguing that a good merchant should possess four characters – wisdom, bravery, benevolence, and strength. Fan Li and Bai Gui were worshipped in later generations as the ancestors of economics. Their economic theories were hailed as authoritative for thousands of years.

During the late Warring States times, great merchants became even more active. Rich and powerful merchants won respect of state leaders because of their enormous wealth. Some merchants made a fortune because of their political speculations, among whom Lü Buwei was a telling example. A conversation between Lü Buwei and his father was recorded in *Zhanguo ce* (*Strategies of the Warring States*):

> [Buwei] asked his father, "What is the profit margin of farming?"[His father] replied, "Tenfold."[Buwei asked,] "What is the [profit] margin of [engaging in the business of] pearls and jades?"[His father] replied, "One hundred fold."[Buwei asked,] "What is the [profit] margin of appointing a monarch and founding a state?"[His father] replied, "Countless." Buwei said, "Today, if [one] industriously works on farming, [he] can't be well-fed and warmly clothed. [If one] helps to appoint a monarch and found a state, the later generations would benefit [from the cause]. I am willing to do it."

This wealthy merchant expended thousands of ounces of gold to help Zichu, the Qin prince in distress and the hostage in the Zhao State. Later, Zichu ascended the throne of the Qin State and appointed Lü Buwei as the prime minister. He also made Lü Marquis of Wenxin with a fief of 100,000 households in Luoyang of Henan.

The periods of Spring and Autumn and Warring States were the golden times of the merchant. However, as soon as merchants pocketed vast social wealth, their clashes with peasants intensified. Consequently, their conflicts with upstarting landlords were aggravated. The seeds of suppressing and devaluing the merchant in the future were thus sown.

## 2   The merchant's dilemma

After the Qin unification, the barriers of inter-state boundaries and local passes were dismantled and traffic obstacles were thereby removed. Furthermore, Emperor Qin Shi Huang repaired highways and unified currencies and measurements, all of which were undoubtedly beneficial to the circulation of commodities. Under a unified regime, had the development of commodified economy maintained the momentum as in the Spring and Autumn and Warring States periods, social and economic history in China would have been entirely different. However, in the two-millennia-long traditional society, ever since Qin Shi Huang's times, all unified autocratic regimes seemed to have an unresolvable "Oedipus complex" when implementing a "pro-agriculture and anti-commerce" policy. In his well-known "Stone Inscription of Langya" (*Langya keshi*), Qin Shi Huang deeply carved eight characters, "*Shang Nong Chu Mo, Qian Shou Shi Fu*" (Prioritizing farming and getting rid of trivial matters [so that] commoners would be rich), making a statement that repressing commerce was the basic state policy. He once viewed merchants and their descendants as criminals and sentenced them to exile to the frontiers to be garrison soldiers. He also relocated rich and influential merchants to Xianyang and Bashu. The Qin Empire was short-lived. Therefore, its anti-commerce policy was not systematically carried out. The systemization of the anti-commerce policy was completed in the times of Emperor Wu of the Han Dynasty.

After Liu Bang unified China, he "ordered that merchants were not allowed to be clothed in silk and take carriages. [He] surcharged rents and taxes to beset and humiliate them." He also mandated that descendants of businessmen "were not permitted to pursue careers of government officials,"[13] to perpetuate the state policy of suppressing the merchant. Because of the longtime unrest in the late Qin, nevertheless, economy was devastated so severely that "people had no shelter, the emperor could not drink fine wines, and generals and minsters had to take oxen-driven carts."[14] Rulers in early Han were compelled to implement a laissez-faire policy known as *wu wei er zhi* (governing by noninterference) to "relax regulations against the merchant."[15] Hence, the merchant gained an opportunity to fully develop themselves under a unified regime. *Records of the Grand Historian* (*Shiji*) stated,

> With the rise of the Han Dynasty, the state was unified. All passes were opened and bans on [developing] mountains and waters were lifted. Therefore, rich and influential merchants traveled all over the country. All goods were circulated without impediment. [Everyone] got what he needed.

Up to the times of Emperor Wen of the Han Dynasty, all strategic passes were abolished and no tariff was imposed. The improvement of conditions of commercial activities enormously raised commercial profits. Sima Qian posited, "For a poor [person] who wishes to make a fortune, [he] would rather [engage in] industry than agriculture; commerce rather than industry; leaning against the door [to sell goods] rather than embroidering and coloring [fabrics]."Thus, more people engaged in trade to reap profits. Great merchants at that time included salt merchants, iron merchants, usurers, transporters, and so forth. The successful ones were as wealthy as rulers and as happy as kings and marquises. They were nicknamed *sufeng*. Even those who sold trivial goods such as rice water and dried meat could acquire wealth. Merchants' rise in power not only shocked people of other classes but also threatened and unsettled the rulers. In Emperor Wu's reign, the state restored its power and consolidated its unity. Therefore, actions were taken to suppress the merchant.

Why would a unified autocratic regime proceed to suppress and devalue the merchant? This resulted from the structure of a traditional society. A unified autocratic regime was usually built upon a small peasant economy. Only with a small peasant economy could such regimes be maintained. As noted earlier, the small peasant economy under the landlord system did not exclude commodified economy but had low tolerance for it. As commodified economy reached a certain limit, commerce would contribute to the disintegration of the traditional social structure. First of all, it would undermine the stability of small peasant economy under the landlord system. Since Qin and Han, as lands could be freely bought and sold, merchants' annexation of lands posed a serious social problem. Peasants who were stripped of lands and forced into exile led to unpaid land taxes. Therefore, state revenues were affected. Meanwhile, it caused social unrest. Some peasants who left their lands were peasants-made-merchants who "attended to the trivialities and neglected the fundamentals" (*sheben zhumo*). The increase in social mobility did harm to the stability of an agricultural society, in which peasants were content to live in their native lands and loathed to move. Second, merchants' swelling power threatened the unified autocratic regime. In early Han, merchants who "got along with princes and marquises and enjoyed more powers than officials" had already invited deep suspicion from rulers. More seriously, some local princes themselves engaged in trade.

> In Emperor Wen's reign, commoners minted coins, smelt iron, and produced salt. Prince Wu was good at profiting from oceans and waters and Deng Tong from western mountains. The crafty and treacherous got together in the Wu State and people from Qin, Yong, Han, and Shu followed Deng. Coins produced by the Wu State and Deng Tong prevailed in [areas] under the heaven.[16]

Up to the times of Emperor Jing of Han, seven feudal states' rebellion almost resulted in the disintegration of the unified Han Dynasty. On account of this, early

Han politicians all preached the pro-agriculture and anti-commerce policy. Chao Cuo once pointed out that in early Han,

> Great merchants hoard [goods] to double profits, while small merchants peddle goods by hoarding [goods] and manipulating the market. They roam around in the metropolises and take advantage of people urgent situation to sell goods at doubled prices. Therefore, men do not farm and women do not raise silkworms and weave. They are clothed colorfully and eat nothing but meat. They are free from miseries of farmers and workers, but obtain the produces from lands. Because of their wealth, they get along with princes and marquises, and their powers are superior to those of officials. They use their money to compete with each other. When they travel long distance, their garments and the circular covering of their carriages are visible. They take fine carts and ride strong horses. Their shoes and clothes are made in silk. That was how merchants can seize farmers' [lands] and why peasants are forced into exile. Now, the law devalues the merchant, but merchants have been rich and influential. [The law] respects the peasant, but farmers are poverty-stricken. Thus, what society appreciates is what the rulers look down upon. What officials despise is what the law reveres. The high and low are contradictory to each other and their preferences are different. So, it is hard to reach [the goal] of making the state rich and the law stand. Today's task is nothing but to impel people to engage in farming.[17]

Discussions as such were countless in ancient classics. It was Emperor Wu of Han who put it into practice.

Emperor Wu of Han launched attack on the merchant by imposing a tax system known as *suan minqian*. "Shihuo zhi" (Treatise of Food and Currency) of *Book of Han* recorded,

> Various merchants, who gained profits from usury, practices of buying cheap and selling dear, hoarding [goods], and commercial activities, reported their properties and were charged at a tax rate of one *suan* for two thousand *guan*, even though they were not registered as merchants. Artisans who paid rents and engaged in smelting were charged at a tax rate of one *suan* for four thousand *guan*.

This new tax was levied universally on manufacturers and merchants, but it hit the merchants the hardest, because merchants usually kept large amounts of cash as circulating funds. Initially, the government mandated that merchants reported their properties at their will. Several years later, Emperor Wu altered the policy by encouraging people to report merchants to the authorities. "[Charges] were brought forward all over the empire against men who attempted to conceal their wealth from the levy; practically every family of middle means or over found itself under accusation."

> The wealth confiscated from the people as a result of their investigations was calculated in billions of cash, with male and female slaves numbering

in the thousands; the confiscated fields amounted to several hundred *qing* in the larger districts, and over 100 *qing* in the smaller ones, with proportionate number of houses. Practically all the merchants of middling or better means were ruined.[18]

When Emperor Wu cracked down on merchants and deprived them of their properties, he also carried out a policy to ban private trade of iron and salt, both of which had been the commodities in highest demand. "Biography of Merchants" of *Records of the Grand Historian* mentioned four merchants "with properties of tens of thousands" and "as wealthy as rulers": Zhuo, Cheng Zheng, Kong, and Cao Bing. All the four engaged in smelting iron. As the ban was enforced, private capital was excluded from the two most significant industrial and commercial sectors. Emperor Wu, moreover, further developed government-controlled manufactures, which had started in the Zhou and Qin Dynasties. Manufactured goods needed by the imperial family and governmental departments (including the army), ranging from luxury goods to military supplies, were in huge amount. If all such goods had been purchased in the market, it would have been a strong impetus towards the development of industry and commerce. Yet the implementation of the system of government-controlled industry allowed for bypassing the market to meet the demands without making purchase in the market. The ban on private investment in the salt and iron industry and the system of government-controlled industry helped to attain the goals of "expelling rich and large-scale traders" and "the wealthy merchants and large-scale traders [being] deprived of any prospect of making big profits."[19] It was during the times of Emperor Wu that the practice of suppressing merchants peaked.

The pro-agriculture and anti-commerce discourses since the pre-Qin times all indicated that agriculture was the essence and commerce was trivial. Overexpansion of commerce was perceived to have resulted in the loss of rural population and therefore crippling the national strength. Prior to the Qin and Han, however, anti-commerce sentiment existed only in writings and discussions. No serious policies to suppress the merchant were put into practice. It was during the times of Emperor Wu of Han that the country was unified and the national power increased. Therefore, the government carried out anti-commerce policies and systemized them. The anti-commerce policies in late generations were merely additions and deductions based on those in Han. For example, the scope of banning private investments could be expanded and punishments could be elevated. During the Tang dynasty, those who privately sold tea for three times and with an amount exceeding 150 *jin* would be sentenced to death. In the early years of the Later Jin, "those who brought over 10 *jin* unauthorized salt would be executed. Those who burned lime and made salt would be executed regardless of the amounts."[20] In the Later Zhou, "violators who brought 5 *jin* salt or wine would be flogged to death."[21] The Song dynasty ruled in 961, "those who smuggled liquor over 15 *jin* and brought 3 *dou* of wines to cities would be executed."[22] Zhu Yuanzhang, Emperor Taizu of the Ming, even killed his son-in-law who smuggled tea. On other occasions, the economic depredation against merchants frequently occurred. Emperor Suzong of the Tang once enforced a *shuidai* policy on wealthy households in Jiang, Huai, Shu, and Han. That is, "powerful merchants and rich families had their properties confiscated. [The emperor] levied taxes on some merchants at a rate of one fifth of their belongings. This was called *shuaidai*, with which tens of thousands [of cash] was received."[23]In Emperor Dezong's reign, practices such as *jiuzhi* (borrowing by force) and *jieshang* (borrowing from merchants) existed. In the times of Emperor Wanli of the Ming, mine supervisors and tax commissioners viciously plundered the merchant. Furthermore, biases against the merchant were rampant. Following the order issued by Emperor Gaozu of the Han to prohibit descendants of merchants from taking office in government, similar injunctions were enacted in later generations. Emperor Wendi of the Sui mandated in 596 that industrialists and merchants should not be officials.[24]The Tang policy ruled that members of industry and commerce were not allowed to join the army.[25]"According to the edict of promotion and selection, a person was not allowed take office in government if his relatives as close as or closer than cousins, who lived with him, engaged in industry and commerce and if his family was specialized in industry and commerce. His existing rank should be abolished. If the situation altered, his career could resume after three years. If the situation did not change after three years, his rank should be removed, as with the rulings for commoners."[26] Not only industrialists and merchants were forbidden from being officials, officials' relatives, who were as close as or closer than cousins and lived with them, would also be prohibited from engaging in industry and business. Zhu Yuanzhang

> redoubled his effort to put emphasis on the essence [agriculture] and destroying the trivial [commerce] by issuing an order to let peasants to wear clothing made in fine yarn and silk and to stipulate that merchants could wear only cloth. In a peasant family, as long as one member was a merchant, no one was allowed to wear clothing in fine yarn.[27]

Pro-agriculture and anti-commerce discourse and practice lingered in traditional society in China. However, the "Oedipus complex" that haunted all unified autocratic regimes – namely, their policies to suppress merchants and advocate farmers – relaxed at times. This was because there existed some fractures in history, although national unity remained a main trend in a two-millennium-long traditional society. Weak monarchs in small countries tried to suppress the merchant but had no power to do so. They counted on commerce to replenish the supply, strengthen the nation, and engage in "international" competitions. During the Three Kingdoms period, rulers of all the states implemented pro-business policies. For example, Emperor Wen of the Wei mandated,

> Passes are [set up] to facilitate trade, and imperial gardens are [maintained for the purpose of] disaster relief. Levying high taxes is not to benefit the people. The ban on building imperial gardens is lifted and tariffs are lowered to ten percent.[28]

The Shu State administered by Zhuge Liang "consolidated the essence and developed the trivial"[29] so that industry and commerce expanded. In the Wu State, tariffs were sometimes exempted, and aristocrats and officials openly engaged in trade. When the three states confronted with one another, commercial activities continued among them. In the Southern and Northern Dynasties, the trade between the South and North did not cease, but markets were opened along boundaries and in strategic positions both on land and in water. For example, Shouchun and Xiangyang of the Southern dynasties were important market towns to attract a large number of merchants. The social conditions in the Eastern Jin and the Southern dynasties were relatively stable. All regimes put premium on trade. The Liu-Song government ruled in 420,

> When the government is in need of goods, it dispatches officials to make purchase in the market based on the current prices and compensating for the values [of goods] fully. [So, the government] no longer made taxpaying people produce them.

Tariffs were also reduced to facilitate commerce.[30] In 464, it was once again mandated, "The eastern territory had a bad harvest last year. It is appropriate to expand trade. Sellers of rice and millet from near and afar should be allowed to stay in the road and levied with sundry taxes." During the Liang and Chen dynasties, edicts were issued to give merchants favorable treatments. For example,

> In the tenth month of 494, an edict was issued stating, "Officials currently in position oftentimes violate old legal codes. [They] have personal advantages to gain and therefore hurt the public interest. [They] actually harm the people. Now, tariffs and temporary borrowings in Shitou cheng, Houzhu, and Fulu must be discontinued."[31]

Therefore, commerce developed faster in the Southern Dynasties than in the Northern Dynasties. It was said, "Merchants were more leisured. Thus, commerce was popular and prevalent in a wider region." "The vast population all gave up on agriculture to make a living."[32] Those comments illustrated the situation. A large number of great merchants emerged then, among whom the most famous one was Shi Chong. Shi "made a living on hundreds of businesses and accumulated a wealth as high as a mountain." Other prominent merchants included Wang Rong, Liu Yin, Sun Sheng, and Diao Da of Jin, Zhu Shudu of Song, Yu Cong of Southern Qi, and Gu Xian of Liang. Compared with the times when the nation was unified, nevertheless, disunity posed problems to commerce. First of all, wars caused by national disunity severely impeded regular circulation of commodities. For example, in the times of the late Eastern Jin, the rebellion of Huan Xuan "led to the blockage of waterway on the Yangzi River and therefore merchants disappeared." For another example, during the Southern and Northern Dynasties, the trade between the South and the North along the Huai River was oftentimes closed for political and military reasons. "In the old times, the Huai River was blocked.

Merchants who did not observe the law crossed the river." Second, there were factors such as the establishment of numerous passes and outposts, numerous tax rates, and non-unified currencies that were in short supply. It is hard to assert whether the relaxed anti-commerce regulation outweighed such negative factors during the times of national disunity. Yet, it is certain that in traditional society, albeit in the era of disunity, the merchant could never restore the golden age of the Spring and Autumn and Warring States. This was due to the structure of traditional society. During the times of the Three Kingdoms, the two Jins, and the Southern and Northern Dynasties, rulers of various states persisted in the monopoly of salt and iron trades. Bans on private investment were ever-expanding. For example, the Wu State monopolized the trade of liquor. During the times of the Northern Wei, the government monopolized the sale of vinegar. Government-controlled industries were not abolished. The Wei State set up *Shaofu* (Chamberlain for the Palace Revenues) to take charge in the governmental manufactures. It supervised three workshops – namely, upper, left, and right – to produce articles used by the imperial palaces. The Shu State appointed a *Sijin zhonglang jiang* (Leader of Court Gentlemen and Master of Metal) to supervise the production of "articles for war and agriculture." A position called *Jinguan* was also set up for the production of silk. The Wu State instituted *Shangfang* (Directorate for Imperial Manufactories) to oversee the making of articles for imperial palaces. Textile rooms were also established for textile production. The Chamberlain for the Palace Revenues was also set up during the two Jins and the Southern and Northern Dynasties to take charge in government-controlled manufacture with offices such as weaponry, iron smelting, fabrics and ribbons, dyeing, and papermaking. The situation was entirely different from that in the Spring and Autumn and Warring State periods. It is true that rulers relaxed policies of suppressing and devaluing merchants. For example, merchants were entitled to purchase official positions and ranks to make their entrance into bureaucracy. Also, there were quite a number of monarchs who were fond of being merchants in the Eastern Jin and the Southern dynasties. Liu Yifu, Emperor Shaodi of the Song, "set up stalls in the Huanglin Garden to personally vend goods."[33] Xiao Baojuan, Marquis of Donghun of the Qi State

> opened a market in the garden to sell wines and meat presented by officials of Directorate for Imperial Manufactories to women in the harem. [Imperial Consort] Pan was named as the manager of the market and the emperor as the market official. It was Pan who took charge in resolving disputes.[34]

Monarchs' mentality to emulate vending merchants testified to a changing ethos of belittling the merchant. However, that did not hint on the restoration of the golden age of the merchant. In this three-century-long period of disunity, the North was ravaged by the longtime warfare. Therefore, commerce experienced ups and downs. More often than not, commerce was in decline. Meanwhile, the South, which was less affected by military actions, boasted a more prosperous commerce. In some areas, the retrogression of the monetized relationship of commodities resulted in the popularity of *gubo huobi* (grain and silk as currency) in the vast territory. In other areas, the prosperity of commerce led to the widespread worshipping of the medium for trade, namely metal currencies. It was in this context that Lu Bao's *Thesis on Money God (Qianshen lun)* was penned.

From the late Tang when warlords divided the country to the Five Dynasties and Ten Kingdoms period, the rise and fall of commerce was commensurate with that in the times of the Three Kingdoms, two Jins, and the Southern and Northern Dynasties. After the establishment of the Song dynasty, the country was reunified only partially, as there existed multiple competing states in China. The Song confronted with the Liao, the Western Xia, and the Jin. The Southern Song dynasty retreated to the Yangzi Delta with a territory of half of China. Such a configuration had a marked impact on commerce. Rulers of the two Songs, on the one hand, expanded their monopoly of salt and tea and enlarged government-controlled manufactures. On the other hand, the regulations on the merchant eased. As soon as the dynasty was founded, policies in favor of the merchant were instituted to exempt various taxes and restructure tax regulations. Therefore, merchants recovered from their initial predicaments. Moreover, as there was no barrier to trading, commerce grew steadily. The situation of unity but with multiple regimes was conducive to overstaffing in the bureaucracy and army. The increase of non-productive expenditures and population was a huge incentive to commerce. The configuration of unity but with multiple regimes resulted in the overspending of military expenditures and "yearly tributes" to other states. In order to balance the books, the government encouraged overseas trades. Emperor Taizong of the Northern Song once dispatched missions to different areas to solicit foreign trades. The Southern Song dynasty retained sovereignty in southeastern China and was therefore more willing to promote international trade. A statistics shows that income of foreign trades in Jiangzhe and Minguang was two million *min* (1,000 copper coins), which amounted to one-twentieth of total government revenues. Commerce in the two Songs was extremely prosperous. The total amount of commercial tax in the Northern Song dynasty after the times of Emperor Renzong reached eight million *guan* (1,000 copper coins). Based on the tax rate of commerce of the day – namely, 2.5% on average with 2% *guoshui* (tax for itinerant traders) and 3% *zhushui* (tax for settled traders) – the total turnover should be 320 million *guan*. Considering other factors to reduce the turnover by half, the amount was 160 million. Based on the population then, each person purchased on average commodities worth more than four and a half *dan* (equivalent to 120 *jin*) of rice. The number was spectacular. In Ming and Qing, two unified regimes, the turnover of commercial activities increased rapidly because of population growth. However, the average trading volume per person did not increase or even decreased compared with that in the two Song dynasties.

In sum, the traditional social structure in China consistently posed the merchant dilemmas.

## A dilemma between unification and suppression of the merchant

China was a vast country with highly diverse productions, climates, and geographical conditions. Therefore, transactions and exchanges of commodities were greatly needed. Merchants' activities strengthened economic ties between different regions and nations. Meanwhile, the commodity was a special agent for culture that strengthened cultural ties between different regions and nations, which was conducive to national unity. A unified nation with policies in favor of commerce was the best case scenario for the merchant. However, such a scenario appeared in short duration only twice in a two-millennium-long traditional society. One in the early Han and the other in the early Tang. In the early Tang when the country had suffered from longtime warfare, social economy was devastated. Therefore, the government also carried out a policy of recuperating and building up strength. All government expenditures relied on *zu* (tax in the form of grains) and *diao* (tax in the form of textile products). In the Kaiyuan reign (713–741), there was no ban on private capital to invest in salt and tea, which gave merchants a lot of leeway. At that time, all important trading routes were extremely busy. Volume 7 of *Tongdian* recorded a trading route between Bianzhou and Qizhou:

> From Song and Bian in the east to Qizhou in the west, there were shops and restaurants along the highway to offer customers fine wines and delicate food. Along the highway of scores of *li*, every shop or restaurant had donkeys for rent. They were called "donkey posts." From Jing and Xiang in the South, to Taiyuan and Fanyang in the north, to the Shu, Chuan, and Liang Prefectures in the west, there were stores for itinerant traders.

As soon as the national power revived, however, rulers hastily carried out harsh anti-commerce policies. Thus, the merchant was drawn into a dilemma between national unity and anti-business policies. In time of national disunity, regulations on the merchant relaxed, but social unrest and barriers to trade limited the development of commercial capital. Anti-business policies enacted in time of national unity similarly crippled the development of commercial capital. This was the dilemma that merchants in traditional society could not keep themselves away from.

## A dilemma between fortune and status

Merchants made a fortune by engaging in "trivial things" – namely, business. Some of them were as rich as kings and dukes. In the traditional social stratum, however, they were the lowest of the four classes. While poverty-stricken scholars usually gained widespread respect, extremely rich merchants were frowned upon. Even farmers enjoyed higher status than merchants. Most of merchants harbored an inferior complex. Why did that happen? The reason was the threat to rulers posed by the merchant's economic power. If merchants were richer than kings and dukes, they could further overpower the rulers. How could the autocratic monarchy tolerate them? Therefore, various anti-merchant stipulations appeared in different dynasties to oppress merchants. For long, concept of social values took shape to establish a criterion of assessing lowliness or nobleness not as wealth but as power. Before the supreme imperial authority, the noble could be relegated as the lowly, and vice versa. The edict issued by Emperor Wu of the Han to urge to report merchants' properties led to the bankruptcy of great merchants. Destitute scholars could accumulate enormous wealth once they graduated from the Civil Service Exam. In traditional society in China, "he who excelled in learning ended up being an official." That was the shortcut to power. Those who possessed power would enjoy unlimited wealth and honor. Therefore, scholars were highest among the four classes. The ban on merchants' taking office in government blocked the avenue for the merchant to power. Even though some merchants had access to officialdom through donation, they possessed mere empty ranks, which were despised by scholars.

In traditional society, the peasant was classified higher than the merchant. In reality, the peasant's life was extremely hard. Cao Cuo stated,

> In a household with five members now, only two can work, and the farmable land does not exceed one hundred *mu*. [Farmers] have to endure the rain in spring, the wind and dust in summer, overcast and rainy days in autumn, and the coldness and freezing in winter. Even though [they] work hard and [lead] painful [lives], [they] still suffer from disasters such as the flood and drought.[35]

If farmers realized that engaging in commerce was more profitable, which could be a shortcut to accumulating wealth, they would flock to do business so that they abandoned the essence (agriculture) in pursuit of the trivial (commerce). That would shake the very foundation of an autocratic monarch – namely, a stable agriculture. To consolidate the foundation of the state, it was necessary to "drive [people] to return to agriculture and work on the essence." To attain the goal of letting peasants come to terms with the hard rural life, it was vital to suppress and devalue the merchant.

From this we can see that the claim that the merchant was the lowest among the four classes stemmed from the traditional social structure. In traditional society, the merchant was drawn into a dilemma between fortune and status. To preserve their wealth, they had to pursue political statuses. The solution was "making a fortune by engaging in commerce, but preserving it by returning to agriculture" – namely, converting themselves into landlords or investing in their children's education in preparation for their entry into the scholar's class. Hence, the merchant was so constrained that they could not become an independent force.

Merchants who were faced with the dilemma intertwined their worshipping and hatred of power. As they engaged in trade, they had to bow to power. Yuan Zhen of the Tang dynasty described a merchant who arrived in Chang'an in his poem, *The Happiness of the Merchant* (*Guke le*): "[The merchant] asked eunuchs first; he then pleaded with various officials. The marquis's residence and the master's house were both decorated nicely. After he returned, he felt settled. He was as powerful as the prince." Merchants suffered from extortion and insult but did not dare to resist. Starting from the Song dynasty, however, the merchant began to challenge the four-class stratification. Some minor merchants, such as Wang Xiaobo, Li Shun, and Lai Wenzheng, joined rebels to fight the rulers.

The dilemma faced by the merchant did not change in modern society.

## Section two: the classification and stratification of the merchant

### 1  The classification of the merchant

The merchant of traditional society could be divided into different types. There were many criteria to classify the merchant, among which ten were the commonest.

First, based on their commercial activities, merchants could be classified as itinerant traders and settled businessmen. The former engaged in long-distance transportation and transaction. Their businesses were highly mobile, large-scale with enormous capital, and risky but extremely profitable. Most rich merchants with great fames in different ages fell into this category. Settled merchants were fixed in one place to engage in trade locally. Some of them were wholesalers, while some others retailers. Some were brokers called *yaren* or *yahang*. *Yahang* or brokers of *yaren* were intermediators who arranged deals between sellers and buyers, determined prices, and received commissions. They played a role in supplying business information and facilitating transactions. Those who arranged deals of purchasing livestock were called *zangkuai* in the early stage of history. Later, their business extended to all kinds of businesses. They were called *yaren*, *yalang*, *yakuai*, or *yashang*. The law of market and trade in 1523 ruled that brokers were issued sealed documents by the government (*yatie*). The fees for *yatie* and taxes charged annually were collectively called *yashui*. Since then, *yaren* acquired special privileges to monopolize the trade of agricultural products. Wholesalers were not allowed to make purchase directly, while petty vendors and producers could not sell products to wholesalers without authorization. Foreign trade was also dominated by *yahang*, such as the 13 Hongs in Qing.

Second, the merchant could be classified as rice, salt, timber, tea, jewelry, or medical herb merchants based on the commodities they dealt with. The constitution of the ancient market allows us to understand the number of trades that merchants engaged in. As early as the Spring and Autumn times, a market area managed by officials was designated at the heart of every city. Since the Han dynasty, the market area expanded substantially. A booth installed inside a market was called *si*. Set in good order, *si* were arranged in rows. Each row was called *sui*. Earlier, the approach of managing a market was to place vendors of the same trade in the same row. Booths of different rows sold different goods. Thus, *hang* (hong) became the alternative name to the classification of goods. Businessmen of the same trade were arranged in the same row so that they were called *tonghang* (in the same row). Inside the Fengdu market of Luoyang in the Tang, there were 120 rows[36] with over 3,000 booths, which means that there were businessmen selling goods of 120 types. On average, merchants of one trade possessed about 30 booths (*si*). The number of trades increased with the development of commodified economy. In the eastern market of Chang'an of the Tang, "there were merchants of 220 rows."[37] In other words, there were 220 categories of goods and merchants of 220 trades. In Hangzhou of the Southern Song, there were 414 types of goods. During the times of Ming and Qing, commodified economy prospered. Therefore, it is hard to estimate the number of types of goods.

Third, based on division of labor among merchants, they could be classified in different specialties. Some large-scale and complex businesses were operated by specialized merchants of different trades. Take the salt trade as an example. After the Hongzhi reign of the Ming, salt merchants diversified into three types. *Bianshang* ("frontier traders") paid salt tax in exchange for the exclusive right of transporting and selling salt, or *yanyin*. They further sold *yanyin* to *neishang* (inner merchants) at a government-set price. After acquiring *yanyin*, *neishang* purchased salt from salt fields before selling it to *shuishang* (water merchants) at a government-designated price. *Shuishang* obtained salt from *neishang* and transported it to government-designated areas (*yin'an*) for sale. During the Qing times, *bianshang* and *shuishang* were transformed into *yunshang* (transportation merchants), while *neishang* into *changshang* ([salt] field merchants). Salt was a state-monopolized commodity. The specialization of salt merchants and its transformations were in accord with the state salt policies.

Fourth, based on their areas of activity, merchants could be classified as maritime traders (*haishang*) and inland merchants (*neilushangren*). Prior to the Yongle reign of the Ming, maritime trade in China was highly developed. Yet, its nature as an ocean commerce controlled by the feudal autocratic regime centering on the emperor dictated that its very existence and development served the ruling clique of feudal bureaucrats with the emperor at the center. Economically, such a maritime trade was purported to gather exotic treasures for the members of feudal ruling groups and meet their desire for luxurious lives. Politically, it served the purpose of "mollifying and grasping the reins of" (*jimi*) various states overseas and establishing China's status as a suzerain. The sixteenth century was also a turning point of China's maritime trade. A new type of maritime traders, whose mainstay goods were raw materials for manufacture and daily life articles and who pursued high profits, constituted the majority of China's maritime trade. Inland merchants were active in not only the continental part of China but also new international trading routes. As early as when Emperor Wu of the Han opened up the road to the Western Region (*Xiyu*, or Central Asia), merchants developed an international trading route connecting Dunhuang, the Yumen Pass, Loulan, Kunlun Mountains, Congling (the Pamirs), Central Asia, the Mediterranean Sea, and Rome, a transportation way widely known as the Silk Road.

Fifth, in accordance with the criterion of merchants' capital, they could be classified as great, medium, and petty merchants. *Shezhi* (*Gazetteer of She County*) of the Shunzhi reign claimed,

> The revenue of a great merchant was equivalent to that of a great [farmer] household's property; the revenue of a medium merchant was equivalent to that of a medium [farmer] household's property; the revenue of a petty merchant was equivalent to that of a petty [farmer] household's property.

The amounts of wealth possessed by great, medium, and petty merchants were not clearly defined. In "*Huozhi*" (Commerce) of *Gazetteer of She County* of the Wanli reign, it was stated, "Take our county as an example. Quite a large number of people own over one thousand [ounces of silver]. Some richer ones have over

ten thousand. The richest boast of a wealth of hundreds of thousands or millions."
Xie Zhaozhe of the Wanli reign commented in his *Wu Zazu* (*Five Miscellanies*),
"Great merchants in Xin'an make a fortune out of fishery and salt. There are people who possess over one million strings of coins. Those who have two hundred
or three hundred thousand are medium merchants." Although they both talked
about Huizhou merchants, "medium merchants" were defined as those who possessed "tens of thousands" of ounces of silver in the first account but as those
who owned 200,000 or 300,000 in the second account. Wang Shixing at the same
historical moment talked about Shanxi merchants who were as famous as those
from Huizhou: "Rich merchants from Pingyang, Ze, and Lu are superior under
the heaven. One who does not possess a wealth of hundreds of thousands is not
regarded as rich." Taken together, medium merchants in late Ming should possess a wealth between tens of thousands and 200,000 or 300,000, while great
merchants' properties were between 400,000or 500,000 and a million. Those who
possessed thousands counted only as petty merchants.

Sixth, in terms of their forms of organization, there were merchants of individual proprietorship and merchants of business partnership. Traditionally, most
merchants were of individual proprietorship and very few sought business partners. In the Northern Song, 16 merchants from Sichuan collectively issued *jiaozi*
(paper currency) for long-distance remittances. This counted as business partnership. During the Ming and Qing times, business partnership, which became a
more common practice, was usually established among relatives. In late Qing, tea
merchants in Huizhou ran large-scale enterprises:

> Those who engaged in green tea trade were mostly from Wuyuan of Huizhou.
> Their tea was produced in local mountains. They usually established business
> partnership. If they lost money, the deficit was shared in accordance with
> stocks. [Hence, they] would not feel the loss unbearable.[38]

Seventh, judging from the relationship between the political power and merchants, merchants could be classified as official-merchants (*guanshang*) and ordinary merchants. Official-merchants took advantage of political privileges to reap
exorbitant profits in areas of circulation. Two types of people could be viewed as
official-merchants. The first type included aristocrats, bureaucrats, and their family members who profited from doing business. The second type was merchants
who gained official titles through donation. In addition, there were privileged
merchants who dealt with state-monopolized commodities. They were merchants
of salt, tea, and so forth. They were remotely related to officialdom, but their
privileges were not stable. Therefore, they needed to invest in their children's
education, intermarry with bureaucrats, or donate wealth to gain access to bureaucracy in order to retain their privileges.

Eighth, based on their multiple identities, merchants could be classified as
merchant-landlords, merchants-cum-bureaucrats (or bureaucrats-cum-merchants),
merchant-usurers, or a combination of all the three. Merchant-usurers adopted
two ways of business. First of all, some engaged in the pawn business. The name

of pawn shops differed historically. They were variously called *zhiku*, *zhisi*, *jieku*, *changshengku*, and so forth. Pawnbrokers received pawners' articles, estimated their values, gave out money, and issued pawn tickets. On a pawn ticket, the address of the pawn shop, the name of the pledged article, the number of articles, the due time, interest rate, and the number of the ticket were all clearly marked. The time limit was usually two years. Pawn shops were entitled to confiscate overdue articles, as they were unredeemed. Short-term pawning was called *duanya* whose pledged articles were usually small in number and low in value. "Small shops for *duanya* accepted trivial things in exchange for cash, wine, or rice. The deal of pawning was done quickly and conveniently."[39] In Volume 13 of *Chuke paian jingqi* (*Slapping the Table in Amazement I*), a certain Zhao Liulao pawned his clothing to his son, Zhao Cong, because of abject poverty. Zhao Cong wrote "a ticket for short-term pawning, on which he put '[After] five months, [the clothing would be] gone'." In other words, if the clothing remained unredeemed in five months, it would belong to the creditor. Second, some practiced moneylending with middlemen. When a merchant granted high-interest loans, he did not accept articles as the pledge. Rather, the borrower was required to have a middleman as his guarantor and to iron out a contract.

Ninth, in line with moral standards, merchants were categorized as good and evil or incorruptible and greedy ones. Good or incorruptible merchants were those who adhered to traditional business ethics that equated righteousness to profits. Evil and greedy merchants were bent solely on profits by hook or by crook.

Tenth, based on education received by merchants, they could be categorized as well-educated Confucian-merchants and insufficiently educated ones. In their commercial activities, merchants were required to command skills of arithmetic and making judgements on goods. Itinerant traders also needed to master knowledge of astronomy, geography, native products, and law. Therefore, merchants usually received some education. Among people of four classes, merchants were second only to scholars.

## 2 The stratification of the merchant

Traditional merchants could also be grouped into higher or lower strata based on certain criteria. Stratification and classification are different. Classification entails differentiating the same objects in line with different standards, whereas stratification uses only one criterion. The classification and stratification of the merchant are two intersecting realms. Different types of merchants could belong to the same stratum, while the same types of merchants could fall into different strata. In addition, it is worth pointing out that although multiple criteria could be applied in stratifying merchants, the connotation of each criterion remains the same. Previous scholarship, which usually takes the merchant's capital as the criterion, confuses stratification with classification. The differentiation of great, medium, and petty merchants is misleading, although it does illustrate strata of merchants in some respects. Those who were classified as great merchants fell into bureaucrat-merchants and commoner-merchants. The former were the rulers, whereas the latter were the ruled. Thus, it is hard to assert that they belonged to the same stratum. Therefore, it is vital to take into account the major factors that hierarchized them to set a multivalent and comprehensive criterion to stratify the merchant. I argue that the criterion of stratifying merchants should be a synthesis of economic, social, and political criteria. The economic criterion refers to capital possessed by merchants. The social criterion refers to reputations and statuses gained by merchants in society. The political criterion refers to the power wielded by merchants. Property, reputation, and power were interrelated and even overlapping. Yet, they were not equivalent to one another. Neither could they be replaced by one another. Based on this multivalent criterion, the merchant could fall into the following four strata.

The first stratum was merchants with property, reputation, and power – namely, bureaucrat-merchants. As early as in the Western Han, some bureaucrats began to engage in trade. But they were in position of secondary importance. Afterwards, more aristocrats and bureaucrats profited from commerce. Starting from the mid-Song, the general atmosphere in society changed remarkably: officials "with high ranks were specialized in commerce to trade state-banned goods such as tea, salt, and fragrant herbs. They counted on ships and vehicles to travel. They were on business trips to travel back and forth to make a fortune regularly."[40] Not only ordinary officials but also eminent bureaucrats were no exception. A few prime ministers "were busy transporting goods for sale."[41] Wang Anshi once pointed out: "High-ranking officials nowadays usually give away bribes to accumulate capital to bear a stigma of corruption. Low-ranking ones trade, beg, and stop at nothing."[42] In late Southern Song times, it was a common practice that family members of high-ranking officials engaged in commerce. At that time, in downtown Lin'an, there were "Pharmacy of Palace Physician Lou," "Official Xu's Scarf," "General Yang's Pharmacy," "Official Fu's Toothbrushes," "Official Zhang's Bookstore for History, Philosophical Writings and Miscellaneous Literary Works," "Supervisor Zhang's Golden Horse-Shape Spoon Pharmacy for Child," and so on. Owners of those stores named after "Palace Physician," "Official," or "General" must be descendants of officials with such titles. Commoners did not dare to counterfeit them in the capital city. In the Southern Song, there were a large number of imperial clansmen who lived as dispersed groups in various areas and engaged in commerce. During Emperor Ningzong's reign, an imperial clansman purchased the exclusive rights in most areas of the Dongting Lake to "monopolize the profits and made a great fortune out of fishing."[43] He practically dominated the local fishery.

In the mid- and late Ming, the prosperity of commoditized economy vastly aroused the emperors, who themselves engaged in trade. During the Zhengde reign, Emperor Wuzong issued an edict to "establish imperial stores."[44]Imperial stores were derived from official stores (*guandian*). Official stores were alternatively known as *tafang* (lodging rooms) built for traveling merchants to get accommodation and store their goods. They were set up as early as in the early Ming. The government relied on official stores to levy commercial taxes and obtain brokerage fees and fees for storing goods. In the mid-Ming, emperors began to pay attention to official stores because official stores had become a major means of reaping profits with the increase of merchants and intensified commercial activities. After official stores were refashioned into imperial stores, their nature as a state-run institution turned into the emperor's private property. Zhu Houzhao, Emperor Wuzong of the Ming, disguised himself as a merchant to do business in imperial stores. *Ming Wuzong waiji* (*An Unofficial Record of Emperor Wuzong of Ming*) recorded that Emperor Wuzong

> once visited the Baohe Store and asked eunuchs to leave their places. He was clothed in the merchant's garment and wore a *guala* hat. He did business in six stores from Baohe to Baoyan by holding an account book. He noisily argued [with other businessmen] and, consequently, a supervisor was asked to mediate.

The most important task of an imperial store was to "monopolize commodities"[45] and "levy taxes on merchants to gain profits."[46] With emperors' edicts and taking actions in the emperor's name, imperial stores acted atrociously against law and reason in the process of collecting taxes. *Ming Wuzong shilu* (the *Chronicle of Emperor Wuzong of Ming*) recorded, "Imperial stores levied taxes on merchants' vessels and vehicles. Even a small load of goods was taxed. [Merchants] both in the capital and elsewhere complained." In order to collect more taxes, "[tax officials] intercepted merchants in the nine sides of the capital city and all the way to places like Zhangjiawan and Hexiwu to extort excessive taxes and levies." Imperial stores everywhere "had their patrollers to extort taxes from trivial goods of peddlers. Officials' baggage was also unpacked for check. No one dared to challenge."[47]Because of imperial stores' close control and intense interception, a lot of goods were seized by imperial stores. According to Liu Ruoyu, eunuch in the Ming, every year, six imperial stores including Baohe of Rongzhengfu Street levied goods annually prior to the Tianqi reign as follows:

> Over 10,000 sheets of marten fur, over 60,000 sheets of fox skins, about 800,000 pieces of flat-bed fabrics, 400,000 pieces of coarse cloth, 6,000 bags of cotton, about 45,000 baskets of stand oil and river oil, about 35,000 baskets of vitex oil, about 40,000 baskets of spirit (not including that brewed in the capital), about 30,000 *dan* of sesame, about 2,000 baskets of grass oil, about 500 horseload of southern silk, about 3,000 horseload of elm barks for incense shops to make incenses, 30,000 *jin* of northern silk, about 100,000 rolls of mixed fabrics, about 35,000 *dan* of sticky rice, about 200,000 pieces of Chinese linen, about 10,000 *dan* of melon seeds, about 200 carload of salted meat, about 10,000 cases of tea from Shaoxing, about 2,000 horseload of Songluo tea, over 30,000 sheets of miscellaneous animal skins, about 500,000 loafs of massive raw starter for alcoholic liquor, about 300,000 loafs of medium raw starter, about 600,000 loafs of raw starter for flour (about 800,000 loafs of petty raw starters were produced in the capital, while raw starters made by aristocrats and officials were not included), 5,000 baskets of

river oil from Sizhi, 200,000 loafs of raw starters from Sizhi, about 5,000 *jin* of jade, about 500,000 pigs, about 300,000 goats – both being taxed – and horses, oxen, mules, and donkeys which were untaxed. Some other items such as the jewelry from Yunnan and Guangdong, gold pearls, lead, copper, granulated mercury, rhinoceros horns, ivories, medical herbs, and silk and velvet fabrics from Jiangsu, Huguang, Fujian, Zhejiang, Shandong, and Shaanxi were untaxed. The amount of tax was about tens of thousands of ounces of silver, which was submitted by season.[48]

From this we can see that imperial stores engulfed quite a lot. The number would be far larger if taxes levied by all imperial stores were taken into account.

Emperors were the greatest bureaucrat-merchants. Those below followed the example of those above. Princes, merited officials, and imperial relatives all engaged in trade. As emperors ran imperial stores, princes opened princely stores. Volume 120 of *Mingshi* (*History of Ming*) recorded that Zhu Yiliu, the fourth son of Emperor Muzong and Prince of Lu, "lived in the capital as the emperor's (Emperor Shenzong) younger brother of the same mother. His princely stores and estates spread all over the capital city." Upon arriving in his fief, Luoyang, Zhu Changxun, Emperor Shenzong's third son and Prince of Fu, established a salt store

> and obtained three hundred salt licenses for salt from Huai. [He] set up stores to sell salt to the people. The central government sent missions to transport salt from Huai and Yang, but [he] seized [the salt] and thereby acquired several times more. Previously, people in Zhongzhou ate salt from Hedong. As they [were asked to] switch to the salt from Huai, the salt that were not from the prince's stores could not be vended. Licensed salt from Hedong was thus stopped and could not be traded.

A vast number of merited officials and imperial relatives engaged in trade. During the Hongzhi reign, distinguished kinsmen and officials "encouraged [their] family members to open stores along great avenues to obtain or intercept commercial goods. [Such stores] prevailed both inside and outside the city."[49] During the Zhengde reign, in the places surrounding the capital such as Zhangjiawan of Tongzhou where merchants got together, "imperial relatives and noble kinsmen ran stores over there to seize goods [from different areas] under heaven so that merchants could not make profits."[50] Under the commodified economy, ordinary gentry and scholars viewed commerce and industry as a significant means of reaping profits. Huang Xing once stated, "Gentry-scholars in Suzhou mostly profited from commerce."[51] Gu Yanwu pointed out, "After the Wanli reign, water conservancy, milling, ferry, and market were all dominated by the powerful gentry. The practice was passed down and became normal."[52] For example, Wang Shizhen, the great scholar and minister of Punishment, ran a large number of pawnshops. In off years, he was able to make a profit of 300,000 ounces of silver annually. The minister of Rites, Dong Fen, who was hailed as the richest person in the Wu area, "owned hundreds of pawnshops" in addition to a large number of fields and estates."[53]

Traditional Chinese society was bureaucracy oriented. Possessing political powers, which were capable of generating wealth, was of utmost importance. Bureaucrat-officials took advantage of their political privileges to engage in lucrative businesses such as salt and tea trades, selling and making of coins and paper money, and commerce in the border areas with ethnic minorities. All those businesses were rigidly banned by the Ming Empire so that ordinary merchants were given little chance to have a hand in them. Although some families of prominent imperial relatives and noblemen were meted out penalties for their violation of injunctions, the number was generally small. Most of them felt assured and emboldened to act willfully because of the power they possessed. For example, salt was a state-monopolized commodity, and revenues from salt tax constituted a vital part of state finance. It was ruled in early Ming that nobles and influential families were strictly prohibited from engaging in the salt trade. However, this injunction could not be carried out. The powerful and influential managed to obtain salt licenses through influence. Hu Song described the Ministry of Revenue's management of salt business during the Jiajing reign as follows:

> Each year when the Ministry of Revenue began to accept yearly incomes and the documentation had yet to arrive, the powerful and influential both inside and outside the capital carried letters asking for help from officials. Officials feared their powers and did not dare to reject. The most powerful would acquire thousands of licenses, and the less powerful one or two thousand. The rest would be given different amounts of [licenses] based on the hierarchy of their powers.[54]

The more powerful gained more licenses, while the less powerful fewer ones. The most powerful requested salt licenses directly from emperors. Zhou Shou, Marquis of Qingyun, and Zhang Heling, Marquis of Shouning, once requested and obtained 800,000 or 900,000 licenses in one meeting during the Hongzhi reign. In actual trades, bureaucrat-merchants resorted to *duozhi* or *jiadai* to profiteer because of their power and influence. *Duozhi* referred to drawing more salt than the amounts designated by licenses. It was stipulated in Ming that each license was equivalent to 220 *jin* of salt. Yet, when bureaucrat-merchants drew salt, the amount far exceeded it. During the Chenghua reign, "families of influential imperial relatives and noblemen . . . acquired five or six hundred *jin* when [they] drew [salt] in Huainan and Huaibei."[55] This alone doubled or tripled the profit. *Jiadai* referred to transporting both authorized salt and salt acquired through *duozhi* or smuggling. Tax posts did not dare to interrogate and examine the businessmen. The eunuch Liu Yun during the Zhengde reign

> requested ten thousand licenses of salt from the Changlu Shipping Bureau and sixty thousand from the Salt Bureau of Huainan and Huaibei. Most of the transporting staff reaped profits [from shipping] because of their power

and influence. They acquired extra ten thousand licenses of [salt] from each place via *douzhi*. Therefore, seventy or eighty thousand licenses of salt was shipped through *jiadai*.[56]

The requested amount of salt was 70,000 licenses, but the amount ended up being 80,000 or 90,000 because of *jiadai*. Bureaucrats who "reaped profits [from the shipping] because of their power and influence" could easily accumulate an enormous wealth. According to Volume 36 of Wang Shizhen's *Yanzhou shiliao houji* (*Historical Materials of Wang Shizhen [Final Part]*),

> [Each time when] Yan Shifan accumulated a wealth of over a million [ounces of silver], [he] held a banquet. Later, he held four such banquets. But [he] did not stop grabbing more [wealth]. Once he [talked to] his favored visitors and enumerated the seventeen top-ranked rich families [in areas] under the heaven. The seventeen families included himself, Prince of Shu, Lord Qian, the eunuchs Gao Zhong, Huang Jin, and Mr. Cheng, Lord Wei, the Commissioner-in-chief Lu Bing, Zhang Erjinyi in the capital (the eunuch Zhang Yong's nephew), three families in Shanxi, two families in Huizhou, and An Xuanwei of Aboriginal Office of Guizhou. Only those with a wealth of 500,000 ounces of silver and above were ranked at the top. Previously, Zou Wang of Wuxi possessed a wealth of almost one million. An Guo's wealth exceeded half a million. Now, the wealth of Minister Dong of Wuxing exceeds one million. The Xiang family of Jiaxing will reach one million. Xiang owns more precious metal and antiques than Dong, but has fewer fields, real estates, pawnshops, and granaries. Powerful eunuchs such as Feng Bao and Zhang Hong possess a wealth of over two million. Marquis Li of Wuqing might have properties over one million.

Among the top 17 "rich families under the heaven" in Yan Shifan's view, only "three families in Shanxi, two families in Huizhou," and Zou Wang and An Guo of Wuxi were merchants. The rest ten were all families of powerful and influential officials. From this we can see that over half of the wealth across the country had been accumulated by households of bureaucrats. Certainly, such enormous wealth was not procured by saving stipends but was gained because of corruption or commercial activities, both of which were derivatives of political power. As far as the seven merchant's households, they had more or less backgrounds of bureaucracy.

Traditional Chinese society was also strictly hierarchized. In this social environment, members of society garnered reputations and respect based on their positions in hierarchy. Here, power and reputation were in direct proportion. Those with higher ranks, greater power, and better reputations won more respect. Bureaucrat-merchants were concurrently bureaucrats so that they received greater respect. The Grand Secretary Heshen of the Qing took office as the Grand Minister of State for 24 years. He was simultaneously a great bureaucrat-merchant. Heshen

> was by nature insatiably avaricious. He solicited wealth extremely anxiously. Supreme Commanders, Provincial Governors, Ministers, and Intendants of

Circuit feared that [Heshen] might plot a frame-up against them. Therefore, they had to deliver goods to his household to gain support.[57]

Despite his misdeeds, he commanded respect because of Emperor Qianlong's trust. After he fell into disrepute as he lost his power, Emperor Jiaqing confiscated all his properties. His 75 pawnshops and 42 native banks vanished with his once respectable status.

At the second level, there were great merchants with both wealth and reputation. Great and medium merchants with a wealth between tens of thousands and millions mostly fell into this stratum. In a traditional society, its members were classified into four identity groups. Merchants, who belonged to the lowest of the "four classes," were deemed as degrading although they might be "richer than a king." Therefore, merchants were motivated to move upward to identify themselves with "scholars" and "peasants." To secure the identification of scholars and peasants and elevate their social statuses, they took the following paths.

The first path was to secure officialdom through donation or investing in children's education. The *juanna* system of donating money and millet in exchange for official titles started in the Qin Dynasty. During the Ming and Qing times, *juanna* prevailed as the governments usually took *juanna* as a means of receiving revenues due to the needs of raising military funds, disaster relief, defending the border, or launching public works. This opened up a new avenue for the merchant's entry into officialdom. "*Huozhi zhuan*" (Biography of the Merchant) of *Zhengxinlu* (*Records for Public Trust*) recorded that during the Wanli reign of the Ming, "the state launched a great project," and the wealthy and influential merchant Wu Yangchun "contributed 300,000 strings of copper coins to assist the project" in exchange for the government's appointment of "five [family members] as Secretariat Drafters within one day." Once a merchant acquired the title or rank, he became a powerful gentry-merchant in the local place. In his "Wenshu sanyou yishu" (Memorabilia of Three Friends of Books and Essays), Hong Liangji narrated the story of Wang Zhong who was in Yangzhou:

> In the year of *jiawu* (1774), I stayed in a Yangzhou hotel for salt businessmen. As I was poor, I studied in an academy. In early evening one day, I led [Wang] Zhong to the place outside the yard. Both riding on a horse, [we] were talking about strengths and weaknesses of *Duli tongkao* (*Biographical Notes on Reading Books of Rites*) written by Xu Qianxue. Suddenly, [we] saw a merchant, who wore the attire of the third rank and took a sedan chair to visit the headmaster of the academy. As soon as he got off the sedan chair, a student rushed to bow to the merchant and said, "I went to your residence yesterday and the day before yesterday to pay you a visit. Do you know that?" The merchant appeared quite arrogant by slightly nodding his head with no response.[58]

The attitude harbored by the student of the Yangzhou academy toward the merchant – namely, his two visits and respect he paid when meeting with the merchant – was typical. The merchant's "attire of the third rank" was, without a doubt, procured through donation. The merchant's paying money to purchase an official title was to buy respectable social statuses and reputations. Another important channel to access the membership of the privileged bureaucratic class was to cultivate their children in an attempt to enter into officialdom. Bao Zidao, merchant-general in Huainan and Huaibei, had two sons. His elder son, Bao Shufang, was originally a student of the National University and appointed as Vice Director through donation. Later, he succeeded to his father to be the merchant-general in Huainan and Huaibei. His second son, Bao Xunmao gained access to officialdom through exams. His highest position was Secretary in the Grand Secretariat with One Added Rank and Probationary Grand Minister of State. The father won honor because of his sons. Bao Zidao was appointed as Gentleman-litterateur and Secretary in the Grand Secretariat with One Added Rank. The secret behind the ability of Bao Zidao and his son to occupy the position of the merchant-general in Huainan and Huaibei was his success in cultivating his son to be an official through the exam system.

The second path was to invest in lands. The merchant's identification with the peasant did not mean that they became farmers. Rather, he returned to his home village to purchase lands to gain a new identity as the landlord. It remained true ever since the ancient times that merchants "made fortune by doing business, but consolidated their wealth by farming." During the times of Emperor Wu of Han, rich merchants had their hundreds of *qin* of lands confiscated in large counties and more than 100 confiscated in small counties because of the edict of reporting merchants' hidden properties and tax evasions. This was a proof that it had been a universal practice to purchase lands. A merchant who brought a stupendous sum of cash to return to his village and buy lands was regarded as "a household of annexing [lands]." During the Qing times, the sons of Liu Zhongwei, a timber merchants from Hengyang, Hunan, possessed over 300,000 *mu* of high-quality lands. The homeland of Huizhou merchants – namely, six counties of Huizhou – lacked arable lands so that people found it hard to live on. Many were compelled to do business elsewhere. Yet, once Huizhou merchants made a fortune, they would return to their home villages to purchase lands. Consequently, land price in Huizhou soared to such an extent that it topped the whole nation. Late Ming novels portrayed the situation of rich merchants' investment in lands. Volume 35 of *Xingshi hengyan* (*Stories to Awaken the World*) told a story of "Xu laopu yifen chengjia" (Old Servant Xu Established a Household Out of Righteousness), which presented a typical example. In the text, the household of Ms. Xu (née Yan) of Chun'an County, Yanzhou Prefecture, Zhejiang, hired a servant called Aji. After Aji made a fortune by engaging in trade, he purchased 1,000*mu* of lands, herds of cattle and horses, and hired hundreds of maiden servants and workers.

Rich and influential merchants exchanged wealth for reputation, and then reputation with more wealth. Although titles procured through donation were usually honorary ones, they qualified them to engage in trading state-monopolized goods. Huizhou and Shanxi merchants who dominated salt businesses in Huainan and Huaibei manipulated wealth and reputation and thereby became the wealthiest merchant groups.

At the third level were merchants who possessed nothing but properties. This stratum consisted of mainly three groups of merchants. The first group was petty merchants. They, who possessed a property under 1,000 ounces of silver, could not emulate powerful and influential merchants to gain official titles through donation or to annex lands. Therefore, they did not win identification of scholars and peasants. Nor could they accumulate an enormous wealth quickly. However, petty merchants had their own ways of making a fortune, that is, diligence, frugality, and emphasis on business ethics. The merchant Zhang Zhou of Ming

> was diligent and did not lax. He made a fortune by being frugal. He brought wealth to Yuhang where he established his character as a faithful, honest, kind, and polite person. He did things with righteousness. Therefore, people liked to hang around with him and his business boomed.[59]

The merchant Ling Jin,

> though as a merchant doing business in streets, was benevolent, righteous, and kind. When he traded with others, sly businessmen took more [goods from him] by deception. He did not bother to argue [with them]. When he mistakenly gave [others] less, he made compensation after he realized [the mistake]. Thus, his business prospered.[60]

The merchant Wu Nanpo once said,

> "Others prefer to cheat, but I prefer to be trustful. I would never cheat a child five *chi* tall by giving false prices." Later, people scrambled [to do business with] Mr. Wu. Every time they visited the marketplace, they took goods labeled with paper strips written by Mr. Wu, regardless of the quality and size of the goods.

The commonality of those merchants was honesty in pursuit of long-term commercial gains. Certainly, after they made fortunes, they were eager to be identified with two groups, scholars and peasants, in order to move up to the second stratum. However, many strived painstakingly to keep their low-capital businesses going. Amid cutthroat commercial competitions, quite a lot of them went bankrupt.

The second group was greedy and evil merchants. Their short-sighted actions to atrociously accumulate wealth typified the predacity of feudal commerce. It was usurers, who not only extorted high interests but also resorted to additional blackmailing means that were most typical. According to the common practice of lending and borrowing, repayment of the Shanxi merchant Wang Laipin's admonition to his sons and grandsons, Li Weizhen of Ming stated in when they arranged loans. In Volume 20 of *Huangming tiaofa shi leizhuan* (*Compilation of Regulations and Laws of Ming*), it was recorded that in early years of Hongzhi reign, a merchant called Li Ji loaned money to Tao Chun.

> In the first two times, the actual amount of the loan was eleven ounces, but [Tao Chun] was forced to write a receipt with an amount of twenty-five ounces. In the fifth month of Hongzhi 2, [Li Ji] lent another five ounces, but

[Tao Chun] wrote that the total amount of the principal and interest was ten ounces.

In his description of usury in Shanghai and other places, Ye Mengzhu of the late Ming and the early Qing also stated,

> In most cases, when [a borrower] borrowed ten ounces of silver, the interest would be deducted [in advance]. [Therefore], the actual amount acquired was nine ounces. [If the amount was calculated with] fine silver (*wenyin*) of standard purity, it was in reality more than eight ounces.[61]

Under this circumstance, a borrower had to borrow more if he expected to obtain the desired amount. The greater the amount, the larger the interest due. Usurers also manipulated purity and weight of silver. In Volume 15 of *Slapping the Table in Amazement*, the pawnbroker Wei "was usually a mean person. When he arrived in Nanjing, he owned no more than a small pawnshop. But he had hundreds of ways of making profits at the expense of morality. For example, when a customer pawned his article, he replaced fine silver with that of 96% or 97%. He weighed silver with a small scale but took off some *dengtou* (amount deductible in weighing). When [the customer] redeemed the article, [Wei] used a big balance-type scale [to weigh silver] and demanded surcharge to make up [the silver's] purity. [He] refused to give back the article if there was slightest disparity." In Volume 22 of the same book, Guo Qilang of Jianglin, a great usurer, acted exactly in the same way. When lending the money, "[he] used large-sized scales [to weigh silver] as he loaned out silver, but used small-sized scales to recover the money. His low-quality silver was taken as high-quality one, while others' high-quality silver was dismissed as low-quality one." Consequently, every borrower "suffered from him and had to swallow insult and humiliation silently." Those accounts were not fiction fabricated by novelists. There were plenty of people like the pawnbroker Wei and Guo Qilang. Pawnshops in Fuzhou of Jiangxi in late Ming were just like this: "When [pawnbrokers] lent money, every ounce of silver was three or four percent lighter. When [they] recovered money, every ounce of silver was required to be three or four percent heavier."[62] Usurers also adopted means of lowering values of pledged articles or even supersede articles surreptitiously to exploit commoners. For example, pawnshops in Beijing "lowered the value of the [pledged] article worth one ounce of silver to three *qian* and article worth one *qian* to three *fen*." Profits were garnered by substituting cheap goods with costly ones and high-quality goods with low-quality ones. The aforementioned pawnbroker Wei was also an old hand of secretly superseding pledged articles.

> [When he] saw a customer to pawn the jewelry and found the purity of the gold was high, he secretly made counterfeits and replaced fine pearl beads with crude ones, precious gems with low-quality stones. He did things like that and it is hard to describe.

Even worse, usurers abused debtors so willfully that they hounded them to death. It was recorded in *Yunjian Zazhi* (*Miscellaneous Information from Songjiang*) that Chen Kan of Shanghai in the Ming

> lived on lending money and afflicted his home village. [He] resented someone's failure to repay his debt. So, [he] caught [the person] back home and beat [him] to death. [He] placed the body in a gigantic pot to rotten it in order to obliterate all traces.[63]

*Zhuzi zhiguai lu* (*Accounts of the Mysterious and Supernatural by Mr. Zhu*) claimed, "Xia Chun, a small peasant, was in heavy debt. [He was] coerced by [creditors] and had to kill himself at home."[64] Pressing for payment of debts and killing people featured as plotlines of some novels. In *Erke paian jingqi* (*Slapping the Table in Amazement II*), there was a callous and cruel powerful pawnbroker, Wang Jun. His uncle of the same clan, Wang Liang, once borrowed two ounces of silver from him. "Although [the uncle] had already repaid the interest twice as much as the principal, he still owed [Wang Jun] two more ounces of silver." Wang Liang resisted but ended up being beaten to death by Wang Jun. Chen Liangmo of Ming painted a picture of evil merchants who engaged in usury. He pointed out that they

> hoard [goods] and gained surplus. [They] are extremely calculative. As for righteous things to comfort and compensate the bereaved, they are too stingy to pull out a hair even to their closest relatives. After several years, they would boast their enormous wealth.[65]

Usurers who "committed atrocities to exploit the people" would invite victims' resistance. *Sangang zhilue* (*Brief Information of Three Ridges*) gave an account of a debtor's robbing and killing of a vicious usurer:

> There were two rich people in Xin'an, Cheng and Wang, both of whom accumulated tens of thousands [of ounces of silver] by trading . . . [They] gained high profits by means of usury. [They] excelled at calculating and excessively mean in their dealings. . . . Cheng had three sons. The eldest son secured nomination from local officials and therefore became even more greedy and insolent by seizing more lands and estates. As a turmoil broke out, his foes rose up against him. [The eldest son] was killed. The rest two sons and five grandsons all died in wars.[66]

The fate of the aforementioned great pawnbroker, Wang Jun, was similar. Wang Shiming, the son of the victim Wang Liang, sought an opportunity to retaliate several years later and stabbed Wang Jun to death. What merits mentioning is the fact that Li Zicheng, the supreme leader of late Ming peasant's uprising army, revolted as he suffered from usury.

The third group was merchants who engaged in illegal trades, such as smuggling salt or tea and crossing the borderline without permission to trade with ethnic minorities outside. Those merchants who violated bans confronted vehemently with feudal regimes. Historically, all smuggling merchants organized their own military forces. Wang Xianzhi and Huang Chao in the late Tang and Zhang Shicheng of the late Yuan were all illegal salt traders. In Chengdu during the Northern Song times, an institution called *Bomaiwu* was set up to prohibit merchants and tea growers from selling silk products and tea. Wang Xiaobo and Li Shun, both tea growers, led the masses to revolt and force the North Song government to abolish *Bomaiwu*. In the mid-Ming, a number of smuggling groups emerged in the coastal area in southeastern China. A host of reputed groups of maritime merchants led by the Xu brothers, Wang Zhi, Xu Hai, Xiao Xian, Lin Bixi, He Yaba, Xu Xichi, Xie Ce, Hong Dizhen, Zhang Wei, Zhang Lian, Wu Ping, Zeng Yiben, Lin Daoqian, Lin Feng, Zheng Zhilong, and others all had close-knit organizations and private military forces to resist the Ming dynasty's anti-maritime trade naval force.

Military forces possessed by smuggling groups were insignificant compared with the war machine of the centralist dynasties. Military forces of salt smugglers had "five or six hundred men at the most and two or three hundred at the least."[67] However, facing the central government's anti-smuggling forces, those scattered and small-sized militarized units did not crumble but increasingly expanded the scope of smuggling. After all, it was because illegal salt was highly popular among consumers. State-monopolized salt was overpriced. In Jiangxi, a peasant had to sell one *dan* of paddy rice in exchange for a small bag of salt (seven *jin* and four *liang*). Tao Shu, Supreme Commander of Jiangsu and Anhui who concurrently took office as the supervisor of salt in Huainan and Huaibei during the Daoguang reign of Qing, once said, "The flesh and blood of the people in Jiangxi and Huguang exhausted because of salt. Poor families of limited means and without powerful connections usually had to endure scores of days or even months of eating food without salt."[68] The high price of salt stemmed from the following four factors. First, feudal regimes levied heavy taxes on salt. Then, "taxes on salt [produced in] Huainan and Huaibei including all principal and miscellaneous items amounted to over six million ounces [of silver] per year."[69] Because of this, it was said, "Taxes levied on salt of Huainan and Huaibei constituted half of all tax revenues [in areas] under the heaven."[70] Second, to tighten the control over salt trade, imperial regimes established a whole set of salt bureaucracy. "The dynasty sent merchants to trade salt and [created positions such as] *Xunyan yushi* (Salt-control Censor), *Yan Yunsi* (Salt Distribution Commission), *Yan fadao* (Salt Control Circuit), *Guanyan tongzhi* (Associate Administrator in Charge of the Affairs of Salt), *Zhishi* (Administrative Clerk), *Jingli* (Registrar), and *Zhubu* (Recorder). People under those officials were innumerable."[71] Salt merchants had to not only cover the expenditure of this immense bureaucratic institution but also cope with various extortions imposed on by different strata of officials when transporting and selling salt. As a consequence, "expenditure for non-business reasons was almost equivalent to half of the cost of salt."[72] Third, salt merchants gave emperors gift silver in order to retain their statues as monopoly businessmen. In total, in years of Qianlong and Jiaqing, salt merchants in Huainan and Huaibei contributed silver amounting to 37,394,951 ounces. Fourth, merchants reaped enormous profits.

According to *Huaicuo beiyao* (*The Essential Huai Salt*), during the Daoguang reign, someone "heard from old people that Huai merchants possessed capital amounting to tens of millions, and the second-tier [merchants] had millions." The margin of profit was astoundingly great. Few merchants of other trades could match their wealth. All such costs eventually factored into salt price. With the increase of the salt price, government-monopolized salt was naturally hard to sell, creating a condition for the prevalence of illegal salt. Illegal salt was untaxed and exempt from the burden of bureaucracy. Therefore, its price was low. Even Bao Shichen, a Qing bureaucrat and scholar, recognized in his *An Wu sizhong* (*Four Items to Pacify Wu*), "Illegal [salt] was inexpensive, pure, and in full measure. Everything that [official] merchants inflicted upon common people was the source of profits for illegal traders." The expansion of illegal salt trade crippled the sale of government-monopolized salt. The smuggling of salt thus dealt a heavy blow to feudal order and rule by disrupting the Qing Empire's salt policy and exacerbating its financial crises. In this sense, illegal salt traders were in confrontation with feudal rulers. Generally speaking, they enjoyed no power and reputation.

The fourth group was petty peddlers without power, reputation, and property. Petty peddlers were originally bankrupted peasants in most cases. For various reasons, they lost lands or were unable to obtain lands. Therefore, they had to rely on small-capital businesses to make a living. They usually borrow capital from wealthy and influential families. In late Ming, Jin Sheng gave an account on Huizhou peasants' relinquishing farming to turn to trade:

> The prefecture [of Huizhou] was situated in the mountains, like rats living in holes. The soil was barren and lands were small. Those who lived on farming did not make up ten percent [of the whole population]. If [one] chose to resign to the circumstance and stay at home for a living, [he] would soon be seen to die. The situation was that [people] had to wander about in different places to earn a living. Therefore, people migrated to all places. They were not born as merchants. [They,] however, still had strong attachment to their ancestral graves and thus reluctant to relocate their whole families [to other places]. So, [they] shipped grains back to [their hometowns], but not for profits. Although [they] possessed money to do business, they did not own it. [They] borrowed it from great families in different places with an interest rate of twenty or thirty percent.[73]

From this, it is not difficult to understand the general situation of petty peddlers. They, who were in great number, adopted various ways of running businesses. Some of them carried baskets or loads and wandered about the streets to hawk their goods. Some "went out as traders" to transport, long distance or short distance, goods for sale. Some others ran restaurants or hotels to sell food and provide lodgings. They "butchered pigs and sold liquor" or vended varieties of daily-use articles. In the realm of circulation, petty peddlers performed a vital function of reinvigorating economy and carrying on the exchange of needed goods. They, as a stratum, were indispensable. The hardworking petty peddlers possessed meager capital and earned small profits, but they were frequently exploited. Feudal states levied heavy taxes on them. During the Wanli reign, provincial governor of Henan, Shen Jiwen, once reported to the emperor, "[Merchants] sell cakes, soups, pig hair, and oxen bones. [They] vend [such goods] all day long, but [earn] very little. [They] are levied heavy [taxes] because they circulate [goods]."[74] In addition, they were oftentimes bullied and extorted by local tyrants, evil gentry, and brokers. Due to their small capital, they could not endure economic setbacks. According to Jin Sheng, when he rested himself in his hometown in Xiuning, he once "surveyed his townspeople from four counties." Seventy percent of those who went out and worked as merchants suffered from adversities and trials so that "they could not return to their business and had to stay at home." Among those who "stayed at home," "no one could luckily escape the fate" of "failing to borrow money to live on before they were seen to die."[75] There were petty peddlers who excelled at running businesses and eventually made a fortune. For example, She Yiwen from She County of Huizhou

> came from a poor family. He became a merchant when he was he was twenty. He was honest and never cheated others. He did not suspect that others were cheating him, either. Usually, he believed hoaxes played by others. Nonetheless, his profits trebled. In his middle age, he accumulated a wealth of several thousand ounces of silver.[76]

Xu Ruxiu from the same county engaged in cotton fabric business in Wuxi. "[He] was initially poor. [Yet, because] he excelled at commerce, he earned thousands [of ounces of silver]."[77] Nevertheless, such petty peddlers who ended up making a fortune constituted a minority.

The strata of merchants in traditional society was a resilient structure. Under certain conditions, the statuses of merchants of the aforementioned strata were interchangeable.

## Notes

1  "Huozhi liezhuan" (货殖列传), in *Shiji* (史记).
2  "Qingzhong yi" (轻重乙), in *Guanzi* (管子).
3  "Youguan" (幼官), in *Guanzi* (管子).
4  "Zhaogong shiliu nian" (昭公十六年), in *Zuozhuan* (左传).
5  "Huozhi liezhuan" (货殖列传), in *Shiji* (史记).
6  "Xianjin pian" (先进篇), in *Lunyu* (论语).
7  "Huozhi liezhuan" (货殖列传), in *Shiji* (史记).
8  Ibid.
9  "Kongcongzi" (孔丛子), quoted in "Huozhi liezhuan" (货殖列传), in *Shiji* (史记).
10  "Huozhi liezhuan" (货殖列传), in *Shiji* (史记).
11  Ibid.
12  Ibid.
13  Ibid.
14  "Shihuo zhi shang" (食货志上), in *Hanshu* (汉书).
15  "Huozhi liezhuan" (货殖列传), in *Shiji* (史记).

16 "Cuobi" (错币), in *Yantie lun* (盐铁论).
17 "Shihuo zhi shang" (食货志上), in *Hanshu* (汉书).
18 "Pingzhun shu" (平准书), in *Shiji* (史记).
19 Ibid.
20 "Wudai yanqu zhi jin" (五代盐曲之禁), *Ershier shi zhaji* (二十二史札记), volume 22.
21 "Zhengque kao er, yantie" (征榷考二, 盐铁), in *Wenxian tongkao* (文献通考), volume 15.
22 "Shihuo zhi" (食货志), in *Song shi* (宋史).
23 *Tongdian* (通典), volume 11.
24 *Zizhi tongjian* (资治通鉴), volume 178.
25 "Zhiguan zhi" (职官志), "Shihuo zhi" (食货志), in *Jiu tangshu* (旧唐书).
26 Entry of "Zhajia guanjia yu renguan" (诈假官假与人官) of "Zhawei pian" (诈伪篇), volume 25, in *Tanglü shuyi* (唐律疏议).
27 *Ming huidian* (明会典).
28 "Wendi ji" (文帝纪), in *Sanguo zhi* (三国志).
29 "Zhuge Liang zhuan" (诸葛亮传), in *Sanguo zhi* (三国志).
30 "Wudi ji" (武帝纪), in *Songshu* (宋书).
31 "Mingdi ji" (明帝纪), in *Nanqi shu* (南齐书).
32 "Zhuan lun" (传论), in *Songshu* (宋书).
33 "Shaodi ji" (少帝纪), in *Songshu* (宋书).
34 "Donghun hou zhuan" (东昏侯传), in *Nanqi shu* (南齐书).
35 "Shihuo zhi" (食货志), in *Hanshu* (汉书).
36 Du Bao (杜宝), *Daye zaji* (大业杂记).
37 Song Minqiu (宋敏求), "Dongshi" (东市), in *Chang'an zhi* (长安志), volume 8.
38 *Tongshang geguan huayang maoyi zongce* (通商各关华洋贸易总册), *Guangxu shiqi nian* (光绪十七年), volume 2.
39 Li Xichong (林西冲), *Yikui lou xuangao* (挹奎楼选稿), volume 1.
40 Cai Xiang (蔡襄), *Cai Zhonghuigong wenji* (蔡忠惠公文集), volume 15.
41 "Lizong san" (理宗三), in *Songshi quanwen* (宋史全文).
42 "Shang Renzong huangdi yanshi shu" (上仁宗皇帝言事书), in *Wang Linchuan ji* (王临川集), volume 39.
43 "Yuezhou hupo" (岳州湖泊), in *Yijian zhi* (夷坚志), volume *xin* (2).
44 "Zhuangtian" (庄田), in *Guochao dianhui* (国朝典汇), volume 19.
45 *Ming wuzong shilu* (明武宗实录), volume 194, the 12th month of Zhengde (正德) 15, 3640.
46 Ibid., volume 197, the 3rd month of Zhengde (正德)16, 3683.
47 Ibid., volume 116, the 9th month of Zhengde (正德)9, 2345; volume 108, the 1st month of Zhengde (正德)9, 2211.
48 "Neifu zhizhang" (内府职掌), in *Minggongshi* (明宫史), volume *mu*.
49 *Mingshi* (明史), volume 300.
50 *Ming Shizong shilu* (明世宗实录), volume 4, the 7th month of Zhengde (正德) 16, 176.
51 *Wufeng lu*(吴风录).
52 "Guilian" (贵廉), in Gu Yanwu (顾炎武),*Rizhi lu* (日知录), volume 3.
53 Fan Shouji (范守己), *Yulongzi ji – Quweixinwen* (御龙子集·曲洧新闻), volume 2.
54 *Ming jingshiwen bian* (明经世文编), volume 246; Hu Song (胡松), "Chen Yuzhong xiaomo yi yibao wanshi zhi'an shi" (陈愚忠效末议以保万世治安事).
55 *Ming Xianzong shilu* (明宪宗实录), volume 181, the 1st month (part I) of Chenghua (成化)21, 4409.
56 *Mingchen zouyi* (明臣奏议), volume 14.
57 Xue Fucheng (薛福成), "Ruxiang qiyuan" (入相奇缘), in *Yong'an biji* (庸庵笔记), volume 3.
58 *Gengshengzhai wen jiaji* (更生斋文甲集), volume 4.
59 *Xin'an Xiuning mingzu zhi* (新安休宁名族志), volume 1.
60 "Wenxing" (文行), in *Shaxi jilue* (沙溪集略), volume 4.
61 *Yueshi pian* (阅世篇), volume 6.

62 Ai Nanying (艾南英), *Tianyongzi quanji* (天佣子全集), volume 6.

63 Li Shaowen (李绍文), *Yunjian zazhi* (云间杂识), volume 8.

64 Zhu Yumming (祝允明), *Zhuzi zhiguai lu* (祝子志怪录), volume 5.

65 *Jianwen jixun* (见闻记训), volume 1.

66 Dong Han (董含), *Sangang zhilue* (三冈识略), volume 8.

67 Bao Shichen (包世臣), *Anwu sizhong* (安吴四种), volume 3 and 5.

68 *Tao Wenyi gong quanji* (陶文毅公全集), volume 19.

69 *Huangchao zhengdian leizuan* (皇朝正典类纂), volume 71.

70 "Beike" (碑刻), part II, in *Xi Huai yanfa zhi* (西淮盐法志) of the Jiaqing (嘉庆) reign, volume 55.

71 "Huzheng" (户政), part 24, in *Huangchao jingshi wenbian* (皇朝经世文编), volume 49.

72 Li Cheng (李澄), *Huaicuo beiyao* (淮鹾备要), volume 3.

73 "Yu Xu antai shu" (与徐按台书), in *Jin Zhongjiegong wenji* (金忠节公文集), volume 4.

74 *Ming Shenzong shilu* (明神宗实录), volume 434, the 6th month of Wanli (万历) 35, 8200.

75 "Yu Xu antai shu" (与徐按台书), in *Jin Zhongjiegong wenji* (金忠节公文集), volume 4.

76 "Lisi xiangxian jishi" (里祀乡贤纪事), in *Yanzhen zhicao* (岩镇志草).

77 "Qian Xi yilai shilue zhuanzhuang" (迁锡以来事略传状), in *Qian Xi Xushi zongpu* (迁锡许氏宗谱).

# 2 The integration of the merchant in early modern times and the rise of merchant groups

In the early modern period, the merchant as a group completed an initial psychological integration because of the rise of the sprout of capitalism. Merchants preached new values such as the equality between scholars and merchants and both agriculture and commerce valued as the root. The integration resulted in the making of merchant groups based on geographic regions. The merchant class began to play an active role in modern China. This chapter also analyzes the areas of activity of individual merchant groups, their commercial networks, and characteristics of their commercial activities.

China's *jinshishehui* (modern society), set in in the sixteenth century, was marked by the emergence of the sprout of capitalism in China. The sprout of capitalism was the primitive form of a capitalistic relation of production inside feudal society. Its creation and maturity was a historical process in which the feudal mode of production transitioned to a capitalistic one. We call the historical stage where capitalism sprouted and then matured as modern society. Here, "maturity" is a relative concept, peculiar to China's actual conditions – namely, merchants' investment in new-style enterprises and the rise of the bourgeoisie. Modern society ended in the twentieth century, with the Opium War being the line of demarcation between the early and late modern times. Merchants in modern society experienced two psychological integrations as a group. In the early modern times, merchants underwent an initial psychological integration with the rise of the sprout of capitalism. It resulted in the making of merchant groups (*shangbang*). Hence, the merchant's class became active in the modern era as a group. In the late modern times when capitalism fully developed, the merchant as a group underwent a psychological integration once again. Its outcome was the establishment of the chamber of commerce (*shanghui*). The merchant, who was incorporated into the bourgeoisie, constituted a vital part of China's upstart capitalists.

## Section one: the merchant's first integration

### 1 The merchant's identification: from kinship to native places

Merchants' psychological integration manifested itself in the transition from their identification with kinship to that with native places. The merchant's psychological integration consisted of two aspects. First of all, the criterion of self-identification among merchants expanded from bondage to patriarchal clans to ties to native soil. During the Jiajing and Wanli reigns, merchants made their footprints across the country with the expansion of the market. No matter where they arrived and what they worked on, they had to strive hard for their survival and thriving. Then, "great merchants must stay in large metropolises." Metropolis referred to "Beijing, Nanjing, and [big cities] in Jiangsu, Zhejiang, Fujian, and Guangdong. The second-tier cities included prefectures such as Suzhou, Songjiang, Huai'an, Yangzhou, Linqing, and, Jining, counties such as Yizhen and Wuhu, and towns such as Guazhou and Jingde."[1] In those metropolises, it was infeasible for one family or clan to cope with issues related to businesses. Nor was it possible to compete with local merchants or businessmen from other regions. Even in villages, towns, and marketplaces, the competition among merchants was intense. Thus, merchants began to put emphasis on unions among different clans. In the criterion of collective identification in China, blood relationship gained more weight than ties to geographical areas. Therefore, the unions of clans actually referred to those among clans with common geographical ties. Such a bond stemmed from inter-clan marriages. In reality, it had been a longtime practice that the commercial relationship among clans was forged because of their marriages. Yet, influential families and gentry all despised this practice. With a traditional feudal concept that prioritized agriculture over commerce, what mattered to a marriage was the political hierarchy and family status. Such a value orientation began to lose ground with the assault of modern commodified economy. Influential families and powerful clans began to value wealth and commercial interests as the most important factor in marriages. The transformation of wedding customs was key to the transition of the merchant's identification from blood relationship to ties to geographical areas. Here, I take the Wang clan, the most prominent family in Huizhou, as an example to make analysis.

The Wang clan was a powerful clan boasting of a long history. "[Wang] Shuju, Commander of the Liu-Song dynasty [during the Southern and Northern Dynasties] and great-great-grandfather of Wang Hua, Duke of Yueguo [during the Tang Dynasty], lived in seclusion in Wang Village and became the ancestor of this village." "The Wang's in the [Huizhou] Prefecture and six counties were all his descendants. [His offspring] spilled over to other provinces and those Wang's also came from here."[2] It was even said, "Among ten households in Xin'an, nine carried the surname of Wang."[3] During the Song times, the major factor behind marriage with this powerful family was status. During the Qianlong and Daoguang times, Hu Shunshen wrote a preface for *Jinzi Hushi jiapu* (*Genealogy of the Hu's of Jinzi*) and mentioned that the Hus and the Wangs "intermarry with each other for generations." He pointed out,

[The Hu's] live in Chongrenfang in the eastern part of the county, while Wang's prosper in Dunlifang. The two clans [live in two opposite zones] in the east and west [like two] ox horns. They intermarry with each for generations. Each of their residential areas occupy half of the county. In Jixi County, only the Hus and the Wangs are known as influential families. The County Magistrate Zhao Xundao (Zhao Qi, whose alternative name was Xundao, once served as the county magistrate during the Daguan reign – from original note) once composed a poem stating, "There were only two clans in Anding and Pingyang." This was an account of the actual situation.

In the mid-Ming, more members of the Wang clan became businessmen. It was stated in *She County Gazetteer* produced in the Wanli reign,

> In this county, it was the Huang clan that initially seized the position as leaders of salt business to dominate in [areas] under the heaven. Later, the Wang clan and Wu clan became prominent. They all possessed [capital of] tens hundreds of thousands and even millions [of ounces of silver].

Xu Chengyao, the last-generation *juren* (provincial level) graduate from She County and author of *Sheshi xiantan* (*Casual Chats on Affairs in She County*), pointed out, "The wealth of Wu's and Wang's peaked during the Ming times. The rise of the Jiang's occurred in the Qing times."[4] It is safe to argue that as a powerful clan that produced the largest number of officials in the county, the Wang clan turned into an influential household of merchants. The marital situation of the Wang's also changed, which was mentioned in *Taihan ji* (*Anthology of Taihan*). I cite some examples to illustrate it.

The Wangs intermarried with the Wus from Xi'nan. The Wus "lived in western She County and made a fortune by means of trading. The most wealthy and influential were called three Wu's." During the Ming times, both the Wang clan and the Wu clan were powerful salt merchants. The great grandson of Wu Rucheng who assumed the position of salt leader during the Zhengde and Wanli reigns, Wu Xunmei married to Wang Daokun's eldest granddaughter. Their son, Wu Qichang, was also a great merchant.

The Wangs also intermarried with the Chengs. Wang Daokun made a statement about his background: "My grandfather and granduncle both thrived as merchants. In my tenth younger brother's generation, [my family] accumulated a fortune of over ten thousand [ounces of silver]." "My grandfather, [Wang] Hang, was the first one to trade salt."[5] The two clans intermarried because of their commercial partnership. "My [Wang Daokun's] late father and your late father were both merchants, and [the families] united in matrimony." Wang Daokun further pointed out that the Cheng clan was extraordinarily rich and enjoyed particularly high status. "Their marriage partners were all [from families of] renowned gentry in the prefecture."[6]

The Wang clan also intermarried with the Sun clan, which produced quite a large number of merchants.

> Mount Yan is in east Xiuning and five *li* away from She County. Mr. Wang Chang is a descendant of Duke of Yueguo. So, he and I descend from the same ancestor. The Sun clan is the most famous among those who live in the

regular marketplace along the riverbank. The two clans intermarry with each for generations.[7]

The Wang and Hu clans continued to intermarry. Wang Daokun's mother was precisely "from the Hu [family]. In his "Nanshan pian" (Essays on Southern Mountains), Wang Daokun not only showed off the background of the Hu clan – namely, "an old and well-respected family in the neighborhood," but took pride in his uncles, who "relied on wealth [accumulated] in the past to accomplish remarkable feats."

It is unnecessary to enumerate all examples of the Wang clan's choices of marriage partners based on commercial interests. The web weaved by marriages among different clans resulted in three patent social effects:

1   The transformation of wedding customs both resulted from the development of commerce and prefigured the further expansion of commerce. The most direct benefit was the further enlargement of sources of capital. Relatives by marriage communicated and cooperated with each to make merchants more skillful in business affairs.

2   The transformation of wedding customs both resulted from merchants' engaging in commercial activities and presupposed the formation of the merchant's groups. Various Huizhou clans were bonded together by marriage because of commercial interests. It not only accelerated the trend of merging families of officials and merchants but also enabled the blood ties among clans to extend and intersect with one another to consolidate collaborations among various clans and groups in commerce. The Huizhou merchant group was both a geographical concept and characterized by strong kinship ties. As a result, merchants from six counties of Huizhou were specialized in different trades, which constituted a salient feature of Huizhou merchants. Among them, merchants from She County were mostly salt traders. Xiuning produced a large number of pawnbrokers. Merchants from Wuyuan engaged in timber and tea trades. Most merchants from Qimen were businessmen of porcelain, tea, and timber. Every county had their specialties due to particular geographical situations and productions. It was also because a web of blood ties constructed by marriages among various clans could cover only one county. Therefore, individual counties had their different principal trades, although those merchants belonged to the same category of Huizhou merchants. Objectively, the specialization of trades allowed various Huizhou merchant groups to develop their own commercial power without external interference and to establish monopoly. Meanwhile, various blood-tied webs intersected with one another, which manifested itself in the fact that merchants from those counties engaged in all kinds of trades and sold all types of commodities besides adhering to their principal businesses. Huizhou merchants exemplified a feudal merchant group built upon factors of kinship and native places.

3   The transformation of wedding customs both resulted from commercial competitions and paved way for further competitions. Merchants' strengthening

of commercial management and cooperation by means of marriages among clans was itself indicative of the existence of an intense competition within feudal commerce due to the development of a commodified economy. The making of merchant groups enhanced merchants' competiveness.

In the process of intermarriage among clans, merchants enhanced a consciousness of collectivity. The scope of their identification expanded from kinship to native places. Accordingly, merchants' organizations expanded from those tied to blood to merchant groups. The establishment of *huiguan* (guild) of merchants marked the creation of merchant groups and the completion of merchants' initial psychological integration. In some sense, merchants' *huiguan* was merely an extension and enlargement of their ancestral temples, which manifested itself in the relationship between Huizhou clans and Huizhou *huiguan*. *Jiali* (*Family Rites*) formulated by Zhu Xi was the prototype of "family codes" or "rules of clan" of various clans in Huizhou. The preface to *Mingzhou Wushi jiadian* (*Family Code of the Wu Clan from Mingzhou*) indicated that rules of the Wu clan "was derived from Zhu Xi's *Family Rites*, and [the compilers] gave [Zhu Xi's work] a new name as *Family Code*." Family Code "held the three cardinal guides and the five constant virtues as its principle" in order to "clarify the ethics of rulers, the ruled, fathers, sons, husbands, and wives and regulate rituals between the intimate and the distant and those between the noble and the lowly." Both Huizhou *huiguan* and Huizhou clans worshipped Master Zhu and maintained their internal relations by means of a patriarchal system, only to different degrees. Xu Chengyao said, "Our Huizhou people believe in fellow townspeople's mutual affection and attach importance to commerce. In any places in which merchants arrive, *huiguan* and coffin homes prevail."[8] All Huizhou *huiguan* across the country enshrined Master Zhu with no exception. In Suzhou, a great commercial metropolis, a Huizhou *huiguan* was established in Changwutu to "worship Master Zhu, the great scholar of the past."[9] In Hankou, "Xin'an *huiguan* worshipped Master Zhu."[10]"Xin'an *huiguan* was established" in Jingdezhen to "be dedicated to Master Zhu in the shrine."[11] In small or medium-sized town such as Liaoliu, "[merchants] followed the examples of Hankou and Suzhou to [establish] a *huiguan* to enshrine Master Zhu."[12]

In Xingsha, "the *huiguan* and Zhu Xi's shrine were repaired and maintained."[13] In the remote South, Zhu Wenwei, a merchant from Wuyuan, "often visited the Pearl River. It happened that the 'Shrine of Master Zhu' was occupied by bandits. Zhu Wenwei brought a lawsuit to the government and stayed in Guangdong for two years before [the shrine] was restored."[14] Huizhou merchants' *huiguan* of different trades also enshrined Master Zhu. Daxing *huiguan* in Xihui of Jiangsu, which "enshrined Lord Guan (Yu) and Master Zhu, was a meeting place of timber merchants."[15]"Huizhou Shrine for Master Zhu outside the Houchao Gate of Hangzhou was precisely the public hall for timber merchants."[16] More interestingly, the Huining *Huiguan* of Shengze Town of Wujiang "had a hall in the east to enshrine Master Zhu of Ziyang Huizhou." In the meantime, the main hall was dedicated to

the "Imposing, Manifest, Benevolent, and Brave Lord who Assists the Heaven."
The eastern hall was a shrine of Lord Wang [Hua], the Prince of Loyalty and Gal-
lantry. The western hall was for Lord Zhang, the Prince of Pacifying the East."[17]
Master Zhu and Wang Hua – the Wang clan's ancestor – were both enshrined.
Considering the Wangs dominated in Shengze Town, merchants worshipped no
one but Wang's ancestor. Here, Wang Hua could also be regarded as the symbol
of the patriarchal force. The enshrinement of the three sworn brothers of the Peach
Garden in the late Han also indicated Huizhou merchants' wish of maintaining
fraternity among them. This was a telling example of the unity between Huizhou
merchants' sense of belonging to the collectivity and that to the patriarchal clans.
The expansion of the criterion of collective identification effectively controlled
the competitions among themselves. Every Huizhou merchant acted for both his
own and his fellow townsmen's maximal profits – namely, "countrymen maintaining harmony and working in concert with each other" or "reaching consensus and
combining talents to study the ways of [doing business] and collectively improve
the skills."[18] When Huizhou merchants were bullied by locals or other merchant
groups in places where they engaged in trade, the Huizhou merchant group would
"use the collective [force] to help the masses." For example,

> merchants from Xindu . . . engaged in trade in other places. Whenever [their
> fellow Xindu merchants] were faced with lawsuits, they felt as if they per-
> sonally underwent [the legal procedures]. So, [they] donated money and put
> up maximal effort to use the collective force to help the masses. This was
> because they were in a place other than their hometown.[19]

## 2  The integration of merchants' values

The second aspect of the merchant group's psychological integration was that of
values. During the Ming and Qing times, traditional values remained the mainstream in social psychology. That is, "accumulating thousands or tens of thousands was inferior to studying."[20]

People "admired that birds flew high in sky" and viewed scholarship as the most
important matter for personal accomplishment and reputation. Espoused by the
rulers, "[the idea was popularized that] farming was the essence [in areas] under
the heaven, whereas manufacturing and commerce were both trivial."[21] Merchants
were disparaged universally in society so that the merchant was at the lowest level
of the four classes. Faced with the enormous pressure resulting from traditional
values, the merchant had to overcome an inferiority complex and establish his
own value system to seek further development. What was central to the merchant's
psychological integration was to pit a new value against the old one and to make
the new value as the psychological foundation for their collective actions and the
ultimate goal in their pursuit. The merchant's psychological integration centered
around the concepts of the merchant (the trivial) and the Confucian scholar (the
essential). In *Merchants and Society in Modern China: From Guild to Chamber of
Commerce*, which is about the merchant's culture, I give fuller details about the

process of integration. The merchant's new values manifested themselves in his estimation of his own social value. When describing the Shanxi merchant Wang Laipin's admonition to his sons and grandsons, Li Weizhen of the Ming stated in "Xiang jijiu Wanggong mubiao" (An Epitaph of Mr. Wang, Chancellor of the Village), "In all four classes, the scholar is the most respectable. However, if [you] cannot make an accomplished [scholar], [you'd] better be a farmer or merchant."[22] Han Bangqi gave an account of the Shanxi merchant Xi Ming in "Daming Xijun muzhiming" (An Epitaph of Mr. Xi of Great Ming):

> When [Mr. Xi] was young, he studied in an attempt to be a scholar, but in vain. [He] did not like farming, either. [He once] said, "How could a gentleman who fails to make his name known to all by being a scholar sweat without establishing an undertaking for his family?"[23]

Gui Youguang stated in "Bai'an Chengweng bashi shouxu" (Preface to the Congratulatory Words on the Birthday of Mr. Cheng of Bai'an),

> Mr. Cheng from Xin'an stayed in Wu when [he was] young. Confucian scholars in Wu all liked to befriend him . . . In ancient times, people of four classes engaged in different businesses. At present, scholars are indistinguishable from peasants or merchants.

The Cheng clan "multiplies, and thousands of descendants live in Haining, She County, and Yi County, many of whom make a living as scholars. Isn't that they are scholar-merchants?"[24] Although Wang Laipin cited the oft-used terms of "farmer" and "merchant," he in reality meant that an unaccomplished scholar was inferior to a merchant. Xi Ming was more candid in claiming that being a merchant was an alternative option if one could not make a scholar. He harbored no intention to be a peasant. Gui Youguang further pointed out that the scholar and the merchant had mixed with each other, making it hard to differentiate them. Thus, according to the concept of the four classes formulated by merchants, the order was supposed to be scholar, merchant, peasant, and artisan. The four classes could further be categorized as two groups: the scholar and merchant belonged to the upperechelon of society, whereas the peasant and artisan were dismissed as the lower strata. In the Qing times, an idea cropped up that the scholar was inferior to the merchant. Gui Zhuang wrote "Chuanyanzhai ji" (Biography of Chamber of Passing Down the Inkslab) for Yan Shungong from Dongtingshan of the Lake Tai, who had a dual identity as both scholar and merchant. The author stated in one paragraph in the text,

> A scholar's son is always a scholar, while a merchant's son is always a merchant. The ancestors of Mr. Yan were both. Shungong has two identities, too. But for Shungong's sake, I consider that Shungong should focus on business and warn his descendants against pursuing careers as scholars. This is because in today's world, the scholar has been exceedingly debased.[25]

Here, Gui Zhuang cited the example of Mr. Yan's ancestors who "were both scholars and merchants" to confirm the observation made by Gui Youguang, his great grandfather, that "scholars are indistinguishable from merchants." However, his advice that Yan Shungong "should focus on business and warn his descendants against pursuing careers as scholars" hinted on the notion that the scholar was inferior to the merchant. In areas where merchants were powerful, new values proposed by merchants gained recognition from members of other social strata in the same areas. It was pointed out in "*She fengsu lijiao kao*" (A Study on Customs and Confucian Ethics in the She County), "The merchant is the lowest among the four classes, but it is not the case in Huizhou's customs." *She County Gazetteer* of the Wanli reign indicated that the status of commerce in Huizhou had changed fundamentally in the Jiajing reign. "In the past, [people] engaging in farming became rich, but now, [those] engaging in trade are rich." It was stated in *Wutai xinzhi* (*New Gazetteer of Wutai*) of Shanxi: "As for the custom in Shanxi, the merchant is more important."[26] Emperor Yongzheng also indicated in his imperial edict, "In Shanxi, the merchant is in the leading position. The second best people work on farming. The next best people join the army, and the lowest ones are made to study."[27] In Fujian, "people [living] in the coast are bent solely on profit. [They] rush to dangerous places like a flock of ducks so that [they] usually reach outlying islets beyond the borderline."[28] Guangdong "people work on trading and gain profits by taking the preemptive opportunities of the time."[29] In Shandong, "people scramble for the smallest profit, and many engage in commerce."[30]

The psychological integration in local societies resulting from the merchant's new values not only transformed the mentality of local people but also produced a current of thought of money worshipping that posed a threat to local society in the late Ming. Xue Lundao described in his essay "Ti qian" (On Money), "People climb the mountains and cross the oceans for you; People seek tigers and look for leopards for you; People lose their lives for you; People sell their bodies for you." "People's morals are rotten for you; People ignore righteousness and mercy for you; People refuse to be filial and incorruptible for you; People forget loyalty and trustworthiness for you." "People feel annoyed and perplexed for you; People are lost in a reverie for you; People change their integrity for you; People disobey the Confucian code of ethics for you." "Without you, heroes devalue; Without you, warriors become sentimental; Without you, the family and the state perish; Without you, [people's] accomplishments fail."

> With you, everyone is happy; With you, everything is marvelous; With you, [people] are positioned above the salt; With you [people] enjoy high standing. At one point when luck disappears and time changes, [people] lower their heads and lock the arms like a chicken soaked through in rain. Just think about that: how much of the past friendship is left?

"[People who are] as changeable as the cloud and rain are so snobbish. The places to pursue profit and chase reputation are like pernicious battlefield." "Everyone is [as greedy as] a snake who wants to swallow an elephant; Everyone is [as aggressive as] a rabbit who runs after a roebuck; Everyone is [as deceptive as] a businessman who hangs dogs but sells lamb."[31] Money worshipping was also illustrated in folk-tales of the day. Zhao Nanxing of the late Ming cited a popular joke: Tang Sanzang went on a pilgrimage to the Western Paradise for Buddhist scriptures. When he arrived in the Thunder Temple, Kassapa aggressively solicited tips. Out of neces-sity, Tang Sanzang gave him a violet gold alms bowl bestowed by the emperor of Tang. Pigsy felt resentful so that he impeached [Kassapa] before Sakyamuni.

> The Buddha says, "Disciples of the Buddha also need to eat and wear cloth-ing. In the past when a master of Sravasti invited Buddhist disciples to come down from the mountain, [I] recited this scripture and asked for three *dou* and three *shen* kernel-shape gold. How much gold does your alms bowl contain? It's not worth mentioning!" The words [shut up] Pigsy [as if] a wild goose's beak was strung up by an arrow. [He] was so upset and walked out by saying: "It turns out that money is needed to see the living Buddha day after day."[32]

The magical power of money was so tremendous that heavenly principles and human relations both bowed to monetary gains. Even Confucian codes of ethics that defied change for thousands of generations decayed and perished. In this trend of money worshipping, more people joined the ranks of the merchant. Encour-aged by the new values and perspectives, merchants entered for the competition confidently to strive for success in their careers. Such common values were an important precondition for the making of the merchant group.

The merchant's values made impact on whole society to such a degree that money worshipping prevailed. However, due to the deep-seated Chinese tradi-tional culture and the Confucian values that had long found its way deep into the hearts of the people, it is not proper to overstate the trend of money worship-ping in the late Ming. In the same time when money worshipping was rampant, a trend of cursing money arose. The merchant's power was a centrifugal force to the existing order with which political power ruled properties. Such a potential crisis of feudal morality aroused the rulers' anxiety. Therefore, as they repeatedly exclaimed, "The power of money is the strongest nowadays,"[33]they assumed a role as the counsellors of the world and heaped curses on money: "[If we] take a look at the composition of the character, it consists of *jin* (metal) and two *ge* (spear), which [means that] it is an instrument to kill people."[34] Someone assumed Confucius's tone to revile the Money God,

> Sage Kong is indignant and curses: "money is a brute! The dynasty's law is manipulated by you. Human relations and codes of ethics are ruined by you . . . As [my anger] comes to mind, [I] cut the Money God with a sword, chop him with an axe, fry him in oil, and steam him in steaming racks."[35]

Some advised,

> People say gold is lovable, but I'm afraid that gold will do harm. How could those who abandon themselves to business prosper long? The golden plat-form has been buried. Where is the money mountain now? [Money] sealed in

purple marks and yellow lists has been ridiculed and admonished for tens of thousands of generations. Brocade bed-curtains and candlewicks are a step to disaster. Ghosts and sickness haunt [people] because of avarice. Generosity makes [people] laugh every time.[36]

The clash between the two trends of money hating and money worshipping indicated, on the one hand, that in modern society when capitalism had sprouted, the power of the merchant class was still too weak to have their values integrate whole society. On the other hand, the formation of the merchant groups did not mean the completion of the psychological integration of merchants. The merchant's inferior complex at the subconscious level drove him to identify himself with the scholar's class, which hampered the merchant's engaging in society as an independent force. Therefore, the integration of the merchant's values occurred throughout modern society and the whole process of transforming the merchant's organizations from blood-tied entities into native-place and trade-oriented ones. In late modern society, the merchant's organizations would undergo another integration and would blossom into an autonomous political force – namely, the bourgeoisie – under the new historical condition of intensified crises both at home and abroad.

## Section two: ten great merchant groups

The merchant groups referred to loose organizations tied by native-place factors. The geographical scope could be as big as several provinces such as the Shan-Shaan merchant group, or West merchant group. It could be as small as several villages such as the Dongting merchant group. The merchant group's structure of organization was *huiguan*. The merchant group was characterized by both kinship relations and business specialties. Generally speaking, the bigger the geographical scope, the less relevant the blood relations were and the more important business specialties became. For example, the Shan(xi)-Shaan(xi) *huiguan* in Hankou included numerous trades and regional merchants in the Shanxi Province such as the Taiyuan group, the Fenzhou group, the Hongrong group, the Herong group, the Juancha group, the Xiyan group, the Wenxi group, the Ya('an) group, the cotton print group, the western pharmacy group, the native fruit group, the imported oil group, the grain group, the machine woven fabric group, the leather group, the native bank group, the walnut group, the Beijing-Tianjin group, the Junzhou tobacco group, the red flower group, the pawn-shop group, the paper group, and the remittance group, most of which were formed based on their business connections. The Dongting group was controlled by a few families.

During the Ming and Qing times, merchants in commercially developed areas relied on the collective power of merchant groups to enter into competition. In various places in China, merchant groups of different sizes are innumerable, among which the most famous ones were the Huizhou, Shanxi, Shaanxi, Jiangxi, Longyou, Ningbo, Dongting, Linqing, Fujian, and Guandong merchant groups. They were collectively known as "the ten great merchant groups." In reality, there were more renowned merchant groups than ten. For example, Suzhou, Shaoxing, Beijing, and Nanjing merchant groups were all powerful ones. Meanwhile, larger merchant groups could be divided into smaller ones. For example, the western merchant group consisted of the Shanxi and Shaanxi groups. The Shanxi group was composed of the Pingyang, Zezhou, and Lu'an groups, whose merchants engaged in ordinary commerce, and Pingyao, Taigu, and Qi County groups, which were specialized in money transfer.

The rise of the merchant group synchronized with the sprout of capitalism. The making of the merchant group indicated that the merchant class went up on the historical stage as a collective force. The merchant group would remain active in the realm of circulation for four long centuries and exerted a huge impact on modern society after the sixteenth century.

### 1 The rise of the merchant group

There were four reasons behind the rise the ten great merchant groups besides the historical context of the development of a commodified economy and intense commercial competitions:

1   Geographical conditions. The rise of merchant groups was closely relevant to geographical conditions. The geographical locations of the ten great merchant groups were largely places with barren and inadequate lands and dense population. The hometown of the Huizhou merchant, the Huizhou Prefecture "is situated in numerous mountains, where transportation by ship and carriage is unavailable. There are few lands but a vast population. With small amounts of land, tax revenues are insignificant."[37] "Towns of the county are situated in numerous mountains, like rats living in holes. The land is barren and small in size . . . The situation is that [people] have to be scattered to make a living elsewhere. Thus, there is an exodus of people."[38]Dongshan and Xishan of Dongting where the Dongting merchant group was produced were also characterized by "narrow lands and dense population." Wang Aozeng, a native of Dongshan, Dongting, and minister of Revenue during the Zhengde reign, said,

[People] from mountains inside the lake live on commerce. The land is small and the population is large. When a person is seventeen or eighteen *sui* old, he went to run a business with a sum of money. [People] go to Chu, Wei, Qi, and Lu. The farther, the better. Someone stays away from home for years.[39]

A statistics shows that in the early Jiajing years, Dongshan and Xishan of Dongting had 18,085 households with a population of 99,971. The size of mountains, forests, lands, and marshes amounted to 1,404 *qin* and 55 *mu*. In other words, the size per person was slightly over one *mu* and four *fen*.[40] The situation compelled people from Dongshan and Xishan to leave their hometowns and do business to make a living. The Longyou merchant group referred to merchants from five counties – Longyou, Changshan, Xi'an, Kaihua, and Jiangshan – all of which belonged to Quzhou Prefecture of Zhejiang. Longyou had more mountains but few lands. Wang Shizhen said, "Lands in Longyou are so infertile that the production is meager and wealth cannot be accumulated. [People] cannot live without going out to trade."[41] The other four counties were faced with the same problem. Take Changshan as an example. *Quzhou fuzhi* (*Gazetteer of Quzhou Prefecture*) mentioned that this place "has small lands and a high population density. [People] maintain a custom of being diligent and frugal. [They] engage in commerce and medicine."[42] The Ningbo merchant group referred to merchants from seven counties under Ningbo Prefecture – Yin County, Cixi, Zhenhai, Dinghai, Fenghua, Xiangshan, and Ninghai. Ningbo prefecture was situated along the coastal area with a vast number of mountains but few lands. For example, Zhenhai County "is built along the ocean. [People] are living in saline and alkaline lands. The soil is poor and the water sources are unavailable. Therefore, farmers fail to harvest all year long."[43] Cixi County "has high population density and tiny lands. Even in years of good harvest, people are short of food by thirty percent."[44] Therefore, "half of Ningbo people reside in elsewhere to live on commerce."[45] The Guangdong merchant group consisted of merchants from Guangzhou, which referred to those from the Pearl River Delta (including all the territories of Panyu, Shunde, Zhongshan, Doumen, and Zhuhai Counties, most territories of Sanshui, Xinhui, Nanhai, and Dongguan Counties, some parts of Gaohe, Zengcheng, and Bao'an Counties, and Guangzhou, Foshan, and Jiangmen Cities). The Pearl River Delta is a densely populated area whose population density topped Guangdong Province. Average acreage per person was 1.8 *mu*. The number in the Nanhai County was merely 1.5.[46] Shanxi, where the Shanxi merchants originated, was also a place where "the soil was infertile, the weather was cold, and produces were rare." This was particularly true to

[the area] south of Taiyuan where people traveled faraway to trade without returning home for several years. This was not because [they] pursued a ten percent profit margin, but because lands could not provide half [of the food]. As the food for a year was unobtainable, [people] had to transport and trade goods in exchange for necessities from other places.[47]

From those accounts we can see that the disadvantaged geographical conditions were directly relevant to peasants' abandoning farming in pursuit of commercial gains and the rise of the merchant groups.

2   Traffic conditions. The rise of the merchant groups was also intimately tied to traffic conditions. Although Huizhou Prefecture, from which Huizhou merchants originated, was surrounded by mountains, it was connected to the external world by waterways. The Xin'an River, the largest river system in Huizhou, ran up eastward to Hangzhou. Going downstream along the Hui Creek and Ru Creek inside Jixi County, one reached the Yangzi Delta. In the

Qimen area in the west, one could sail to the Boyang Lake along the Chang River. The Yangzi Delta, arguably the richest place in China, was the area in which Huizhou merchants were particularly active. Situated along the Grand Canal, Linqing boasted of a uniquely favorable natural condition to facilitate exchange and trade of goods from both the South and the North. Longyou occupied a place at the crossroad of three provinces (Zhejiang, Fujian, and Jiangxi). Xu Fuchu of the Ming said, "The county was built on a vital passage. The incoming carriages and vessels and the transported commercial goods were in large crowd and crammed [the passage]."[48] Ningbo, Fujian, and Guangdong merchants all hailed from the coastal areas. Good harbors and easy access to rivers and oceans were key factors behind the rise of those merchant groups. Ningbo was built by the East China Sea and was situated at the middle point of China's coastal line. Sailing from the Ningbo Port, commercial ships could take advantage of the ocean circulation to travel back and forth between the South and the North by dint of wind. Or, they could pass along the Yong River, Yuyao River, Cao'e River, and canals in eastern Zhejiang to reach Hangzhou and then enter the Grand Canal. The Pearl River Delta faced the sea in three sides with ports branching off each other and waterways clustering together. Therefore, the water transportation was highly developed. In 1522, when the Ming government closed the Quanzhou and Ningbo ports, Guangzhou became the sole great port of the nation for international trade. From Guangzhou, one could reach places like Fujian and Southeast Asia. In addition, the Pearl River Delta was also the convergence of the East River, the West River, and the North River. The three rivers and their tributaries, such as the Gui River, the He River, the Pa River, the Sui River, the Tan River, the Han River, the Nanxi River, the Jian River, the Hanyang River, and Nandu River, collectively formed an inland traffic network to connect places from all directions. The Fujian coastal area, from which Fujian merchants originated, featured a highly irregular coastline. It had natural harbors such Quanzhou and Zhangzhou and more than 1,100 islands, which were beneficial to international trade. Its varied topography was conducive to smuggling. Shanxi, a hinterland province, also enjoyed certain geographical advantages. Shanxi was situated at the connecting point between the Northwest and the Southeast – that is, "[The place] was in an important passage."[49] To the east, there were Beijing, the nation's capital city, and Tianjin, a commercial metropolis. The province connected to Mongolia. One could exit Datong and arrive in Kyakhta via Suiyuan and Guihua. This was a significant international commercial route during the Qing times. To the west, one could reach Xinjiang and Central Asia via Xi'an, a route better known as the Silk Road. To the south, the province connected to Henan and then to the prosperous southeastern China. Such an advantaged geographical position, which was "accessible from all directions and convenient for getting to anywhere," allowed Shanxi to be an important distributing center for goods in northern China and paved the way for the rise of merchants of the Shanxi group.

3   Government policies. The Ming government's *kaizhong* policy was a crucial to the rise of Shanxi merchants and their fast development into a giant commercial entity. In the early Ming, when the government proceeded to solve the problem of supplying provisions and funds to military garrisons in the North and minimize the cost of transporting grains by non-government parties, it took advantage of the state-controlled monopoly of salt and ruled that merchants were entitled to obtain certificates of salt, with which they could draw salt from designated salt fields and then sell it in state-designated marketplaces, as long as they shipped grains to granaries in the border areas. In the early Ming, all northern garrisons in the border areas were built along the Great Wall, which was very close to Shanxi. Therefore, Shanxi merchants took action faster than anyone else to make their way to marketplaces in northern garrisons by dint of the policy of transporting grains in exchange for salt. According to volume 447 of *Ming jingshi wenbian* (*Anthology of State Affair Management in Ming*),

Troops and horses who crowded in Yansui Town all relied on merchants to supply provisions and necessities. Every year a quota was set to summon merchants from Shanxi. [Shanxi merchants] acquired rights to buy salt from Huai and Zhejiang in exchange for their shipment of grains to various granaries, before they went to the Jiangnan Salt Distribution Commission to draw salt for sale. They gained huge profits.

This laid a foundation for Shanxi merchants to have access to the national market. It was in mid-Ming times that the Shanxi merchant group officially came into existence. In 1492, when Ye Qi, minister of Revenue, launched a reform to change *kaizhong* to *zhese* – that is, turning *bense* (actual grains) into *zhese* (silver). Thus, Shanxi merchants, who originally were very active in the market of northern garrisons, turned their attention to the inland part of China, especially the areas of Huainan, Huaibei, Jiangsu, and Zhejiang whose salt businesses topped the whole country. Then, a large number of Shanxi rich merchants migrated to Huainan, Huaibei, and Zhejiang to pay silver to related government institutions in exchange for certificates of salt. They were thereby transformed into inland merchants. Aside from Huainan and Huaibei, places where salt was produced such as Changlu, Shandong, and Hebei were all visited by Shanxi merchants. Hence, taking Huainan and Huaibei as the center and Yangzhou, the distributing center for salt, as the base area, Shanxi merchants consistently enlarged their scope of business and penetrated into markets nationwide. A vast merchant group took shape.

The transformation from *kaizhong* into *zhese* was also of great importance to Huizhou merchants. Huainan, Huaibei, and Zhejiang had been Huizhou merchants' sphere of influence. After the reform to implement the *zhese* system was launched, Huizhou merchants enjoyed the geographical advantage to turn themselves into inland merchants and eventually became the mainstay of inland merchants in China. Volume 11 of the *Yangzhou fuzhi* (*Gazetteer of Yangzhou Prefecture*) printed during the Wanli reign gave an account of the composition of inland merchants: "Inland merchants were mostly from Huizhou and She County and Huai-Yang sojourners who originally hailed from Shanxi and Shaanxi." It is thus clear that the former were in larger number than the latter. The preface to *Gazetteer of Yangzhou Prefecture* printed in Wanli 11 also indicated, "Yangzhou, a water town, . . . gathered people from [places of] all directions. [Among them, people from] Huizhou were the most numerous, and those from Shaanxi and Shanxi were second [to Huizhou people.]" In a similar fashion, chapter "Huozhi" (Trade) of the *She County Gazetteer* also mentioned, "Nowhere else [produced] more widely known great merchants than our county. Even merchants from Shaanxi and Shanxi who sojourned in Huai-Yang were concerned that they can find very few peers." In addition, the following statistics can also be cited for reference. First, according to "Liezhuan" (Biographies) of *Liang Huai yanfa zhi* (the *Chronicle of Salt Business in Huainan and Huaibei*) printed during the Guangxu reign, between the Jiajing times of the Ming and Qianlong times of the Qing, there were 80 famous sojourning merchants in Yangzhou, among whom 60 were from Huizhou and ten each came from Shanxi and Shaanxi. Second, according to the statistics provided by "Shangji" (Registry of Merchants) of the *Chronicle of Salt Business in Huainan and Huaibei* printed in the Jiaqing times, there were 35 famous salt merchants in Zhejiang in Ming and Qing. Among them, 28 were Huizhou merchants. Therefore, the reform of turning *kaizhong* into *zhese* was of utmost importance to Huizhou merchants' prosperity. During the times of Jiajing and Wanli, the Huizhou merchant group, which was dominated by salt merchants, finally came into being and led the circle of businessmen.

After Shanxi and Shaanxi merchants headed for the South, their strength weakened because they were far away from their hometowns and their business lines stretched too thin. Things were even worse when they encroached into Huizhou merchants' sphere of influence in the South. They underwent marginalization, suppression, and assault. This was particularly true in the area of Huainan and Huaibei where they failed to put their feet on. Under this circumstance, Shanxi and Shaanxi merchants united by marriage – namely, "the union between Qin and Jin"[50] – to form a trans-provincial Shan-Shaan merchant group. Certainly, this was a relatively loose merchant organization. In the process of trading salt, Shanxi merchants accumulated enormous capital. In early years of the Daoguang reign, Shanxi merchants, who excelled at grasping opportunities, began to run exchange shops. After that, Shanxi merchants played a leading role in commerce.

The governments' ban on maritime trade also had great impact on the formation of Ningbo, Fujian, and Guangdong merchant groups.

4    Cultural backgrounds. The rise of merchant groups had its factors of cultural backgrounds. The higher the educational level in a local area, the more merchants in this area became intellectuals. Take Dongshan and Xishan of Dongting as an example. Although it was a tiny place, its people's success in the Civil Service Exam was remarkable during the Ming and Qing times.

Dongshan was home to two first-place and one third-place graduates of the palace exams, two first-place graduate and 28 graduates of metropolitan Civil Service Exams. Xishan also produced 12 graduates of metropolitan Civil Service Exams and a larger number of graduates of provincial and county level exams.[51] The number of scholars who ended up graduating from the exams and gaining access to officialdom was small. Most had to find other careers, such as farming. However, as Dongshan and Xishan were mountainous areas with few lands and a large population, farming was undesirable. The only feasible way of success was commerce. In genealogies discovered in Dongshan and Xishan in Dongting, there were a lot of descriptions such as "abandoning Confucian [scholarship] to do business," "stopping schooling to learn to trade," "quitting a student's career and realize his aspiration anywhere all over the country," and "stopping schooling to embark on a career in the marketplace." Therefore, among Dongting merchants there were a vast number of decently educated ones who learned skills of accomplished merchants. They were thus different from ordinary merchants. Dongting merchants had wide visions, great judgments, and good credits. They particularly placed emphasis on relations bonded by native places and patriarchal clans so that the fellow townspeople liked to get together to devise plans of further developments. Therefore, Dongting merchants, though in small numbers, were always successful. Given the fact that so many scholars engaged in trade, it is hard to differentiate scholars from merchants in Dongshan and Xishan of Dongting. The first Dongshan-native first-place winner of the Civil Service Exam, Shi Pan, "followed his father to do business in the Huai River area."[52] Yan Jing, who graduated from the metropolitan exam and earned the degree of *jinshi* in 1496 and once took office as the prefect of Zhangde, had been "a merchant in Pei when he was young."[53]There were graduates of provincial level of exams with a degree of *juren* who engaged in trade. In the Jiangjing reign,

A certain Mr. Jiang, a native of Xiaoxiawan of Xishan, Dongting and a *juren* degree holder, repeatedly failed exams in springs and then quitted. He emulated those who made profits in the market. [After he] rose when cocks crowed, he carried counting rods [all day long] to calculate money until sunset. He was concerned with only goods. [He] hoarded goods and gained surplus. [He] was extremely calculative. As for righteous things to comfort and compensate the bereaved, they were too stingy to pull out a hair even to his closest relatives. After several years, he would boast of his enormous wealth.[54]

After Wang Ao, minister of Revenue and Grand Secretary of the Hall of Literary Profundity, was retired and returned to Suzhou, his son, Wang Yanze, who had accompanied him and stayed in Beijing, openly "developed his business. After a few years, [he] acquired massive properties. His money-lending shops, melting furnaces, and hotels were numerous so that [he] built a grand residence in western part of the city."[55] Wang Ao wrote a vast number of biographies, epitaphs, and memorials for Dongting merchants in his *Zhenze xiansheng wenji* (*Anthology of Mr. Zhenze*). The union of merchants and scholars led to a virtuous cycle among them. Therefore, Dongshan and Xishan of Dongting produced not only great scholars but also a strong merchant group.

Culture was closely tied to the rise of merchant groups. Places where merchant groups prospered were usually areas boasting of cultural sophistication. During the Ming and Qing times, "[Places] under heaven with the most Confucian academies were Donglin, Jiangxi, Guanzhong, and Huizhou."[56] Those four places were precisely home to Jiangsu, Jiangxi, Shan-Shaan, and Huizhou merchants. The flourishing of Confucian academies resulted from merchants' generous donations. *Liang Huai yanzheng quande ji* (*An Account of the Virtuous in Salt Business of Huainan and Huaibei*) addressed the situation of She County, Huizhou Prefecture's seat:

> She County was situated inside the mountains with inadequate lands. Those who stayed studied, and those who traveled engaged in trade. Places for studying were usually Confucian academies, with the exception of colleges run by the prefecture and the county. There were ten academies, with Ziyang being the biggest. Merchants got to everywhere in the country. [Among them,] salt merchants in Huainan and Huaibei were the most famous. . . . In places as big as metropolises and as small as villages, how could customs come into being if there were no schools? How could people get together if there was no money? Once a teacher was invited, building must be repaired and refashioned and grains must be supplied. [The cost incurred by] offering sacrifice to the door-god and giving teachers gifts was not paid by [the income] from farming.

Since the expenditure of Confucian academies was not covered by "farming," it had to be met by subsidies provided by those who "engaged in commerce in lieu of farming." Assertions such as "How could customs come into being if there were no schools?" and "How could people get together if there was no money?" were indicative of the relationship between culture and commerce.

There were others reasons behind the rise of the merchant group. Yet, by and large, the aforementioned four constituted the major factors. Past studies on reasons of the rise of merchant groups usually highlighted geographical conditions, which is misleading. Every geographical unit was a relatively independent ecosystem that played a function of the whole. Such a function of the whole resulted from intersections and syntheses of multifarious factors. Whether a certain area was able to produce a strong merchant group depended on factors such as geographical condition, traffic, opportunity, and culture.

## 2 Merchant groups' areas of activity and commercial networks

Because merchant groups participated in commercial competitions as a collective force, the platform of their activities was big. Accounts about various merchant groups usually highlighted that their workings spread all over the country. Huizhou merchants were said to "[have been to] anywhere under the heaven."[57] They set foot on "the distant border areas and dangerous ocean islands. Their itineraries included almost everywhere in China."[58]Longyou merchants were famous for "traveling to everywhere."[59] According to Volume 12 of *Compilation of Regulations and Laws of Ming*, Yao'an Prefecture (west of today's Chuxiong Yi Autonomous Prefecture) of Yunnan alone hosted 35,000 merchants from Longyou and Anfu of Jiangxi. Hence, the assertion of "everywhere" was not an overstatement. Shanxi merchants "made a fortune thousands or tens of thousands of *li* away, and they did not work on farming."[60] Fujian merchants "who had an ingenious mind viewed surge billows as lands and sails and masts as forks and shovels. The rich used their wealth and the poor traveled to transport goods from China to foreign countries in exchange for their native products."[61] Guangdong merchants also "formed groups of scores or hundreds of people to sail two-masted ships and bring illegal goods to travel between East and Southeast Asia and the West."[62] Ningbo merchants "could reach extremely distant foreign countries."[63] Mr. Sun Yat-sen pointed out,

> Ningbo was opened to foreigners after Guangdong was. However, Ningbo was not inferior to Guangdong in terms of its liberal social ethos. All port cities in China featured Ningbo people's businesses. Even in European countries, there were footprints left by Ningbo merchants. Their ability and impact were unmatched.[64]

Although merchants set foot everywhere, individual merchant groups had their focused areas of activity. Dongting merchants were active mainly in four regions: first, the Yangzi Delta centering around the Lake Tai Valley; second, the northern region north to the Yangzi River and along the Grand Canal; third, the western region in the middle reach of the Yangzi River centering on the Hunan and Hubei area; fourth, Fujian, Guangdong, and abroad.[65] Jiangxi merchants had five main areas of activity: first, Yunan, Guizhou, and Sichuan; second, Hunan and Hubei; third, Beijing and various northern provinces; fourth, Jiangsu, Zhejiang, Fujian, and Guangdong; fifth, Liaodong and Tibet.[66] Shanxi merchants were active in the North, Mongolia, and the Northwest, with Beijing, Tianjin, Zhangjiakou, Wuhan, Nanjing, Suzhou, Guangzhou and other port cities as their base areas. Their businesses were even extended to Russia, Japan, and Southeast Asia.[67] Because the headquarters of Huizhou merchants were the Yangzi Delta, there was a saying, "It doesn't make a town with Huizhou merchants." They were active in five areas: first, Zhejiang, Fujian, and Guangdong; second, Hunan, Hubei, Yunnan, Guizhou, and Sichuan; third, Shanxi, Shaanxi, Hebei, and Henan; fourth, Japan and Southeast Asia; fifth, all great commercial metropolises. The headquarters of Ningbo merchants were eastern Zhejiang and Shanghai. In addition, they were influential in the Lake Tai Valley, Hunan, Hubei, Sichuan, and Beijing. Merchants of Ningbo, Fujian, and Guangdong groups were particularly specialized in international trade.

With their focused areas of activity, merchants were not limited to those regions but traveled all of the country. In this fashion, a commercial network that covered the whole of China was constructed. All-important commercial cities such as Beijing, Nanjing, Jinan, Linqing, Huaian, Yangzhou, Wuhan, Suzhou, Hangzhou, Fuzhou, Guangzhou, Foshan, Changsha, Nanchang, Chengdu, and Chongqing were all areas that gathered great merchant groups. They thus became pivots and bases of a national network of commerce. In those pivots and bases, there were *huiguan* run by various great merchant groups. Let's take Changsha Prefecture (including Changsha and Shanhua Counties) of Hunan, one of the commercial metropolises, as an example for our analysis.

Merchant groups from 14 provinces congregated in Changsha Prefecture. Aside from the border areas, Shandong, Zhili, and Guangxi were the only three provinces whose merchants sojourning in Changsha did not find mention in written accounts. Given the fact that Zhili and Guangxi had yet to form their own merchant groups, therefore, virtually all merchant groups across the country – with the exception of that of Shandong – established their footholds in Changsha. In Changsha, it was the Jiangxi merchants who dominated because of the geographical advantage they enjoyed. In "Fengsu" (Customs) of *Shanhua xianzhi* (*Gazetteer of Shanhua County*) of the Jiaqing reign, it was pointed out, "People in Hunan and Hubei were simple . . . who were outwit by their counterparts from Jiangxi." Therefore, in towns and villages alike, those who "hoarded goods to reap profits" were exclusively Jiangxi merchants. "Fengsu" (Customs) of *Changsha xianzhi* (*Gazetteer of Changsha County*) indicated that, in Changsha County, "those who traded currencies, golden or jade curios, and ran shops in busy neighborhoods were . . . all merchants from Jiangxi." There were also vast numbers of Guangdong merchants who did business in Changsha, the provincial capital, and Shanhua. In the Jiaqing reign, Shanhua County

> did not produce surplus goods in the countryside. Therefore, goods in the market and warehouses were all supplied from cities. When [people from this county] relocated, [they] loaded grains to travel. Very few went to distant cities or provinces to engage in trade. As merchants from various provinces came to town, . . . merchants from Guangdong dominated in the city and village.[68]

In years of the Guangxu reign, there were two Guangdong *huiguan* in the Shanhua city. One was *Yuedong huiguan* (East Guangdong *Huiguan*), which was on Shipufusheng Street and built by Guangdong merchants. The other one, *Shuidu bing guan* (Shuidu Guesthouse), which was situated on Shiyipulexin Street, was built by Guangzhou merchants.[69] Merchants from Shanxi and Shaanxi were also highly influential. "Their goods such as felts and furs" "[made] splendid and profitable businesses."[70] As early as 1664, Shan-Shaan merchants established the Shan-Shaan Huiguan on Xishisanpupozi Street inside the Changsha city, after which the *huiguan* "underwent repair repeatedly" in 1794 and 1845.[71] The number of Jiangsu and Zhejiang merchants in Changsha and Shanhua was not small. During the Qianlong times, in Changsha, "southern merchants from Suzhou and Hangzhou [sold] such goods as silk and antiques."[72] There were three *huiguan* in Shanhua run by Jiangsu merchants – namely, Suzhou Huiguan on Shipufusheng Street established by Suzhou merchants during the Kangxi years, *Jiangnan Huiguan* (Yangzi Delta Huiguan) on Shiputaiping Street established by Jiangsu and Zhejiang merchants, and Shangyuan Huiguan behind Shisanpuxianwei established by Nanjing merchants.[73] Fujian merchants founded the *Tianhou gong* (Palace of the Heavenly Goddess) on Shierpuxinjiekou in Shanhua County.[74] Hubei merchants (including Puqi, Huangzhou, Wuchang, and other groups) established in Shanhua Hubei Huiguan and *Huangzhou gongyu* (Huangzhou Public Residence).[75] Huizhou merchants ran Taiping Huiguan in Shanhua. Yunnan and Guizhou merchants established *Yungui huiguan* (Yunnan and Guizhou Huiguan) on *Shisanpu xi pailou* (Western Archway of Shisanpu) in eastern Shanhua. Henan merchants (including Wu'an, Huaiqing, and Zhongzhou groups) established Zhongzhou Huiguan on Shipufusheng Street of Shanhua.[76] Although Sichuan merchants did not make a strong group, Sichuan is close to Hunan. Therefore, Sichuan merchants also did business in Changsha. From this we can see that Changsha Prefecture was one the pivots and bases of commercial network in Ming and Qing. Merchants of all groups came to establish *huiguan* and shops. Itinerant traders and settled merchants of all groups coordinated with each to transport goods from all over the country into Changsha and then shipped products of Hunan to different places in China. Merchants of various groups had their specialties. Therefore, they placed emphasis on different long-distance trading routes. Through waterways and inland routes (prior to the rise of the railroad, inland transportation remained a supplementary means of transportation), merchants constructed a giant commercial web to connect all commercial metropolises, the pivots and bases. The web was extended to neighboring villages, towns, marketplaces, and country fairs from those pivots and bases. A Huizhou merchant in the Ming once said, "Even in mountains, corners of oceans, isolated villages, and distant places, there were people from our town."[77] In the remotest townlets, there were commercial activities and *huiguan*. Those *huiguan* constituted small bases of this commercial network, which linked otherwise isolated local markets. In the Ming, such linkage took place principally between the South and the North, along the Grand Canal or from Gan River to Guangdong and Guangxi via Yuling Mountain. The linkage between the West and East concentrated in the middle and lower reaches of the Yangzi River. Up till the Qing times, the connection between the eastern and western markets underwent great transformations. This was particularly true to the linkage between the upper and middle reaches of the Yangzi River. In the mid-Qing, such a commercial network almost covered the whole country. This web was loosely knit but missed nothing. It reached Tibet in the west, the ocean in the east, Liao and Shen in the north, and Guangdong, Guangxi, Yunnan, and Guizhou in the south. In the Yangzi Delta, Pearl River Delta, and areas along the Grand Canal and the Yangzi River where a commodified economy fully developed, the network was closely knit. With the formation and expansion of the commercial network, a megamarket that transcended local regions – or a market nationwide, an equivalent to a national market in Europe – took shape gradually. The rise of the megamarket was a vital precondition for the transition from the sprout of capitalistic relation of production to a mature capitalism.

## 3  Characters of business activities of merchant groups

Due to differing geographical and cultural backgrounds that made various merchant groups, individual merchant communities had entirely different psychological conditions. For example, Shanxi merchants were meticulous, precise, and simple. Guangdong merchants were radical, adroit, and bold. Ningbo merchants shared the strengths of their Shanxi counterparts but were not conservative. They were less decisive but more surefooted and dependable than their Guangdong competitors. Huizhou merchants endeared themselves to Confucian scholarship and liked to associate with the powerful. Dongting merchants earned a sobriquet as "zuantian Dongting" (Dongting merchants, the sky driller) for their ability to drill a way through to fame and profit. Jiangsu merchants were intelligent, while Jiangxi merchants excelled at calculating. Their different psychological conditions led to the difference in their running business. However, the ten merchant groups shared some common characteristics.

First, a transition from local markets to the megamarket. The timing of the rise individual merchant groups and the goods dealt in by them were usually limited by the geographical conditions. Huizhou was a mountainous area, abounding with timber and tea. It had few lands and a vast population to such a degree that the yearly production of grains could not support the whole population for one month. Initially, Huizhou merchants mostly dealt in timber, tea, and food industry. Their area of activity was limited to the local market in the Yangzi Delta. Huizhou's manufacture was also related to its native products. Huizhou ink was made of pine soot, *Longwei* (Dragon-tail) Ink Slab was produced in Wuyuan, and Chengxintang paper was made of bamboo and wood. After the sixteenth century, nevertheless, Huizhou merchants got out of their local market and began to engage in long-distance transportation and trade. Long-distance trade of this kind was one of the preconditions for developing a capitalistic relation of production, because the massive accumulation of commercial capital entailed long-distance trade. Meanwhile, the making of merchant groups also depended on the rise of a large number of merchants who possessed copious amounts of currencies. For example, Huizhou timber merchants mainly traded Huizhou timber before the mid-Ming, with their main markets being Zhejiang and southern Jiangsu. With the formation of the merchant group after the sixteenth century, Huizhou timber merchants went eastward to Chun, Sui, and Qu of Zhejiang, southward to Fujian and Guangdong, northward to the Hetao region, and westward to the western part of the Yangzi River to Jiangxi, Hunan, Hubei, Sichuan, and Guizhou. The goods sold were no longer limited to Huizhou timber. For information of Huizhou timber merchants' entry into the megamarket, please see Table 2.1.

Table 2.1 Long-distance timber trade of Huizhou merchants

| Name and Place of Origin | Areas of Activity | | Sources |
|---|---|---|---|
| Huang Shiquan (Wuyuan) | Fujian | "[Huang] possessed a huge amount of money and brought his old friends to sell timber in Fujian." | "Biographies: Righteous Activities" of *Gazetteer of Wuyuan County* (printed in the Guangxu reign), volume 31. |
| Cheng Zhaoshu (Wuyuan) | Hetao | "[Cheng] abandoned his career as a scholar and embarked on timber trade. Assigned by his superiors to purchase raw materials, [he] went to the Hetao area and Beijing." | Same as above, volume 35. |
| Dong Changyuan (Wuyuan) | Jiangxi | "[Dong] purchased timber in southern Jiangxi, but came across flood. [He] lost over half of the goods." | "Biographies: Virtuous Activities" of *Gazetteer of Wuyuan County* (printed in the Guangxu reign), volume 38. |
| Dong Bangchao (Wuyuan) | Jiangxi | "[Dong] embarked on timber trade. [He] once stayed in Nankang." | "Biographies: Righteous Activities" of *Gazetteer of Wuyuan County* (printed in the Guangxu reign), volume 34. |
| Ni Guoshi (Qimen) | Jiangxi | "[Ni] did business and earned a fortune. [He] sold timber in Raohe." | *Qimen Nishi zupu (The Pedigree of the Ni Family of Qimen)*, volume 2. |
| Hong Zhihui (Wuyuan) | Jiangxi | "[Hong] once shipped timber to Xunyang." | "*Xiaoyou*" (Filial Sons and Loyal Friends) *Wuyuanxiancaiji (Collected and Compiled Information of Wuyuan County).* |
| Ni Wangquan (Qimen) | Jiangxi | "[Ni] traveled back and forth between the Boyang Lake and the Chang River to sell timber." | *The Pedigree of the Ni Family of Qimen*, volume 2. |
| Shan Qipan (Wuyuan) | Jiangxi | "[As Shan] began to sell timber in Jiangxi, [his] family became rich." | "Biographies: Righteous Activities" of *Gazetteer of Wuyuan County* (printed in the Guangxu reign), volume 34. |
| Sun Huiwu (Wuyuan) | Hunan | "[Sun] once traded timber in Hunan and reached the Xun River." | "Biographies: Righteous Activities" of *Gazetteer of Wuyuan County* (printed in the Guangxu reign), volume 33. |

| | | | |
|---|---|---|---|
| Bi Xing (Wuyuan) | Hunan | "[Bi] sold timber in the border area between Wu and Chu." | "Filial Sons and Loyal Friends," *Gazetteer of Wuyuan County* (printed in the Guangxu reign), volume 30. |
| Wang Renzu (Wuyuan) | Hunan | "[Wang] traded timber between Wu and Chu." | "Biographies: Righteous Activities" of *Gazetteer of Wuyuan County* (printed in the Guangxu reign), volume 34. |
| Jiang Rongdong (Wuyuan) | Hunan | "[Jiang's] family members were timber merchants who did business in Wu and Chu. [They] might sell thousands of huge timbers." | "*Jiang xianshengjiazhuan*" (The Biography of Mr. Jiang and His Family), *Damishanfangji* (*Anthology of Damishanfang*), volume 72. |
| Wang Jie (Wuyuan) | Hunan | "[Wang] brought his cousin to trade timber in Chu. Each had a boat." | "Filial Sons and Loyal Friends," *Gazetteer of Wuyuan County* (printed in the Guangxu reign), volume 30. |
| Huang Fa (The She County) | Hunan | "[Huang] sold timber in Hunan." | "Huang Ketangshi" (Poems of Huang Ketang) *Casual Chats on Affairs in the She County*, book 3. |
| Huizhou merchants | Sichuan, Guangdong, and/ or Guizhou | "Huizhou produced a lot of timber merchants who did business in Sichuan and Guangdong." | "A Study on Customs and Confucian Ethics in the She County," *Casual Chats on Affairs in the She County*, book 18. |
| Hong Tingmei (Wuyuan) | Sichuan, Guangdong, and/ or Guizhou | "[Hong] led his relatives and planted wood thousands of *li* away [from home] in Fujian, Zhejiang, Hunan/Hubei, and Sichuan." | "*Qinghuaxuezhai gong zhuan*" (Biography of Lord QinghuaXuezhai), *Dunhuang Hongshitongzongpu* (*General Genealogy of the Hong Family in Dunhuang*) of Wuyuan, volume 58. |
| Cheng Zhipan (She County) | Sichuan, Guangdong, and/ or Guizhou | "[Cheng] traded in Sichuan and arrived at the family of Dong Pu, Pacification Commissioner of Jianchang and Yazhou. [The place] was ruled by chieftains. [It] was in deep valleys and steep mountains with a huge volume of timber. [Cheng] cut it to make profits." | "*Cheng Zhifanzhuan*" (Biography of Cheng Zhifan), *Dai Nanshanxianshengquanji* (*Anthology of Mr. Dai Nanshan*), volume 8. |

(Continued)

Table 2.1 (Continued)

| Name and Place of Origin | Areas of Activity | | Sources |
|---|---|---|---|
| Wang Shiji (She County) | Sichuan, Guangdong, and/ or Guizhou | "[Wang] accompanied his father, Wang Huashun, to travel to Sichuan to sell timber." | "Renwuzhi – xiaoyou" (Biographies: Filial Sons and Loyal Friends), She xianzhi (She County Gazetteer), printed in the Republican times. |
| Shi Tingzhao (Wuyuan) | Sichuan, Guangdong, and/ or Guizhou | "[Shi] traded timber to Hmong's territories." | "Filial Sons and Loyal Friends," Gazetteer of Wuyuan County (printed in the Guangxu reign), volume 30. |
| Wang Rong (Wuyuan) | Sichuan, Guangdong, and/ or Guizhou | "[Wang] was hired by timber merchants to traverse rivers and lakes and reached Hmong caves." | "Yixing" (Righteous Activities) Collected and Compiled Information of Wuyuan County. |
| "Huizhou people" | Zhejiang | "There were few lands in Kai [Kaihua of Quzhou]. People counted on felling cedars to make a living. A great cutting event every thirty or forty years was called pinshan. . . . Yet, [Kaihua people] relied on capital from Huizhou merchants so that goods in shops in Jiangsu would not be in poor demand." | "Wuchan" (Native Products) Zhejiang tongzhi (Annals of Zhejiang), volume 6. |
| Cheng, the old guy (Wuyuan) | Zhejiang | "Cheng, the old guy, was a timber merchant. He often felled trees in places such as Quzhou and Chuzhou Prefectures and sold the timber to eastern Zhejiang and Nanzhili. Therefore, he lived in Kaihua." | Chapter 4 of Zuixingshi (Stone of Drunken and Sober). |

Longyou merchants also sold native products from mountains initially. Longyou abounded with forestal products such as tea, timber, bamboo, dye, tobacco, and oil. Therefore, early Longyou merchants were mostly forestal goods or paper dealers. After the mid-Ming, Longyou merchants began to break through this small market in eastern Zhejiang. Accordingly, their goods were no longer limited to native products.

Silk products were not massively produced locally in Longyou. Longyou merchants purchased silk knitting goods from Suzhou and Hangzhou to sell them to Hunan and Hubei. Li Weizhen gave an account in *Anthology of Damishanfang*: "Li Ruheng, or Li the twelfth, was a native of Longyou, Zhejiang. Since the time when his father, Li Heting did business in Jiangling, it had been two generations. Both the father and son were adept at scheming and grasping the timings without slightest loss. In Li Ruheng's generation, [his family] became even more affluent. He hoarded silk, grains, hemp, and wool fabrics in his residence and sought the exotic and precious from all places. He [owned and used] hundreds of vessels and carts. Caps, belts, clothes, and shoes [that he sold] spread 15prefectures in Hunan." From this we can see that Longyou silk merchants accumulated enormous capital in their long-distance trades. Longyou produced paper and accordingly books massively. Booksellers from Longyou were active in everywhere in Jiangsu and Zhejiang. Longyou was not by the ocean, but there were quite a large number of maritime traders from Longyou. During the Jiajing reign, some smugglers at sea were Longyou natives. According to Wang Wenlu's *Ceshu* (*Key Strategies*), smugglers at ocean "were mostly people from Fujian, Guangdong, Ningbo, Shaoxing, Wenzhou, Taizhou, and Longyou." Longyou merchants also engaged in long-distance trade of the jewelry. Wang Shixing stated, "Longyou people were good at trading. They mostly traded light and soft goods such as pearls, treasures, gems, and cat's eyes. It took only one merchant to bring goods worth thousands of ounces of silver to the capital."[78] The jewelry dealt in by Longyou merchants was imported from overseas. Therefore, Longyou maritime merchants and jewelry traders were related to each other. Because they transcended the local market as well as the limitations of native products, Longyou merchants were said to "spread all over [the country]" and thus became a great merchant group. Ningbo, Fujian, and Guangdong groups were all composed of mainly maritime traders. Therefore, it goes with saying that they participated in long-distance trade.

Second, different trades inside individual merchant groups interpenetrated with and boosted each other to create huge commercial systems. Take the Ningbo merchant group as an example. Although its businessmen engaged in all kinds of trades, it could be summarized that there were mainly four categories. First, shipping was the main and the most accomplished business of Ningbo merchants. As early as in the Ming, Ningbo shippers had already constituted a major force in maritime trade in southeastern China. In the Qing, Ningbo shippers divided into the northbound and southbound groups. "Southbound vessels were often used to ship sugar, indigo, Chinese pachysandra, black pepper, medical herbs, jelly fish, cedar timber, and foot-long planks." "Northbound ships were usually loaded with cotton, ox bones, peach, dates, fruits, and sand to Sichuan, Hunan/ Hubei, Shandong, and Nanzhili." Ningbo shippers were active on rivers, along the coastal lines, and at oceans. During the Daoguang reign, Ningbo shippers encroached into the large junk industry centering in Shanghai and Chongming and gradually ousted large junk shippers along the Jiangsu coastline before taking control of most affairs in *Shanghai shangchuan huiguan* (Shanghai Commercial Shipping *Huiguan*). The second one was native banks. Ningbo merchants began to run native banks as early as the Qinglong reign. During the Daoguang reign, Ningbo merchants began to open their native banks in Shanghai and underwent a rapid development. According to *Shanghai qianzhuang shiliao* (*Historical Materials of Shanghai Native Banks*), among leading Ningbo merchants in the industry of native bank, there were "Zhao Puzhai, Zhang Baochu, Zhuang Erxiang, and Feng Zefu initially and later Yuan Lianqing, Li Mojun, and so forth." All of them "were top talents of the times and won confidence in people."[79]Later, there were nine renowned native banking capitalists, among whom there were Ningbo merchants. Thus, Ningbo native bankers largely dominated in Shanghai's native banking industry in late Qing. In addition, Ningbo merchants founded quite a vast number of influential native banks in Hankou, Hangzhou, Tianjin, and other cities. The third one was *minxin ye*. *Minxin ye* referred to a civilians' postal institution to deliver chiefly monetary instruments and parcels. According to *Zhongguo haiguan yu youzheng* (*Customs and Postal Services in China*), *minxin ye*, "which prevailed in the Yangzi River and South and North Ocean, was initially set up during the Qianlong reign." *Yinxian tongzhi* (*Annals of Yin County*) recorded that after the Qianlong and Jiaqing reigns, "there were thousands of *minxin* firms across the country in not only metropolises and towns in China, but also Southeast Asian islands. Our Ningbo groups were the widely acknowledged leader."[80] The development of *minxin ye* was premised upon the proliferation of Ningbo firms, which enjoyed tremendous strength and unrivalled reputation. After the rise of Shanghai, the center of *minxin* institutions shifted to Shanghai, but the business was still dominated by Ningbo merchants. All eight Ningbo *minxin* firms such as Yongli, Zhenghe, Guangda, Furun, Quansheng, Xiexing, Qingshun, and Zhengda established branch offices in Shanghai. The widely known saying, "*Piaohao* (a firm for money exchange and transfer) was dominated by the Shanxi people, while *minxin* firms were monopolized by the Ningbo people,"[81] vividly illustrated Ningbo people's unique status in *minxin ye*. The fourth one included fishing, salt, seafood, sundry merchandises, medical herbs, silk fabrics, clothing, timber, grains, straw mats, and straw hats. Ningbo merchants were extremely active in all those trades. The four aspects of business collectively made a massive commercial system. In this system, shipping facilitated transportation, which became the mainstay of Ningbo merchants' business. Native banks accommodated the needs of financing. *Minxin ye* was a provider of information, while other trades focused on long- or short-distance purchase and selling. All trades mutually interpenetrated and boosted to become a sustaining power to develop the Ningbo merchant group. Here, native banking was of considerable significance. Xin Jiang ming, author of

*Ningbo qian ye hui guan beiji* (*Inscriptions on Tablets of Ningbo Native Banking Huiguan*), pointed out,

> I heard from the elders that over a century ago, [people] upheld frugality as their customs and diligently purchased goods cheap to sell them dear. Those who possessed huge wealth were usually merchants. People traveled long distance and their businesses spread in all provinces. Money was too heavy to be carried, but money shops [provided means] of capital turnover. Money shops must be run by the extremely wealthy, whose influence reached different provinces.

Native banks accommodated the needs of long-distance traders' capital turnover so that their "influence reached different places." Meanwhile, native bankers provided their fellow townspeople with basic functions of capital loans. It is fair to argue that any merchant groups would not have built up a commercial system to back up their long-distance trade and to sustain long-term commercial prosperity, had they not possessed their own finance. The Longyou merchant group, once enjoying a high reputation, gradually disappeared in the mid-Qing because its merchants rarely engaged in finance and failed to establish the mainstay of their businesses.

The longevity of Shanxi and Huizhou merchant groups stemmed in part from the fact that an enormous trading commercial system was established from inside. The main force of the Shanxi merchant group was initially salt traders and then *piaohao* dealers. The main force of Huizhou merchants included salt, pawn shop, tea, and timber merchants. Both of them had their own finance. After the sixteenth century, industries of finance and pawn shops were essentially controlled by Huizhou and Shan-Shaan merchants. Volume 434 of *Ming Shenzong shilu* (the *Chronicle of Emperor Shenzong of Ming*) recorded, "Pawn shops run by Huizhou merchants spread all over the area north of the Yangzi River." "In Henan, there were 213 [pawn shops] run by Wang Ke and others." Those accounts indicated that Huizhou pawnbrokers in the Ming and Qing controlled finance in areas north and south of the Yangzi River. Entering into the Qing Dynasty, pawn shops run by Shanxi merchants actually outnumbered those by their Huizhou competitors. In 1795, Li Sui, secretary of Shanxi Provincial Education Commissioner wrote in his diary that in terms of pawnbrokers nationwide, "those in south of the Yangzi River were all Huizhou people, who were called Huizhou merchants, while those who were north of the Yangzi River were all Shanxi people, who were called Shanxi merchants."[82] After the Qianlong times, Shanxi merchants established *zhangju* and *piaohao*, which were a transitional form between pawnshop and banking. *Zhangju* were credit agencies that ran money depositing and lending for urban manufacture and commerce, while *piaohao* engaged in remittance of *huipiao* (bills of exchange). The rise of *zhangju* and *piaohao* served the needs of long-distance transportation and trades of goods. On the one hand, long-distance trades resulted in the reduction of speed of commodity circulation and capital turnover.

The cost of advance expenditure increased. Borrowing was necessary in light of insufficient self-owned capital. On the other hand, the circulation between cities became more frequent and the turnover of currency expanded accordingly. Loan settlements between cities, however, depended upon the shipping of silver, which was neither convenient nor safe. Merchants urged to transform the shipping of silver into money transfer. *Piaohao* of Shanxi set up their branch offices in more than 80 cities in Chia to make a remittance network that linked everywhere across China. That was beneficiary to the development of a commoditized economy. Certainly it was Shan-Shaan merchants who benefited from it most. Shanxi *piaohao* spread all over the country, and accordingly, Shan-Shaan merchants prevailed everywhere. Long-distance trades, in which they engaged, such as grains, salt, cotton fabrics, tea, and timber, were all prosperous. Hence, it is clear that the powerfulness of Shanxi and Huizhou merchant groups was intimately related to its rational and sophisticated internal structures.

Third, merchant groups placed emphasis on kinship in patriarchal clans. Native-place organizations of merchant groups did not undermine the basis of conception of patriarchal clans. Instead, they strengthened blood ties of patriarchal clans, which was to a great extent conducive to the development of merchant groups and enhanced their cohesiveness. Shan-Shaan merchants laid special significance on blood ties in their commercial activities. Zhang Siwei recorded in "Haifeng Wanggong qishi ronggui xu" (Preface to the Return of Mr. Wang of Haifeng at the Age of Seventy), "The young-generation people in the clan were given capital so that they carried money to live in various places. [All those places] were jam-packed with [fellow kinsmen]."[83] This constituted a part of a biography of a certain Mr. Wang from Puzhou, Shanxi, who earned substantial profits from trading salt produced in Changlu. We understand that quite a lot of young kinsmen obtained capital from him. Li Weizhen in his "Zeng Luotian ling Wanggong mubiao" (Epitaph of Mr. Wang, Magistrate of Luotian) gave an account that Wang Kejian, who hailed from Gaoling County, Xi'an Prefecture of Shaanxi, was successful in his salt trade and then sponsored his fellow kinsmen to engage in trade: "Anyone who were able to trade would be given capital without asking for interests. [He sponsored] scores of people in total, all of whom were renowned for their vast wealth."[84] In Lü Nan's "Nanyang fujiaoshou feng Hanlinyuan jiantao Wang xiansheng mubei" (Epitaph of Mr. Wang, Instructor of Nanyang Prefecture and Examining Editor of the Hanlin Academy), there was an account about a certain Confucian scholar, Wang, from Hu County, Xi'an Prefecture of Shaanxi. He subsidized 36 people from his clan to do business. Aside from providing financial assistance to the poor from the same clans for their engagement in trade, Shan-Shaan merchants ran businesses with their fellow kinsmen. Shan-Shaan merchants who traded salt in Yangzhou basically came from ten great families. Volume 12 of *Jiangdu xian xuzhi* (*Sequel to Gazetteer of Jiangdu County*) recorded,

There were a large number of sojourners who registered in Yangzhou. Although [they] lived in Yangzhou for generations, they were tied to their native places. In the mid-Ming when the law on salt was implemented,

Shan-Shaan merchants crowded into [Yangzhou]. The Liangs of Sanyuan and the Yans and the Lis of Shanxi took exams [in Yangzhou] for two centuries. The Lius of Hejin Lanzhou, the Qiaos and the Gaos of Xianglin, the Zhangs and the Guos of Jingyang, the Shens of Xi'an, and the Zhangs of Lintong kept their registry in their native places, although they actually lived in Yangzhou.

In the late Ming and early Qing, eight Shanxi merchants monopolized trade in Zhangjiakou. According to Volume 10 of *Wanquan xianzhi* (*Gazetteer of Wanquan County*), "All eight merchants hailed from Shanxi. They came to Zhangjiakou for trade in late Ming. They were: Wang Dengku, Jin Liangyu, Fan Yongdou, Liang Jiabing, TianShenglan, Zhai Tang, and Huang Yunfa. Since our dynasty rose to prominence in Liaodong and sent people to Zhangjiakou to do business, the eight families dominated." Fourteen influential families (all from Jiexiu, Pingsheng, Taigu, Qi County, and Yuci) concentrated wealth of Shanxi *piaohao* during the Qing times. According to "Shanxi duo fushang" (Rich merchants were numerous in Shanxi), volume 5 of *Qing baileichao* (*Anthology of Petty Matters in Qing*), during the Guangxu reign (1875–1908), families with a wealth over 300,000 ounces of silver included Yang (300,000 ounces), Meng (450,000 ounces), Wu (500,000 ounces), Liu (one million ounces), and Cao (between four and five million ounces) from Taigu County; Ji (300,000 ounces) and Hou (between seven and eight million) from Jiexiu County; Hao (300,000 ounces), He (400,000 ounces), Wang (500,000 ounces), Hou (850,000 ounces), and Chang (one million ounces) from Yuci County; Qu (one million ounces) and Qiao (between three and four million ounces) from Qi County. In 1853, Imperial Censor of Guangxi, Zhang Siheng, pointed out in his memorial,

> The Sun family from Taigu County of Shanxi possessed a wealth of 200,000 [ounces of silver], and the Cao family and the Jia family four or five million each. The Hou family of Pingyao County and the Zhang family of Jiexiu County each possessed a wealth of three or four million [ounces of silver]. In Yuci County, the Xu's and Wang's lived together as clans. The wealth of each clan amounted to ten million. Ten families in Jiexiu County and scores of families in Qi County possessed a wealth of one million.[85]

Thus, we can see that Shanxi merchants were closely tied to clans in terms of both their commercial activities and wealth accumulation.

The Ningbo group also boasted of a large number of family-controlled conglomerates such as the Yan Xinhou family of Cixi, the Ye Chengzhong family of Zhenhai, the Fang Jietang family of Zhenhai, the Dong Dilin family of Cixi, the Yu Xiaqing family of Zhenhai, the Qin Jun'an family of Ningbo, the Zhu Zhiyao family of Fenghua, the Song Weichen family of Zhenhai, and the Zhu Baosan family of Dinghai. All those families possessed substantial financial powers and a solid and broad social base, making them the mainstay of the Ningbo group. Take the Fang family of Zhenhai as an example. Ever since Fang Jietang established the Yihe Sugar Firm in Shanghai during the Jiaqing reign, the whole Fang clan engaged in commercial activities. The Fangs had two branches, the new Fangs and the old Fangs. The new Fangs established 17 native banks in Shanghai and seven more in Hankou and Ningbo. The old Fangs had eight native banks in Shanghai and ten in Ningbo and Hankou. Both the new and old Fangs ran businesses such as sugar, large junk, jewelry, silk, cotton fabrics, medical herbs, sundry goods, fishery, books, and real estate. Centering on Shanghai, their area of commercial activity included Hangzhou, Ningbo, Shaoxing, Hankou, Nanjing, Shashi, Yichang, Huzhou, and Zhenhai. Because of the role of the great cohesive power of clans in commercial activities, Ningbo merchants, with no exception, donated money for public good of their respective clans after they achieved prosperity. According to their genealogies, the Fangs of Zhenghai purchased 1,200 *mu* of land to found the Baoshantang Charitable Estate with 57 rooms. The Ye family of Cixi spent over 63,000 ounces of silver to buy 1,400 *mu* of land to establish Ye's Charitable Estate. Chen Zuzhao from Zhenhai indicated in "Yitian ji" (An Account of Charitable Lands) of *Cixi Hongmen Zhang shizongpu* (*Genealogy of the Zhang Family from Hongmen of Cixi*), "Ningbo merchants established charitable estates, compiled genealogies for their clans, and built clan shrines." On the one hand, they intended to gain a reputation as philanthropists, and their social statuses thereby won recognition from their fellow townspeople and clansmen. On the other hand, they consolidated relations and reconfirmed concepts of the patriarchal clan so that their commercial activities could secured support and attention in preparation for further development. Putting premium on ties to patriarchal clans constituted a shared characters of all merchant groups. For details of the role of ties to patriarchal clans in merchants' commercial activities, please see Section 1 of Chapter 3 about kin's organizations.

Fourth, merchants placed emphasis on commercial credit and management. Huizhou merchants' management was conducted at four levels: agents, deputies, shopkeepers, and employees. Internally, Huizhou merchants relied on the patriarchal system to take control of their business groups by emphasizing loyalty of different management levels to merchants (who were usually the eldest sons of clans). Shanxi merchants adopted a different approach. Although Shanxi merchants also stressed relationships of native place and clan, they were strict about management. During the Ming and Qing times, Shanxi merchants developed *huoji zhi* (partnership), *lianhao zhi* (head office branch), *jingli fuze zhi* (manager responsibility system), and *gufen zhi* (shareholding system). *Huoji zhi* was the earliest management system created by Shanxi merchants. Shen Sixiao stated in *Jinlu* (*Records of Shanxi*),

> Merchants from Pingyang, Ze, Lu, and Hao were richest across the country. Those who did not possessed a wealth of hundreds of thousands of silver did not dare to claim themselves rich. They adopted a fine way of management. They valued people's behaviors. Those who joined hands to do business were called *huoji* (partners). One person contributed capital, and all merchants worked together. Although they did not take an oath, they were selfless. [There was a case where] the grandfather borrowed money and owed

the principal and interests, but he died halfway. The lender had given up [the loan] decades before. [If] his grandson knew the situation, he toiled to pay off the debt. Thus, other wealthy people strove to hire this person to be their partner, because [people] thought that as he did not forget the dead person, he would not betray the living people. Hence, this person paid a small amount of interests before he gained enormous profits later. Therefore, there were people who did not initially possess wealth, but ended up making a living. In addition, the rich people did not hide wealth at home, but distributed to their partners. To estimate a person's property, [one can] count the number of his major and minor partners. Thus, his wealth of hundreds of thousands or even millions of [ounces of silver] could be known. Consequently, the rich would not fall into poverty all of a sudden, while the poor could become rich. [That was because merchants adopted] fine way of management and [people] were of superb moral characters.

This piece of historical material tells us that *Huoji zhi* of Shanxi merchants was built upon a mutual trust between investors and their partners (managers of enterprises). Merchants contributed capital and selected people of high moral standards as partners, to whom businesses were consigned. Partners loyally fulfilled their obligations to investors. Hence, investors and partners mutually benefited from this system. After the founding of the Qing Dynasty, with the development of the Shanxi merchant group, the management system further improved and perfected. *Huojizhi* was transformed into *lianhao zhi. Lianhao zhi* was similar to parent company-subsidiary system in western European capitalism. In most cases, an investor contributed the whole or the majority of capital. To control branch firms in different geographical areas and specialized in different trades, investors adopted an approach of running parent firms and subsidiaries. All head offices were set up in Shanxi, while branch firms were spread to other commercial cities and towns. For example, firms run by the Cao family from Taigu County of Shanxi were managed through three branch firms. The first one was Lijinde Account's Office which managed firms in Taiyuan, Lu'an, and various areas in the Yangzi Delta. The second one was Yongtongyu Account's Office which managed firms in Manchuria. The third one was Sanjinchuan Account's Office to manage firms in Shandong. Here, there existed three layers. Lijinde Accountant's Office was a subsidiary for the Cao family, but it functioned as a parent firm for various firms in Taiyuan, Lu'an, and the Yangzi Delta. The managerial levels of *lianhao zhi* actually multiplied into more than three strata. For example, Caixiawei, which was managed by Lijinde Account's Office, was the largest-scale silk fabric firm owned by the Cao family. Meanwhile, Caixiawei controlled Jintaiheng in Zhangjiakou, Ruixiadang in Licheng, Guangshengdian in Yuci, Jinshengwei in Taigu, and other firms. It was not the Cao family, the investor, but Caiweixia, who supervised those firms' profit and loss. Caiweixia was responsible for Lijinde Account's Office. If the manager of Jintaiheng, which was a subsidiary of Caiweixia, wanted to pay a visit to the investor, he needed to be led by the manager of Caiweixia to see the manager of Lijinde first. Then, the manager of Lijinde could lead him to see the investor.

Although all firms under the Cao family were independent accounting units, they, under the leadership of the parent firm at the upper level, mutually supported in terms of information exchange, material procurement, and marketing. Between a parent firm and a subsidiary, a letter was sent every three or five days in order to exchange information. If necessary, funds were appropriated to help other firms.

*Jingli fuze zhi* (manager responsibility system), *xuetu zhi* (apprenticeship system), and *hegu zhi* (shareholding system) were established to match *lianhao zhi*. In *Jingli fuze zhi*, the investor personally hired a general manager and consigned all capital of the firm to the manager he signed. The investor would no longer intervene in the firm's affairs thereafter. The investor neither devised plans nor supervised the firm. When the settlement day (every three or five years) arrived, the manager was required to report to the investor loss and profit of the firm. After the settlement day, the investor made a decision on whether renew the contract with the manager. *Xuetu zhi* stipulated that every apprentice get recommendation from a relative or a friend, who served as a guarantor. He would be admitted after interviews. After he was hired, the head office of the firms sent senior employees to train the apprentice. There were two types of training. The first one included vocational skills, mainly using an abacus, writing, foreign languages, familiarity with properties of commodities and business skills, copying letters, writing letters, and keeping accounts. The second one was about work ethic, mainly trustworthiness, candor, restraining desire, cultivating morality, loyalty, selflessness, fraternity, being unenvious, enduring hardships, and simplicity. After the probationary period expired, more investigations were in need before an apprentice could be officially hired. Approaches of investigation included sending him on a long-distance trip to observe his aspiration, having him stay with the manager of the head office to examine his respectfulness, asking him to cope with difficult businesses to gauge his ability, letting him handle financial matters to see his honesty, prohibiting him from returning to his native place to visit his relative to ensure within a two-year probationary period to check whether he observed rules and regulations, and sending him to busy metropolises to see his composure. The strictness of the apprenticeship allowed Shanxi merchants to cultivate a lot of talents. Quite a large number of apprentices went through stages of partners and *ding shengyi* (granted shares) and became the backbone of Shanxi merchants by being promoted as deputy managers and managers. When *lianhao zhi* was implemented, *gufen zhi* was introduced to expand the sources of capital. *Gufen zhi* could be categorized as *yingu* (shares in the form of silver) and *shengu* (shares in the form of body). Namely, "those who contributed money would be given *yingu*, while those who contributed labor would gain *shengu*." *Shengu* referred to a process in which "a teenager boy who could write and calculate was selected to work as a partner before he was given *shengu* but not salary with the exception of money purchasing clothing because he was found to be a promising talent after several years. A settlement was made after three years to pay dividends in accordance to the amounts of shares. The better the business, the more the dividends paid. The amount of *shengu* increased accordingly. Thus, everyone worked for his own [interest]. He was diligent and frugal without resorting to responsibility and regulation."[86] Shanxi merchants' management system, particularly *lianhaozhi*, paved the way of their running of *piaohao*.

All great merchant groups placed an emphasis on commercial credit and its management, which corresponded to the expansion of businesses in the modern times. Among them, Shanxi merchants' management system, arguably the most sophisticated one, was the embryo of capitalistic enterprises.

Fifth, the organizational form of merchant groups was *huiguan* and *gongsuo*. Each merchant group worshipped its country sages or deities. For details, please see Chapter 3 about merchants' organizations.

Sixth, merchant groups were tinted with strong feudalism and weak capitalism, which manifested itself in the flow of capital of various great merchant groups. The merchant groups' capital was directed to the following destinations:

1   Land purchase. Merchants of various groups spent a sizable portion of their profits to purchase lands. In Jiangxi where "produces were limited but population was huge," merchants struggled to buy landed properties after they became rich. For example, Nie Rugao from Qingjiang did business in Pingxiang and "made a fortune by trading medical herbs." "[He] was by nature frugal so that [he] would eat one chunk of fermented bean curd for two meals. [He] abhorred extravagance [to such a degree] that he wore crude clothing." However, he was not stingy with "purchasing lands."[87] In Shanxi, rich and influential merchants "mostly purchased lands."[88] During the Kangxi reign, the great salt merchant Hang Baiwan "was the leader of Shanxi merchants. In his hometown, Linfen, [he owned] such a great number of houses as if [his family] were a noble and powerful one."[89] In one year of severe drought, everyone was in a panic. Hang Baiwan, however, elatedly claimed, "Just as there is heaven up there, there is Hang Baiwan down here. [Even though] it doesn't rain in the next three years, [I] still have ten thousand *dan* of surplus grains."[90] His possession of a large volume of lands was self-evident. Shanxi merchants also took advantage of bad years to carry money to purchase lands in Henan. A memorial sent by Bi Yuan, Provincial Governor of Henan was recorded in volume 1255 of *Qing shilu* (the *Chronicle of Qing*) stating,

The Henan Province had bad harvests in a few years in a row. Those with properties had to sell their belongings in exchange for food. More recently when food was in short supply between two harvests, [people] sold at low price lands in which wheat was about to mature. Rich families from Shanxi learned the news and crowded in Henan to lend money and thereby acquired landed properties.

Zheng Zhilong, the great maritime trader in the late Ming, also "owned lands and estates all over Fujian and Guangdong."[91] The merchant's capital was monetized capital in circulation. As merchants strove to buy lands, the merchant's capital rapidly flowed to lands, which means it was frozen on lands and withdrew from circulation. Great amounts of the merchant's capital thus quietly turned into feudal real estate.

2   Currency hoarding. Metal coins possessed by Huizhou merchants were sometimes buried underground as the fortune and therefore withdrawn from circulation. It was not until the times when Zeng Guofan suppressed the Taiping army and "connived at his troops' plunder" in Huizhou that "cellars which stored [money] were emptied."[92] It was also universal for Shanxi merchants to hoard currencies. For example, Qu Xiaozhou from Qi County possessed a wealth of three or four million ounces of silver. When the firms he invested during the Qianlong reign made profits, he withdrew a sizable portion of shares to store a vast amount of money in cellars on the grounds that "[he] could earn ten thousand today, but might lose twenty thousand tomorrow." After the 1911 Revolution, Yan Xishan once borrowed from the Qu family 300,000 ounces of silver, all of which had been stored in cellars. The hoarding of currencies testified to, on the one hand, merchants' worshipping of money and, on the other hand, the lack of outlets of the merchant's capital.

3   Luxury consumption. Rich and influential merchants also expended enormously for their luxurious lives. Volume 6 of *Yangzhou huafang lu* (*A Record of Painted Pleasure Boat in Yangzhou*) had a quite typical account:

Salt traders in Yangzhou all pursued extravagant [lifestyles]. [Events like] a wedding or a funeral featured housing, food, clothing, and transportation, all of which usually cost hundreds of thousands [ounces of silver]. A certain merchant [required] cooks to cook dozens of kinds of dishes. When eating, the [newlywed] couple sat side by side, and waiters carried dishes before them. [The couple chose from] tea, wheaten food, meat, and vegetarian food. For food [they] did not intend to eat, [they] shook their heads. Waiters changed dishes according to their facial expressions. Some were fond of fine horses. They raised hundreds of horses, each of which cost scores of ounces of silver every day. [Each day, they] exited the city from the city gate in the morning and returned from the suburb at night. Horses looked so splendid that spectators felt dizzy. Some liked orchids. [They] placed orchids everywhere from outside their residences all the way to their inner chambers. Some made wooden naked women, which were driven by gears to move. As they were placed inside rooms and halls, the panicked guests would escape. The early richest merchant was An Lücun. Those who became rich later behaved even more oddly. Some tried to expend ten thousand [ounces of silver] at one time. His clients used gold to buy gold foils and transported them to the pagoda on Mountain Jinshan to fly them in the wind.[Those gold foils] instantly scattered and were dotted along the river, grasslands, and trees without a chance to be retrieved. Some spent three thousand [ounces of silver] in buying self-righting dolls in Suzhou and placed them in the river. The river was thereby blocked. Some preferred good-looking people to such an extent that they selected no one but pretty teenagers to fill positions ranging from doorkeepers to servants in the kitchen. Conversely, there were people who prioritized the ugly. Those who looked into the mirror and found themselves disqualified disfigured their own faces and plastered them with paste before exposing the faces under the sun. Someone was fascinated by large-sized stuff. He had a five- or six-*chi* tall bronze night stool made. At night when he urinated, he used it. There were countless examples of how [merchants] competed with one another for oddity.

Although the author did not give the surnames of those rich and influential merchants, those Yangzhou-based merchants who controlled salt business in Huainan and Huaibei in the Qing Dynasty and who were lavish with their money must be salt traders from Huizhou or Shanxi-Shaanxi.

4    Almsgiving and donation. Between late years of the Wanli reign and the early Qing, the state-monopolized salt trade was carried out in the name of *gang-yanzhi* (a system limiting salt traders to trade salt in specified geographical locations [or *gang*]). Salt traders had to submit their enormous profits to the imperial courts in the name of almsgiving, military expenditures, costs of repairing rivers, costs of repairing city walls, disaster relief, and gifts to governments in order to retain their monopolizing privileges. According to a statistics in *Liang Huai yanfa zhi* (*Chronicle of Salt Business in Huainan and Huaibei*), within over a century between 1671 and 1804, salt traders in Huainan and Huaibei contributed 39,302,196 ounces of silver, 21,500 *dan* of rice, and 329,460 *dan* of cereals. It was Huizhou merchants who mostly undertook the contributions. In 1831, salt fields in Huainan and Huaibei switched from *gangyanzhi* to *piaoyanzhi* (namely, merchants acquired salt based on *piao* or coupons but not limited geographical locations) and thereby abolished salt merchants' privileges. Consequently, Huizhou salt traders went bankrupt. Under this circumstance, the Qing government turned its attention to Shanxi merchants as the chief almsgivers. In 1843, when the Qing government needed to pay an indemnity in the wake of the Opium War, Shanxi merchants were apportioned "over two million ounces [of silver]."[93] In 1853, the Qing government once again urged merchants nationwide to make contributions because of its suppression of the Taiping Rebellion. Shanxi merchants topped the whole nation by contributing 1,599,300 ounces of silver, or 37.65% of all contributions across the country.[94] People of the day said, "The Shanxi province made their contributions for five or six times with a total amount over ten thousand [ounces of silver]." Under high pressure of contributions, most of merchants' profits were transferred to the government. The expenditure of donations in exchange for official titles was also immense. In Ming, merchants obtained official ranks by donating in the name of "being awarded titles for their zeal for public good." During the Wanli reign, Wu Yangchum, a merchant from She County donated 300,000 ounces of silver to the Ming government so that "[the government] appointed "five [family members] as Secretariat Drafter within one day." During the Qing times, *najuanzhi* was implemented to set prices of official titles for sale. Studentship in the Imperial Academy could also be procured by donation. In order

to make their way to the gentry class, merchants had to pay a portion of their commercial gains. As a merchant bemoaned, "Donating money in exchange for studentship in the Imperial Academy and official titles required enormous expenditure."[95]

In addition, other expenditure was incurred to sponsor their patriarchal clans and cover the costs of investing in cultivating talents in feudal society. The aforementioned uses of merchants' wealth were main flows of the merchant's capital and profits, which led to the merge of bureaucrats and merchants in modern society. Take Zhang Siwei, Wang Chonggu, and Ma Ziqiang during the Longqing and Wanli reigns as examples. Zhang Siwei earned the *jinshi* degree in 1553. Upon Zhang Juzheng's recommendation in 1574, he served as minister of Rites, Grand Secretary in the East Hall, and Grand Adjutant. After Zhang Juzheng's death, he took Zhang Juzheng's place to administrate state affairs. Zhang Siwei came from a powerful salt merchant family. His father, Zhang Yun-ling, possessed a wealth between hundreds of thousands and two million ounces of silver.[96] His brother, Zhang Sijiao, was a salt merchant in Changlu and later donated to earn the title of Assistant Commander of the Longhu Garrison. Wang Chonggu earned the *jinshi* degree in 1541 and was appointed as the Supreme Commander of Xuanda and Shanxi, making him the highest leader of national defense in the North. His younger brother was a salt merchant who was closely related to the *kaizhong* policy in the North. Ma Ziqiang graduated from the Civil Service Exam as a *jinshi* in 1544 and was later appointed as Minister of Rites. His son, Ma Zixiu, was also an influential merchant. All the three families of Zhang, Wang, and Ma possessed landed properties in Shanxi and were connected to one another by marriage. It is thus clear that inside merchant groups, rich and powerful merchants, the core of those groups, were heavily feudalistic. Not only did those merchants command a triple identity, the core part of merchant groups also formed a triple identity by marriage, which became an advantage of various merchant groups in feudalistic commercial competitions. However, that also explains why the majority of merchant groups could qualify only as a "scavenger" of capitalism. As capitalism was on the rise, they declined with the demise of feudalism.

It is vital to understand that merchant groups were disinclined to develop a capitalist economy in two ways. First, only a minority of great merchant groups' capital and profits were directed to production. Second, the majority of merchant groups, including the powerful Shanxi and Huizhou groups, declined in the late nineteenth century. Only a small number of merchant groups kept up with the times to transform themselves into capitalist merchant groups. For example, the Ningbo merchant group, which was composed of medium or petty merchants, had no intimate relationship with the government. Its development was predicated on Ningbo's local products and traffic conditions and the growth of a commodified economy. Therefore, it differed from Shanxi and Huizhou groups and represented an alternative direction of the development of merchant groups. Thus, the outcome was entirely different. The Guangdong and Dongting merchant groups were similar and later transformed themselves into new-style capitalist industrial and commercial groups.

The decline of most merchant groups was marked by the bankruptcy of their backbone businesses. The switch between *gangyanzhi* to *piaoyanzhi* during the Daoguang reign signaled the decline of Huizhou merchants. Within a decade after the 1911 Revolution, *piaohao* went out of business, which symbolized the collapse of Shanxi merchants. However, some merchants in various merchant groups did invest in capitalist enterprises and succeeded in transforming themselves. For example, Qu Benqiao, a rich merchant from Qi County of Shanxi, invested in 1906 5,000 ounces of silver to take over the previously government-run *Shanxi huochaiju* (the Shanxi Match Firm) and renamed it as *Shuangfu huochai gongsi* (the Shuangfu Match Company), the first industrial enterprise controlled by national capitalism in Shanxi. In 1907, Qu further raised an enormous fund of 1.5 million to redeem the right of mining of coal locally in Shanxi from the Peking Syndicate Limited of Britain. He later made arrangements to establish *Baojin kuangwu gongsi* (the Baojin Mining Company) and personally took office as the general manager. Although such merchants were no longer members of individual merchant groups, their commercial activities were still defined by strong kinship and native-place ties.

China's merchant groups have yet to disappear until today but are active all over the world. For example, members of the Ningbo merchant group migrated from Shanghai to Hong Kong, Macau, and Taiwan and then to Japan, Korea, Southeast Asia, Thailand, Brazil, Argentina, Australia, the United States, Canada, and various countries in Western Europe. They established native-place and trade-oriented associations so that the overseas Ningbo groups came into existence. A statistic shows that there are over 73,000 members of Ningbo groups, among which 17,800 are in Taiwan, 42,500 in Hong Kong and Macau, and 12,700 in 50 countries and regions abroad.[97] In Chinatowns where there is sizable population of Chinese immigrants, all kinds of *huiguan* are still playing a role as a nexus of native-place ties.

## Notes

1 "Huozhi" (货殖), in *Shezhi* (歙志) of the Wanli (万历) reign.
2 *Jixi xianzhicaifangbiao* (绩溪县志采访表), 1933.
3 Cheng Shangkuan (程尚宽), *Xin'anmingzuzhi* (新安名族志) (Hefei: Huangshan-shushe, 2007).
4 XuChengyao (许承尧), "Wu Shiqi*Zhengxinlu*zhongzhi 'huozhizhuan'" (吴士奇《征信录》中之《货殖传》), in *Sheshixiantan* (歙事闲谭), volume 4 (Hefei: Huang-shanshushe, 2001), 109.
5 Wang Daokun (汪道昆), "Shoushidijiqixu" (寿十弟及耆序), in *Taihanji* (太函集), volume 17, *Xuxiusikuquanshu – jibu* (续修四库全书·集部), book 1347, 9.
6 Wang Daokun (汪道昆), "Haiyang Cheng Cigongqishishouxu" (海阳程次公七十寿序), volume 16, *Xuxiusikuquanshu – jibu* (续修四库全书·集部), book 1346, 691; "Ming gutongyidafu Nanjing hubuyoushilangChenggongxingzhuang" (明故通议大夫南京户部右侍郎程公行状), in *Taihanji* (太函集), volume 43, *Xuxiusikuquanshu – jibu* (续修四库全书·集部), book 1347, 292.

7  Wang Daokun (汪道昆), "Ming chushiYanshan Wang Changgongpei Sun ruren-hezangmuzhiming" (明处士兖山汪长公配孙孺人合葬墓志铭), in *Taihanji* (太函集), volume 55, *Xuxiusikuquanshu – jibu* (续修四库全书·集部), book 1347, 419.

8  Xu Chengyao (许承尧), "Beijing Shexianyizhuang" (北京歙县义庄), in *Sheshixiantan* (歙事闲谭), volume 11, 357.

9  Jiangsu sheng bowuguan (江苏省博物馆) ed., *Jiangsu sheng Ming Qing yilaibeikeziliaoxuanji* (江苏省明清以来碑刻资料选集) (Beijing: Sanlianshudian, 1959), 378.

10  Shi Guozhu (石国柱) and Xu Chengyao (许承尧), "Renwuzhi – yixing" (人物志·义行), in *She xianzhi* (歙县志), volume 9, edition of 1937.

11  "Renwushi – Yixingsi" (人物十·义行四), in *Wuyuan xianzhi* (婺源县志) of the Guangxu (光绪) reign, volume 32, 5–6.

12  "Shangyi" (尚义), in *Yi xianzhi* (黟县志) of the Jiaqing (嘉庆) reign, volume 7.

13  "Renwushi – Yixing qi" (人物十·义行七), in *Wuyuan xianzhi* (婺源县志)of the Guangxu (光绪) reign, volume 34, 21.

14  "Renwushi – Yixingba" (人物十·义行八), in *Wuyuan xianzhi* (婺源县志)of the Guangxu (光绪) reign, volume 35, 2.

15  Jiangsu sheng bowuguan (江苏省博物馆) ed., *Jiangsu sheng Ming Qing yilaibeikeziliaoxuanji* (江苏省明清以来碑刻资料选集), 101.

16  "Xu" (序), in *Huishanggongsuozhengxinlu* (徽商公所征信录).

17  Jiangsu sheng bowuguan (江苏省博物馆) ed., *Jiangsu sheng Ming Qing yilaibeikeziliaoxuanji* (江苏省明清以来碑刻资料选集), 449.

18  Suzhou lishibowuguan (苏州历史博物馆) ed., *Ming Qing Suzhou gongshangyebeikeji* (明清苏州工商业碑刻集) (Nanjing: Jiangsu renminchubanshe, 1981), 357.

19  GuYanwu (顾炎武), *Zhaoyuzhi* (肇域志), book 3 (Shanghai: Shanghai gujichubanshe, 2004).

20  Yan Zhitui (颜之推), "Mianxue" (勉学), in *Yanshijiaxun* (颜氏家训), interpreted and annotated by Tan Zuowen (檀作文) (Beijing: Zhonghuashuju, 2007), 101.

21  *Qing shizongshilu* (清世宗实录), volume 57, the 5thmonth of Yongzheng (雍正) 5 (Beijing: Zhonghuashuju, 1985), 841.

22  Li Weizhen (李维桢), "Xiang JijiuWanggongmubiao" (乡祭酒王公墓表), in *Damishanfangji* (大泌山房集), volume 106, *Sikuquanshucunmucongshu – jibu* (四库全书存目丛书·集部), book 153, 154.

23  Han Bangqi (韩邦奇), *Yuanluoji* (苑洛集), volume 6, *Qindingsikuquanshu – jibu* (钦定四库全书), book 1269, 37b.

24  GuiYouguang (归有光), "BaianChengwengbashishouxu" (白庵程翁八十寿序), in *Zhenchuanxianshengji* (震川先生集), volume 13, *Sibucongkan – jibu* (四部丛刊·集部), book 1597, 11a.

25  GuiZhuang (归庄), "Chuanyanzhaiji" (传砚斋记), in *GuiZhuangji* (归庄集), volume 6 (Beijing: Zhonghuashuju, 1962), 360.

26  XuJishe (徐继畲), "Shengji" (生计), in *Wutai xinzhi* (五台新志), volume 2.

27  *Yongzhengzhupiyuzhi* (雍正朱批谕旨), book 47.

28  GuYanwu (顾炎武), "Fujian" (福建), in *Tianxiajunguolibingshu* (天下郡国利病书), volume 96, collated and annotated by Huang Kun (黄坤)(Shanghai: Shanghai gujichubanshe, 2012), 2996.

29  QuDajun (屈大均), "Shiyu" (食语), in *Guangdong xinyu* (广东新语), volume 14 (Beijing: Zhonghuashuju, 1985), 371.

30  "Fengtu" (风土), in *DaoguangJiningZhilizhouzhi* (道光济宁直隶州志), 17.

31  XueLundao (薛论道), "Ti qian" (题钱), in *Linshiyixing* (林石逸兴), volume 5 (Kunming: Yunnan daxuechubanshe, 2010), 189; "Fenshi" (愤世), *Linshiyixing* (林石逸兴), volume 3, 111.

32  "Xiaozan" (笑赞), *Zhao Nanxingquanji* (赵南星全集).

33  Huang Xingzeng (黄省曾), "Yuyuan" (语苑),*Wuyueshanrenji* (五岳山人集), volume 21, *Sikuquanshucunmucongshu – jibu* (四库全书存目丛书·集部), book 94 (Bieji lei别集类) (Jinan: Qilushushe, 1997).

34 Tao Zongyi (陶宗仪), "Qian" (钱), in *Shuofu* (说郛), volume 77 (Beijing: Zhongguoshudian, 1986), 3.

35 Zhu Zaiyu (朱载堉), "Xingshi ci – ma qian" (醒世词·骂钱),in *Mingdaigequxuan* (明代歌曲选), ed., Yu Lugong (于路工) (Beijing: Gudianwenxuechubanshe, 1956), 77.

36 XueLundao (薛论道), "Cai" (财), *Linshiyixing* (林石逸兴), volume 1, 32.

37 "Shihuo" (食货), in *Huizhoufuzhi* (徽州府志) of the Hongzhi (弘治) reign, volume 2.

38 "Juanzhen" (蠲赈), in *Huizhoufuzhi* (徽州府志) of the Kangxi (康熙) reign, volume 8.

39 Wang Ao (王鏊), "Fengsu" (风俗), in *ZhenzeJi* (震泽集), volume 3.

40 See Lü Zuoxie (吕作燮), "Ming Qing yilai de Dongtingshangren" (明清以来的洞庭商人), in *Pingzhunxuekan – Zhongguoshehuijingjishiyanjiulunji* (平准学刊 – 中国社会经济史研究论集), volume 1, ed., Sun Yutang (孙毓棠) (Beijing: Zhongguoshangyechubanshe, 1985), 259.

41 Wang Shizhen (王世贞), *Yanzhoushanrenxugaobeizhuan* (弇州山人续稿碑传), volume 72, *Mingdaizhuanjicongkan – zonglu lei* (明代传记丛刊·综录类), book 55 (Taipei: Mingwenshuju, 1991), 15.

42 "Liandian" (礼典),*Quzhoufuzhi* (衢州府志) of the Tianqi (天启)reign.

43 "Fengsu" (风俗),*Dinghai xianzhi* (定海县志) of the Jiajing (嘉靖) reign, volume 5.

44 "Fengsu" (风俗), *Ningbo fuzhi* (宁波府志) of the Yongzheng (雍正) reign, volume 5.

45 Lu Ji (陆楫), *Jianjia tang zazhuzhaichao* (兼葭堂杂着摘抄) (Beijing: Zhonghuashuju, 1985), 3.

46 Liang Fangzhong (梁方仲), *Zhongguolidaihukou, tianmu, tianfutongji* (中国历代户口、田亩、田赋统计) (Shanghai: Shanghai renminchubanshe, 1980).

47 Kang Jitian (康基田), *Jinshengweilue* (晋乘蒐略), volume 2, carved and printed in Jiaqing (嘉庆), 16.

48 Xu Fuchu (徐复初), *Chongjianxianzhiji* (重建县治记).

49 *Qing Gaozongshilu* (清高宗实录), volume 1261, the leap 7th month (second half), Qianlong (乾隆) 51 (Beijing: Zhonghuashuju, 1985), 974.

50 Feng Congwu (冯从吾), "Fengshijiacheng" (冯氏家乘), in *Shaoxuji* (少墟集), volume 20, *Qindingsikuquanshu* (钦定四库全书), Section *ji*, book 1293. There was a quotation as "Qin and Jin are territories [linked by] marriages."

51 Jin Youli (金友理), "Xuanju" (选举), in *Taihubeikao* (太湖备考), volume 7, annotated by Xue Zhengxing (薛正兴) (Nanjing: Jiangsu guji chubanshe, 1998).

52 Weng Peng (翁澎), "Zaji" (杂记), in *Juquzhi* (具区志), volume 15.

53 "Dongshundafuzhi Henan ZhangdefushiYanjunmuzhiming" (东顺大夫知河南彰德府事严君墓志铭), in *Zhenzexianshengwenji* (震泽先生文集), volume 30.

54 WengPeng (翁澎), "Zaji" (杂记), in *Juquzhi* (具区志), volume 15.

55 "Shangbao gong muzhiming" (尚宝公墓志铭), in *MoliWangshiJiawei* (莫厘王氏家谓), volume 13.

56 "Yingjianzhi – Xuexiao" (营建制·学校), in *Huizhou fuzhi* (徽州府志) of the Daoguang (道光) reign, *Zhongguofangzhicongshu* (中国方志丛书) (Taipei: Taiwan chengwenchubanshe, 1975).

57 "Fengsu" (风俗), in *Yi xianzhi* (黟县志) of the Kangxi (康熙) reign, volume 1.

58 "Fengsu" (风俗), in *Xiuning xianzhi* (休宁县志) of the Kangxi (康熙) reign, volume 1. *Zhongguofangzhicongshu* (中国方志丛书) (Taipei: Taiwan chengwenchubanshe, 1975).

59 "Dilikao" (地理考), in *Longyou xianzhi* (龙游县志) of the Republican times, volume 3.

60 "Shengji" (生计), in *Wutai xinzhi* (五台新志), volume 2.

61 "Fengtu" (风土), in *Chenghai xianzhi* (澄海县志) of the Republican times, volume 15. It cites the old gazetteer of Ming.

62 "Yiwen" (艺文), in *Chaozhoufuzhi* (潮州府志) of the Qianlong (乾隆) reign, volume 40.

63 Wan Biao (万表), "Wanlutinggao" (玩鹿亭稿),*Jiushacaotangzayan* (九沙草堂杂言), volume 9, collected in *Simingcongshu* (四明丛书), ed., Zhang Shouyong (张寿镛).

64 *Mingguoribao* (民国日报), August 25, 1916.

65 See Lü Zuoxie (吕作燮), "Ming Qing yilai de Dongtingshangren" (明清以来的洞庭商人).

66  See Fang Zhiyuan (方志远) and Huang Ruiqing (黄瑞卿), "Ming Qing Jiangyoushang de jingyingguannianyutouzifangxiang" (明清江右商的经营观念与投资方向), *Zhongguoshiyanjiu* (中国史研究, Journal of Chinese Historical Studies), No. 4 (1991).

67  See Zhang Zhengming (张正明), "Jinbang de dingshengshiqi – Qingmo" (晋帮的鼎盛时期 – 清末), unpublished manuscript.

68  "Fengsu" (风俗), *Changsha xianzhi* (长沙县志) of the Jiaqing (嘉庆) reign, volume 14.

69  "Huiguan" (会馆), *Shanhua xianzhi* (善化县志) of the Guangxu (光绪) reign, volume 30.

70  "Fengsu" (风俗), *Changsha fuzhi* (长沙府志) of the Qianlong (乾隆) reign, volume 14.

71  "Huiguan" (会馆), *Shanhua xianzhi* (善化县志) of the Guangxu (光绪) reign, volume 30.

72  "Fengsu" (风俗), *Changsha fuzhi* (长沙府志) of the Qianlong (乾隆) reign, volume 14.

73  "Huiguan" (会馆), *Shanhua xianzhi* (善化县志) of the Guangxu (光绪) reign, volume 30.

74  Ibid.

75  Ibid.

76  Ibid.

77  Xie Bi (谢陛), "Huozhi" (货殖), *Shezhi* (歙志) of the Wanli (万历) reign.

78  Wang Shixing (王士性), "Jiangnanzhusheng" (江南诸省), in *Guangzhiyi* (广志绎), volume 4 (Beijing: Zhonghuashuju, 1997).

79  Zhongguorenminyinhang Shanghai shifenhang (中国人民银行上海市分行编) eds., *Shanghai Qianzhuangshiliao* (上海钱庄史料) (Shanghai: Shanghai renminchubanshe, 1960), 53.

80  "Zhengjiaozhi – youzheng" (政教志·邮政), *Yinxiantongzhi* (鄞县通志).

81  Lou Zuyi (楼祖诒), *Zhongguoyouyishiliao* (中国邮驿史料) (Beijing: Renminyoudianchubanshe, 1958), 54.

82  Li Sui (李燧) and Li Hongling (李宏龄), "Shanxi piaoshangchengbaiji" (山西票商成败记), in *Jinyouriji – tongzhouzhonggao* (晋游日记 – 同舟忠告), annotated by Huang Jianhui (黄鉴晖) (Taiyuan: Shanxi jingjichubanshe, 2003), 73.

83  Zhang Siwei (张四维), *Tiaolu tang ji* (条麓堂集), carved by Zhang Taizheng (张泰征) in Wanli (万历) 23 of Ming, collected in the library of the Shanxi University, volume 21.

84  Li Weizhen (李维桢), "Zeng Luotian ling Wanggong Biao" (赠罗田令王公表), in *Damishanfangji* (大泌山房集), volume 106, *Sikuquanshucunmucongshu – jibu* (四库全书目丛书·集部), book 153, 149.

85  *Junjichulufu – Guangxidaojianchayushi Zhang Sihengzouzhe* (军机处录副·广西道监察御史章嗣衡奏折), the 13th day of the 10th month of Xianfeng (咸丰) 3.

86  XuKe (徐珂), *Qing baileichao* (清稗类钞), book 5 (Beijing: Zhonghuashuju, 1986), 2308.

87  Zhang Han (张瀚), *Songchuangmengyu* (松窗梦语), annotated by Sheng Dongling (盛冬铃) (Beijing: Zhonghuashuju, 1985), 84.

88  "DayingbingzhiBingbofulaodarenzhuan" (大饮宾之宾伯父老大人传), *QingjiangXiangtianNieshichongxiuzupu* (清江香田聂氏重修族谱), volume 1.

89  Yinfulaoren (蟫伏老人), *Kangxinanxunmiji* (康熙南巡秘记) (Shanghai: Shanghai jinbushuju, 1910), 87.

90  Ma Guohan (马国翰), "Hang baiwan" (亢百万), in *Zhu ruyi* (竹如意), volume 2.

91  Letianjushi (乐天居士), *Tongshi – di shiqizhong – Longwuyishi* (痛史•第十七种•隆武遗事), edition of 1911.

92  Chen Qubing (陈去病), *Wushizhi* (五石脂).

93  The Qing Dynasty Archives, "Yushi Zhang Wei Xianfengyuannianshiyueershibarizouzhe" (御史张炜咸丰元年十月二十八日奏折).

94  The Qing Dynasty Archives, "Guanlihubushiwu Qi GuizaoXianfengsannianzhengyueershiliurizouzhe" (管理户部事务祁寯藻咸丰三年正月二十六日奏折).

95 *Jiushuqidi* (阄书契底) of Huizhou (徽州), collated in the Institute of History Studies, Chinese Academy of Social Sciences, No. 1000461.
96 Wang Shizhen (王世贞), "ZhanggongJuzhengzhuan" (张公居正传), *Guochaoxianzhenglu* (国朝献征录), volume 17.
97 See Ge Guopei (葛国培), "Ningbo bang de xingchengchutan" (宁波帮的形成初探), *Ningbo shiyuanxuebao* (宁波师院学报), No. 2 (1990); Zhang Shouguang (张守广), "Ming Qing shiqi Ningbo shangrenjituan de chansheng he fazhan" (明清时期宁波商人集团的产生和发展), *Nanjing shidaxuebao* (南京师大学报), No. 3 (1991).

# 3 The merchants' organizations

The merchants' organizations went through three stages: the clan, the kinship organization; *huiguan*, the geographically based organization; and *hanghui/gongsuo*, the business related organization. As Chinese society was defined by a tradition of kingship and native-place ties, the three types of organizations did not replace one another in history. Rather, they coexisted and overlapped in their organizations.

With the intensification of market competition in modern society, merchants participated in commercial wars as a group. Therefore, merchant organizations came into being. The earliest form of the merchant organization was a natural one, overlapping with merchants' kinship ties in the patriarchal clan. Organizations based on blood ties further developed into those based on native-place and trade relations. Relatively speaking, *huiguan*, a native-place organization, was a progress in comparison with the patriarchal clan, an organization tied to kinship. While native-place organizations – particularly those tied to kinship – were not created out of their members' self-conscious choice and thus fell into the category of involuntary entities, trade-oriented organizations were formed of their members' own volition. Therefore, the transformation from organizations tied to geographic and blood factors to those related to trade was an inevitable trend because of both the social development and the growth of commodified economy. However, those three organizations did not replace one another in proper sequence. Temporally, they coexisted with one another. Organizationally, they overlapped with one another. As ties to the patriarchal clan and the native place were a defining character of traditional Chinese society, virtually all merchants' trade-oriented organizations and trans-trade entities in the late modern times – namely, chambers of commerce – were imprinted, to varying degrees, with kinship and geographic factors.

## Section one: the merchant kinship organization – the patriarchal clan

The household was a basic cell and the most fundamental economic unit of society. Ever since the ancient times, merchants in China ran businesses with the household being a unit. Such household-related business usually took the form of cooperations between fathers and sons or brothers. For example, the merchant Cheng Tingzhu

> followed his father to travel along the Yangzi River and assisted him in running business. After his father died, he succeeded to his father's cause and was kind to his younger brothers. He took care of business in Yushan and increased landed properties. His second younger brother, [Cheng] Tingbo, was assigned to supervise oil trade in Lanyi. [Cheng] Tingzi, the third younger brother, stayed in Hangzhou to retail goods. His fourth younger brother, [Cheng] Tinghuan, traveled along the Yangzi and Han Rivers to do business. [He] established pawnshops and estates in Longyou, engaged in salt trade in Jinhua and Lanxi, ran stores in Longyou, and traded salt in Fengkou in our county. [He] thereby expanded his ancestor's properties and made them even greater.[1]

In the mid-Ming, with the flowering of a commodified economy, commercial competition grew more intense. Merchants found it hard to depend solely on the power of single households to engage in larger-scale competitions. Thus, kinship organizations played an increasingly important role in commercial activities. The kinship organization or clan (*zongzu*) referred to the patriarchal organization whose members had definite blood ties, were economically connected to one another, and lived together. A clan usually possessed an ancestral hall, clan lands, genealogies, regulations, schools, military force, and a cemetery, and so forth. A single-surname village was created when a clan was bonded in a specific geographical area. Therefore, a typical kinship organization was at once a ritual, economic, and legal unit. It was also an educational, self-defense, and geographical unit. A clan's leaders were *zongzi* (eldest son of the principal wife) and *zuzhang* (the chief of a clan). *Zongzi*, who was in charge of sacrifices of the whole clan, was assumed by the eldest sons inside the clan generations after generations. *Zuzhang*, who took care of affairs of the whole clan, was usually chosen by election. However, *zongzi* and *zuzhang* could be taken by the same persons. The blood-oriented clan was an extension of the household and had strong cohesive power. Therefore, engaging in commerce by relying on the kinship power immensely enhanced merchants' competitiveness.

## *1 The patriarchal clan's function in commercial management*

Here, I take Huizhou merchants as an example to make an analysis of the function performed by the kinship power in commercial activities.

### *Obtaining financial and personnel supports by relying on kinship power*

Huizhou merchants' seed capital funds were usually related to patriarchal clans. Those who "saved stipends from their careers as officials" or "possessed additional money as merchants" oftentimes funded their clansmen to do business. For example, a certain Huizhou person "whose ancestor came to Yangzhou to seek refuge with relatives when he was poor." "When [he] arrived in Yangzhou, the relatives provided financial support and gave him [a position] in a pawnshop" so that he was able to do business.[2] Some invested their money in businesses of merchants in the same clan. For example, Jiang Guozheng, a merchant from She County during the Ming and Qing times, engaged in trade in Huaiyin. "[His] relatives and friends found that he was meticulous and honest so that they contributed thousands [of ounces] of silver to [consign to] him [to do business]."[3] There were cases where clansmen ran joint ventures. For example, Cheng Suo, a merchant from Xiuning in the Ming, "collaborated with ten wise and influential [clansmen], each of whom brought three hundred [ounces of silver], to trade in Xinshi of Wuxing."[4]The Japanese professor Fujii Hiroshi once summarized that capital of Huizhou merchants fell into seven categories: collective capital, consigned capital, capital by assistance, capital by marriage, capital by inheritance, labor capital, and bureaucratic capital. It is worth pointing out that all but labor capital were related to kinship. Moreover, there was borrowed capital, which constituted another important source of Huizhou merchants' capital. For example, Xu Jiqing, a She County native during the Tianshun reign of the Ming, "considered wealth as an irrelevant matter. Inside the clan, he lent money to poor merchants without asking them to pay interests."[5] There were countless cases where Huizhou people gained loans from their fellow clansmen to do business.

The clerks hired by Huizhou merchants were mostly their fellow clansmen. "Choosing [the right] people and taking advantage of [the right] timing" were a recipe for commercial success. Certainly, the most trusted clerks were clansmen. During the Jiajing and Wanli reigns of the Ming, the She County merchant Wu Liangyou did business elsewhere. "[The number of his] fellow clansmen who followed him to engage in trade increased year by year." Wu Deming, a She County person,

> stayed at home but [accumulated a wealth] of one hundred thousand [ounces of silver]. [He] never took care of the business personally, but was good at using wise and capable youngsters from [his] relatives' families. [He] assigned them to the posts without caring for slight profits.

"Throughout [his] life, [Wu] assigned poor clansmen to jobs, allowing them to pursue vocations."[6] Wang Xuanyi, great granduncle of Wang Daokun, the author of *Anthology of Taihan*, "gathered grains for three months" as his seed capital to "trade in Yan and Dai. Later, [he] embarked on salt trade and stayed in various prefectures in the coastal area in the East." As his business expanded, "dozens of young clansmen [followed him] to be merchants." Under Wang Xuanyi's direction, they participated in running business. "All purchases and sales must be decided by Lord [Wang] before they could be conducted." Wang Xuanyi later made a great fortune and ascended to be the leader of salt traders. Clansmen who followed him also became rich. "Some might be several times wealthier than Lord [Wang]."[7]

The financial and personnel supports provided by the clan made Huizhou merchants' commercial activities long-lasting. Before the Ming, it was well known in society that Huizhou people excelled at trading, even though the concept of "Huizhou merchants" was not recorded in official texts. In the mid-Ming, com-modified economy fully developed and commercial capital was unprecedentedly active. Huizhou merchants took advantage of the timing and rose to prominence quickly. After the Chenghua and Hongzhi reigns, more and more Huizhou people engaged in commerce. "Seven or eight out of ten [Huizhou people] did business."[8] The scope of their business expanded increasingly so that "[those merchants were able to] reach anywhere across the country."[9]

*Resorting the power of the clan to establish commercial monopoly*

The predatory nature of feudal commerce was to reap profits by buying commodi-ties at low prices and selling them at high prices. In markets in various places, settled merchants participated in competition to achieve the goal of selling goods expensively. In order to maximize profit margins, it was necessary to reject com-petition and establish monopoly. Settled merchants from Huizhou monopolized the market in two ways. First, they controlled all trades in urban markets and fairs. Second, they monopolized all businesses in one specific trade.

Monopoly was established with the full support of the clan. When a Huizhou merchant did business elsewhere and managed to settle down in the urban market or fair, his fellow kinsmen would follow him and then his fellow townspeople would come, too. Hu Shi, a Huizhou native and famous scholar, stressed the con-nection between Huizhou people's migration as a clan and the establishment of monopoly in his letter to the compiler of the gazetteer of Jixi County. He said,

> The county gazetteer should focus on the distribution and history of our townspeople's migration for commercial purposes. The gazetteer should avoid only giving accounts of the little Jixi by ignoring the "greater Jixi," which was of more profound significance. If there were no "greater Jixi," the little Jixi would not have been relevant. The new gazetteer should set up a chapter of the "greater Jixi," in which various clans drew roadmaps to explore their routes of migration and their trades. For example, Jinhua and Lanxi constituted one route; Xiaofeng and Huzhou another one; Hangzhou another one; Shanghai another one; and from Jixi to the Yangzi River another one. But [each clan] had its preferred [trades]. For example, although the noodle trade started in various villages, it would become a specialty of merchants from Shiwudu. For example, although Hankou was opened up by our clan, [merchants who worked in Hankou] were not limited to those from Beixiang. However, the Tongzhou trade was initiated by the Cheng family from Renli, and no one else participated in it. Trades in Henggang were mostly monopo-lized by people from Lingnan.[10]

Hu Shi was justified to propose a concept of the "greater Jixi." As Jixi people migrated as clans to do business elsewhere, they established monopoly organiza-tions in some cities and towns. Those places became "greater Jixi' beyond Jixi proper. To further Hu Shi's proposition, there was "greater Huizhou" beyond the little Huizhou. The saying that "there were no towns without Huizhou [merchants]" also indicated Huizhou merchants' monopoly of local markets.

*Shangchuan Mingjing Hushi zongpu* (*The Genealogy of the Hu Family of Mingjing, Shangchuan*) of Jixi traced a history of commercial activities of Hu Shi's ancestors and clearly showed a trend of migration as a whole clan:

> Prior to the thirteenth generation, [people] of our clan rarely engaged in commerce. Later, Mr. [Hu] Wenlan went to Fujian, Mr. [Hu] Zhaokong to Shanghai, and Mr. [Hu] Hansan to Guangdong. Their businesses were all remarkable of the day. During the Daoguang and Xianfeng reigns, Mr. [Hu] Duanzhai rose to prominence by earning a reputation in the business of stationery and ink. Meanwhile, clansmen who ran stores in Shanghai included Zhaokong, who had thirteen stories under the name of "Wan," Zhijun, who opened nine stores under the name of "Ding," and also my clansmen. During the Tongzhi and Guangxu reigns, in Shanghai there were Dingmao run by Mr. Zhenhai, Wanshengduan by Mr. Yuting, and Songmao by Mr. Zhenchun. In Nanjing, there was Hengzhi run by Mr. Fangkai. In Sanxi, my great granduncle, Yinlin, ran Jinglong. Their businesses were closely connected to one another, making them as rich as the noble and the influential. They thus earned a reputation of excelling at trading among sojourning merchants. . . . In addition, my clansmen mostly sojourned in Shanghai and its neighboring areas. The number reached several hundred. I heard that the first one [who did business in Shanghai] was Mr. [Hu] Zhaokong. Today's sojourning merchants in Shanghai should worship him as the Christopher Columbus [of Huizhou merchants].[11]

Later, a vast number of merchants poured into Yangzhou. Chen Qubing recently said, "The prosperity of Yangzhou stemmed from [the arrival of] Huizhou merchants. Yangzhou was actually a colony of Huizhou merchants."[12]

When Huizhou merchants established regional monopoly, they resorted the power of clans to create personnel and financial advantages. For example, the Wuyuan merchant Cheng Dong "reaped quite good profits and purchased landed properties" in Hankou. "His relatives and fellow townspeople could live [in his residence] for several months without having to pay the cost of food. [He] even made recommendations [for them] to find jobs."[13] Another example was Wucheng Town of Jiangxi, which was "a place where Huizhou merchants congregated." Zhu Chengxun, a merchant from Yi County, "made recommendations based on their talents" for "his fellow townspeople who came to look for a job or who were poor because of unemployment."[14]Consequently, the power of the clan expanded incessantly, and the goal of excluding outsiders was attained. During the Jingtai and Hongzhi reigns in Ming, the Huizhou merchant Xu Mengjie did business for over 20 years in Zhengyang, an important town that "connected the Huai River and the Sishui River." As his clansmen came to seek refuge with him, Xu "was particularly kind to his relatives and friends" and, consequently, his kinsmen made a fortune because of him. Gradually, Huizhou merchants monopolized the market. "Hence, Zhengyang's market prospered because of Mr. [Xu Mengjie]." When Xu Mengjie died on alien soil in Zhengyang, "nearly three thousand people participated in his funeral, and ten thousand spectators mourned him. Even high-ranking officials and noblemen paled in comparison with this merchant to move a massive population."[15]We can thus see the power of the Xu family. One can also understand Huizhou merchants' monopoly of cities and towns by taking a look at their registry for residence. In Linqing, known as "the fair of Shandong and the pivot of China,"[16]"Huizhou merchants constituted ninety percent of those who registered for residence."[17] Huizhou merchants monopolized trades of general merchandises to reap high profits in cities, towns, markets, and fairs they controlled. In Nanxiang Town in Ming, "Huizhou merchants sojourned and hoarded general merchandises. [So, this town] was busier than all other towns."[18] Luodian Town "gathered Huizhou merchants so that its commerce was almost as prosperous as that in Nanxiang."[19]

Huizhou merchants' success in establishing monopoly resided in the support of the clan. Take the pawn business as an example. "Most pawnbrokers were people from Xiuning."[20] Their strategy was to have clansmen and fellow townspeople to engage in the same trade. They thereby relied on their solid capital and took actions in concert in order to lowered pawn-broking interests and beat merchants from other groups, who possessed small funds but sought higher interest rates. It was recorded in volume 3 of *Jinling suoshi shenglu* (*The Remnant Record of Trivial Matters of Jinling*),

> [In Jinling], there were five hundred pawn shops. Those run by Fujian [merchants] possessed smaller funds and asked for an interest rate of thirty or forty percent. Shops run by Huizhou merchants enjoyed more abundant capital and asked for an interest rate of merely ten, twenty, or thirty percent, which was beneficial to the poor. People did not like [shops run] by Fujian [merchants], but had no option.

In the Ming times, a certain Mr. Wang made a fortune by opening pawn shops in Shanghai. Then he ran more shops in the surrounding counties and sent his clansmen to take charge.

> This gentleman exhorted his clansmen [that when they] lived in other counties, [they] should not abuse the right to make profits. [When they] lent money. [They] should not substitute low-quality metal money for high-quality one or give inadequate amounts of cash. [When they] demanded interests, [they] should not seek high profits or ask for interests daily.

The outcome was "[that] everyone flocked to do business [with those pawn shops]. Even [people from] other counties also came. After a while, he became extremely wealthy, and no one in town was richer than he was."[21] Mr. Wang attracted the poor by giving low interest rates and thereby expanded his business.

In Pinghu County of Zhejiang, "whose city wall stretched several *li*, rich people from Xin'an possessed enormous funds to loan money and earn interests. They settled down in [the county seat] and multiplied into dozens of families. Half of magnificent houses owned by officials' families were occupied by them."[22] In Taixing of Jiangsu, "most pawn shops were run by Xin'an people. They were opened in [areas] close to the five city gates and other towns."[23] Hence, Huizhou pawnbrokers gradually expanded their spheres of influence in different regions and thereby established the monopoly of the trade.

### *Participating in market competition by resorting to the power of the clan*

Aside from settled merchants, there were itinerant traders. Rich merchants from Huizhou traveled across the country. They left their traces in Tibet, Taiwan, Manchuria, Fujian, Guangdong, and overseas. Itinerant traders earned profits from price differences through buying cheap and selling dear and from exploiting transporters. Commercial activities of itinerant traders were much more complicated than those of settled merchants. Their margins of profit were dictated by the following factors: a right judgement and the ability to predict market demands, turnover rates of goods, correct estimation of the influences of seasons and phenological character on the prices, wages of transporters, and so forth. Constrained by such factors, the transporting trades usually took the form of groups. The larger capital was, the more effective the organization was, the more competitive the merchants became, and the higher the profits were. When rich and powerful merchants from Huizhou engaged in shipping trade, they also gained support from the clan.

A right judgement and right prediction of market demands were necessary to the shipping trade. Huizhou merchants paid exclusive attention to the investigation of local markets. Cheng Jigong, a Huizhou merchant during the Hongzhi and Wanli reigns in Ming, "traveled eastward from Shaoxing and to Songjiang. Along the coastal line, [he reached] the Huai-Yang area and then traveled northward to the You-Ji area. Thus, [he] observed the situation of ten thousand goods."[24] However, the market was in a constant state of flux. In order to "be good at examining the rise and fall of market demands to raise and lower the prices in accordance with the timing," it was inadequate to merely rely on experiences or general knowledge of the market. Huizhou merchants' judgement and prediction of market demands were made based on the information supplied by their assistants and their clansmen who did business locally in different regions. Therefore, Huizhou merchants attached great importance to compiling genealogies. Zhang Bitai, a merchant from Jixi "lived a life obscurely by trading and traveled back and forth in Jiangsu and Zhejiang."

> [He] once paid visits to his clansmen for compiling the genealogy and happened to meet with [Zhang] Han, his fellow clansman from Pucheng, Fujian, in Suzhou. They spoke of reconstructing the ancestral shrine in Nanfeng. Hence, [they] together sent notices to notify clansmen in different areas.

"Later, [he] arrived at Pucheng and checked the difference between the general genealogy of all clans and the Xiguan genealogy."[25] In some sense, genealogies became the liaison for itinerant traders from Huizhou. "Clansmen in different areas" were important sources from which they could gain access to reliable information. It was because of this that Cheng Jigong was able to "sit and devise plans" to direct his clansmen to engage in multiple shipping trades simultaneously.

> Suzhou was rich in cotton. So, cloth was traded. Huai-Yang was situated in the middle of our country. Therefore, plans of salt trade were made. [Lands] in our prefecture was infertile. Thus, [merchants] engaged in money lending. All merchants from the Cheng clan got together and followed Cheng Jigong. Only Cheng Jigong made decisions. . . . In a decade, the initially poor Cheng's gained prominence. Cheng Jigong's wealth rose multiple times, and [he] became the richest person in Changyuan.[26]

To raise profit margins, itinerant traders had to accelerate the turnover rate of shipping trades to ensure that capital could yield the maximal benefit in the same period of time. It was crucial to make arrangements beforehand to connect water and land transportations and select traffic routes. Some trades were distinctively seasonal. For example, when timber merchants purchased timber locally in Huizhou, "[they] had [trees] chopped down in wintertime. In the fifth or sixth month when the rainy season set in and the water rose, [the timber] was shipped to Zhejiang through Yanzhou and to the Yangzi Delta through Jixi. [As the logs] were drifting down the river, it did not entail much work."[27] If one missed the rainy season, his capital would remain stagnant for another year. On the other hand, it was vital to shorten the stay in areas of purchasing and selling. During the Jiajing and Wanli reigns in the Ming, Wang Zicheng, a merchant from the She County, was trading in Sichuan. Some merchants from Xin'an shipped goods to Sichuan but failed to sell them at right prices. The goods, which were stored in warehouses, were subject to tax. Meanwhile, the goods they were eager to buy were unobtainable because they had invested all funds in those unsold goods. Hence, Wang Zicheng was commissioned to sell the goods and lent them money to make purchases.[28] From this we can see that to enhance their competitiveness, itinerant traders had to build up commercial conglomerates under their full control and establish commercial networks so that they could install their trusted people in key links of purchasing, selling, and shipping. All records of Huizhou itinerant traders indicated that they garnered supports from their clans in this respect. For example, Wang Fuxian of Xiuning

> traded salt in the Yangzi and Huai Rivers with thousands of ships. [He] led clansmen to [tread the water and] travel [to different places] as though walking upon flat ground. [He] excelled at choosing talents and taking advantage of the timing. [His] calculations always paid dividends. Consequently, he accumulated a wealth of tens of thousands [of ounces of silver]. . . . Those who knew him understood the way he made a fortune. Therefore, his fellow

townspeople strove to use his business tactics to grow and thrive. After several decades, among all townspeople, the Wang clan from Ximen was acknowledged to be extremely rich.[29]

With thousands of vessels, Wang controlled an immense business. Under his direction, his clansmen engaged in shipping trades, and he garnered "a wealth of tens of thousands [of ounces of silver]." Thus, the Wang clan of Ximen prospered.

To raise profit margins, itinerant traders kept transporters' salaries as low as possible. In his essay, *"Jianwen jixun"* (Record of and Comments on What is Seen and Heard), the Ming person Chen Liangmo gave an account of Huizhou merchants' pernicious exploitation of transport workers:

> Xu Aai, Yang Da, and Wan Zhong from Tongli were extremely poor and had to make a living by poling rafts and shipping commercial goods. Because the three people argued with Cheng Lin, a Huizhou merchant, over the fees of transportation, they offended [Cheng]. [Cheng] lodged a false accusation against them of stealing rice, fabrics, and dried fish by taking a bag of dried fish as the stolen goods to show Lang Sheng, the chief of *li*, asking him to accept it as the proof. The case was presented to the prefectural government, where the prefect, Lin Yunxi, believed [Cheng] and [punished the three] by severely flogging them. Xu Aai committed suicide by hanging himself in prison. Yang Da and Wan Zhong were both meted out a penalty of having their faces tattooed and sent into exile. Both died in guesthouses on their way. Aai's old parents suffered from hunger and cold without a son to help. They later died one after another.

To maximize profit margins, Huizhou merchants revived the remnant of slavery – namely, the bondservant system, which remained intact under the patriarchal clan system. Bondservants were driven to engage in transportation. For example, *Lishi fenjia wenyue* (*A Written Note of the Li Family on Dividing Up Family Property and Living Apart*) of Qimen indicated,

> The above-mentioned bondservants should be ordered about according to the circumstances, with the exception of important occasions such as weddings, funerals, and rituals held in various households. Don't issue duplicate orders for their long-distance trips to county and prefecture seats to assemble rafts, ship logs, and cut firewood. Arrangements should be made after they settle down in specific households. All [households] should contribute wages for them.

The written note stipulated that assembling rafts, shipping logs, and cutting firewood be included as the required labor service of bondservants. Their "long-distance trips to county and prefecture seats" also constituted a part of their labor service to ship goods. This was a unique advantage enjoyed by Huizhou merchants who counted on the power of the patriarchal clan to make higher profits in market competition.

*Controlling commercial partners by means
of the patriarchal clan system*

Usually, Huizhou merchants held dual identities as settled merchants and itinerant traders. As they shipped goods in distant places and ran multiple stores, they needed to hire numerous clerks. Yu Yue recorded in *Youtaixian guan biji* (*Notes of Youtaixian Chamber*) that Mr. Xu, a merchant from She County, owned "over forty [pawnshops] with almost two thousand clerks." In order to perpetuate their market success, Huizhou merchants had to strengthen internal controls over their commercial conglomerates and establish a rigorous management system. They hired clerks under multifarious names, but in terms of the strata of management, there were four levels: agents, assistants, shopkeepers, and employees.

Agents were given authorization by merchants to do business. For example, Jiang Chengfeng was

> consigned by his clansmen to trade salt, but never meddled in it. Sometimes, the business went down and therefore lost money. [Jiang] was willing to compensate for the loss with his own properties. His clansmen had faith in his selflessness and therefore always pardoned him.[30]

Assistants were aides to merchants. They performed three functions. First, they were the intermediaries and coordinators between merchants and shopkeepers. For example, Li Shifu, a Wuyuan native during the Jiajing and Wanli reigns, "followed senior clansmen to trade in Jiangning. He was good at calculating and devising plans. He assisted senior merchants above him and, simultaneously, supervised shopkeepers below him. The business prospered gradually."[31] Second, they were informants who enabled merchants to "be clear-sighted to anticipate price surge of goods and lower the costs of transportation."

> An influential merchant usually [possessed] hundreds of thousands of ounces of silver and hired a number of assistants to help them gather information. They were selfless persons who would not embezzle a penny. Therefore, they could win favor and trust from the powerful merchant. When the merchant earned surplus out of usurious loans, the property would be divided, allowing assistants to become merchants themselves. Therefore, to become a rich and influential merchant entailed [the cooperation] of more than one person.[32]

Third, assistants were assigned to be the liaison of the government. In *Rulin waishi* (*The Scholar*), it was recorded, "*Dasike* referred to a person consigned by a salt trader to get in touch with the government, meet with guests, and pay visits to clients with a pay of hundreds of [ounces of] silver."[33]

Shopkeepers were managers of stores who undertook the tasks of purchasing and selling. For example, Min Shizhang from Yan Town "traveled to Yangzhou and kept shops for his fellow townspeople. He won the trust because of his loyalty and trustworthiness. Later, he saved thousands of [ounces of] silver and engaged in salt trade to accumulate a wealth of tens of thousands."[34] Bao Zhitong, a merchant from She County,

> learned salt trade with my uncle, Mr. [Bao] Fengzhan, when he was young. Soon, he assumed a position as the teller. [He] was so talented that he remained in the position for more than two decades without switching to other employers. His family thereby gradually prospered.[35]

Moreover, there were cases where bondservants served as shopkeepers. For example, Huang Yanxiu's father "dispatched his bondservant, Bao Qiu, to be a shopkeeper in Jinling."[36]

Fellow townspeople or bondservants were usually hired as clerks and laborers.

Hence, we can see that clerks of different levels were basically composed of clansmen and fellow townspeople. Rich and influential merchants demanded them to be "loyal and trustworthy," "selfless," "not embezzling a penny," or "not meddling in [the business]." For a clerk, as long as they were meticulous in their jobs and then "won favor from great merchants," they could expect to "garner a portion of [the merchants'] wealth and become merchants themselves." For example, Bao Zhidao, who enjoyed a reputation in Huainan and Huaibei as a great merchant,

> used to assist others to trade salt in Yangzhou. Those who were assisted by Mr. [Bao] thrived, and Mr. [Bao] himself accumulated a wealth and engaged in commerce. His revenues unusually exceeded his expectations. After a long time, he became rich. Therefore, he did business by himself in Huainan and no longer served as an aide to others.[37]

Even lower-level employees had a chance to "be promoted as shopkeepers in charge of money" and "glorify their families by founding their own businesses."[38]

However, only a minority of people could "garner a portion of [the merchants'] wealth and become merchants themselves." There were cases that employees cheated and lied. For example, when Wu Liang you was a powerful merchant, "his clansmen followed him in the business. After many years, [they] embezzled more than thousands of [ounces of silver]."[39] A certain Mr. Huang from Xiuning "consigned a wrong person, who illegally appropriated [his properties] and returned to destroy houses to cover up his dishonesty. [Properties worth] ten thousand [ounces of silver] were burned down."[40] There were also a vast number of cases that bondservants stole properties and absconded. Huang Yanxiu's father hired his bondservant, Bao Qiu, as the shopkeeper, but Bao Qiu "appropriated tens of thousands of [ounces of silver] and then burned down the house to escape." Cheng Suo hired his bondservant as the shopkeeper, but he "stole money and absconded."[41]

In light of this, Huizhou merchants resorted to the patriarchal clan system to tighten their control over employees (mostly clansmen) of different levels. Volume 3, "Fengsu" [Customs], of *Yixian zhi* (*Gazetteer of Yi County*) stated,

"Huizhou people lived together as clans and placed a great emphasis on patriarchal relations." In areas of their commercial activities, Huizhou merchants retained their custom of living together with clansmen. For example, the Wu clan, who "engaged in commerce in more than two centuries between the Ming and this (Qing) dynasty,"[42] had quite a vast number of its members migrate to Yangzhou. Its offshoots multiplied. The Wu clan "gathered clansmen and took care of neighbors" in Yangzhou.[43] It was indicated in *A Record of Painted Pleasure Boat in Yangzhou*,

> The Wu clan was respected and influential in Huizhou. They were spread out in villages such as Xixinan, Changqiao, Beian, and Yan Town. Those who sojourned in Yangzhou were also divided [into subgroups] in accordance to the villages [they originally came from].[44]

Huizhou merchants were active in building clan shrines to worship their ancestors in areas where they engaged in trade. For example, it was written in the preface to *Wangshi pucheng* (*Genealogy of the Wang Clan*),

> The offshoots of our Wang clan were spread out across the country. Those who came from She County and sojourned in Yangzhou and who traded salt in Huainan and Huaibei were particularly numerous. [Our clansmen] who live in Yangzhou could not return to the native place yearly to perform rituals. Thus, [they] built a public shrine. On occasions of commemorating ancestors, clansmen were ordered to display sacrifice containers and offer seasonal food. Every year, clansmen were assigned special tasks individually. After several decades, the population increased, but they had never become slack in [performing] rituals and [displaying] utensils.

Fang Shituo, a Huizhou merchant during the Qianlong reign, "sojourned in Yangzhou and could not return to hometown soon. Thus, [he] built an ancestral hall to set up sacrifice lands in Yangzhou. [He] gathered Yangzhou merchants from the same clan to diligently participate in rituals."[45] Zheng Jianyuan, a Huizhou merchant, "took charge of salt trade for more than ten years" during the Qianlong and Jiaqing reigns. "His ancestors migrated from She County to Yizheng because of the salt policy, then to Jiangning and to Yangzhou, where [the Zheng] clan registered their residence." He not only "built the clan hall of the Zheng's in Hongqiao of She County and the Patriarch Shrine of Haigong, the Distance Ancestor, in Shanglüsi by installing a sacrifice field," but also constructed shrines in areas where he engaged in trade. He "built a patriarchal hall for his grandfather and set up three fields for sacrifice" in Nanjing. In Yangzhou, he built the Qinle Hall behind his residence "for his descendants to perform rituals timely."[46]Huizhou merchants' activism in promoting ancestral worship was driven by their intention to take control over clansmen – namely, they managed and disciplined their fellow clansmen as *zongzi* in an attempt to maintain the rigidly stratified managerial levels in accordance to degrees of kinship. In the epitaph written by Wang Daokun for Wu Rongrang, a Huizhou merchant, a picture was portrayed about the relationship between the Huizhou merchant and the clerk – namely between *zongzi* and ordinary clansmen. When Wu Rongrang was 16*sui* old, he "followed clansmen to do business in Songjiang." Because of this extraordinary ability to trade, he independently developed his own business and migrated to Jiaoshan of Tonglu, Zhejiang to create new enterprises. In Jiaoshan, he "established an ancestral hall to enshrine ancestors and set up a field for ritual matters following the previous ways." "[He] summoned poor people in the clan and gave them jobs so that they could survive. Hundreds of fellow clansmen, who acted just like his clients, [were under him.]" All clerks were his clansmen. In order to tighten his grips on them, Wu Rongrang gathered together those clansmen – namely, clerks – in every first and fifteenth day of the lunar month to "carry *Yanshi jiaxun* (*Admonitions for the Yan Clan*) in the courtyard. As a rule, all clerks were in military uniform and awaited order."[47]

Huizhou merchants also took advantage of the patriarchal clan system to strengthen their control over bondservants who were assigned to do business. Bondservants in Huizhou suffered an extremely low social standing. It was said, "The master and the servant distinguished from each, allowing no room for confusing their hats and clothes."[48] "The hierarchy between the master and the servant was strictly [enforced] and would not change after ten generations. [With this system,] rascals did not dare to behave wantonly."[49]

> A bondservant who served [the master] would not violate [the rule]. Once he violated, [he] would be seized and turned over to the court. Even though he accumulated a wealth and behaved well to become an official, he would not gain higher ranks.[50]

In *The Scholars*, it was mentioned that Wan Xuezhai, the boy attendant of Cheng Mingqing, a Huizhou merchant, made a great fortune of hundreds of thousands by dealing in salt certificates. Later, Cheng Mingqing went bankrupted and returned to his hometown. In the wedding where Wan Xuezhai married to the daughter of an imperial academician, Cheng Mingqing happened to pass by. Wan Xuezhai could not help kneeling down to greet him. Eventually, Wan spent 10,000 ounces of silver to send his ex-master away.[51] Even though the episode was from a mere novel, it reflected the social reality. The Huizhou merchant Sun Wenlin traded in Wuxing and "had many highly disciplined servants, who never tried to tell jokes."[52] Here, "highly disciplined servants" referred to bondservants who were handcuffed by the patriarchal clan system.

*Collaborating with the feudal regime by resorting to the patriarch clan system*

Sandwiched between the anti-commerce policies and state-monopoly trade implemented by the ruling groups, commercial capital barely developed during the Ming and Qing times. Like all other merchants, Huizhou merchants were also bullied by feudal politics, such as the appropriation of properties by imperial relatives and aristocrats. For example, "in the seventh month of 1603, Cheng Sichan, a great merchant, carried a large amount of money and goods to Luoyang, all of which were appropriated by the Prince of Runing."[53] In other cases, merchants were extorted by bureaucrats. "Officials intimate to the emperor traveled around to levy taxes. They inflicted damage on the whole country. Xin'an suffered the most for their extortion."[54] In addition, there were local tyrants and evil gentry who victimized merchants. The Huizhou merchant Wang Quanye traded in Zhejiang. "Zhang Shi, a local tyrant in the county, sent vicious servants to create disturbances in merchants' [place]. Those servants lodged false accusations against people. Even influential officials' families and powerful gentry succumbed themselves to [Zhang]."[55] In order to avoid being bullied by the feudal political power and sustain their own development, Huizhou merchants were willing to collaborate with the feudal regime.

Huizhou merchants enjoyed a uniquely favorable condition to seek refuge with the feudal regime, because Huizhou's patriarchal force had a natural linkage to the latter. Most powerful clans in Huizhou originated from "officials' clans in the Central Plains." Their first immigratory ancestors "had usually taken office here and ended up staying put because of their love of the mountains and waters here." The rise and fall of the patriarchal power was predicated on the number of clansmen who served as officials in the court. For example, "among all clans in various counties, it was the Cheng and Wang clans that were most time-honored and prosperous."[56] This was because, first of all, they had prominent ancestors. The ancestor of the Cheng clan, Cheng Yuantan, was the chief of Xin'an during the Eastern Jin dynasty, who was bestowed lands and residences to stay in She County.[57] The first immigratory ancestor to She County of the Wang clan was Wang Shuju, the commander-in-chief in the military of the Liu-Song dynasty. During the Sui-Tang transition, "[he] and Wang Hua, Duke of Yueguo, rose from Chengyuan (a village of Jixi, original note) to protect six counties. [He] later surrendered to the Tang dynasty and was awarded special honors and titles." Second, those clans had their clansmen serve the government continually throughout various dynasties. The Wang clan "had numerous descendants take office in the dynasties. Therefore, the Wang clan thrived with the multiplication of progeny all over She County."[58] Hence, all clans in Huizhou placed great emphasis on their children's education in pursuit of a positon in the government, which topped all items of the rules of the clans.

> Young people from the clan with unusual deportment and deep wisdom but incapable of receiving education should be recruited and taught. They could be either taught in the clan's school or given subsidies. If one talent or two were cultivated, they could be the paragons of the future [generations]. This was the hope of our clan and the glory of the ancestors, which was of great relevance.[59]

Huizhou influential and powerful clans invested heavily in establishing academies and schools, and Huizhou merchants expended huge amounts of money to sponsor those schools. Consequently, Huizhou became "Zou and Lu in the Southeast." According to a statistics in *Jiudian beizheng* (*Old Texts for Reference*) authored by Zhu Pengshou, among all provinces, Anhui was ranked the third (nine in total) in producing *zhuangyuan* (the first rank) degree holders. Anhui featured 13 prefectures, among which Huizhou Prefecture produced four. The fact that a large number of Huizhou natives ascended to bureaucracy paved the way for Huizhou merchants to cooperate with the feudal force by means of "talking about friendship among clansmen." Meanwhile, some Huizhou merchants themselves were culturally sophisticated. They were both Confucians and merchants. The marriage between Confucianism and business was beneficial to their dealings with the government.

One of the most commonly used approaches was to "lend money to the noblemen so that the latter would usually show merchants favor."[60]*Xiguan Zhangshi zupu* (*Genealogy of the Zhang Clan of Xiguan*) indicated that Zhang Bilin from Jixi

> had an uncle who assumed the position of Registrar of Salt and was awaiting a vacancy in officialdom to fill in Zhejiang. Later he was assigned his original position and took care of affairs in various salt fields. [Zhang Bilin] always accompanied him to take office and hanged around with him day in and day out. For this reason, [Zhang] earned a reputation among salt officials. At that time, half of salt traders from Jixi started their businesses because of him. In times of difficulty, [people] counted on his well-devised plans [to survive]. Therefore, countless people felt grateful to him.

His younger brother of the same clan, Zhang Bihuan (whose style name was Dounan) "enjoyed a high reputation in Zhejiang. Those who came from Jixi and traded salt acknowledged Dounan as the harbinger." The Zhang clan depended on the power of their clansmen who took office in the government to act in collusion with the government and dominate in the salt business in Zhejiang. Merchants from the same county also benefited from this. Li Weizhen of Ming pointed out, "Huizhou merchants possessed enormous funds, but excelled at private fighting. They kept fighting until they triumphed. Moreover, they were good at fawning on the powerful."[61]"Fawning on the powerful" enabled them to "excel at private fighting and keep fighting until they triumphed."

The collusion between Huizhou merchants and political powers manifested itself particularly in trading state-monopolized commodities. Karl Marx pointed out, "competition was engendered by feudal monopoly."[62] Ever since the ancient times, salt was a state-monopolized commodity. During the Wanli reign of Ming, *gangyan zhi* was implemented, and merchants registered in the system became hereditary merchants with exclusive rights. "Among all commercial activities that entailed buying cheap and selling dear, nothing was more [lucrative] than salt trade."[63] Merchants of different groups engaged in intense competitions to gain the privileges of salt trade. The key to their success in competitions was the degree to which they collaborated with feudal political forces. For merchants within the system of *gangyanzhi*, it was vital to acquire the qualification of the "official-merchant" in order to retain their monopoly. *Chronicle of Salt Business in Huainan and Huaibei* printed during the Jiaqing reign recorded that there were two avenues through which a person could become an "official-merchant." First, "a merchant in Huainan and Huaibei secured a registry in officialdom and registered his residence elsewhere as an official-merchant. He was not given what other officials were entitled to get or other unnecessary costs." Second, "a salt merchant had his sons or grandsons serve in the government. He thereby established himself as an official-merchant. He was given half of office expenses. In some cases, he was not given any expense at all." Those were two viable ways for Huizhou merchants. Thanks to Huizhou clans' emphasis on education, Huizhou merchants were both Confucianists and businessmen, among whom there were people who initially engaged in trade and later gained registry as officials. For example, Jiang Lianru, son of the great salt merchant Jiang Zhaomin,

> was intelligent by nature and liked to study. Because of busy family affairs, he did business in Shaoxing. Mr. [Jiang Zhaomin] pondered over glorifying the clan. . . .[Therefore, Jiang Lianru was] called back to resume his study. He earned a great fame in the school. In 1698, he gained the status of tribute student, which met his father's expectation.[64]

Huizhou merchants hired tutors to teach their children. Huizhou merchants sojourning in Yangzhou "multiplied into officials' households and produced celebrities generations after generations." Many talented people and refined scholars recorded in Li Dou's *A Record of Painted Pleasure Boat in Yangzhou* were the scion of Huizhou merchants. Therefore, it was relative easy for Huizhou merchants to be incorporated into officialdom. Above official-merchants, there were merchants-general (*zongshang*). "All merchants who sold salt should have the merchant-general as the guarantor."[65] The merchants-general led all the businesses of salt merchants within *gangyanzhi* and undertook tax farming for the state. A merchant-general was either elected by merchants or appointed by the government. Generally speaking, merchants-general enjoyed more powerful political backing. For example, Bao Zhidao and his son, Bao Shufang, were both merchants-general, while his second son, Bao Xummao, assumed positions as high as the Secretariat in the Grand Secretariat with One Added Rank and Probationary Grand Minister of State.[66] Cao Wenzhi, father of Cao Qi, the merchant-general, who "lived in Yangzhou and on whom people from Huaibei often relied," took office as the Minister of Revenues. His younger brother, Cao Zhenyong, assumed the position as the Grand Councilor.[67] Huizhou merchants' tradition of cultivating their children was beneficial to their fight for the position of the merchant-general. A closer look at *Chronicle of Salt Business in Huainan and Huaibei* shows that most merchants-general were native of She County. *Shexian zhi (Gazetteer of the County)* recorded, "Among eight merchants-general, four came from our county." The early Ming government carried out the *kaizhong* system, under which "outside merchants" (merchants shipped goods to the border areas) were mostly merchants from Shanxi and Shaanxi, while "inside merchants" (those who dealt in salt in the hinterland) were Shan-Shaan and Huizhou merchants sojourning in Yangzhou. In the early Jiajing years, "hundreds of merchants hailing from the Northwest lived in Yangzhou,"[68] making them more powerful than their Huizhou competitors. After *gangyanzhi* was implemented, Huizhou merchants rapidly gained momentum. "Huozhi" (Commerce) of *She Gazetteer of County* printed during the Wanli reign claimed, "Nowhere else [produced] more widely known great merchants than our county. Even merchants from Shaanxi and Shanxi who sojourned in Huai-Yang were concerned that they could find very few peers." The reason why Huizhou merchants outshone Shan-Shaan merchants in market competition and took the leading role was, aside from their geographical proximity, the intimate relationship between Huizhou merchants and the patriarch clan system and between merchants and political regimes.

## 2 The collaboration between merchants and the force of the patriarchal clan

Given the vital importance of kinship organizations in commercial activities, it was universal that modern merchants colluded with the force of the feudal clan. The period after the fifteenth and sixteenth centuries witnessed the emergence of a prosperous commodified economy in southern China and the development of the patriarchal clan. Scholars both in China and abroad have conducted studies on the Pearl River Delta and point out that the development of kinship organizations synchronized with the growth of commodified economy.[69] For example, in Foshan Town, where manufacture and commerce thrived, all influential clans underwent similar processes of development: making a fortune by engaging in commerce and manufacture, emphasizing education, cultivating youngsters to pursue careers in officialdom, establishing ancestral halls, and reclaiming ancestral fields, stores, and other public properties to gather together descendants under earliest ancestors and the first immigratory ancestors. The Xian clan of Foshan was composed of five families in Shixiang, Baikan, Heyuan, Fenshui, and Dongtou. Among them, the fifth generation of Heyuan, Haotong made a fortune by engaging in the manufacture of iron pots. According to volume 6 of *Heyuan Xianshi jiapu* (*Genealogies of the Xian Family of Heyuan*),

> Mr. Yuesong, whose real name was Haotong and style name Xiangfu, was Mr. Helü's eldest son . . . His most significant business in Foshan was manufacture of iron pots. Powerful merchants from various provinces learned about his trustworthiness and came to do business with him. He appointed his brother as the manager, who coped with the clientele carefully. All his customers were given adequate goods without delay. Everyone was pleased and presented him grand rewards. Because he was very wealthy, he was not stingy and distributed all gifts to his younger brother. . . . He owned about fifty *mu* of housing and over two hundred *mu* of lands. He also set up lands for sacrifice and lands for education, both of which were unprecedented in the village.

Haotong's sons divided the property into three. Guiqi, the eldest son who was born by a concubine,

> earned the *jinshi* degree in 1535 and proposed to build a great ancestral hall. Zongxin was appointed as *zongzi* to take charge in rituals of worshipping ancestors and thereby unifying all clansmen. . . . In the first month of 1550, [he donated] his own land in Guluo, whose taxable amount was one *mu* even, to build a grand ancestral hall.[70]

This ancestral hall united five Xian families in Foshan. Afterwards, kinship organizations of the Xian clan continued to develop and expanded to the Lingnan area. Volume 2 ("*Zongmiao pu*" [Genealogy of Ancestral Hall]) of *Lingnan Xianshi zongpu* (*Genealogy of the Xian Clan in Lingnan*) claimed,

> Ancestral halls of our clan were mostly built during the Jiajing years. In the early Tianqi times, twenty-eight households got together to build an ancestral shrine in Huiyuan to offer sacrifice to Duke of Qujiang County, Lord Zhongyi and worship him as the earliest ancestor.

The Li clan of Foshan was similar. According to *Lishi zupu* (*Genealogy of the Li Clan*), the Li clan's first immigratory ancestor, Guangcheng migrated from Lishui to Foshan and lived on iron smelting. His descendants also engaged in iron smelting for generations. Among them, Mr. [Li] Tongye made a fortune by smelting iron and "gained a huge wealth." Over 60 members of his family also lived on iron smelting. Tongye's grandson, Daiwen, earned the *jinshi* degree and took office as the Secretary in the Ministry of Rites, Provincial Governor of Nanjing, Yingtian Prefecture, and Minister of Revenue. In 1626, Li Daiwen established a shrine for Lord Guangcheng, the first immigratory ancestor, and set up lands for the clan and education. According to a statistics in Foshan *Zhongyi xiangzhi* (Gazetteer of Zhongyi Village, Foshan) printed during the Republican times, among numerous local shrines, the founding dates of 85 could be determined: four were established during the Song and Yuan dynasties, three in the early Ming, five between the Xuande and Zhengde reigns, 31 between the Jiajing and Chongzhen reigns, 22 between the Shunzhi and Qianlong reigns in the Qing, and 20 between the Jiaqing and Daoguang reigns. Those numbers indicated that shrines built in the Song, Yuan, and early Ming were small in number and were intermittently established. After the mid-fifteenth century, an increasingly large number of shrines were built. The vast majority were built after the sixteenth century, and the trend continued into the Qing dynasty. The full development of kinship organizations in the sixteenth century was an outgrowth of several factors, but the development of commerce was undoubtedly a driving force. Commercial activities were conducive to the development of the patriarchal clan and vice versa. The sprout of capitalism had already manifested itself in Foshan's pot casting manufacture in the late Ming. The saying, "Foshan's iron smelting prevailed across the country," actually referred to pot casting. In the Qing times, Foshan blossomed from a village into a booming city. According to volume 4 of Liu Xianting's *Guangyang zaji* (*Miscellanies of Guangyang*), "There were four [places] where [people] gathered together: Beijing in the North, Foshan in the South, Suzhou in the East, and Hankou in the West." As the representative in the South, Foshan outshone Guangzhou, the provincial capital, because of its prosperity. Kinship organizations gained prominence across Guangdong with the rise of Guangdong merchants. According to Chen Hanshen's investigation, until the early twentieth century,

> over eighty percent of Guangdong peasants lived together with their clansmen. In rural Chaoan, half of villages were single-surname ones. Even in multi-surname villages, people of the same surnames lived together. In Huiyang, over half of villages were dominated by single surnames.[71]

The synchronized development of feudal kinship organizations and commodified economy took place not just in the South. According to a statistics issued in 1764, there were 89 ancestral halls collectively built by clans sharing the same surnames. The branch shrines set up by various clans amounted to 8,994.[72] It was a defining characteristic of modern Chinese merchants to resort to kinship organizations to participate in commercial competition.

## Section two: *huiguan*: merchants' native-place organizations

*Huiguan* referred to sites built by sojourners living in other places for compatriots to convene and stay. They were also a native-place organization of merchant groups. The predecessors of *huiguan* were guesthouses in the capital city set up by people from prefectures for their compatriots during the Han dynasty, *Jinzouyuan* set up by the Ministry of Personnel in the capital in the Tang, and *Chaojiyuan* in the capital set up for compatriots in the Song. The earliest *huiguan* was established in Beijing. The Hangzhou native Liu Shijun said, "The establishment of *huiguan* originated in Beijing."[73] *Huiguan* was initiated in the sixteenth century. It was stated in volume 4 of *Dijing jingwu lue* (*A Brief Record of Landscapes and Matters in the Imperil Capital*), "My study shows that in ancient times there were no *huiguan* in the capital. They began to exist during the Jiajing and Longqing reigns."

### 1  Types of huiguan

In terms of the statuses of their members, *huiguan* could be classified into three categories. The first type centered on bureaucrats and functioned as sites for officials, gentry, and exam candidates to stay and convene. The second type referred to those collectively built by officials and merchants. In most cases, it was the officials who took the initiative and the merchants who covered the expenditure in order to build such *huiguan*. Usually, officials dominated in those *huiguan*. The third type was controlled by merchants. According to a statistics, in Beijing, the political center, there used to be 392 *huiguan*, among which 92% could be

categorized as the first type and only 8% fell into the second and third categories. In commercial cities outside the capital city, *huiguan*'s targeted clients were
mostly traveling merchants from the native places. "Wu Yue fengtu lu" (Customs
of Wu and Yue) of *Xiaowanhu zhai yudi congchao* (*Collected Writings about
Geography of the Xiaowanhu Chamber*) indicated,

> [The purpose of] building *huiguan* was to provide means of traveling back
> and forth [between the hometowns and areas of doing business] and facilitate
> trades. [*Huiguan* were places] to store goods or for merchants to stay. [*Hui-
> guan*] was indeed an indispensable place for merchants to get together and
> engage in trade.

Therefore, quite a number of *huiguan* had their mission statements in establishing them as: "*Huigan* is the very place for [people from] our prefecture to discuss
business."[74] Those *huiguan* were precisely organizational institutions of merchant groups. In Suzhou, an industrial and commercial metropolis, *huiguan* of the
second and third types constituted about 90%.[75] The situations in industrial and
commercial strongholds such as Hankou, Shanghai, Foshan, and Hangzhou were
similar to that in Suzhou.

In terms of geographical factors, *huiguan* could be categorized as five types.
First, *huiguan* covered one or several villages, such as *Dongting huiguan* or
*Dongting Dongshan huiguan* in Suzhou and Shanghai and *Jinting huiguan* in
Hankou and Shanghai. *Jinting huiguan* was established by Xishan natives of
Dongting, whereas *Dongting huiguan* by Dongshan natives of the same county.
Both Dongshan and Xishan of Dongting were small in size. Today, Dongshan of
Dongting is no bigger than a town in the countryside, while Xishan of Dongting
is as big as three towns. Areas as small as them actually had their *huiguan* estab-
lished in great metropolises. That was because of the rise of influential merchants
from Dongshan and Xishan of Dongting in the Ming and Qing times. They were
called Dongting merchants. The second type of *huiguan* represented one or more
counties. For example, She County *Huiguan*, Ying County *Huiguan*, and Pingyao
*Huiguan* in Beijing were built on the basis of one county. Gao-Bao *Huiguan* and
Yuan-Ning Huiguan in Suzhou, Ma-Gang-An Tri-County *Huiguan* of Hankou,
and Chao-Hui *Huiguan* in Shanghai included multiple counties. The third type
featured one or more prefectures. The most typical and numerous ones were those
built on one prefecture, but there were many *huiguan* that included multiple prefectures, such as Hui-Ning Huiguan, Quan-Zhang *Huiguan*, and Jian-Ting *Huiguan* in Shanghai. The fourth type of *huiguan* was built based on one or more
provinces. Eight-province *Huiguan* in Chongqing featured the largest geographical scope we know. *Huiguan* that covered smaller geographical areas included
Yun-Gui *Huiguan*, Guangdong-Guangxi *Huiguan*, and Feng-Zhi *Huiguan* of
Eight Banners in Suzhou. The fifth type was *huiguan* for the whole nation, which
were built only abroad, such as China *Huiguan* set up by overseas Chinese in
Japan and Southeast Asia.[76]

## 2 Functions of huiguan

Although *huiguan* was a native-place organization, it performed functions of business-related and blood-tied ones. Merchants from the same native-places usually embarked on the same businesses. Then a *guihuan*, a geographical organization established by merchants, was highly relevant to business. Its ties of blood manifested itself in the fact that the system of the "chief of *huiguan*" (*huishou*) was deeply imprinted with the clan system. The Jiangnan *Huiguan* of Chongqing stipulated, "The chief of *huiguan* should be approved and managed collectively by five families . . . Those who initially led should be one who had paid *lijin* tax." "[A]pproved and managed collectively by five families" means the expansion of single households. The approval of the chief must be based on the fact that "[t]hose who initially led should be one who had paid *lijin* tax," hinting at the possibility that people other than the five families could also assume the role as the chief. In addition, the Jiangnan *Huiguan* also took on significance as an "association for sons and grandsons." The membership of the older generations could qualify their younger generations. It was ruled by the *huiguan*, "Compatriots whose ancestors were proved to have paid *lijin* tax and paid membership fees could be admitted into the *huiguan*."[77] The larger a *huiguan*'s geographical scope, the weaker its blood ties, and the more intimate its relationship to business. Conversely, the smaller a *huiguan*'s geographical scope, the stronger its blood ties, and the more distant its relationship to business.

*Huiguan* performed five main functions. First, it was used to "repay the blessings of the gods and deepen rapports of fellow townspeople."[78] In festivals, *huiguan* gathered together fellow townspeople to collectively offer sacrifice to deities worshiped in their native places in order to enhance their relations. After rituals of sacrifice, fellow townspeople usually dined together. They "strengthened their attachment to hometowns and advocated a moral quality of credibility through feasting and chatting."[79] Here, deities worshiped was switched from ancestors of the clan to sages or gods of native places, indicating the scope of merchants' self-identification extended from kinship to native-place ties. The Zhengyi Shrine (*huiguan* for native banks) of Zhejiang in Beijing unequivocally indicated in *Regulations Publicly Approved* enacted in 1721 that this *huiguan* placed an emphasis on worshipping sages and deities of the native place. It ruled,

> Worshipping deities [serves the purpose of] gathering fellow townspeople and enhancing the fraternity among people of different surnames. Therefore, a person is in trouble would be given relief. When things turn unfavorable, timely help is in particular need. [Only in so doing] can [we] live up to the grand occasion of establishing this shrine. In terms of matters under public discussion, those who make mischief and who do not participate in the *huiguan* would not be allowed to discuss. Loyal and honest persons who suffer from unexpected calamities will gain support from fellow members. Once a notice is delivered, one should come instantly in person. Everyone should rush to rescue out of a sense of righteousness and without a fear of danger. This is the brotherhood of *huiguan* members – that is, overcoming difficulties

and helping those in distress. Those who refuse to come after public discussion or those who avoid risks would be fined ten ounces of silver.[80]

To conform to the folk tradition, every place across the country worshipped their respective sages or gods. Thus, based on deities enshrined in their *huiguan*, one can make a judgment on merchants' hometowns. The Huizhou merchant group worshipped Zhu Xi, the sage of their native place. The Jiangxi group worshipped Xu, the Perfected Person. The Shaanxi and Shanxi groups worshipped Guan Yu. The Hunan group worshipped Qu, the Perfected Person. The Hubei group worshipped Yu, the Great, who earned a reputation for taming rivers. The Guangdong group worshipped Saintly Emperor Guan (Guan Yu). The Fujian group worshipped Heavenly Imperial Consort. All *huiguan* across the country featured a hall to enshrine immortals, which constituted the main building of *huiguan*. Occasionally, the names of halls for worshipping deities were used to name *huiguan*. For example, *huiguan* for Jiangxi merchants were mostly called Palace of Longevity. Those for Fujian merchants were alternatively known as Temple of Heavenly Imperial Consort, Palace of Heavenly Imperial Consort, or Temple of Heavenly Empress. Those of Shaanxi and Shanxi merchants were called Palace of the Saint of War or Palace of Three Saints, Palace of Three Spirits, Shrine of Three Officials, or Temple of Three Officials because of the collective worshipping of Liu Bei, Guan Yu, and Zhang Fei. Those of Hunan merchants were called Temple of Qu, the Perfected Person. Those of Hunan and Hubei merchants were called Palace of King Yu, Temple of King Yu, or Temple of Yu, the Great. What merits mentioning is the fact that in some local gazetteers, it was clearly marked out under entries of palaces, shrines, and temples as such and such *huiguan*. For example the Palace of the Perfected Martial "is Chang(de)-Li(zhou) *huiguan*"; the Palace of Various Saints "is Zhejiang *huiguan*"; the Palace of Three Righteousness "is Shanxi *huiguan*"; the Shrine of Lianxi "is Yongzhou *huiguan*";[81] the Palace of Imposing Soul "is Huangzhou *huiguan*"; the Palace of Zhaowu "is Fuzhou *huiguan*"; the Palace of Jade Emperor "is Changde *huiguan*";[82] the Palace of Saint Guan "was collectively built by people from Hunan and Hubei. Its plaque reads 'Huguang *Huiguan*.'" The Palace of Heavenly Empress "was built by Guangdong natives and was alternative called Guangdong *Huiguan*." The Palace of Heavenly Holy Mother "was collectively built by Fujian people and was alternative called Fujian *Huiguan*. The Palace of Longevity "was collectively built by Jiangxi people and was alternative called Jiangxi *Huiguan*."[83] When *huiguan* enshrined deities from their respective native places, they also worshipped other immortals. For example, it was recorded in *Xinjian Yuzhang huiguan shimo bei* (*A Stele on the Full Story of the New Construction of Yuzhang Huiguan*) that this *huiguan*

> enshrines Xu, the Perfected Person in the main room and Five-route Money Gods in the wing-room. In the hall, numerous idols of deities including the God of Culture and Literature are enshrined [in this *huiguan*] to allow our fellow townspeople to offer incense in festivals and to admire the kind aura [of gods] and invoke spirits of Perfected Persons and Masters of Fortune. After a long time with many visits, one score will surely success in his business.[84]

Such a polytheistic worshipping centering on sages of native places was a testimony to merchants' geography-oriented conception and wishes of securing blessings from various deities.

The second function performed by *huiguan* was to deliver philanthropic services for compatriots. Merchants sojourning in other places could not avoid "illnesses and pains." Therefore, *huiguan* conducted a philanthropic events for compatriots in distress: to provide money and medicine for poor and sick compatriots; to offer righteous cemeteries to those who died on foreign soil and were unable to be buried in their hometown. It was also ruled that every year in "late spring, colleagues were summoned to inspect [the cemeteries]. In the seventh month, mulberry barks and food were offered to ensure that there was no hungry ghosts."[85] Some *huiguan* set up righteous private schools to educate the descendants of their compatriots. Because of such philanthropic activities, merchants "enhanced their intimate relations and communicated their feelings." Compatriots were linked together in a common cause and shared joys and sorrows.

The third function was to unite merchants to cast off the control of brokers. Some merchants who intended to get out of brokers' control became brokers themselves. For example, Ruan Bi, who engaged in paper dyeing in Wuhu, had triple identities as broker, itinerant trader, and settled merchant.[86] However, they constituted the minority. Merchants' *huiguan* aggregated merchants' force and gained support from the government to gradually grab the monopoly privilege from brokers. *Huiguan* usually possessed stores, warehouses, and dockyards to accommodate the needs of merchants. When *huiguan* were constructed, such facilities, clashes with brokers and other local forces intensified. For example, Xin'an *Huiguan* of Hubei during the Yongzheng reign

> intended to widen the road and rename it as "Xin'an Alley."[They] opened a dockyard to enable settled merchants and itinerant traders to go out and come in. local people stopped them and filed a lawsuit in the next six years. [The *huiguan*] spent tens of thousands [ounces of silver] without accomplishing the goal. The wealth finally exhausted [to such as degree that] rituals could not be performed.

In 1733, Xu Dengying, a native of She County, was appointed as the magistrate of Shaoling.

> Mr. [Xu] initiated the practice of contributions by merchants and obtained fifteen thousand [ounces of] silver, with which [he] purchased stores and houses and widened the road. [He] had "Xin'an Alley" inscribed on a stone and opened the Xin'an Dockyard.[87]

The fourth function was to launch great pro-commerce works. Such projects could not be completed by a single family or clan. For example,

> Two floodgates, Heng and Yue, in the Dantu River were broken. The water overflew to jeopardize vessels in traffic. During the Daoguang reign, directors

of the Daxing *Huiguan* proposed to devise a plan to rebuild the two flood-gates and dredge the Tang and Meng Rivers. After the project was completed, the water was pacified so that [people on boat] felt as though they were walking upon flat ground.[88]

The fifth function was to negotiate with the governments regarding commercial affairs on merchants' behalf. Directors of *huiguan* discussed commercial affairs as the representative of merchants' interests. For example, when shipping logs along rivers, timber merchants were troubled by an excessively large number of tax posts and extra tariffs under various pretexts. Consequently, "merchants were in great trouble. Some was stuck [in a place] and could not pass for months." When Huizhou merchants shipped timber from Huizhou to Hangzhou for sale, they passed two posts in Dongguan and Wenyan in Yanzhou. Hence, the Huizhou Timber Merchants' Society (a business-oriented *huiguan*) represented timber merchants to negotiate repeatedly with bureaus, offices, and *daotai* so that Huizhou timber merchants gained a privilege of exempting from inspection. "When passing the two posts, [merchants] had their government-issued certificates, or *zhaopiao*, exempted and were released upon submitting the documentation." "As soon as logs were shipped to Hangzhou, the Jianggan post checked *juanpiao* (certificate of tax paying)."[89] Hence, the "distress faced by merchants" was released.

In addition, *huiguan* also performed functions such as paying *lijin* tariff for merchants, dispute arbitration, money lending, warehouse building, and formulating commercial rules.

The institution to lead a *huiguan* was the board of directors. All members to join the *huiguan* were required to pay an amount of membership fee, fulfill certain obligations, observe rules of *huiguan*, and participate in social activities of *huiguan* and religious ceremonies. This was vital for merchants to gradually get out of the limited sphere of kinship. With the expansion of the scope of self-identification, a consciousness of a greater group was a progress.

Because of so many functions the *huiguan* performed, they were in great number and were distributed extremely widely. According to a statistics in the early twentieth century, in 17 provinces where there were *huiguan* organizations, the number reached 1,042, among which Hebei had 375, Hunan 114, Hubei 88, Anhui 81, Jiangxi 64, Jiangsu 49, and Zhejiang 44.[90] According to a survey in 1956, there were 849 overseas*huiguan* in total, among which 251 were in Malaysia, 74 in Singapore, 78 in Indonesia, 70 in Philippines, 63 in Thailand, and 55 in the United States.[91]

## Section three: *hanghui* and *gongsuo*: the merchant's trade-oriented organizations

### 1 The rise of the merchant's trade-oriented organizations and their characteristics

*Hanghui* and *gongsuo*, the merchant's trade-oriented institutions, were organizational forms established spontaneously or self-consciously by merchants based on their trades. The earliest trade-oriented organizations in China appeared in the Sui and Tang. Fengdu of the Sui featured 120 types of trades and over 3,000 stores. In the Tang, such organizations increased in terms of not only the number of types of trades but also stores in each trade. In the Northern and Southern Song dynasties, trade-oriented organizations underwent unprecedented growth. However, those organizations, just like their counterparts during the Sui and Tang times, were created under the auspices of the government and undertook the task of levying taxes, making them entirely different from the guild in Europe. During the Yuan and early Ming times, governments revived a system to control artisans by establishing artisan registry. Under this circumstance, it was hard for a spontaneous organization by manufacturers and traders to emerge. Generally speaking, organizations similar to the guild in the West did not come into existence until the Qianlong and Jiaqing periods in the Qing. The Qianlong and Jiaqing times were the heyday of *hanghui* and *gongsuo*. For example, in Shanghai 26*gongsuo* were built prior to the Opium War, among which one each was established during the Shunzhi and Yongzheng reigns, two during the Kangxi reign, ten during the Qianlong reign, and six during the Jiaqing reign. Those built during the Qianlong and Jiaqing years constituted 62% of the total number. *Hanghui* and *gongsuo* did not emerge *en masse* until the Qianlong and Jiaqing years because, first of all, after the sprout of capitalism died prematurely during the Ming-Qing transition, it began to come back to life again during the Qianlong and Jiaqing periods. With the further expansion of the domestic market and the intensification of market competition then, division of labor became more elaborate, and the merchant became more specialized. The clash between merchants and manufacturers also intensified. It was impossible to rely on merely kinship or native-place relations to reconcile conflicts caused by sharing interests or competitions for interests within specific trades. *Hanghui* or *gongsuo* were precisely products at a point where commodified economy developed. On the one hand, merchants and manufacturers parted ways with each other and established their respective *hanghui* or *gongsuo*. On the other hand, the emergence of those institutions was intended to attain the goal of easing conflicts caused by sharing interests or competitions for interests within a larger scope of business and thereby enforcing monopoly. Second, the rise and development of trade-oriented organizations were a manifestation of the growth of commodified economy and the professionalization of the merchant. They enjoyed advantages of concentrating manpower and capital and making right judgments on the market to motivate merchants to engage in larger-scale and longer-distance commercial activities. Third, their emergence resulted from the government's loosening of manufacture and business. In every dynasty, the government sent specially assigned persons – namely, *hangtou* – to control organizations of manufacturers and merchants. *Hangtou* were agents of the government, who took charge in levying taxes and soliciting contributions but hardly undertook the task of struggling for the benefits of fellow manufacturers and merchants. Merchants and artisans both opposed the establishment of *hangtou*. During the Kangxi reign, merchants began to free themselves from the fetter of the government and organized their own *hanghui* by themselves, making the government rule "to ban all governmental titles such as *hangtou*."[92] After the government's control ended, *hanghui* underwent a rapid growth. Fourth, *hanghui* in the earliest stage were derivatives of *huiguan*. As a native-place organization, *huiguan* possessed some characteristics of a trade-oriented institution. There were natural divisions of labor among various merchant groups. For example, in Beijing in the Qing, native banks, clothing, and medical herbs were traded by eastern Zhejiang merchants, spices and the jewelry by Guangdong merchants, used clothing, restaurants, and silk by Jiaodong merchants, and *piaohao*, pawnshops, and sundry goods by Shanxi merchants. All those merchants' *huiguan* evolved into local *hanghui* because of the needs of market competition.

Although *hanghui* and *gongsuo* were trade-oriented organizations, they still possessed features of native-place and kinship ones. After the Qianlong reign, *gongsuo* that blended geographical and trade factors came into being. For example, Huizhou Timber *Gongsuo* in Hangzhou was both a native-place and trade-oriented organization whose members were limited to Huizhou natives who traded timber. Meanwhile, this *gongsuo* possessed the feature of a kinship organization. According to *Zhengxin lu* (*Records for Public Trust*), 216 Huizhou timber traders engaged in the activities of the *gongsuo* in 1908, among whom 124 surnames were knowable. There were 21 Zhan families, 20 Wang families, 17 Wang families, 14 Cheng families, seven Jiang families, six Wu families, five Hong families, four Zhang families, three families each of Zhou, Hu, Zhu, and Dai, and two families each of Song and Yao. Other families carried only one surname. The Zhan family constituted over one-sixth of all merchants, while the seven surnames of Zhan, Wang, Wang, Cheng, Jiang, Wu, and Hong slightly exceeded three quarters. All such surnames could be found in *Xin'an mingzu zhi* (*Chronicle of Influential Clans in Xin'an*). Among them, the Zhan clan originated from Wuyuan, while others were not limited to Wuyuan but spread across all counties in Huizhou. Taking the Zhan clan as an example, it had ancestors of great reputations: a prefectural governor in Tang, a scholar of imperial academy, and a Minister of Personnel in early Ming. Thus, the Zhan clan was a great family in Wuyuan. All families from those surnames dominated in the timber *gongsuo*. The members of the board of directors were elected, but most seats were occupied by the rich ones from those clans or merchants who garnered official titles through donation. *Piaohao* of Shanxi merchants in Qing was divided into three groups, Qi County, Pingyao, and Taigu, all of which took leading roles in China's finance and exerted enormous influence. However, all employees of the three groups were fellow clansmen or from the same counties. The development of trade-oriented organizations were predicated on the weakening of kinship organizations and the expansion of relations tied to geography. With the growth of commodified economy and merchants' emphasis on their common interests, their identification with kinship and narrow-minded conception of native-place ties loosened, but the conception tied to trades strengthened. Consequently, not only the original trade-oriented organizations, which had been built on the basis of kinship, dramatically changed, *hanghui* and *gongsuo*, which had been tied to geographic identifications, also transcended geographic factors and transformed themselves into trade-oriented organizations. For example, the Jijin Society of Guisui in Inner Mongolia was initially an organization of Shanxi merchants. As it expanded, it absorbed merchants of different native places and nationalities. Among those merchants, Muslims constituted about one quarter. In the Qing, silk merchants from Suzhou, Hangzhou, Henan, Fujian, Shandong, and other places initially established their *huiguan* based on their native places to compete with one another. In 1843, however, silk merchants from different places collectively established Qixiang *Gongsuo*. In 1680, Daxing *Huiguan* was established in Suzhou to include timber merchants only from the Jiangsu Province, but in 1871, the restriction on native place was lifted, and Xunzheng *Gongsuo* was founded to include timber merchants from Jiangxi, Huguang, Fujian, and Zhejiang.

Trade-oriented organizations usually worshipped the ancestors or deities of their trades in order to pursue good fortune and avoid disaster and to achieve solidarity. Huizhou Timber Merchant *Gongsuo* in Hangzhou still worshipped Zhu Xi. The preface to *Records for Public Trust* claimed, "The Wengong Shrine, situated outside the Houchao Gate, is precisely Huizhou Timber Merchant *Gongsuo*." "Fanli" (Guide) to *Records for Public Trust* stipulated, "The fifteenth day of the ninth month is the birthday of Mr. Zhu, the late sage. The *gongsuo* prepared candles, incenses, and sacrifice to devoutly worship [him]." That was the evidence of the transformation of this *gongsuo* from a native-place organization and the strong legacy of blood and native place ties. Some deities that possessed characters of trade-oriented or native-place organizations, such as the Heavenly Imperial Consort or Heavenly Empress, evolved into the guardian deities for trade-oriented organizations of maritime traders. Shanghai Commercial Shipping *Huiguan*, which was founded by large junk industry owners from Chongming during the Kangxi reign, included a main hall to worship the Heavenly Imperial Empress. The site of Shanghai Zhe-Ning *Huiguan* was the Palace of the Heavenly Empress originally invested in and built by shipmasters from Ningbo, Zhejiang. Thus, we can see that the Heavenly Empress was not merely the guardian goddess of Fujian merchants but for all navigators. Other *hanghui* had their own guardian gods, who were usually ancestors of their respective trades and were not relevant to their native places. For example, pigment *hanghui* worshipped two immortals, Ge and Mei; jade *hanghui* worshipped Qu, the Perfected Person; masons and carpenters enshrined Lu Ban; copper, iron, tin, and coal groups worshipped the Grand Supreme Elderly Lord; shoemakers worshipped Guiguzi; brewers worshipped Du Kang; pharmacists worshipped Sun Simiao; lacquerers worshipped Monk Pu'an; candle workers worshipped Saintly Emperor Guan; cotton traders worshipped the God of Tuanhua; and finance *hanghui* worshipped Zhao Gongming, the Perfected Lord of Xuantan. The transition from the past sages or deities of the native places to forerunners of the trades testifies to the fact that merchants' self-identification had already transcended blood and native places. However, in China where conception of the patriarchal clan and provincialism were deep-seated, it was hard for trade-oriented organizations to keep themselves away from the network of kinship and native places. A special emphasis on kinship and connections by native places constituted the most salient feature of Chinese merchants' commercial activities.

This never changed either in the process of the sprout of capitalism or in the development of modern capitalist enterprises.

## 2 Functions of the merchant's trade-oriented organizations

*Hanghui* of Chinese merchants and guilds in the West performed similar functions. First, it minimized competition inside *hanghui*. One of the basic items of hanghui regulations in Qing was to strictly limit the number of apprentices and helps. The waxed paper *hanghui* in the Wu County of Jiangsu stipulated, "A time limit is enforced for accepting apprentices." "An apprentice is allowed to be accepted in every six years."[93] The punishment to those who illegally accepted more apprentices was severe. For example,

> gold foil industry in Suzhou [was known as] short of hands, but highly profitable. [Every master] was allowed to accept only one apprentice. It had been the practice because [gold foil manufacturers] did not want to expand the business. A certain master Dong violated the rule by accepting two apprentices. His colleagues knew about the situation and asked him to get rid of one. He did not listen. People were upset so that they made an appointment to summon members of the board of directors to discuss it in the *gongsuo*. When Dong came, more than one hundred people had already got together, who were led by four people. They told the crowd, "Dong violates the rule of *hanghui*. He deserves a penalty of having his body cut into pieces." They thus tied the naked Dong to a pillar and asked people to bite his body until the flesh was gone. The four people led the crowd to approach Dong. After a short while, his whole body from head to foot was badly mutilated like a festered and corrupt corpse, but he kept screaming. When local officials came and broke in, those hundreds of people stood still and were all arrested. It was decided to punish the four leaders for the crime.[94]

Although the action taken by directors against those "violating the rule of *hanghui*" was beyond the realm of *hanghui*'s authority, it reflected a strong desire of manufacturers and merchants to limit the scale of operation and minimize competition. Other measures of *hanghui* and *gongsuo* to limit intra-trade competition included unifying standards and prices of manufactural goods, limiting sizes and locations of workshops, and specifying salaries.

The second function was to protect regular business activities of merchants of *hanghui* and enhance their competitiveness – particularly large-scale and long-distance ones. Directors of *hanghui* and *gongsuo* usually resorted the government to "enact laws" by petitioning the government to approve of requests of merchants, making written laws and regulations, and urging various parties to follow the government's instructions. In this regard, a vast amount of materials could be found in *Ming Qing yilai Beijing gongshang huiguan beike ji* (*Collection of Stone Inscriptions of Manufactural and Commercial Huiguan in Beijing since Ming and Qing*), *Jiangsu sheng Ming Qing yilai beike ziliao xuanji* (*Selected Materials of Stone Inscriptions in Jiangsu Province since Ming and Qing*), *Ming Qing Suzhou gongshangye beike ji* (*Collection of Stone Inscriptions of Manufacture and Commerce in Suzhou in Ming and Qing*), and *Shanghai beike ziliao xuanji* (*Selected Materials of Stone Inscriptions in Shanghai*). Such materials included a large number of trades, allowing us to fully examine functions of *hanghui* and *gongsuo*. A minor weakness is that such materials are inadequate for us to explore in depth the role played by *hanghui* and *gongsuo* in specific trades. *Records for Public Trust* by Huizhou Timber Merchant *Gongsuo* in Hangzhou can make up for the weakness of stone inscriptions. *Records for Public Trust* revealed the protection afforded by *gongsuo* in numerous segments of timber merchants' commercial activities. Commercial activities of timber merchants, who engaged in long-distance trade, were far more complicated than those of settled merchants or workshop owners. Therefore, *Records for Public Trust* enables us to arrive at an understanding of the capacity of *hanghui* and *gongsuo* to safeguard merchants' regular activities and enhance their competitiveness.

Itinerant merchants who engaged in timber trade dealt with three portions of their business: purchase, shipping, and sale. Among them, the most difficult was shipping. In the process of long-distance transportation, timber merchants were faced with not only the threat of the nature but also disputes provoked by commoners along the rivers, local authorities, and other itinerant merchants. Members of Huizhou Timber Merchant *Gongsuo* undertook long-distance shipping and sales of logs from Huizhou. Its shipping route was through the Xin'an River eastward to Hangzhou, from which logs could be transshipped elsewhere. Huizhou Timber Merchant *Gongsuo* owned 3,690 *mu* of sandy lands to store timber only for Huizhou merchants but not those from other places. *Records for Public Trust* recorded clashes such as "the dispute over drifted logs," "the dispute over vessels and logs," and "the dispute over sandy lands." Such disputes could not be resolved by individual timber merchants but by the collective force of the timber *gongsuo*, which negotiated with the government to protect *gongsuo* members' regular commercial activities.

"The dispute over drifted logs." In 1902 and 1903, the government of She County issued "Public Notice on Salvaging Logs along the Hui River" at Huizhou Timber Merchant *Gongsuo*'s request. The notice reported the hardship of Huizhou timber merchants' "floating logs":

> The Huizhou timber is procured in the mountain. The mountain is dangerously steep, and it is difficult to move the timber. It is shipped along the river, but the river is so perilous that shipping logs is not easy. [Logs] are shipped to Zhejiang through thousands of mountains and tens of thousands of rivers and in months or years after tariffs are paid in tax posts. The river ebbs and flows. When it flows, the flood strikes. When it ebbs, the river becomes stone walls and dry beaches so that logs grounded on the river without being able to move. Once it floods, [the logs] would be washed away. It happens frequently that [timber merchants] lose their money and suffer from unspeakable troubles.

When logs drifted away and picked up by people along the river, usually it was timber merchants who paid for those people's labor to retrieve logs. In summer of 1902,

> A large amount of [logs] were scattered in the Shexiu River and were picked up by [people] in villages and neighborhoods close to the river. The directors [of the timber *gongsuo*] went to bring the logs back, but those people were controlled by local rascals and were unwilling to give logs back. [They] cut wood into pieces and hid it. When [the directors] went to argue with [those people], [they] armed themselves and used violence.

The dispute over drifted logs could not be resolved by merchant's own forces. Therefore, the *gongsuo* resorted to the government to "enact a law" and "publicize an injunction":

> Everyone resident and other people along the river: next time when logs are washed away to rivers in various villages, please salvage them and keep them, awaiting timber merchants to pay to retrieve them based on rules. Hoarding and profiteering logs and extorting the merchants are prohibited. Cutting wood into pieces to hide it is not allowed either. Violators, once found or reported, would be arrested and severely punished. Don't blame us for not having forewarned you.

"Public Notice on Salvaging Logs" reiterated the price of redemption set by the Zhejiang Provincial Governor in 1871: "The labor for salvaging one regular log is priced at three *fen* and that of a pointed one is one *fen*."

"The dispute over vessels and logs." When Huizhou logs entered into the Grand Canal, the disputes arose between logs and ships sailed by other itinerant merchants, because of the narrowness of the river. Huizhou Timber Merchant *Gongsuo* usually put itself under the government's protection for an arrangement in its favor:

> Cargo vessels should observe the past rule, that is, the vessels sailing on the east side and logs floating on the west side. On days of shipping logs (namely, days ending with the numbers of three, six, and nine of each month for long-distance traders' logs and days ending with the numbers of one and eight of each month for logs of local timber firms and other minor traders), cargo vessels are prohibited from intersecting [with those logs] or moving across the river. Overloading a light ship, stopping over [in the middle of the waterway], or obliquely anchoring [a ship] to block the waterway are all forbidden.

"There are two horizontal rivers under the Nanxing Bridge, which are the strategic passage for logs to enter *Choufenchang* (government office in charge of tariffs on timber, bamboo, and firewood). No passing vessels are allowed to stop over to avoid congestion."

"The dispute over sandy lands." During the Qianlong reign, when Jiang Yang-yan, a timber merchant from Wuyuan, established the *gongsuo*, he purchased 3,690 *mu* of sandy lands located outside the Houchao Gate between Zhakou and the Qiutao Palace. It was a place to "store, dismount, and inspect logs that passes through the tax posts for purposes of taxation and avoiding losses caused by being drifted away." Nevertheless, local residents provoked a dispute over the owner-ship of the sandy lands. They reclaimed sandy lands nearby so that logs could not be stored, and the *gongsuo*'s business was suspended. Huizhou timber merchants filed a series of lawsuits against local people to "the provincial level all the way to the ministry." *Records for Public Trust* recorded a written accusation by Huizhou timber merchant in 1784:

> Merchants brought money and logs to the provincial city and stored them in the sandy lands near Zhakou and Longkou. . . . Now, the sandy lands are being reclaimed by [local] people, precluding [the government officials] from levying taxes from timber merchants. [We hereby] petition to ban land recla-mation to benefit both merchants and tax officials.

In 1790, merchants finally won the lawsuit:

> The salt office publicizes an announcement: "I was assigned by the provincial governor to collaborate with related offices to investigate the dispute between merchants and [local] people in the sandy lands along the Qiantang River filed by Qian Weishan and other people. We inspected [the site] on the third day of the fifth month. [We] learned that the area between Zhakou and the Qiutao Palace, which was all sandy lands, was a passage for timber merchants to ship logs. Although there were roads for carts, it was after all a hindrance to shipping logs. All logs were stored along the river. If the tide turned in the river, there would be a concern of drifting away logs. In addition, the lands [of timber stor-age and those of farmers] were adjacent to each, the crops would be damaged, and more disputes would arise. This sandy area is a significant place to store logs. Now, [farmers] are hurting the tax revenue of tens of thousands of ounces of silver for land tax worth hundreds of ounces of silver. If [we] calculate and check carefully, the difference is enormous. [Therefore, the lands] should be managed by merchants. The merchants should make up for the tax for newly reclaimed lands, and all households should share the amount. The amount of tax that has been paid [by farmers] and the cost of reclaiming lands should be repaid in favor [of farmers], which has been acknowledged by Chen Tianlu and other people. Although the lands belonged to merchants, the merchants should not take them as their private properties. Rents should be collected, and houses are to be built. Although [this place] is convenient for storing logs, it should meet the demands of various merchants to store and ship goods. In this place, sand continues to well up. So, no one is allowed to reclaim the lands. [The injunction] should be inscribed on the stone for people to follow. That is beneficial to government's management, but does not hurt harvest of grains."

The lawsuit between timber merchants and local forces lasted several years and cost huge amounts of money. Directors of the *gongsuo* were "mentally and physically exhausted" to "preserve the properties." Without the collective strength of Huizhou timber merchants, it was impossible to triumph over the local forces. Certainly, the feudal rulers made a verdict in favor of timber merchants on account of "the tax revenue of tens of thousands of ounces of silver." Meanwhile, the rulers did not fail to remember to impose the "land tax worth hundreds of ounces of silver" on timber merchants. The sandy lands were of special significance to all portions of timber merchants' commercial activities. Piling up logs, storing and shipping goods, inspection, and delivery all took place in the sandy lands. Timber merchants toured the whole country. Wherever there was a timber merchant *gongsuo*, there was a sandy-land warehouse. The disputes between timber merchants and local forces occurred frequently. Without *hanghui* or *gongsuo*, there was no collective strength. Thus, merchants could not compete with local forces or engage in regular commercial activities.

The third function performed by *hanghui* and *gongsuo* was to collude with the government to suppress workers' strikes. To increase their profit margins, Huizhou merchants always lowered, as much as possible, the salaries of rafters and dyke maintainers. *Records for Public Trust* features a public notice issued by the supervisor of the branch office in Hangzhou, Zhejiang in charge of salt, grains, and irrigation in 1902, revealing rafters' and dyke maintainers' work-to-rule to strive for pay increase. The Yongchang Dyke outside the Wangjiang Gate of Hangzhou was the key passage between the Qiantang River and inland rivers. When it ebbed, the water gate opened so that logs could go through to enter the inland rivers. When it flowed, logs were dragged to inland rivers by dyke maintainers. If logs did not enter the inland rivers timely and was kept floating in the middle of the river, merchants ran the risk of having logs scattered when the river flowed. As timber merchants rushed to send logs to the inland rivers, dyke maintainers and rafters used the timing to demand higher salaries. "It is recently revealed that the sly rafters collude with dyke maintainers to control the dyke. As the logs in the front are stuck, the logs behind stop. It is impossible to move [the logs] first." Huizhou Timber Merchant *Gongsuo* "issued an injunction" "to reiterate the order" and to exert high pressure on rafters and dyke maintainers in the name of the government: "In the case of shipping wood through the Yongchang Dyke, it is required that dyke maintainers send more people. Backlog of work is not allowed. In busy seasons when the demands are high, [dyke maintainers] should not create difficulties under pretexts. [Otherwise, dyke maintainers] should be held accountable."

> Later, if rafters and dyke maintainers collude to make logs stuck, they would both be punished, if verified. If a rafter stops over mid-way and ignores any prompting, he should be arrested instantly. He would be severely penalized after the misdeeds are ascertained by being imprisoned in the county. Merchants are allowed to hire rafters to ship logs by themselves. After a while, the malpractice is rectified.

The fourth function performed by *hanghui* and *gongsuo* was to deliver philanthropic services to colleagues, such as raising relief funds to provide relief to old, weak, poor, and sick colleagues and building righteous gardens and lands as the cemeteries for deceased colleagues who could not afford to return to their native places and be buried. Huizhou Timber Merchant *Gongsuo* ruled, "Merchants donate money for coffins and burial sites. As a rule, one *qian* and five *fen* are deducted from every one hundred silver dollars by timber firms to submit to the Weishan Hall." "On the first day of the tenth month of each year, *gongsuo* held the Yulan ceremony to offer sacrifice to lonely ghosts."

*Hanghui*, *gongsuo*, and *huiguan* performed quite similar functions, but their differences were also manifest. Regulations of *huiguan* addressed principles of worshipping gods, mutual supports, and philanthropic services but failed to specify regulatory rules of manufactural and commercial activities, which was a manifestation of its nature as a loosely organized entity. Rules of *hanghui* and *gongsuo* had strong binding force for colleagues of the same trades. Any rules to restrict intra-trade competitions, once discussed and passed by all members of an individual trade, would have the force equivalent to law. The organization of *gongsuo* was more tightly knit. For example, *gongsuo* placed a great emphasis on elections of directors. "Guide" to *Records for Public Trust* stipulated, "The elected directors should be upright. [The candidates] should be listed on *zhidan* (notices) beforehand, and [their candidacy] could be determined if everyone approved."

> The term of directors was three years for fear that the situation changed after a long while. When the three-year term expired, the director summoned all merchants to hand over account books and documents before he could retire without having his reputation tarnished. If the director was upright and kept clean account books, merchants insisted on his resumption of the position. He consented.

With elections and fixed terms of office, the system seemed akin to democracy. However, those who made the roster on *zhidan* were only rich and influential merchants in clans. To enhance the directors' status as uniting and inspiring leaders, *gongsuo* highlighted the directors' quality of "uprightness" and formulated some detailed regulations for them to follow. For example, "no director was allowed to overdraw his account besides receiving his salary. Everyone should pay attention." "Directors were not allowed to cover expenditures of irrelevant social activities by using funds of *gongsuo*." "Directors were not allowed to use funds for rickshaw unless in case of attending meetings in government offices for *gongsuo*'s businesses." Directors were subject to merchants' supervision:

> The first day of the sixth month of every year was the date for settling accounts. All merchants got together to burn incenses and pay respect before the idol of Mr. Zhu. Then, [merchants] began to check the accounts and make comments.

This system raised merchants' confidence in *gongsuo* and enhanced the cohesive force. Inside *gongsuo*, directors worked to settle disputes among merchants, while outside *gongsuo*, directors negotiated with governments on behalf of merchants. Compared with *huiguan*, therefore, *hanghui* and *gongsuo* were more similar to guilds in western Europe.

However, compared with guilds in western Europe, trade-oriented organizations of Chinese merchants were weak in exclusivity and monopoly. One of functions performed by guilds in the West was to protect local manufacturers and merchants and to expel exogenous ones. In medieval Europe, every city was relatively independent, with insignificant movement of population. It was easy for guilds to attain the goal of protecting their members. However, in China the cities and countryside were linked to each other with considerable movement of population. This was particularly true to traders, which were mostly made of by outsiders. Therefore, it was hard to differentiate local and outside merchants. Because of this, trade-oriented organizations took on different forms. Some were *gongsuo* for single trades. Some were joint entities for different trades. In some other organizations, factors of trades and native places overlapped. Even in single-trade *gongsuo* or *hanghui*, there existed different subgroups. For example, Jingdezhen Porcelain *Hanghui* consisted of three subgroups: cosmopolitan, Huizhou, and miscellaneous. The Suzhou silk industry could also be divided into Beijing and Suzhou subgroups. Shanghai's cotton fluffing *gongsuo* was composed of *benbang* (local) and *kebang* (outside) subgroups. In Hankou, the carpenter *gongsuo* was split into civil (carpenters from Hanyang) and military (carpenters from Wuchang) subgroups. Under this circumstance, *gongsuo* could not achieve exclusivity and monopoly. Local manufacturers and merchants could not expel their competitors from outside.

Merchant organizations' transformation from kinship and native-place into trade-oriented entities was a natural outgrowth of the development of commodified economy and the intensification of competitions. In the process of developing commodified economy, merchants transformed society and themselves. The evolution of merchant organizations testifies to the strengthening of merchants' collective consciousness, which made merchants in modern society different from their counterparts in traditional society. With the expanded scope of their identification, the merchant class in the modern times grew more mature and finally incorporated themselves into the bourgeoisie.

## Notes

1 "Cheng Tingzhu zhuan" (程廷柱传), in *Chengshi Meng Sungong zhipu* (程氏孟孙公支谱) of She (歙) County.
2 Zhu Jiaxuan (褚稼轩), "Baishui tongyin" (白水铜印), in *Jianhu miji* (坚瓠秘集), volume 5.
3 "Qing gu chushi Guozheng gong zhuan" (清故处士国政公传), in *Jiyang Jiangshi zupu* (济阳江氏族谱) of She (歙) county, volume 9.
4 Wang Daokun (汪道昆), "Ming chushi Xiuning Cheng changgong mubiao" (明处士休宁程长公墓表), in *Taihan ji* (太函集), 478.

5  "Gaofeng fengzheng dafu Tanzhai Xu gong xingzhuang" (诰封奉政大夫坦斋许公行状), in *Xushi shipu* (许氏世谱) of She (歙) County, book 5.

6  Wu Jihu (吴吉祐), "Liangyou gongzhuang" (良友公状), "Deming gongzhuang" (德明公状), in *Fengnan zhi* (丰南志), book 5.

7  Wang Daokun (汪道昆), "Xian dafu Zhuang" (先大父状), in *Taihan fumo* (太函副墨), volume 1.

8  Wang Daokun (汪道昆), "Fucheng pian" (阜成篇)," in *Taihan ji* (太函集), volume 17, 12.

9  Quan De (全德), "Huizhou Ziyang shuyuan suigong ziyong ji" (徽州紫阳书院岁贡资用记), in *Huizhoufuzhi* (徽州府志) of the Daoguang (道光) Reign, volume 3, edition of Daoguang 7, in *Zhonghua fangzhi congshu* (中华方志丛书), Huazhong (华中) No. 235, 225.

10  Hu Shi (胡适), "Hu Shizhi xiansheng zhi Hu bianzuan han" (胡适之先生致胡编纂函), in *Hu Shi jiashu* (胡适家书) (Beijing: Jincheng chubanshe, 2013), 235.

11  "Shiyi (拾遗)," in *Shangchuan Mingjing Hushi zongpu* (上川明经胡氏宗谱) of Jixi (绩溪), volume 2.

12  Chen Qubing (陈去病), *Wushizhi* (五石脂).

13  "Xiaoyou" (孝友), in *Wuyuan xian caiji* (婺源县采辑).

14  Xie Yongtai (谢永泰) et al., *Yixian sanzhi* (黟县三志), volume 7, *zhongguo difang zhi congshu* (中国地方志丛书), photocopied edition of the Tongzhi (同治) 9 version (Taipei: Chengwen chubanshe, 1970).

15  "Chushi Meng Jiegong xingzhuang" (处士孟洁公行状), in *Xushi tong zongpu* (许氏统宗谱).

16  Wu Jihu (吴吉祐), "Baisui weng Zhuang" (百岁翁状), in *Fengnan zhi* (丰南志), volume 5.

17  Xie Zhaozhe (谢肇淛), "Shibu er" (事部二), in *Wu zazu* (五杂俎), volume 14.

18  "Shizhen" (市镇), in *Jiading xianzhi* (嘉定县志) of the Wanli (万历) reign, volume 1.

19  Ibid.

20  Xu Chengyao (许承尧), "She fengsu lijiao kao" (歙风俗礼教考), in *Sheshi xiantan* (歙事闲谭), volume 18, 604.

21  Wang Daokun (汪道昆), "Wang chushi zhuan" (汪处士传), in *Taihanfumo* (太函副墨), volume 4.

22  "Fengsu" (风俗), in *Pinghu xianzhi* (平湖县志) of the Kangxi (康熙) reign, volume 4.

23  "Fengsu" (风俗), in *Taixing xianzhi* (泰兴县志) of the Kangxi (康熙) reign, volume 1.

24  Wang Daokun (汪道昆), "Ming gu Mingweijiangjun Xin'anwei zhihui qianshi Hengshan Cheng jigong muzhiming" (明故明威将军新安卫指挥佥事衡山程季公墓志铭), in *Taihanji* (太函集), 391.

25  *Xiguan Zhangshi zupu* (西关章氏族谱) of Jixi (绩溪), volume 24.

26  Wang Daokun (汪道昆), "Ming gu Mingweijiangjun Xin'anwei zhihui qianshi Hengshan Cheng jigong muzhiming" (明故明威将军新安卫指挥佥事衡山程季公墓志铭), in *Taihanji* (太函集), 391.

27  Zhao Jishi (赵吉士), *Jiyuan ji suoji* (寄园寄所寄), volume 11, carved in Kangxi (康熙)35.

28  Wang Daokun (汪道昆), "Shouyu pian wei zhangzhe Wang Feng jun shou" (寿域篇为长者王封君寿), in *Taihan ji* (太函集), 478.

29  "Yifu dianshan Fuguang gong ji pei Jin ruren muzhiming" (益府典膳福光公暨配金孺人墓志铭), in *Xiuning Ximen Wangshi zupu* (休宁西门汪氏族谱), volume 6.

30  Jiang Dengyun (江登云) and Jiang Shaolian (江绍莲), "Renwu – yinde" (人物·隐德), in *Chengyangsanzhi* (橙阳散志), volume 3.

31  "Huanchou Dong Shifu gong xingzhuang" (环畴东世福公行状), in *Santian Lishi tongzongpu* (三田李氏统宗谱) of Wuyuan (婺源).

32  Gu yanwu (顾炎武), "Huizhou fu" (徽州府), in *Zhaoyu zhi* (肇域志).

33  Wu Jingzi (吴敬梓), *Rulin waishi* (儒林外史) (Nanjing: Fenghuang chubanshe, 2011), 178.

34  Xu Chengyao (许承尧), "Min Xiangnan – Wu Youfu" (闵象南·吴幼符), in *Sheshi xiantan* (歙事闲谭), 998.

35 "Lishou Feng Zhi dafu zhoutongzhi xian jia erji Mingqi Zaicong shu xingzhuang" (例授奉直大夫州同知衔加二级鸣岐再从叔行状), in *Xinguan Baoshi zhucuntang cipu* (新馆鲍氏著存堂祠谱) of She (歙) county, volume 2.

36 "Gu guozisheng Huang Yanxiu muzhiming" (故国子生黄彦修墓志铭), in *Tandu Huangshi zupu* (潭渡黄氏族谱) of She (歙) County, volume 9.

37 "Zhongxian dafu Kenyuan Baogong xingzhuang" (中宪大夫肯园鲍公行状), in *Tangyue Baoshi Xuanzhong tang zhipu* (棠樾鲍氏宣忠堂支谱) of She (歙) County, volume 21.

38 *Taoyuan suyu quanshi ci* (桃源俗语劝世词) of Huizhou (徽州).

39 Wu Jihu (吴吉祐), "Liangyou gongzhuang" (良友公状), in *Fengnan zhi* (丰南志), book 5.

40 *Xiuning Gulin Huangshi chongxiu zupu* (休宁古林黄氏重修族谱).

41 Wang Daokun (汪道昆), "Ming chushi xiuning Cheng Zhanggong mubiao" (明处士休宁程长公墓表), in *Taihan ji* (太函集), volume 61, 478.

42 Wu Jihu (吴吉祐), "Huang Qing lifeng YirenTanen Gaofeng taiyiren jinfeng taigongren xianbi Qiao taigongren xingshu" (皇清例封宜人覃恩诰封太宜人晋封太恭人显妣乔太恭人行述), in *Fengnan zhi* (丰南志), book 5.

43 Xu Chengyao (许承尧), "Zheng Jianyuan" (郑鉴元), in *Sheshi xiantan* (歙事闲谭), volume 25 (Hefei: Huangshanshushe, 2001), 883.

44 Li Dou (李斗), "Qiaoxi lu" (桥西录), in *Yangzhou huafang lu* (扬州画舫录), volume 13 (Yangzhou: Jiangsu Guanglin guji keyinshe, 1984), 282.

45 Shi Guozhu (石国柱) and Xu Chengyao (许承尧), "Renwu – yixing" (人物·义行), in *Shexian zhi* (歙县志), volume 9.

46 Xu Chengyao (许承尧), *Sheshi xiantan* (歙事闲谭), volume 25.

47 Wang Daokun (汪道昆), "Ming gu chushi Wugong ruren Chenshi hezang muzhiming" (明故处士吴公孺人陈氏合葬墓志铭), in *Taihan ji* (太函集), 338.

48 Xu Chengyao (许承尧), "Cheng Qieshuo *Chunfan jichen*"(程且硕《春帆记程》), in *Sheshi xiantan* (歙事闲谭), 258.

49 Zhao Jishi (赵吉士), *Jiyuan ji suoji* (寄园寄所寄), volume 11, 485 (lower row).

50 "Fengsu" (风俗), in *Qimen xianzhi* (祁门县志) of the Wanli (万历) reign.

51 Wu Jingzi (吴敬梓), *Rulin waishi* (儒林外史), chapter 23.

52 Li Weizhen (李维帧), "Xiting Sun Zhanggong jiazhuan" (溪亭孙长公家传), in *Dami shanfang ji* (大泌山房集), volume 72, 258.

53 *Xin'an Zhangshi xuxiu zongpu* (新安张氏续修宗谱).

54 Li Weizhen (李维帧), "Wang neishi jiazhuan" (汪内史家传), in *Dami shanfang ji* (大泌山房集), volume 69, 179.

55 Wang Daokun (汪道昆), "Ming chengshilang Wang jun muzhiming" (明承事郎王君墓志铭), in *Taihan ji* (太函集), volume 45, 313.

56 Shi Guozhu (石国柱) and Xu Chengyao (许承尧), "Yudi zhi – fengtu" (舆地志·风土), in *Shexian zhi* (歙县志).

57 *Xin'an Chengshi tongzong buzheng tuzuan cun* (新安程氏统宗补正图纂存).

58 Chen Qubing (陈去病), *Wushizhi* (五石脂).

59 *Mingzhou Wushi jiadian* (茗州吴氏家典), volume 1.

60 Wang Daokun (汪道昆), "Ming chengshilang Wang jun muzhiming" (明承事郎王君墓志铭), in *Taihan ji* (太函集), 313.

61 Li Weizhen (李维帧), "He zhongcheng jiazhuan" (何中丞家传), in *Dami shanfang ji* (大泌山房集), volume 66, 139.

62 *Makesi Engesi xuanji* (马克思恩格斯选集), volume 1 (Beijing: Renmin chubanshe, 1995), 211.

63 "Huzheng" (户政),*Huangchao jingshiwen bian* (皇朝经世文编), volume 50.

64 "Qing houxuan jingli Zhaomin gong zhuan" (清候选经历肇岷公传), in *Jiyang Jiangshi zupu* (济阳江氏族谱) of She (歙) County, volume 9.

65 *Huangchao jingshiwen xubian* (皇朝经世文续编), volume 51.

66 *Tangyue Baoshi Xuanzhongtang zhipu* (棠樾鲍氏宣忠堂支谱) of She (歙) County.

67 Li Dou (李斗), *Yangzhou huafang lu* (扬州画舫录), volume 10.

68 "Yanli" (閭里),*Chongxiu Yangzhou fuzhi* (重修扬州府志) of the Kangxi (康熙) reign, volume 25.

69 Ming Qing Guangdong sheng shehui jingji yanjiuhui (明清广东省社会经济研究会), *Ming Qing Guangdong shehui jingji yanjiu* (明清广东社会经济研究) (Guangzhou: Guangdong renmin chubanshe, 1987).

70 *Lingnan Xianshi zongpu* (岭南冼氏宗谱), volume 3.

71 Chen Hansheng (陈翰笙), *Guangdong nongcun shengchan guanxi yu shengchan li* (广东农村生产关系与生产力) (Shanghai: Shanghai Zhongshan wenhua jiaoyu guan, 1934), 18.

72 Fude (辅德), "Fuzou chaban Jiangxi citang shu" (复奏查办江西祠堂疏),*Huang Qing zouyi* (皇清奏议), volume 55.

73 Jiangsu sheng bowuguan (江苏省博物馆), *Jiangsu sheng Ming Qing yilai beike ziliao xuanji* (江苏省明清以来碑刻资料选集), 24.

74 "Qianlong sanshiqi nian Wu Chang Qianjiang huiguan beiji" (乾隆三十七年吴阊钱江会馆碑记), in *Jiangsu sheng Ming Qing yilai beike ziliao xuanji* (江苏省明清以来碑刻资料选集), 24.

75 See "Shilun Ming Qing shiqi huiguan de xingzhi he zuoyong" (试论明清时期会馆的性质和作用), in *Zhongguo ziben zhuyi mengya wenti lunwen ji* (中国资本主义萌芽问题论文集).

76 Zhao Lingyu (赵令瑜), "Zhongguo huiguan zhi shehuixue de fenxi" (中国会馆之社会学的分析), Bachelor's degree thesis, Department of Sociology, Yenching University, 1937.

77 Dou Jiliang (窦季良), *Tongxiang zuzhi zhi yanjiu* (同乡组织之研究) (Nanjing: Zhengzhong shuju, 1946), 29.

78 Li Hua (李华), *Ming Qing yilai Beijing gongshang huiguan beike xuanbian* (明清以来北京工商会馆碑刻选编) (Beijing: Wenwu chubanshe, 1980), 14, 19.

79 Ibid.

80 Jiangsu sheng bowuguan (江苏省博物馆), *Jiangsu sheng Ming Qing yilai beike ziliao xuanji* (江苏省明清以来碑刻资料选集), 351.

81 *Kaixian zhi* (开县志), volume 9, carved in Xianfeng (咸丰) 3.

82 Liangshan xianzhi (梁山县志) of the Jiaqing (嘉庆) reign, volume 7.

83 *Zhongjiang xianzhi* (中江县志), volume 4, reprinted in 1930.

84 Shanghai bowuguan (上海博物馆), *Shanghai beike ziliao xuanji* (上海碑刻资料选辑) (Shanghai: Shanghai renmin chubanshe, 1980), 336.

85 Li Hua (李华), *Ming Qing yilai Beijing gongshang huiguan beike xuanbian* (明清以来北京工商会馆碑刻选编), 14.

86 Wang Daokun (汪道昆), "Ming ciji Luan Zhanggong zhuan" (明赐级阮长公传), in *Taihan ji* (太函集), 401.

87 "Guancha Puyuan gong shishi" (观察逋园公事实), in *Chongxiu gu She Dongmen Xushi zongpu* (重修古歙东门许氏宗谱).

88 "Renwu – yixing" (人物·义行), in *Wuyuan xianzhi* (婺源县志) of the Guangxu (光绪) reign, volume 34.

89 *Huishanggongsuo zhengxin lu* (徽商公所征信录) of the Xuantong (宣统) reign.

90 Tōa Dōbunkai (东亚同文会), *Shina shōbetsu zenshi* (支那省别全志) (Tokyo: Tōa Dōbunkai, 1917–1920).

91 He Bingdi (何炳棣), *Zhongguo huiguan shilun* (中国会馆史论) (Taipei: Taiwan xuesheng shuju, 1966), 98.

92 Huizhou Timber Merchant *Gongsuo*'s *Zhengxin lu* (徽商木业公所《征信录》) is now collected in the Anhui Provincial Museum (安徽省博物馆).

93 Suzhou lishi bowuguan (苏州历史博物馆) et al., *Ming Qing Suzhou gongshangye beike ji* (明清苏州工商业碑刻集) (Nanjing: Jiangsu renmin chubanshe, 1981), 104.

94 Huang Junzai (黄钧宰), "Jinbo zuo" (金箔作),*Jinhu qimo* (金壶七墨), volume 2 (Shanghai: Shanghai guji chubanshe, 2002).

# 4 The merchant and the sprout of Chinese capitalism

Since the late fifteenth century, the great geographical discovery and the establishment of the world-market began to influence the coastal area in China. Militarized maritime merchants and smugglers exemplified by Wang Zhi connected markets in northeastern Asia, Southeast Asia, and even North Africa and Europe. The expansion of the overseas market stimulated the growth of production of silk, cotton fabrics, porcelain wares, and iron wares, which were all in huge demand overseas. In the field of circulation, capitalism sprouted with the massive influx of silver and the booming of cities and towns in the Yangzi Delta.

In the sixteenth century when a completely new capitalism started, the bud of capitalism speared out of the earth in the ancient China. It was weak and germinated with great difficulty in its birth. Its road to development was slow and bumpy. Hence, some scholars outright rejected the theory of the sprout of capitalism in China.[1] An examination of the uneasy process of the sprout of capitalism in China enables us to arrive at a deeper understanding of the notion that pre-capitalist merchants were the elements, "with whom its revolution was to start."[2]

## Section one: the rise of the private maritime trade

### 1 Productivity, social economic structure, and the world-market

The sprout of capitalism resulted from a comprehensive factor. Traditional studies are usually limited to the examination of productivity and social economic structure but rarely address the world-market. It was true that the most fundamental premise of the sprout of capitalism was productivity and the social economic structure that corresponded to it. However, if we study such preconditions alone, we cannot make reasonable explanations on why the sprout of capitalism took place in the sixteenth century, and it would thereby be hard to make a right assessment to the merchant's historical roles.

Chinese society was precocious. Its social economy peaked as early as the Song dynasty. A lot of sectors such as agriculture, manufacture, and science and technology were in the lead in the whole world. In terms of productivity, the Song times had the material foundation for the sprout of capitalism. According to Su Shi's *Xuzhou shang huangdi shu* (*A Memorial Submitted by Su Shi to the Emperor*),

> *Liguojian* has been a place to gather together iron smelters and merchants since the ancient times. People are affluent and happy. There are thirty-six iron smelting households, each of which is an influential family with a wealth of tens of thousands [of ounces of silver]. . . . Each household hires hundreds of workers to mine iron and coal. They are poor, desperate, strong, and ferocious people.

Scholars usually assume that *Liguojian* was precisely a manufacturing workshop characterized by the sprout of capitalism. However, capitalist manufacturing workshops existed only sporadically and prematurely (aside from *Liguojian* in Xuzhou, also the silk factory in Xu Yikui's "Zhigong dui" [Conversations with Weavers]), which is insufficient to be taken as the start of the sprout of Chinese capitalism.

The sprout of capitalism was a new relation of production inside traditional society. It had tenacious vitality. Once it came into existence, it would not have died prematurely but led to a new mode of production had there not been irresistible causes. Therefore, the authentic sprout of capitalism should have been sustainable and conducive to a mode of production. China's sprout of capitalism took place in the sixteenth century, namely, during the Jiajing and Wanli reigns. This theory has gained widespread recognition. But why did it occur in the sixteenth century? In terms of productivity, farming tools and skills in the Ming were similar to those in the Song. Manufactural technologies were slightly improved on the basis of those in the Song. In many aspects, such improvements were merely a quantitative change. For example, weavers used in the silk weaving industry in the Ming remained the same as those in the Song. The differences included the specialization of the weaving machinery, improved weaving technologies, and greatly diverse products.[3] Thus, the Ming's productivity was an improvement compared to that in the Song but by no means a breakthrough. If this was the case, why did the sprout of capitalism spear out of the earth in the Ming?

As we know, above a certain level of productivity, the social production scale is restricted by the market. Only when demands from society increase remarkably, traditional small-scale production of commodity would be replaced by capitalist production of commodity. The domestic market is restricted by the specific social economic structure. What defined Chinese social economic structure was a small-peasant economy under the landlord system. Landlords controlled large quantities of lands and leased them to peasants. One peasant household (not only a tenant peasant, but also a landholding peasant) was a production unit. There was a division of labor inside the household – namely, "men farming and women weaving." That was in reality a combination of agriculture and manufacture. After paying rents and taxes, a household kept products from farming and manufacturing for their day-to-day consumption. The portion left for circulation in the market was insignificant. Because they achieved self-sufficiency, they did not have to rely on the market. The vast majority of Chinese population was the rural one. The small-sized market in the countryside considerably restrained the development of the scale of commodity production. Although productivity in the Song had paved the way for a factory mode of manufactural production, China's social economic structure handicapped the development of a rural market. Therefore, the scale of a small-peasant economy could not achieve a breakthrough, and the sprout of capitalism could hardly take place (although in sporadic and premature way occasionally). Karl Marx said, "The economic structure of capitalist society has grown out of the economic structure of feudal society. The dissolution of the latter set free the elements of the former."[4] Were there some signs of the dissolution of traditional economic structure in the Ming in the sixteenth century? In reality,

> China still has scattered and individual agriculture and handicrafts, constituting about 90 per cent of her entire economy; this is backward, this is not very different from ancient times – about 90 per cent of our economic life remains the same as in ancient times.[5]

It was the case in 1949 on the eve of the Liberation, not to speak of during the Ming times. The traditional economic structure in China was extremely sturdy. As Marx has indicated,

> The obstacles presented by the internal solidity and organization of pre-capitalistic, national modes of production to the corrosive influence of commerce are strikingly illustrated in the intercourse of the English with India and China. The broad basis of the mode of production here is formed by the unity of small-scale agriculture and home industry, to which in India we should add the form of village communities built upon the common ownership of land, which, incidentally, was the original form in China as well.[6]

If that held true, why did the sprout take place in sixteenth-century China? We need to not only investigate China's internal situation but also turn our attention to the world environment to answer the question by exploring the dialectical relationship between the internal and external causes.

When he studied the development of European capitalism, Karl Marx pointed out, "when in the 16th and partially still in the 17th century the sudden expansion of commerce and emergence of a new world-market overwhelmingly contributed to the fall of the old mode of production and the rise of capitalist production."[7] He further stated that with the great geographical discoveries in the late fifteenth and early sixteenth centuries, isolation of different parts of the world was broken. "The . . . exploitation of the world-market [gave] a cosmopolitan character to production and consumption in every country."[8] That is to say, the impact of the world-market was not limited to Europe. Did the Ming's ban on maritime trade and traveling separate China from the world-market? It is fair to argue that scholars in China have underestimated the impact of the world-market on Chinese social economy. When we examine Ming's maritime trade, it is clear that 1514 was a turning point. Before that, Ming and other countries did have commercial relations but limited to government-sanctioned trades in the form of tribute boats. In the early Ming, 15 countries including Korea, Japan, Great Ryukyu, Minor Ryukyu, Annam, Chenla, Siam, Champa, Sumatra, Western Ocean, Java, Pahang, Battak or West Java, Srivijaya, and Brunei were designated as "not to be invaded" and were allowed to "pay tribute" in China. Such a legitimate, official trade was strictly limited by the Ming dynasty. In terms of its time limit, the shortest interval of tributes was every two years for countries like Ryukyu. The longer one was every six years for countries like Siam. The longest one was every ten years for countries like Japan. In terms of their scales, the number of ships could not exceed three, and the number of envoys could not be more than 300. This situation would undergo drastic change in the first half of the sixteenth century when the world-market expanded eastward. In 1514, colonizers from Portugal, the "marine overlord," began to spy on China's domestic market. Later, they purchased the bulk of silk products in Guangdong to transship them to Goa of India, Japan, the Philippines, and Portugal for sale to seek enormous profits at a margin over 100%. Accordingly, smuggling became unstoppably rampant in the coastal area in southeastern China. In 1553, the Portuguese occupied Macau as their base area of commerce in the name of leasing. As merchants from China, Japan, and various countries in Southeast Asia crowded into Macau and settled down, it became an important pivot where the world-market and Chinese market met. Subsequently, Spanish colonizers also knocked at the door of China to look for "gold-like" Chinese porcelain. Since 1565, they, taking Manila as the transshipment port, sold Chinese porcelain wares and silk in Spain and its American colonies. Later, the Dutch, known as the "Sea Coachmen," also encroached upon the Chinese market. The situation became increasingly entangled and messy. While the Ming's close-door policy did not isolate China from the world-market, its tributary system was out of order. Colonizers from the West ignored the tributary system. Portuguese colonizers even controlled the China-Japan trade for a while. Along the long coastal line in southeastern China, colonizers' three-masted gunboats colluded with militarized maritime traders from China to break through restrictions of maritime trade and traveling and link China to the world-market. Even though China's participation in the world-market was passive and limited, it exerted profound impact on China's social economy.

The world-market performed an obvious function in nurturing the sprout of capitalism in China. However, when we examine how exogenous factors acted upon internal factors, it is essential that we not ignore the political structure – the centralized imperial power and its robust controlling force – that was built upon the traditional economic structure. The anti-commerce policies and bans on maritime trade and traveling implemented by the Ming dynasty served the purpose of maintaining and strengthening the traditional economic structure. The bans on maritime trade and traveling effectively precluded an outward expansion of market and commodity production and made China a closed system. In the sixteenth century when private overseas trades rose to break through such restrictions, this closed system and the external environment (the world-market) connected to each other. The overseas market prompted the increase of production capacity in some areas in China, which further led to the change of the mode of production and the sprout of capitalism. This was the starting point of a series of chain reactions in China's modern social economy. Here, maritime traders played an indispensable role. They were the starting point of social transformations. They were the middlemen between China's closed society and the external environment, without whom the exogenous could not act on the indigenous factors.

## 2 Maritime traders' smuggling activities and the world-market

How did maritime traders play their role as the middlemen? Let's take Huizhou maritime traders, the backbone force of smuggling activities during the Jiajing and Longqing reigns, as an example to make an analysis.

How could Huizhou maritime traders, who stayed far away from their hometown, compete with their counterparts from Zhejiang and Fujian and thereby become the backbone force of smuggling trades during the Jiajing and Longqing times? By examining Huizhou maritime merchants' business management, we can see that they were not isolated at the ocean but gained empowerment from their connection with Huizhou settled merchants, itinerant traders, and manufacturers. In a broad sense, Huizhou maritime traders' commercial activities were not limited to the ocean but included three levels. The core level referred to Huizhou merchants who dominated the sea. The peripheral level featured Huizhou settled merchants and manufacturers in towns and cities in the Yangzi Delta. In between, there were Huizhou itinerant traders. The three levels collectively constituted a coherent whole of maritime trade. Let's examine the three levels individually and discuss their interrelationship.

First, let's examine the core level. Huizhou merchants who sailed at the ocean ran the greatest risk but made the highest profits. Ming rulers enforced bans on maritime trade and traveling rigidly by stipulating "those who dared to trade with barbarians would be severely punished by law."[9] The strictness of the maritime ban was also reflected in Huizhou's local history. Bi Maozheng, a Huizhou merchant,

> once traveled to Fujian. . . . He met with a merchant who lost his money and was about to sail overseas. At that time, the fine for traveling in the sea was enormous. Bi Maozheng gave him traveling expenses and brought him back.[10]

Bi Maozheng sponsored his compatriot to free him from "the fine for traveling in the sea." This was hailed as "righteous act," revealing the rigor of law and regulation. Another risk that Huizhou maritime traders ran was the hardship at sea. It was a common practice that maritime traders were plunged by pirates. During the Jiajing and Wanli reigns, Xu Gu, a Huizhou maritime merchant "sailed in the sea to trade silk." "When the ship was approaching Kinmen, a crowd of bandits came to pillage."[11] The merchant BaoWenyu from Huizhou

> engaged in business outside his hometown and traveled between Wenzhou and Guangdong. At that time, commercial ships sailing at sea were oftentimes

plunged [by pirates]. Wenyu traveled for several times, but he was so lucky that he did not come across [pirates].

Because of the frequency of pillage, the author of "Baojun Wenyu zhuan" (Biography of Mr. Bao Wenyu) referred to merchant Bao's not being robbed as "lucky" and "assisted by deities when traveling at sea."[12] When traveling at sea, merchants were prone to sickness because of harsh natural conditions. There was a story recorded in "Jingci si" (Jingci Temple) of *Huruan zaji* (*Lakeside Notes*):

> In the Ming, the merchant Zhao from Xiuning sailed abroad and fell sick. His fellow boatmen discarded him on a waste island. . . . [He happened to meet with a monk, who rescued him and brought him back]. After the merchant returned, he donated money to build the Jianchu Temple. He had the divine monk's deeds painted on the murals to illustrate the power of the Buddha.

In other accounts, there were capsized ships that had been forced to deviate because of hurricane. According to a survey recorded in the entry of March 24, 1547, in volume 321 of *Jiajing shilu* (the *Chronicle of Emperor Jiajing*), over 1,000 maritime traders who engaged in the trade between China and Japan had their ships drifted to the territory of Korea. Those merchants were lucky not to lose their lives. Despite high risks, Huizhou merchants flocked to engage in maritime business because of enormous profits of overseas trade. The aforementioned Xu Gu, who "sailed in the sea to trade silk," "did business in the islands and earned a profit rate of 100 times." When he was in the foreign territory, BaoWenyu "put all goods on the ground and people strove to take them. There was no overstocking of goods, and [he] earned several times of profits." Wang Tang, a Xiuning merchant during the Wanli times, "went to the ocean to engage in business and always garnered double profits."[13] Xu Chengjiang, a merchant from She County during the Jiajing reign, "sailed in the ocean and traveled along the rivers. [He] was completely free and very satisfied. [He enjoyed] fertile lands and abundant wealth, making him a fine merchant who resembled ancient hermits."[14] Driven by high profits, more and more Huizhou merchants rushed ahead into danger to navigate in the ocean. Jin Sheng, a Huizhou scholar in the Ming, pointed out, "Our fellow townspeople left their footprints in places [ranging from] great metropolises, to underdeveloped and bleak countryside, to the remote places [inhabited by] barbarians, and to foreign soil out of the reach of the tributary system."[15]Most Huizhou maritime traders during the Jiajing and Longqing reigns were natives of She County and Xiuning, which corresponded with the fact that commerce in the two counties took off earlier than other four counties in Huizhou. According to *She County Gazetteer* of the Wanli reign, "even in mountains, oceans, isolated villages, and remote countryside, there were people from our county." "Merchants from She County spread to nine provinces and four seas. Fifty or sixty percent of them *jiji* (registered their residence locally)." Huizhou maritime traders, who were not tolerated by feudal rulers, naturally fell into the category of the remaining 40%or 50%. *Xiuning xianzhi* (*Gazetteer of the Xiuning County*) also stated that people from that county "went to so far to travel in the border areas and ventured to sail to islands at ocean. They left their footprints across the country." Huizhou merchants did not establish their fixed residence but traveled about in the border areas and on islands. Some of them migrated to foreign countries. Volume 6 of Zheng Shungong's *Riben yijian* (*Guide to Japan*) recorded that the Huizhou merchants Xu Er and Xu San married into families in Malacca, before Xu Yi and Xu Si "went there to trade." Hu Zongxian, who gained his fame for suppressing the Japanese pirates and strictly enforcing bans on maritime trade and traveling, said in *Chouhai tubian* (*Atlas for the Marine Stratagem*), "Thousands of shameless and unruly people from Fujian, Guangdong, Huizhou, and Zhejiang hid in Japan and they named the streets they lived in as the Great Tang." "[Those people] colluded with Japanese pirates to trade."[16] He thus acknowledged that there were Huizhou merchants among Chinese immigrants in Japan.

As many Huizhou merchants engaged in maritime trade, what were their approaches of business administration? Maritime traders' business administration was constrained by the following factors. First, they had to face feudal rulers' ban on maritime activities. Second, they needed to possess enormous capital. At that time, building a seagoing ship entailed "thousands of ounces of silver." Hiring clerks, sailors, and helmsmen and repairing ships required huge investments.[17] Therefore, there were not many single proprietorship ventures. In most cases, Huizhou merchants established joint ventures. The merchant Zhao from Xiuning, whom "his fellow boatmen discarded on a waste island," ran a joint venture. In 1540, Wang Zhi, a Huizhou merchant, cooperated with Ye Zongman, XuWeixue, Xie He, and Fang Tingzhu to "build sea-going ships and sell contraband goods such as sulfur and silk and cotton fabrics in Japan, Siam, and various countries in the Western Ocean. He traded on foreign soil for five or six years and made a great fortune."[18]Moreover, there were merchants trading in groups. In order to resist the Ming's military suppression and expand their business, maritime traders gradually formed militarized commercial groups. They

> built their ships individually and elected a powerful merchant as the chief of ships. [The groups] consisted of either fifty or one hundred ships. [They] acted in groups, but were divided into cliques to occupy ports for mooring [their ships]. They traveled at ocean in multitude.[19]

Those chiefs would transform into serval major militarized maritime trader's groups amid competitions. Among them, the maritime traders' groups of the Xu brothers, Wang Zhi, and Xu Hai were the three most famous groups led by Huizhou merchants.

Maritime traders engaged in a two-way trade. They shipped China-made silk floss, silk fabrics, porcelain wares, cotton fabrics, iron tools, tea, and medical herbs to Japan and various countries in Southeast Asia and then shipped sapanwood, pepper, ivories, rhinoceros horns, tortoiseshells, and silver coins produced overseas back to China. The overseas trade consisted of three segments: purchase, shipping, and sale. Purchases and sales on foreign soil were unaffected by the

Ming's marine bans but welcomed by foreign countries. For example, to obtain Chinese goods, Matsuura Nobutaka, daimyo of Hirado of Japan "made use of Wang Zhi so that Chinese commercial ships kept coming. . . . Therefore, influential merchants from Kyoto and Sakaiko all gathered together in this place. People called it "western capital."[20] He even permitted Wang Zhi to control Matsuura Tsu, where Wang "arrogated the title as the Song and called himself as the 'Prince of Huizhou.' His subordinates were all given titles. [He] controlled sites of strategic significance, and barbarians on the thirty-six islands obeyed his orders."[21] Wang Zhi remained active in Hirado for 15 years, making Hirado a place to appeal Chinese maritime traders. Daimyo of Hirado also earned enormous tax revenues through such commercial activities. In terms of shipping, maritime traders of single proprietorship or joint ventures were impotent to resist the Ming's military suppression. However, the Ming court did not focus on developing a navy. Its defensive strategy remained traditional – namely, relying on heavy infantry and cavalry to defend the continent. Therefore, important marine passages during the Jiajing and Longqing reigns were all controlled by militarized maritime trader's groups led by the Xu and Wang families. Merchants of single proprietorship or joint ventures also paid for those groups' armed protection. The third factor behind maritime traders' business administration, that is, purchases and sales in the coastal or inland areas in China, was the most crucial one. There were quite a number of provisions on marine bans in the *Great Ming Code*. Here, I record two provisions to show the difficulty in fulfilling the aforementioned third factor:

> Those who build illegal two-masted ships or bigger without authorization, ship contraband goods by sea to foreign countries for sale, and secretly collaborate with pirates by colluding with them and serving as guide for them to pillage law-abiding people shall be sentenced to death for sedition. The prime culprit shall have his cut-off head displayed to the public, and the whole family shall be sent to exile to frontier garrisons.

"When foreign goods arrive, [those] who sell over one thousand *jin* Sappanwood or pepper without authorization" "shall be sent to exile to frontier garrisons."[22] On the one hand, selling contraband goods (including silk floss and iron tools) abroad was strictly forbidden. On the other hand, it was illegal to sell imported goods in China. The coastal area of Zhejiang, Fujian, and Guangdong was under tight surveillance of the Ming government, but the third factor behind maritime merchants' success in their seagoing trade – namely, purchases and sales in China – must be fulfilled in this area. This was the difficult part of maritime trade. If this was blocked, the other two could not function.

The militarized maritime trader's groups fulfilled the task by two means. First, they occupied sea islands as the marketplace for overseas trade and attract foreign merchants and Chinese traders of single proprietorship or joint ventures to exchange goods. The militarized maritime trader's groups guaranteed the safety of traveling routes at sea and the security of transactions. They also played a role as the middlemen who "commanded confidence of both merchants and barbarians"[23] – namely, they "controled the contracts."[24]Shuangyu, Damao, and Liegang, islands near the coastal area of Zhejiang, all became transshipment ports of international trade. *Guide to Japan* recorded that in 1540, the Xu brothers "lured barbarians from Portugal to trade in the sea near Zhejiang and opened Shuangyu, Damao, and other ports." In 1545, Wang Zhi traded in Japan and "called the Japanese Hakata Tsu, Yamatosuke, and Saimon for doing business in Shuangyu."[25] Volume 12 of *Atlas of the Marine Stratagem* indicated that in 1540, the Xu brothers "sent his vicious rascals to Nanzhili, Suzhou, and Songjiang to deceive law-abiding people and purchase goods before shipping to the ports." The Xu and Wang families levied transaction taxes to play a role similar to brokers. Second, they made purchase by themselves in the continent. Some members of the militarized maritime trader's groups sneaked to the continent to make purchase. They relied on their wealth and military might to solve problems. "[They] entered the passes without any barrier and openly traveled freely between Suzhou and Hangzhou."[26] "[They] sneaked to the inland to collude and trade with evil people."[27] For merchants of single proprietorship or joint ventures, making purchases and sales in China's coastal and inland areas – the third key to maritime traders' success – was far more difficult. They had no option other than cooperating with itinerant traders to acquire goods for export from the latter and sell the latter imported goods. Smuggling maritime traders not only ran the risk of being arrested and punished when they bought and sold goods in the inland but also failed to make more profits by taking advantage of the turnovers of seagoing ships. Smuggling maritime traders risked losing all their wealth and lives once they were reported. Therefore, their transactions with itinerant traders were conducted secretly, and such transactional relations were usually tinted with kinship and native-place ties. For example, those who were contacted by Huizhou maritime traders were usually Huizhou itinerant traders (I shall elaborate on this later). The militarized maritime trader's groups similarly had to count on itinerant merchants. They recruited maritime traders for the purpose of cooperating with itinerant merchants. They were able to "travel freely between Suzhou and Hangzhou" precisely because of the help of settled merchants and itinerant traders in different places. From this we can see that Huizhou maritime traders did not engage in commercial activities only by themselves. Itinerant traders were an indispensable contributor.

Second, let's examine the level in between: itinerant traders. Huizhou maritime merchants' ability to dominate the overseas market stemmed from Huizhou itinerant traders' continuous supply of goods and promotion of imported goods in the affluent Yangzi Delta and other places nationwide. During the Jiajing, Longqing, and Wanli times in the Ming, Huizhou itinerant merchants were extremely active.

[They] carried money to travel to all metropolises. They transacted goods to make up what the specific places lacked and observed the harvests to calculate losses and profits. They reached sea islands secretly and went to the desert where people rarely arrived. They left their footprints to half of the country.[28]

There were mainly two trading routes for Huizhou itinerant traders. The first one was a horizontal route to sail upstream along the Yangzi River to Hunan, Hubei, Sichuan, Yunnan, and Guizhou. The other one was a vertical route connecting the South and the North. At that time, the South-North route was more profitable because of the flourishing of smuggling trade, for which reason it became Huizhou merchants' principal trading route. For that matter, "Commerce" of *She County Gazetteer* printed in the Wanli reign claimed that merchants from the county traveled to capital cities, provinces like Jiangsu, Zhejiang, Fujian, and Guangdong, prefectures including Suzhou, Songjiang, Huainan, Huaibei, Yangzhou, Linqing, and Jining, counties such as Yizhen and Wuhu, and towns like Guazhou and Jingdezhen. All those metropolises, prefectures, counties, and towns, when taken together, constituted a network of business routes of Huizhou itinerant traders. The two capitals, Jiangsu, Zhejiang, Fujian, and Guangdong were situated precisely on the South-North trading route, while the aforementioned prefectures, counties, and towns were mostly in the Yangzi Delta area, showing an intimate relationship between Huizhou itinerant merchants and overseas trade. As for the horizontal route, it did not become a mainstream one until the war broke out during the Ming-Qing transition and the implementation of the policy of locking up the sea in the early Qing. There exist a large amount of archival materials about Huizhou itinerant traders during the Jiajing and Wanli Reigns. Let's select some for a close examination. The merchant Huang Yong from She County during the Jiajing reign "traveled to Fujian, Zhejiang, and Shandong for business for over thirty years. He gained profits at a rate of ten percent and thereby made a great fortune."[29] Huang Shizheng, a She County merchant during the Zhengde and Jiajing times, "won a reputation in Jiangsu, Zhejiang, and Shandong because he possessed an enormous amount of money to engage in transactions of goods." His son, Huang Mingfang, helped him "travel in the South and the North. He was adept at calculating. Those sophisticated merchants were no match to him." Thus, he enjoyed a peerless reputation in the home village."[30] Jiang Xixian, a She County merchant in the Ming, "carried money to travel to Zhejiang and Jiangsu without fearing the hardship."[31] The She County merchant Cheng Qixian in the Ming "traveled to engage in trade when he was sixteen *sui*. [He] went to Fujian, Zhejiang, Hubei, and Henan. He insisted on being an honest [merchant] not to pursue inappropriate profits. His business boomed."[32] Although various Huizhou merchants took different trading routes, the direction they took was largely the same.

Huizhou itinerant merchants shuttled between the Yangzi Delta where silk, cotton fabrics, and porcelain wares were produced and the coastal areas of Zhejiang, Fujian, and Guangdong to connect the way of exchange between the South and the North. *Songyuan Ji'anji* (*Anthology of Gentleman Ji'an of the Pine Garden*) recorded that Cheng Rugai, a Huizhou merchant during the Jiajing and Wanli reigns,

traveled with his father to engage in trade. He was fond of reading. He was not hungry for money and [knew] what to give and take. Wherever he arrived, he befriended famous scholars. [He] once traveled to the rural areas in Shandong and Hebei, then to Wenzhou and Fujian. He arrived in Zhangzhou and Quanzhou, where he traded with foreign maritime traders and then returned.[33]

This account conveys two messages. First, Cheng Rugai exchanged goods that overseas market demanded with imported goods. Second, "trading with foreign maritime traders and then returning" means that he started a new round of business. The activities of Huizhou itinerant traders were of special significance to maritime traders. Their bonds to clans and native places were a guarantee of safe smuggling trades in the times of strict marine bans. Meanwhile, Huizhou itinerant merchants maintained close relationship with settled Huizhou merchants and owners of manufacturing workshops who sojourned in the Yangzi Delta because of kinship and native-place ties in order to obtain commodities that were unpermitted to export and sell imported goods. Huizhou itinerant traders, as the broker between indigenous producers and overseas trade, enjoyed the advantage of achieving quick turnovers and gaining high profits so that more Huizhou merchants were drawn to the engagement in the smuggling-related trade between the North and the South. *Minshu* (*Book of Fujian*) indicated, "The town of Anping was close to the ocean. Merchants were hired by people from She County of Huizhou. They sailed across the sea to trade with barbarians, and their money was barely enough."[34] That reflected the prosperity of Anping Town of Quanzhou, one of the key ports of smuggling trade, in which Huizhou merchants crowded.

Third, let's examine the peripheral level of Huizhou maritime trade – namely, Huizhou settled merchants and owners of manufacturing workshops prevalent in the Yangzi Delta. Huizhou maritime merchants' success, to a great degree, should be ascribed to "the continuous supply of running water from the source." The Yangzi Delta, in which "a town could not prosper without Huizhou merchants," was precisely the source to supply running water. *Jianzhi bian* (*Writings of What Is Seen and Known*) gave an account of commodities produced in Ming China that Japan needed: "Rouzhou's porcelain wares, Huzhou's silk floss, Zhouzhou's spun silk yarn, and Songjiang's cotton fabrics were particularly popular in that country."[35]Raozhou, Huzhou, and Songjiang, all of which were important places of origin of China's manufactured goods, were precisely the area concentrating Huizhou merchants. As early as the Song, it was recorded that Huizhou merchants were active in the area of Suzhou, Songjiang, Hangzhou, Jiaxing, and Huzhou. It was not until the Jiajing and Wanli reigns in the Ming when cities and towns rose, however, that their key role in regional economy was established. With the expansion of the overseas market, more Huizhou merchants were drawn to the Yangzi Delta to engage in trade. The situation that "a town could not prosper without Huizhou merchants" came into existence because of the full support of Huizhou patriarchal forces. Huizhou people had a habit of migrating as a whole clan to engage in trade. Once a Huizhou merchant settled down in a city, town, market, or fair, his clansmen or fellow townspeople would follow his footsteps. Then, they relied on their personnel and financial advantages to establish their monopoly of a city, town, market, or fair, or a trade. This was beneficial to their control of hotly sought-after commodities in overseas trade. Let's take an overview of Huzhou silk, Songjiang cotton fabrics, and Rouzhou porcelain. All towns in the Tai Lake Valley where Huzhou silk was produced were areas for Huizhou merchants to do business. *Hangzhou fuzhi* (*Gazetteer of Hangzhou Prefecture*) indicated, "The market where Huizhou goods piled was called Huzhou, just like *Huizhou tang*, [which was named because it was] the place along the Qiantang River where Huizhou merchants disembarked.[36]*Jiashan xianzhi* (*Gazetteer of Jiashan County*) stated,

> In old times, merchants did not leave their hometowns indiscreetly. Now, there are businessmen who go to distant places. . . . Those carrying large amounts of money and making enormous profits are mostly Huizhou merchants. People from our native place do not do this.[37]

*Tangqi zhi* (*Gazetteer of Tangqi*) quoted *Tangxi fengtu ji* (*Account of Customs of Tangqi*) of Hu Yuanjing of the late Ming and said:

> This town is forty-five *li* away from the Wulin Gate with a long river surrounding and converging. It is fifty-four *li* away from Chongde in the east, which can also be reached through waterway. The town is situated in the midway. A stream of official and commercial ships pass by or moor as if it were a town of great significance. Wealth and goods are gathered. Therefore, merchants from Huizhou and Hangzhou consider it a source of profits. [Those who] open pawn shops, store grains, trade silk, and run spinning wheels flock in and get together.[38]

Huizhou merchants not only purchased natural silk produced in the rural areas nearby but also "ran spinning wheels" to reel silk to produce silk products. Wujiang County's Shengze and Wujiang, which were specialized in producing silk products, were also "places of gathering"[39] for Huizhou merchants. Silk products produced by textile households fell in hands of Huizhou merchants continuously. Songjiang, known as a place "giving clothes to the whole country," was dominated by Huizhou merchants. A story was recorded in *Yunjian zazhi* (*Miscellaneous Information of Songjiang*):

> In the late Chenghua years, an influential official returned with a considerable wealth. An old man personally came to visit and bowed to him. The official felt surprised and asked the reason. [The old man] replied, "The fortune of Songjiang has been moved away by Huizhou merchants. Now luckily you returned. How can I dare not to thank you?" The official felt abashed and did not reply.

We can see the dominant power of Huizhou merchants. In Nanxiang, a stronghold of cotton fabric production, "there were a large number of Huizhou merchants sojourning in town. With all kinds of goods piling up, [Nanxiang] surpassed all towns." In the neighboring town, Luodian, "Huizhou merchants got together, and its prosperity could be compared with that of Nanxiang."[40] Huizhou merchants infiltrated deep into some small markets or fairs and the countryside. For example, Qianmentangshi was famous for its Dingcun fabric during the Wanli times. "Huizhou merchants rented houses in the neighborhood to purchase [fabrics] for trade." Consequently, the town "looked like a small metropolis, as prosperous as Nanxiang."[41] In Jingdezhen of Raozhou, the capital of porcelain manufacturing, there were a lot of Huizhou merchants. *Yixian sanzhi* (*The Third Gazetteer of Yi County*) recorded, "There were more mountains and fewer lands in Huizhou. Over half of men were away from home to engage in trade. [It] bordered on Raozhou so that many got together in Raohzou."[42] Goods that settled merchants from Huizhou "obtained and purchased" were "shipped and sold" by Huizhou itinerant traders, creating a business mechanism of supplying inexhaustible "running water from the source" to Huizhou maritime traders. This mechanism was two-way – namely, a revere process of business was underway from maritime traders to itinerant traders and then to settled merchants. Volume 4 (*Song Taibang gong* [Eulogy of Lord Taibang] of *Wenyuan* [Literary Circle]) in *Panchuan Wangshi jiapu* (*Genealogy of the Wang Family in Panchuan*) had an account: "Lord [Wang] Taibang, my ancestor, engaged in trade in Jiangsu and set up a store in Zhouzhuang to emulate Duanmu Ci. He traded tea in springtime and imported goods in wintertime." Since selling imported goods without authorization was a violation of law, the author of the genealogy did not specify what goods Wang Taibang sold. According to Gui Youguang, a scholar during the Jiajiang and Wanli reigns, Huizhou merchants traded mainly,

> salt [like what] Yi Dun [of the Spring and Autumn times did], livestock [like what] Wu Luo [of the Warring States times did], fine wood and bamboo, and treasures such as pearl, rhinoceros horns, ivories, tortoise shells, and other miscellaneous goods. [They also sold] inexpensive goods such as hot water and meat.[43]

Among them, "pearl, rhinoceros horns, ivories, tortoiseshells, and other miscellaneous goods" fell into the category of imported goods. Wang Taibang, a settled merchant, acquired such imported goods from Huizhou itinerant traders. Wang Shizhen once gave an account of the commercial activities of a Huizhou itinerant merchant in the early Wanli times:

> Mr. Cheng was a Xin'an native. The Huizhou custom had it that [a merchant] spent thirty percent of his time in the native place and seventy percent elsewhere. He placed ten percent of his savings in his hometown and ninety percent elsewhere. As a child, he followed his uncle to trade in the Yangzi and Huai River areas as a lower-level merchant, and later became a mid-level merchant. [When] his family had trouble, he returned. Then he transferred his funds to Hunan and later to Guangdong and Guangxi to trade pearl, rhinoceros horns, ivories, spices, medical herbs, and other miscellaneous goods. After a few years, he became a great merchant.[44]

Mr. Cheng sold "pearl, rhinoceros horns, ivories, spices, medical herbs, and other miscellaneous goods" to settled merchants such as Wang Taibang and thereby became the middleman between maritime traders and settled merchants. Thus, the channel for the reverse process of business went through.

The aforementioned two-way business by Huizhou maritime merchants created a positive circle that allowed for the interaction between production and circulation. The production of agricultural and sideline products and manufactural goods in the Yangzi Delta provided smuggling trades with a source for sufficient and marketable commodities. Conversely, the expansion of the overseas market stimulated and promoted, to a great extent, the development of production in the Yangzi Delta. The rise of towns and cities in the Yangzi Delta almost synchronized with the flourishing of smuggling trades. In some sense, the idiom, "a town could not prosper without Huizhou merchants," was not only indicative of the significance of Huizhou merchants in economy in Yangzi Delta towns and cities but also an acknowledgment of the role of Huizhou merchants' commercial activities in pushing for the rise of Yangzi Delta towns and cities.

In this system, what linked and integrated Huizhou merchants' three levels of commercial activities was the patriarchal clan system and a strong regionalism in Huizhou. The reason why Huizhou maritime dominated in intense competitions could not be explained solely in terms of their business administration. A more significant underlying reason was the special advantage that Huizhou merchants had: they managed to incorporate their deep-seated kinship ties and strong regionalism into their commercial activities so that they turned "fellow people of the native places" into the Huizhou merchant groups whose members "spoke with one voice, made the same demands," and "engaged in the same business by resorting to the same skills." Gu Yanwu, author of *Zhaoyu zhi* (*The Annals of Founding the Territories*), pointed out,

> People from Xindu . . . stayed away from their native places to engage in trade. When their fellow townspeople were involved in lawsuits, they felt as they were personally [in legal trouble]. [They] donated money and put up considerable efforts to use the collective force to help each other. This was because they were not in their native places.

Huizhou maritime traders and itinerant traders resorted to such tenets as "putting up considerable efforts" and "to use the collective force to help each other" so that they were able to break through marine bans and advance the smuggling trades. The intersections of ties to blood and native places and the three levels of trade made Huizhou maritime traders' commercial activities a reticular whole. Kinship and native-places relations were a stabilizer with special significance in Huizhou maritime traders' commercial activities when the system was in an adverse environment (that is, rigid marine bans). This could be corroborated by the Huizhou maritime trader Wang Zhi's commercial activities. Let's begin with identifying and correcting Wang Zhi's name. Mr. Dai Yixuan posits, "Wang Zhi's 汪直 name had always been written as Wang Zhi王直 in various Ming historical materials. Only *Ming shi* (the *History of Ming*) sought to be different and changed it to "Wang Zhi汪植," which was indeed unnecessary. When Wang Zhi asked Hu Zongxian to submit a memorial on his behalf, he called himself in the memorial "Wang Zhi王直, the sinner, whose alternative name is Wang Wufeng, a native of She County of Huizhou Prefecture, Nanzhili." (See CaiJiude, *Wobian shilue [Brief Accounts of Japanese Pirates' Uprisings]*, volume 4). As he himself recognized the name as Wang Zhi王直, there is no need to change it to 'Wang Wufeng,' not to speak of 'Wang Zhi汪直'."[45] I argue that the *History of Ming*'s change Wang Zhi王直 to Wang Zhi汪直 was not purported to appear unconventional but was really necessary. The dispute over the surname was a manifestation of Huizhou merchants' opportunism. Jin Sheng, a Ming scholar, pointed out,

> People in She County did not own lands and had to engage in trade everywhere in the country. Since the pirates staged armed rebellions, over half of the households went bankrupt. Because people in this county lived on commerce, they brought relatives and friends to work together. Therefore, once one family prospered, they would not feed their family members only. The wealthiest supported thousands of families, while the less wealthy could support several or scores of families. People sojourned in other places year in and year out, with very few people staying in the native place. If one family unfortunately went bankrupt, many other families followed to be broke, too.[46]

"Bringing relatives and friends to work together" was a defining characteristic of Huizhou merchants' approach of doing business. They rose together and supported each other. If one was honored, everyone else was. If one was injured, everyone else was. The account – "since the pirates staged armed rebellions over half of the households went bankrupt" – referred to the harassment of Japanese pirates. A lot of families that went bankrupt were those of Huizhou merchants who received commendation for their resistance to "Japanese pirates." Xu Guo, Grand Secretary of Ming and a She County native, once said,

> Huizhou merchants sojourned in other places to engage in trade. They did not own lands. So, they appeared to be rich, but in reality, they were poor. In the past when various prefectures in the Southeast improved armament and constructed city walls, [the governments] relied on sojourners [as a financial resource], ninety percent of whom were Huizhou people.

During the Jiajing and Longqing reigns, the financial resources of Zhejiang's and Jiangsu's budgets of "improving armament and constructing city walls" for the sake of "resisting the Japanese [pirates]" were Huizhou merchants, who made up "ninety percent" of the donors. Thus, Xu Guo felt alarmed, "[If] the outside money (sojourning merchants' funds) was exhausted," "how could commoners stand that?"[47] Huizhou merchants' investment in resisting the Japanese pirates, on the one hand, demonstrated their feudal character to maintain a feudal order that was beneficial to their commercial activities. On the other hand, merchants, who inherently sought after only profit, were forced to do so. Many of them were exploited and extorted by local officials. Xu Guo's text illustrated those merchants' grief and indignation. Some families that "went bankrupt" were Huizhou merchants who engaged in overseas trade and therefore falsely accused of colluding with the Japanese pirates. Hu Zongxian pointed out in *Atlas of the Marine Stratagem* that Huizhou merchants were compelled to act under the banner of "Japanese pirates" because, first, they capitalized on the rulers' fear of Japanese pirates to enjoy the freedom in sailing at ocean. Second, "Only pretending to be Japanese could hide [their identities] so that their families and clans could be preserved." With this understanding, it is easy to comprehend why Huizhou maritime traders hid their names and changed their surnames. The reason why Wang Zhi hid his real surname was because of the severity of the *Great Ming Code* to punish traders who engaged in overseas trades and their families. His aging mother and wife were both in his hometown, She County. Moreover, this ensured that those merchants maintained close relationship with their relatives and friends and gained their support without implicating them. Today, we are unable to identify Wang Zhi's name in the genealogy and cite it as the evidence of his surname. According to the regulation of the Huizhou clan, those who did not die a natural death would not have their names shown up in the genealogy and their memorial tablets enshrined in the ancestral hall. Wang Zhi was executed by Hu Zongxian, which fell into the category of unnatural death. However, Wang Zhi's surname of Wang could be corroborated by numerous sources other than the *History of Ming*. A statistic shows that *Wang Zhizhuan* (*Biography of Wang Zhi*), *Jieyueshan fang huichao* (*Collected Writings of the Jieyueshan Chamber*), *Wokou shimo* (A Full Account of Japanese Pirates) of *Tanwang* (*Remarks on the Past*), *Brief Accounts of Japanese Pirates' Uprisings*, and *Ping Wo* (*Suppressing the Japanese Pirates*) of *Yongchuang xiaopin* (*Essays of Yongchuang*) all featured the same records as that of the *History of Ming*. "Suppressing the Japanese Pirates" of *Essays of Yongchuang* called him Wang Zhi王直 first and then changed to Wang Zhi汪直 later, which was appropriate. When Wang Zhi dominated in the sea and tried to hide his name, the author called him Wang Zhi 王直. After Wang Zhi was captured, the surname was changed to Wang 汪. When the author introduced Wang Zhi, he was certain "Wang Zhi, a former owner of ships, were a Huizhou native." From this we can see that Wang confessed his real surname. Mr. Dai cites *Brief Accounts of Japanese Pirates' Uprisings*, in which it was recorded, "Wang Zhi, the sinner, whose alternative name is Wang Wufeng." He then jumps to his conclusion: "As he himself recognized the name as Wang Zhi, there is no need to change it to 'Wang Wufeng,' not to speak of 'Wang Zhi'." In fact, the citation and the conclusion did not have a logical relation. Mr. Dai's cited text came from the memorial drafted by Wang Zhi. Wang Zhi submitted his memorial to request a permission of trade on accounts of Hu Zongxian's promise to granting him the rank of nobility. Since the prospect of glorifying his ancestors was at sight, he certainly did not have to conceal his real surname. Furthermore, Hu Zongxian was also a Huizhou native, and Wang's wife, daughters, and aging mother were all under custody. It was not possible for him to hide his real surname. Therefore, Wang Zhi confessed, "Wang Zhi王直 is Wang Wufeng汪五峰" in his memorial.

The reason that Wang Zhi was able to take the leading role in maritime merchant groups was his surname. Wang was the largest surname in Huizhou, where there was a saying, "Out of ten families, there were nine Wang's." *Wu shizhi (Five-color Stone Ester)* stated, "There were many surnames with large population, whose members lived together as a clan. Among them, Wang and Cheng were the most eminent with thousands of second-tier shrines each." "A galaxy of their descendants took office in the government. Thus, the scion of the Wangmang state became more prominent and prevailed in She County. Their custom was to engage in trade. [So, they] traveled around to do business and stayed away without returning. Therefore, influential clans in prefectures in southeastern China, not just the Wang and Cheng clans, usually originated from She." The Wangs spread over in southeastern prefectures (Jiangsu, Zhejiang, Jiangxi, Fujian, and Guangdong, etc.). For example, the Wang family, "an influential family in Hongcun," "had a large number of its members who traded in Hanghzou and Shaoxing of Zhejiang. Wearing silk shoes and clothing, their attire looked magnificent. They thereby fed their families."[48] Although Hongcun belonged to Yi County, it "originally came from She." Therefore, Wang Zhi's ability to "pass posts without hindrance to travel openly and freely between Suzhou and Hangzhou" and "hide himself in the islands and secretly sneak back to the hinterland to trade with vicious persons" was enhanced by the cover-up provided by his relatives and friends. Gu Yanwu once said,

> Guesthouses in Hangzhou coveted heavy profits so that they allowed [merchants] to store goods as they wished and made arrangements or provided protection for them. For example, copper coins that were used to produce guns, lead used to make bullets, saltpeter for gunpowder, iron used to make swords and spears, animal skins to make armors, and other goods such as cotton fabrics, silk fabrics, silk floss, oil, hemp, liquor, and rice were all supplied. Those who stayed in the inland were just Japanese pirates' collaborators.[49]

Here, "Japanese pirates' collaborators" who "made arrangements and provided protection" and "supplied goods" were mostly Wang Zhi's clansmen and fellow townspeople. In 1556, Wang Bo, Vice Commissioner of Sea Transportation, "established rules and disciplines for sojourning merchants, particularly for those from Guangdong, Huizhou, and Quanzhou."[50] When Professor Fujii Hiroshi of Japan explained in *Shin'anshounin no kenkyū* (Studies on Xin'an Merchants) why Wang Bo used Huizhou people as the models to discipline and regulate merchants in Guangzhou, he pointed out,

> Wang Bo was born in Fuliang County of Jiangxi, in which the famous Jingdezhen was one of the places where Huizhou merchants conducted commercial activities. Therefore, Wang Bo worked for Huizhou merchants' benefits, possibly because they maintained certain a special relationship.

Fujii's conjecture is right. Wang Bo also "originated from She." Thus, Huizhou maritime merchants' commercial activities gained secret support from eunuchs. The dispute on Wang Zhi's surname indicated that the domination of Huizhou merchants, who were kept away from the mountainous area in Southern Anhui, in overseas trade was made possible not only because of Huizhou merchants' various advantages such as rich experiences in commerce, cultural sophistication, and commercial ethics but also the special effect of ties of blood and native places to maritime merchants' commercial activities. The kinship and native-place ties maintained the three levels of maritime merchants' commercial activities, making it an entity to sustain the two-way movement of production, supply, and sales that enhanced Huizhou maritime merchants' competiveness.

In the sixteenth century, Zhejiang, Fujian, and Guangdong merchants also engaged in smuggling trade in the coastal areas in southeastern China. They all placed emphasis on kinship and native-place ties. For example, Lin Guangtian, a maritime merchant from Longxi of Fujian who sojourned in Luzon, "planned to gather wealth and earn interests for his clan. As he accumulated thousands of ounces of silver, he brought it back to build the ancestral shrine and purchase properties for the shrine and lands for education."[51] Li Yuxi, a maritime trader from Anping,

> was upright and straightforward. He kept good faith and did not break his promises. He liked to help those in emergency and relieve people of poverty. At home, he stressed filial piety and fraternity. His grandfather's uncle and my grandfather were buried together. He covered the expenditure from his pocket to build tombs and offer sacrifice in the wintertime. [He] called his clansmen for putting an emphasis on [burying and offering]. People thought highly of this. . . . [He] indeed attached great importance to the ancestors, the clan, and filial devotion.[52]

Accounts like this were innumerable in local gazetteers and anthologies in the Ming and Qing. Maritime smugglers in China constructed a channel to the world-market in their unique way. The soaring demands for China-made goods and enormous profits impelled more maritime merchants to risk their lives to engage in smuggling trade. It was precisely because of the brokerage of maritime traders that a new chapter of Chinese economy unfolded in the sixteenth century.

## Section two: the merchant: "revolution was to start"

### 1 The rise of the sprout of capitalism

The sprout of capitalism was a social phenomenon resulting from both the comprehensive development of social economy into a certain point and a certain historical environment. The demands of Chinese goods from the world-market after the sixteenth century stimulated the comprehensive development of new socio-economic factors such as the growth of commodity production, the rise of cities and towns in the Yangzi Delta, the wide circulation of silver, the precious metal, as a currency, and the transformation of the merchant capital into industrial capital, all of which enabled the sprout of capitalism. Such a development of new socio-economic factors testifies to merchants' role as an agent "with whom its revolution was to start." We can understand this in the following aspects:

1   Taking production and circulation as a whole process. Affected by the conventional trichotomy of relation of production, scholars have long focused on the realm of production – namely, manufacture, agriculture, and mining – and their organizational modes and employment relationship in studying the sprout of capitalism inside China's feudal society. Studies on the realm of production in the research of the sprout of capitalism, without a doubt, were of vital importance to determine whether there was a sprout of capitalism in feudal society in China and when the sprout of capitalism started. Recently, researches of the sprout of capitalism in the realm of production are gradually deepening. Researchers no long sporadically look for some related evidence based on theories proposed by classical Marxist writers but made remarkable headway by proceeding from the historical realities to investigate and study in depth specific regions and trades. However, in order to further improve the research into the sprout of capitalism, it is necessary to expand the horizon beyond the realm of production. Marx indicated in "Introduction to a Contribution to the Critique of Political Economy" that relations of production include relations of all aspects of the production, distribution, exchange and consumption of means of production by people. "[T]hey are links of a single whole, different aspects of one unit."[53] Frederick Engels summarized in *Anti-Dühring* that relations of production are "the conditions and forms under which the various human societies have produced and exchanged and on this basis have distributed their products."[54] That is to say, a study on relations of production could not be kept away from researches into exchange and consumption. Production and circulation mutually supported and collectively constituted "links of a single whole, different aspects of one unit." In the past, the weakness of studying the sprout of capitalism was an exclusive focus on production but to ignore circulation. We ought to achieve a breakthrough in both theory and methodology to take production and circulation as a single whole or a system to examine the sprout of capitalism.

    As we examine production and circulation as a single whole, it is not hard to discover that, first of all, industrial sectors that produced commodities with the largest demands in the world-market, such as silk, fabrics, iron tools, and porcelain wares, took the lead to create capitalistic mode of production. Second, maritime traders' commercial activities directly led to the birth of the sprout of capitalism. Once the mode of production of the sprout of capitalism was created, it determined that the circulation activities, which were directly related to it, would also have the character of the sprout of capitalism. Therefore, maritime merchants' business activities had the character of the sprout of capitalism.

2   The rise of cities and towns in the Yangzi Delta. The urbanization trend began during the Song dynasty. Because of the development of commodified economy, some regular fairs were gradually transformed into gathering places of commerce. Some towns whose main functions had been administration or military also underwent metamorphosis and became commercial and trading centers. However, this was an extremely slow process. In the early sixteenth century, it was still in its inceptive stage. During the Jiajing and Wanli reigns, cities and towns rose quickly in the Yangzi Delta. According to *Wujiang xianzhi* (*Gazetteer of Wujiang County*), the county originally featured only three cities and four towns before the Hongzhi reign. During the Wanli Reign, it included ten cities and seven towns. Among them, Shengze Town had only 50 or 60 households in the early Ming, making it nothing but a village. During the Jiajing times, it became a city. During the Wanli times, it blossomed into a large town with 50,000 households. This was not unique to Wujiang. According to a statistics in five prefectures of Suzhou, Songjiang, Hangzhou, Jiaxing, and Huzhou, there were four cities or towns with a population over 50,000, one with a population of 35,000, seven with 10000 or 20,000, and countless with fewer than 10,000 during the Wanli reign. The rise of Yangzi Delta cities and towns was coeval with the expansion of the world-market. Huzhou silk, silk products, cotton fabrics and other products from the Yangzi Delta were massively exported through smuggling trade. The export of Huzhou silk to West Europe began in the Jiajing times. In the late Ming, Portuguese shipped over 43 pounds of Chinese silk (mainly Huzhou silk) each year to Goa and Cochin of India. Afterwards, the Dutch, British, and Frenchmen also imported large quantities of Huzhou silk. More Huzhou silk was shipped to Japan. In the late Ming, about 100,000 kilos of Huzhou silk was exported to Japan annually. According to *Dictionnaire universel de commerce* authored by Savary Brothers in the eighteenth century, "Zhejiang Province of China produced the largest amount of silk in the world. Its production matched the total production of Europe and Asia." We can see Huzhou silk's significant status in the world-market. The export of silk products was similar. According to the Japanese, in 1641, Nagasaki imported Chinese 134,936 *tan* of silk fabrics (a *tan* is 10 × 0.34 square meters), most of which were produced in the Yangzi Delta.[55] In 250 years after 1565, the Spaniards used Manila as a transshipment port to ship massively Chinese silk to Latin America. "Chinese silk not only prevailed in the American market and took share away from Spanish silk, but also traveled half of the globe to be sold in Spain proper and directly destroyed the production of Spanish silk."[56]Cotton fabrics in the Ming were mainly exported to Japan and Southeast Asia. The major place of production of Yangzi Delta cotton fabrics was Songjiang, which annually exported 15–20 million bolts of fabrics. Between 1786 and 1833, British, American, French, and Dutch fleets purchased 44 million bolts of nankeen in Guangzhou, among which American commercial ships bought about 1.2 million bolts each year on average.[57] The huge demands for silk, silk products, and fabrics produced in the Yangzi Delta greatly stimulated the development

of the commodity production and commerce in the Yangzi Delta and thereby sped up the process of urbanization.

The rising towns and cities in the Yangzi Delta could be classified into two categories: commercial and specialized ones. Commercial towns were situated in the main traffic thoroughfares with a function of gathering and distributing goods. The expanded market for silk, cotton fabrics, and silk products altered the narrowness of towns ever since the times of the Song and Yuan. Massive and bulk transactions took place in towns. In those towns, there were all kinds of firms, such as silk firms, flower firms and cloth shops, which purchased goods from neighboring villages, brokers who served as middlemen between sojourning merchants and peasants, and *Yakuai* or *Hangba*, who controlled brokers. There were various stores that supplied consumer goods to peasant households in the neighboring villages and workshops that produced farm equipment and manufactural goods. Moreover, there were subsidiary facilities such as teahouses and restaurants, which were indispensable to towns. Such a structure showed the special function of a town as the commercial center. The thriving of commerce enabled those towns to be hustle and bustle all year long. This was particularly true when silk floss was on the market. Boats and oars blocked ports and people jostled each other in the streets. Silk markets in Jiaxing and Huzhou were usually established after *xiaoman* (from May 20 to 22). For example Nanxun Town's "silk markets became most prosperous after *xiaoman*. Noises abounded in all stores, and roads were blocked."[58] In Shuanglin Town during the Longqing times, "in the fourth or fifth month [each year], villagers' ships used to sell silk moored in rows on the creek."[59]

There were not many purely commercial towns in the Yangzi Delta. Most were concurrently specialized towns, such as towns specialized in silk weaving in the Jiaxing and Huzhou area and those specialized in cotton industry in the Taicang and Songjiang area. Puyuan Town of Jiaxing Prefecture was nothing but a marketplace outside the city wall prior to the Southern Song times. It became a town in Yuan. In the Wanli times of Ming, it blossomed into a town of great significance specialized in silk production with "over ten thousand households" and "a production of silk over one thousand *jin* each day."[60] In the Wanli years, Wangjiangjing had "[households] which weaved satins and profited from silk. There were over seven thousand households not engaging in farming."[61] Tangqi Town, which were collectively administered by Huzhou and Hangzhou Prefectures, was originally an unknown village during the Song and Yuan times. In the Longqing years of Ming, it

gathered wealth and goods. Influential merchants from Huizhou and Hangzhou viewed it as a source of profits. [Those who] opened pawn shops, stored grains, traded silk, and ran spinning wheels flocked in and got together. Those who observed it all called [the town] as the place of wealth and tax revenue.[62]

The flourishing of Yangzi Delta cities and towns also synchronized with the development of specialized agriculture and sideline industries in this area. With the rise of Puyuan Town, peasants in the adjacent areas "mostly engaged in weaving. Very few who farmed hired people from Xitou to do it."[63] The situation in Shengze was similar. During Jiajing and Wanli reigns, "in [a region] of forty or fifty *li* long between Shengze and Huangxi, people gained profits from silk and satins" to such a degree that "the abundant or poor production of silk and the fluctuations of silk prices" dictated "the differentiation between good and bad years."[64] In Zhenze Town under Wujiang County, Suzhou Prefecture, "prior to Song and Yuan, silk industry was conducted by people from this prefecture (Suzhou). Beginning in the Hongxi and Xuande times, when people from Wujiang County gradually engaged in silk weaving, [they] continued to hire people from the prefecture to weave. After the Chenghua and Hongzhi reigns, some peasants in the neighboring areas excelled at it, and [silk weaving] gradually became a custom [of Zhenze people]." Hence, people from Zhenze and villages nearby "all profited from silk and satins."[65] The extension of commodity production from cities and towns to the neighboring rural areas was coeval with the expansion of market (mainly the world-market). The extension of commodity production to the countryside shook the monolithic feudal economic structure and thereby effected a series of changes of social economy. Peasants' engagement in planting mulberry trees and raising silkworms was not limited to the 40 or 50*li* long area in Shengze and Huangxi. The Yangzi Delta had been a fertile region that produced grains. Because of the specialization of cash crop production, it became a region short of grains and in need of the import of grains. Historically, the saying had it, "when Suzhou and Hangzhou were harvesting, everyone across the country was fed." After the Zhengde and Jiading reigns, the saying became "when Hunan and Hubei were harvesting, everyone across the country was fed." After the late Ming, rice produced in Hunan and Hubei was shipped via long distance to Jiangsu, Zhejiang, Fujian, and Guangdong where cash crops were grown. The development of cash crops and a series of ensuing changes in long-distance shipping were the chain reaction resulting from the destabilized economic structure. Such changes were conducive to the sprout of capitalism. The early form of capitalism thus sprouted out in Yangzi Delta cities and towns.

3　The wide circulation of silver. Historically, the creation of a capitalist relation of production was premised on two conditions. First, a handful people accumulated a monetary wealth necessary for the organization of a capitalist production. Second, laborers lost their means of production but enjoyed personal liberty. The creation of the two conditions was both related to the widespread circulation of silver. However, because China did not enjoy a substantial reserve of silver and the circulation of gold, and silver in China was outlawed in the Yuan Dynasty, China-made silver, which was purchased with paper currency, was shipped to Central Asia and West Asia. The outflow of silver resulted in a short supply of silver. Thus, it was hard for silver to become a major medium of exchange and means of circulation. Before the Ming, if we focus on currency itself and leave out other social conditions, it was difficult to achieve a massive accumulation of a monetary wealth. In the mid-Ming, Chinese commodities made their way to the world-market in an unprecedented scale, triggering a dramatic transformation. That is, through all channels of commerce, silver, which was originally produced in Latin America, flowed into China steadily. It was recorded in history, "Merchants [shipped] silk, cotton, satins, fabrics, porcelain, and iron to foreign countries in exchange for not goods, but gold and silver only."[66] Within 72 years between 1573 and 1644, silver dollars imported from various countries into China amounted to 100 million. During the Jiajing reign, the state's main means of payment had mostly been silver. Not only had "paper money long been out of circulation," "the use of copper coins was also obstructed. [People] were more willing to use silver."[67] The circulation of silver in the market became so extensive that the majority of commodities were priced with silver. "Even in obscure villages, there were scales for silver."[68] At that time, block trading entailed the payment with silver, while retailing used silver pieces. *Maiyoulang duzhan huakui* (The Oil Peddler Courts the Courtesan) in volume three of *Stories to Awaken the World* told the story of an oil peddler's business with tiny capital: incomes from selling oil were usually small pieces of silver weighing two or three *fen*. In his *Wanshu zaji* (*Miscellaneous Notes in the Wanping Office*), Shen Bang who was active during the Wanli reign gave a comprehensive and detailed account of prices of commodities in the Beijing area: pork two *fen* of silver per *jin*; beef and lamb one *fen* and five *li* per *jin*; fresh fish two *fen* per *jin*; large goose two *qian* of silver per *jin*, and so forth. The circulated silver currencies in the market included 50 *liang* horseshoe-shaped silver ingot, one-*liang* smallshoe-shaped silver ingot, small silver ingots variously weighing one, two, three or four *liang*, and silver pieces. Spanish dollars minted in Mexico also functioned as currency in some areas. Silver is a precious metal with a relatively high value. Therefore, only after the sixteenth century when monetary wealth was massively accumulated did it begin to be provided with appropriate material prerequisites. The use of silver as the means of payment brought considerable convenience to rich and influential merchants. Their commercial activities expanded because of the use of silver as hard currency. Long-distance trade broke the geographical restrictions and linked domestic markets, with silver being the lubricant of China's inner market. Meanwhile, because of the nature of silver as a world currency, it further connected Chinese and world markets, making areas where China-made goods were produced for export partially depended on the world-market. In the overseas trade and land-distance trade in China, merchants accumulated enormous monetary wealth.

The emergence of employed labor force with personal liberty was also related to the massive influx of silver. In the early Ming, it was forbidden to use gold and silver in transactions in society. In the mid-Ming, with the development of commodified and monetary economy, people were more or less involved in the transactions of commodities. As a means of circulation and a measurement of value, the precious metal silver became a hotly sough-after article of emperors and officials of various ranks alike. Feudal rulers demanded currencies for a sizable portion of taxes. Even corvée could be paid in the form of silver. In 1581, the "Single Whip Method" was implemented nationwide, with which the government combined land taxes, corvée, and other miscellaneous taxes. Taxes were paid in the form of currencies based on the acreage of lands – namely, "the way in which people paid the government was nothing but silver."[69] The payment of land taxes and corvée in silver loosened the political authorities' fetter on individuals. Therefore, when the development of commodified economy polarized peasants and handicraftsmen, a vast number of poor and bankrupted peasants and handicraftsmen were relegated to be "free" hired laborers who sold their labor to make a living.

4    The transformation of the merchant's capital into industrial capital. Merchants' active role in the sprout of capitalism manifested itself in not only creating the preconditions for the sprout of capitalism but also transforming the merchant's capital into the industrial one. The transformation of the merchant's capital into the industrial one took on four forms. The first was the "payment by the merchant with the particular kinds of goods that are needed by the 'handicraftsman' for production"[70] to small commodity producers. Hence, small commodity producers were divorced from markets of production and raw materials and thereby became dependent upon merchant's capital. In the Ming and Qing, there were a large number of such putting-up merchants in southeastern China where economy was developed. Zhu Guozhen stated in his *Essays of Yongchuang* stated, "Merchants purchased cotton from neighboring prefectures and placed it on our soil. Ordinary people wove yarns or fabrics and sold them in the market in the morning in exchange for cotton. [They] continued to weave [with cotton]. In the next morning, [they] still took [textile products] in exchange for [cotton]." In *Xijin zhixiao lu* (*Records of Trivial Things in Wuxi and Jinkui*), Huang Yang mentioned the same situation in Wuxi during the Qianlong reign:

There were three grades of fabrics. A bolt [of fabric] as long as three *zhang* was called long head, and a bolt [of fabric] as long as two *zhang* was called short head. Both were traded for cotton. A bolt [of fabric] as long as two *zhang* four *chi* was called extra-long, which was traded in exchange for rice and money. The settled merchants purchased them and bound them to trade in places like Huai, Yang, Gao, and Bao. The turnover of a year exceeded tens of thousands or millions of bolts.

Zhou Fengchi gave a more detailed account in *Jinze xiaozhi* (*Little Gazetteer of Jinze*) on such a business administration:

In Jinze, women, rich or poor, all engaged in textile weaving. Stores in the market that purchased cloth was called *huabusha zhuang* (shops of cotton, fabrics, and yarns). After fabrics were woven, they were used to exchange for cotton. Sometimes, cotton was directly used in exchange for yarns. The profits multiplied with transactions of several times. Some leftovers were saved in preparation for keeping the whole family warm and were also traded to purchase rice and salt.

Here, "leftovers" in the text meant the in-kind wages paid by putting-up merchants to small commodity producers. Thus, putting-up merchants were transformed into capitalists who exploited workers. Second, "payment [was made] by the merchant with the particular kinds of goods that are needed by the 'handicraftsman' for production (raw or auxiliary materials, etc.)."[71] Merchants purchased products regularly and paid small commodity producers certain amounts of wages based on the quantity and quality of products. In mid- and late Ming, summer sock stores run by Songjiang merchants adopted this approach. In *Yunjian jumu chao* (*Collected Writings about Songjiang [Based on What Was] Seen*), Fan Lian said,

In the past, there was no summer sock stores. In the summertime, many wore socks made of felt. Ever since the Wanli reign, Youdun cotton fabrics were used to make summer socks. [Because] they were light-weighted, [people from] far away came to buy them. In the western suburb of the prefecture, hundreds of summer sock stores were opened. Men and women of the whole prefecture lived on making socks. They got pays from the stores, which was a convenient way for the new business.

The "men and women of the whole prefecture," who made a living on making socks, became hired laborers who "got pays" from socks stores, while owners of summer socks evolved into capitalists. *Zhangfang* (loom household) of in the Qing times was also of a character of the non-concentrated capitalist handicraft manufacture. In 1896, Liu Kunyi stated in his report about taxes on silk looms in Suzhou, "Merchants possessed looms and gave them to weavers to weave. That was called *zhangfang*."[72] "*Nongshang lei*" (Category of Agriculture and Commerce) of *Anthology of Petty Matters in Qing* compiled by XuKe contained an account of *zhangfang* in Zhenjiang: "[The owners] ran dozens of firms. All silk was distributed to weavers through firms. [Weavers'] wages were paid based on the amounts of silk fabrics [produced by weavers]." Owners of *zhangfang* were all silk merchants with enormous capital.[73] The relationship between silk merchants and weavers was precisely that between capitalists and hired laborers. Third, merchant-manufacturers stood out in competitions and became capitalists. In the Ming and Qing, independent small commodity producers were usually both manufacturers and merchants. They directly sold their products in the market. Volume 18 of Feng Menglong's *Stories to Awaken the World*, "Shi Fu Encounters a Friend at Tanque" narrated the story:

During the Jiajing reign, there was a man called Shi Fu in Shengze Town. . . . [He] operated a few silk looms at home and raised several baskets of silkworms every year. With the wife winding silk and the husband weaving silk, [they] led a decent life. . . . People saw that [silk fabrics] were sleek and glossy. So, they strove to purchase them by increasing the price. [They] paid some more silver for every bolt of silk fabric. Because of such a smooth development, the household added three or four silk looms, and the family became quite rich. . . . [He] wanted to buy more looms, but the house was so small that there was no room for [extra] looms. . . . It happened that a neighbor was in a rush to sell two small chambers because their business of mulberry leaves and silkworms failed. This benefited Shi Fu. . . . The couple saved money on food and expenses as usual and worked hard day in and day out. Less than ten years, [they] accumulated a wealth of several thousand [ounces of silver]. [They] bought another big house in the nearby place and operated thirty or forty looms.

Although the story came from a novel, the author was a contemporary of Ming. Therefore, he would not fabricated it. The story of Shi Fu was a testimony to society in late Ming Shengze, which was representative. Shi Fu transformed himself from a small commodity producer-trader into an owner of manufacture workshop with 30or 40looms. Such a transformation was made possible because of the flourishing of commodified economy and the intensification of commercial competitions. Fourth, merchants directly opened manufacture workshops to hire workers to conduct capitalist production. In this case, merchants became bona fide industrial capitalist, while producers were entirely turned into hired laborers. The merchant's capital directly became industrial capital. For example, private copper mines in Yunnan in Qing were invested in and run by rich and influential merchants from other provinces. According to Tang Jiong, a Qing person,

In the past, those who ran [copper mines in Yunnan] were powerful merchants from Sichuan, Hubei, Jiangsu, and Guangdong. Each time they opened a new mine, it would cost one hundred or two hundred thousand ounces of silver. At that time, they hired mining specialists to examine the geographical positions, the depth of the tunnels, the size of the mine pits, and the quality of ores. After investigations were done, the project started. Once it started, the mines would not be exhausted in decades.[74]

Prior to the Daoguang reign, there were 85 furnaces in iron smelting workshops run by Guangdong merchants in 30 counties, mainly in four prefectures of Guangzhou, Shaozhou, Huizhou, and Jiayingzhou. Guangxi merchants ran 64 furnaces for iron smelting in 11 counties. The merchant's capital was also invested in the shipbuilding industry. In the Kangxi times, Suzhou ship builders built thousands of ships for overseas trade and possessed an enormous wealth. Generally speaking, however, the merchant's capital that was transformed into industrial capital constituted a tiny minority. The vast majority of the merchant's capital was disposed of in conventional ways.

The four functions performed by merchants as noted above testify to what Karl Marx has stated, "The merchant was the revolutionary element in this society where everything else was stable – stable, as it were, through inheritance. . . . [W]ith [the merchant,] its revolution was to start."[75]

## 2 The fragility of the "sprout" and the weakness of the merchant

The sprout of capitalism in China did not take place spontaneously. The growth of the sprout of capitalism illustrated by classical Marxist writers on various occasions was a natural historical process – that is, the development of productivity widened the social division of labor, the growth of commodified economy, the rise and independence of cities, commodified economy's destruction of the natural economic structure in the countryside, the expansion of the market, and the rise of manufacture workshops. The observation was made based on the evolutionary mode of the history of late medieval West Europe. However, the historical processes toward capitalism in various countries did not follow a same mode. It is true that the sprout and growth of capitalism in China were closely related to the enhancement of productivity, but social productivity in the Ming and Qing was not an obvious upgrading of that in the Song and Yuan. Chinese cities were centers of administration of different levels. Even in the Ming and Qing, Yangzi Delta cities and towns did not break away autocratic rules and achieve autonomy. The economic structure that combined household manufacture and agriculture was still indestructible, leading to a limited domestic market. All those historical conditions differed from those in Western Europe. More seriously, the countryside in China did not undergo a major transformation. In the past, we usually ignore such differences and therefore apply the western European mode of historical evolution to the sprout of capitalism in China by emphasizing that the sprout of capitalism in China was a natural outcome of a historical process. Thus, it is impossible to provide a scientific explanation of why the sprout of capitalism occurred in the Jiajing and Wanli years. Of course, without the external stimulation from the world-market, capitalism could still sprout from China's traditional society. Yet, the process would have undoubtedly been significantly postponed. Therefore, it is fair to argue that the opening of the world-market and the rise of smuggling trade in the sixteenth century afforded a great opportunity to the sprout of capitalism in China. Because the sprout of capitalism in China was heavily reliant on the overseas market, it was inherently fragile. The vicissitude of the sprout of capitalism in China was dictated by policies of foreign trade implemented by rulers of dynasties. When the marine ban was lifted during the Longqing and Wanli reigns, the sprout of capitalism grew. After 1592, the marine ban tightened because of Toyotomi Hideyoshi's invasions of Korea, and the sprout of capitalism was constrained. In late Ming and early Qing, the incessant warfare and early Qing's policy of evacuating the coastal areas led to the temporary demise of the sprout of capitalism. In 1684, the marine ban was lifted, and Guangzhou, Zhangzhou, Ningbo, and Yuntaishan were designed as the port cities to conduct international trade. Later, as Guangzhou became the sole port city for international trade, the level of production with a character of the sprout of capitalism revived and surpassed that in Ming. On the eve of the Opium War, the Qing rulers carried out a national policy of locking up the country. Therefore, the sprout of capitalism remained nothing but a sprout throughout the history.

The fragility of the sprout of capitalism led to the merchant's weakness. After the sixteenth century, although the merchant went up on the historical stage as a collective force, they were unable to put forth their own political views. Moreover, when they fought for their economic interests, they showed the signs of their weakness. For example, the aforementioned Huizhou merchants' struggle against the marine ban demonstrated the merchant's weakness and duality. On the one hand, Huizhou merchants struggled against the marine ban for their interests and thereby dealt a heavy blow to the rulers. Moreover, to put it in perspective, maritime merchants' struggles were tied to the economic forces of the sprout of capitalism, suggesting its nature as a social revolution. In this sense, the significance of maritime traders' resistance was greater than that of the peasant's warfare. On the other hand, when maritime traders were struggling for their interests, they could not be disenchanted with the rulers. Wang Zhi, the leader of the militarized maritime trader's group who was falsely accused by the Ming dynasty of being "the pirates' head and being seditious,"[76] brought proposals of lifting the marine ban to strengthen commercial relationships for several times: "In Japan, silk and cotton are in short supply. The marine ban must be lifted so that the trouble at ocean could be resolved." "They [Japanese] do not have great aspiration other than paying tribute and engaging in trade." He also expressed his willingness to lay down arms in exchange for an official title. Maritime traders failed to put forth political views in relation to their economic interests, revealing their failure to elevate themselves from a "class-in-itself" to a "class-for-itself." Huizhou merchants had a strong feudal character, as they relied on feudal relations of kinship and native places to enhance their competitiveness. Their feudal ties foreclosed the possibility of their participation in further competitions. Huizhou bureaucrats capitalized on the relations of blood and native places to deceive those who were eager to reopen international trade to eliminate the maritime merchant's groups led by Wang Zhi and Xu Hai. The force of Huizhou maritime traders were dealt with a fatal blow with Hu Zongxian's crackdown. In 1617, the Ming government implemented *gangyanzhi*, and consequently, merchants began to enjoy a hereditary power of shipping and selling salt. The main force of Huizhou merchants therefore turned to the salt trade, which was risk free but highly lucrative. Afterwards, although some Huizhou merchants continued to navigate at the ocean, they were as impotent as a spent bullet and could not compete with their Zhejiang, Fujian, and Guangdong counterparts. The weak sprout of capitalism in Huizhou merchants further waned, but their feudal characters greatly strengthened. Huizhou maritime merchants' weakness and duality was correspondent with the fragility of the sprout of capitalism. The period between the establishment of the Chinese merchant's collective consciousness and their accomplishing political independence lasted for three or four long centuries, which again corresponded with the slow and winding path of development of the sprout of capitalism in China.

## Notes

1 See Max Weber, *The religion of China* and *The protestant ethic and the spirit of capitalism*.
2 Karl Marx, *Thecapital*, volume 3 (Beijing: Renminchubanshe, 2006), 1019.
3 See Wu Chengming (吴承明), "GuanyuZhonguozibenzhuyimengya de jigewenti" (关于中国资本主义萌芽的几个问题), *Wen shizhe* (文史哲), No. 5 (1981).
4 *Makesi Engesi xuanji* (马克思恩格斯选集), volume 2, 221.
5 *Mao Zedong xuanji* (毛泽东选集), volume 4 (Beijing: Renminchubanshe, 1991), 1434.
6 *Makesi Engesi quanji* (马克思恩格斯全集), volume 26 (Beijing: Renminchubanshe, 2006), 373.
7 *Capital*, volume 3, 387.
8 *Makesi Engesi xuanji* (马克思恩格斯选集), 312.
9 *Ming taizushilu* (明太祖实录), volume 231, the jiayin (甲寅) day of the 5th month of Hongwu (洪武)27, 3374.
10 Shi Guozhu (石国柱) and Xu Chengyao (许承尧), "Renwu – yixing" (人物·义行), in *She xianzhi* (歙县志), volume 9.
11 "XuQuanshanzhuan" (许全善传), in *Chongxiugu She DongmenXushizongpu* (重修古歙东门许氏宗谱), volume 9.
12 "BaojunWenyuzhuan" (鲍君文玉传), in *She TangyueBaoshiXuanzhong tang zhipu* (歙棠樾鲍氏宣忠堂支谱), volume 21.
13 "ChushiTanggongzhuan" (处士镗公传), in *XiuningXimenWangshizongpu* (休宁西门汪氏宗谱), volume 64.
14 "LianxiChenjiangzexu" (练溪辰江则叙), in *Xin'anShebeiXushidongzhishipu* (新安歙北许氏东支世谱), volume 5.
15 Jin Sheng (金声), "Yanyigeji" (燕诒阁集), volume 7, 81.
16 Hu Zongxian (胡宗宪), *Chouhaitubian* (筹海图编), edition of complete library of the four treasuries in Wenyuan (文渊) pavilion of Qing, 284.
17 Zhang Xie (张燮), "Zhoushikao" (舟师考), in *Dongxiyangkao* (东西洋考), volume 9, edition of *Xiyinxuancongshu* (惜阴轩丛书) of Qing, 99.
18 Yan Congjian (严从简), "Dongyi" (东夷), in *Shuyuzhouzilu* (殊域周咨录), carved in the Wanli (万历) reign of Ming, 44.
19 Fu Weilin (傅维麟), *Mingshu* (明书), volume 162, Biography 20, edition of *Jifucongshu* (畿辅丛书) of Qing, 1917.
20 Yasuhiko Kimiya (木宫泰彦), *RiZhongwenhuajiaoliushi* (日中文化交流史) (Beijing: Shangwuyinshuguan, 1980).
21 Hu Zongxian (胡宗宪), *Chouhaitubian* (筹海图编), volume 9.
22 Shu Hua (舒化), "Da Ming lüfuli" (大明律附例) of "Bing lü san" (兵律三), in *Da Ming lü* (大明律), volume 15, carved in the Jiajing (嘉靖)reign of Ming.
23 "Jiajingsanshiliunianshiyiyue" (嘉靖三十六年十一月), in *Ming shizongshilu* (明世宗实录), volume 453, 7676.
24 Ibid.
25 Zheng Shungong (郑舜功), "Haishi" (海市), in *Ribenyijian* (日本一鉴), volume 64, photocopied edition of 1939.
26 Fu Weilin (傅维麟), *Mingshu* (明书), volume 162.
27 GuYanwu (顾炎武), *Tianxiajunguolibingshu* (天下郡国利病书), 3910.
28 "Yudizhi – fengsu" (舆地志·风俗), in *Xiuning xianzhi* (休宁县志) of the Wanli (万历) reign.

29 "Songjian Huang chushizhuan" (松涧黄处士传), in *TanduHuangshizupu* (潭渡黄氏族谱) of She (歙) county, volume 9.

30 "ShuangquanHuangjunxingzhuang" (双泉黄君行状), in *SongtangHuangshizongpu* (竦塘黄氏宗谱) of She (歙) county, volume 5.

31 "Ming chushiXixianxingzhuang" (明处士希贤行状), in *JiyangJiangshizupu* (济阳江氏族谱) of She (歙) county, volume 9.

32 *Yanzhenzhicao* (岩镇志草).

33 Cheng Jiasui (程嘉燧), "MingchushiChengjunmuzhiming" (明处士程君墓志铭), in *Songyuanji'anji* (松园偈庵集), volume 2.

34 He Qiaoyuan (何乔远), "Fengsu" (风俗), in *Minshu* (闽书), volume 38.

35 Yao Shilin (姚士麟), *Jianzhibian* (见只编), volume 1.

36 "Shizhen" (市镇), in *Hangzhou fuzhi* (杭州府志) of the Qianlong (乾隆) reign, volume 5.

37 "Fengsu" (风俗), in *Jiashan xianzhi* (嘉善县志) of the Jiaqing(嘉庆) reign, volume 6.

38 "Fengsu" (风俗), in *Tangqizhi* (塘栖志) of the Guangxu (光绪) reign, volume 18.

39 Suzhou lishibowuguan (苏州历史博物馆) et al., *Ming Qing Suzhou gongshangye-beikeji* (明清苏州工商业碑刻集), 356–357.

40 "Shizhen – Nanxiangzhen" (市镇·南翔镇), "Shizhen – Luodianzhen" (市镇·罗店镇), in *Jiading xianzhi* (嘉定县志) of the Wanli (万历) reign, volume 1.

41 "Wanggangzhi" (外冈志), in *Qianmentangxiangzhi* (钱门塘乡志).

42 XieYongtai (谢永泰) et al., "Yiwenzhi – renwu lei – ShujunZungangzhuan" (艺文志·人物类·舒君遵刚传), in *Yixiansanzhi* (黟县三志).

43 Gui Youguang (归有光), "BaianChengwengbashishouxu" (白庵程翁八十寿序), in *Zhenchuanxianshengji* (震川先生集), volume 13.

44 "Zeng Chengjunwushixu" (赠程君五十序), in Wang Shizhen (王世贞), *Yanzhoushan-rensibugao* (弇州山人四部稿), volume 61.

45 Dai Yixuan (戴裔煊), *MingdaiJia Long jian de WokouyuZhongguozibenzhuyimengya* (明代嘉隆间的倭寇与中国资本主义萌芽) (Beijing: Zhongguoshehuikexuechu-banshe, 1982), 10, note 2.

46 Gugongbowuyuan (故宫博物院) ed., *Jin taishiji* (金太史集) (Haikou: Hainan chu-banshe, 2000).

47 XuGuo (许国), "Yu Lin Xianfu" (与林宪副), in "XuWenmu gong ji" (许文穆公集), in *Chongxiugu She Dongmenxushizongpu* (重修古歙东门许氏宗谱), volume 10, red print edition of *SunshiJiansutang* (孙氏简素堂)of Wuxi (无锡)in 1924.

48 "Yiwen – Wang Wenxuezhuan" (艺文·汪文学传), in *Yixianxuzhi* (黟县续志), volume 15, in *Zhongguodifangzhijicheng Anhui fuxianzhiji* (中国地方志集成安徽府县志辑), No. 56 (Nanjing: Jiangsu gujichubanshe, 1998).

49 GuYanwu (顾炎武), *Tianxiajunguolibingshu* (天下郡国利病书), 2464.

50 GuoPei (郭裴), "Zaman" (杂蛮), in *Guangdong tongzhi* (广东通志), edition of Wanli (万历), 30.

51 "Ming renwu" (明人物), in *Zhangzhoufuzhi* (漳州府志), volume 23, carved in Guangxu (光绪),3.

52 Li Guangjin (李光缙), "Yuxixiongboshouxu" (寓西兄伯寿序), in *Jingbiji* (景壁集), volume 3 (Fuzhou: Fujian renminchubashe, 2012).

53 *Makesi Engesi xuanji* (马克思恩格斯选集), volume 2, 53.

54 Ibid., 526.

55 YamawakiTeijirō (山脉悌二郎), *Nagasaki no Tōjinbōeki* (长崎的华人贸易) (Tōkyō: Yoshikawa Kōbunkan, 1964).

56 Yan Zhongping (严中平), "SichouliuxiangFeilübingbaiyinliuxiangZhongguo" (丝绸流向菲律宾白银流向中国), *jindaishiyanjiu* (近代史研究), No. 1 (1981).

57 See QuanHansheng (全汉昇), "Yapianzhanzhengqian Jiangsu de mianfangzhi ye" (鸦片战争前江苏的棉纺织业), in *Zhongguojingjishiluncong* (中国经济史论丛), book 2.

58 Wang Rizhen (汪日桢), *Nanxunzhenzhi* (南浔镇志), volume 24, the edition of Tong-zhi (同治), 2.

59 Dong Sizhang (董斯张), "Wuxingcongshu" (吴兴丛书), in *Wuxingbeizhi* (吴兴备志), volume 31.

60 Li Pei (李培), "Xiangyunguanbeiji" (翔云观碑记), in *Puchuansuowenji* (濮川所闻记), volume 4.

61 *Xiushui xianzhi* (秀水县志) of the Wanli (万历) reign, volume 1, reprinted in 1925.

62 "Tangqizhi" (塘栖志), cited from Hu Yuanjing (胡元敬), *Tangqifengtuji* (塘栖风土记).

63 Xia Xinming (夏辛铭), *Puyuanzhi* (濮院志), edition of 1928.

64 *Wujiang xianzhi* (吴江县志), in *Zhongguodifangzhijicheng* (中国地方志集成),Jiangsu fuxianzhiji (江苏府县志辑),No. 20.

65 Ibid.

66 "Tongfanboyi" (通番舶议) of "Feng Yangxuji" (冯养虚集), in *Ming jingshiwenji* (明经世文编), volume 280.

67 "Shihuozhi" (食货志), in *Mingshi* (明史), volume 81.

68 Gu Yanwu (顾炎武), *Tianxiajunguolibingshu* (天下郡国利病书), 3119.

69 Gu Yanwu (顾炎武), *Rizhilu* (日知录), volume 11.

70 Lelin, *Eguozibenzhuyi de fanzhan* (俄国资本主义的发展) (Beijing: Renminchubanshe, 1960), 328.

71 Ibid.

72 Liu Kunyi (刘坤一), *Liu Kunyizhoushu* (刘坤一奏疏) (Changsha: Yuelushushe, 2013).

73 Liu Jinzao (刘锦藻), "Shiyekao" (实业考), in *Qingchaoxuwenxiantongkao* (清朝续文献通考), volume 385 (Hangzhou: Zhejiang gujichubanshe, 1988).

74 Tang Jiong (唐炯), "ChouyikuagnwunizhaojishangguyanpinDongyangguangshishu" (筹议矿务拟招集商股延聘东洋矿师疏), in *Huangchaojingshi wen xubian* (皇朝经世文续编), volume 26.

75 *The Capital*, volume 3, 1019.

76 Wang Shizhen (王世贞), "Jiang Chen ershengzhuan" (蒋陈二生传), in *Wozhi* (倭志).

# 5    The merchant and the communal life

The detailed studies on the interaction between the merchant and the communal life in this chapter deepen our understanding of peculiar social roles played by merchants in the modern times. This chapter selects Huizhou society as a case study to make an in-depth analysis and exploration of four aspects – merchants and women, merchants and the family, the structure of patriarchal clans, and the expansion of the living space of the merchant and community.

"The merchant and the communal life" is a micro-history topic. The community is a unit of social life tied by certain geographical relations. It is a concrete and self-evident social entity. By using detailed and authentic materials, the study on the community allows to demonstrate the merchant's social functions and social roles. An in-depth exploration of the interaction between merchants and their communal life shall deepen our understanding of their unique social functions and social roles in modern society.

We select Huizhou merchants and Huizhou society as the subject of study not only because Huizhou merchants were one of the most powerful merchant groups but also because the Huizhou community was a typical one. The area of the Huizhou community was stable and closed. It was situated on the border of Anhui, Zhejiang, and Jiangxi Provinces. After the Qin's unification of the six states, the whole country was divided up into 36 prefectures. In the Huizhou area, Yi and She Counties were set up under Kuaiji Prefecture. Historically, the Sui dynasty was an exception as the southeastern part of She County was partitioned and Shixin (today's Chun'an) and Suian were established. Apart from losing Shixin and Suian, the Huizhou area retained other regions. Since 769, She Prefecture featured six counties: She, Xiuning, Yi, Wuyuan, Qimen, and Jixi. With the exception that Wuyuan was once promoted as a prefecture, everything else remained unchanged. The Huizhou community after the sixteenth century included essentially the territory of Yi and She Counties in the ancient times. In terms of the geographical environment, "Huizhou as a prefecture was situated in rugged mountains and valleys."[1] Mountainous areas and hills constituted 90% of the territory, making it a relative independent society. This had a profound impact on the relative independent development of its politics, economy, and culture. According to *She County Gazetteer* of Wanli, during the

Chenghua reign in the late fifteenth and early sixteenth centuries, communal life in She County was:

> All households had adequate supplies and people lived in contentment. Those who lived here owned houses. Those who farmed could rent lands. Woodcutters went to the mountains. Horticulturists had gardens. Tax collectors did not harass [the community], and bandits did not prevail. Marriages were arranged in accordance with the right timing. Neighbors lived in peace. Women wove and men planted mulberry trees. Servants served and neighbors maintained good relationships.

It was pointed out in *She County Gazetteer* that the medieval idyllic life in the Huizhou community was an extension of a traditional social life: "It is true that [the golden times like] the Three Dynasties [in the ancient times] were not just the Taiping reign of the Song, the Zhenguan reign of the Tang, and the times of Emperor Wen and Emperor Jing of the Han." In the first half of the sixteenth century, the communal life in Huizhou underwent drastic changes:

> Those who went out as merchants became numerous, and the ownership of land was no longer esteemed. As men matched wits using their assets, fortunes rose and fell unpredictably. The capable succeeded, the dull-witted were destroyed; the family to the west enriched itself while the family to the east was impoverished. The balance between the mighty and the lowly was lost as both competed for trifling amounts, each exploiting the other and everyone publicizing himself.

The change took place extremely fast. In the Wanli years of the second half of the sixteenth century, the Huizhou community featured

> one percent of rich people and ninety percent of poor people. The poor could not compete with the wealthy, but the minority could control the majority. The gold commander ruled the heaven and the money god managed the earth. [People] were extremely greedy and engaged in fratricidal fighting.

*She County Gazetteer* pointed that the dramatic change like "rivers becoming hills and mountains becoming earth and ocean" in Huizhou's communal life resulted from "the rise of numerous merchants" and "most being not rich." Therefore, it is of vital importance to understand the merchant's social functions and social roles to explore Huizhou merchants' impact on the relatively independent but closed communal life.

Huizhou merchants' impact on the relatively independent but closed communal life was omnipresent. This chapter takes a sociological angle to explore major issues such as women's issue, the fundamental communal structure, and the expansion of the community's living space, with which I shall further explore the interaction between the merchant and the community.

## Section one: the merchant and the woman

### *1 The social functions of merchants' wives*

Huizhou women were intimately linked to commerce ever since the ancient times. In Huizhou, "[the place] was situated inside the mountains. The grains produced were not enough [to feed people for] a month. Ninety percent [of the grains] needed [to be imported] from outside."[2]Therefore, "Huizhou people relied on trade to make a living."[3] The earliest commodities of Huizhou commerce were tea, timber, and other products from the mountains in exchange for grains. Women mostly engaged in production. *She fengsu lijiao kao* (*An Investigation of Customs and Morality in She*) claimed, "In the [busy] seasons for tea, even women did not have time to rest." *Xin'an zhuzhici* (*Lyrics of Bamboo Shoots of Xin'an*) described the customs of the day: "During the Qingming times, the ethereal grasses begins to sprout. In the summertime, the taste of Songluo tea turns awful. So many married ladies who returned to visit their natal families followed their mothers to pick new teas." The consciousness of commodity made its way into women's daily life. *Xin'an zhi* (*Xin'an Gazetteer*) printed in the Chunxi times described the customs of Huizhou in the Song: "When a girl is born, cedars are planted for her. When she is about to get married, the trees are cut [in exchange for goods] of diverse uses. For this reason, girls make savings by themselves." Therefore, after the Chenghua and Hongzhi reigns of the Ming, when commodified economy developed to pave the way for the rise of Huizhou merchants, Huizhou women readily played their roles as merchants' wives. In the Ming and Qing times, when traders constituted 70% or 80% of the population in Huizhou, merchants' wives also made up the majority of the Huizhou women. Huizhou merchants' careers could not thrive without those women. Therefore, it does injustice to history to underestimate merchants' wives' social functions.

### *Supplying to Huizhou merchants source capital*

There were three types of capital provided by merchants' wives. The first was dowry. For example, Wu Liefu, a merchant from She County in Ming, "brought his wife's dowry to engage in trade and accumulated tens of thousands [of ounces of silver] and several *qin* of lands."[4] The She County merchant Xu Dongjing "was not a merchant when he was poor. His wife contributed her hair claps, ornaments, clothes, and hemps as the source money." "[He] thrived because of salt trade. [His] houses and lands were entirely different [from what he had] in the past. He gained great reputation in the home village."[5] Xu Fu, the father of Xu Guo, Ming's Grand Secretary and Minister of Rites, also rose to prominence with his wife's dowry. In "Mu ruren shishi" (An Authentic Account of My Mother, Child Nurturess), Xu Guo indicated,

> [Wang] Fuying is Child Nurturess's real name. As Child Nurturess married to my late father, they were poor. [She] advised my late father to engage in trade. As my late father considered that he did not have money, [Child Nurturess] gave all her dowry to finance him. Hence, my late father followed my uncle, Mr. Youshan, to do business in Jiangsu.[6]

There were people who resorted to their sisters-in-law's dowry as capital. *Yanzhen zhicao* (*A Draft of Yan Town Gazetteer*) recorded, Zheng Xian's "brother, Zheng Duo, engaged in trade but had no money. Zheng Xian talked to his wife and gained her permission to give all the dowry to Zheng Duo to trade in Jingzhou and Yangzhou. The business thrived." Hence, Wang Daokun recorded that Jin's mother "donated money to Jin Zhanggong for his business in Huai. After a few years, Zhanggong began to prosper and eventually became rich." Wang thus commented, "The mother made the initial contribution."[7] It was a common practice in Huizhou to use dowry as source capital. There are quite a lot of records in the respect. The second one was the bride price. "Hunyin lei" (The Category of Marriage) of *Anthology of Petty Matters in Qing* stated,

> A certain Mr. Cheng had been influential in the hometown because of his wealth for generations. He had a son who was born a fool. . . . No one was willing to marry him. In the past, the Cheng family ran a broker's shop in Wuxi, with a certain Mr. Wang being the accountant for generations. Wang had a daughter of the same age.

In order to obtain the bride price as his capital, Wang married his daughter to this mentally challenged man. The Cheng family "divided its wealth and gave [Wang] tens of thousands [of ounces of silver]," but the young woman "remained alone in the rest of her life." The third was labor capital. "Fengsu" (Customs) of *Huizhou fuzhi* (*Gazetteer of Huizhou Prefecture*) claimed that Huizhou

> women were particularly frugal. When [they] stayed in the village for several months, [they] did not eat fish or meat. Every day, [they] used needles to sew and mend. The customs in Yi and Qi Counties were weaving kapok. [Women] in the same neighborhoods got together to weave at night [as if they could] work forty-five days a month. Huizhou's customs prioritized saving money. [They] did not squander their money, because of their inherent virtues.

There were many examples that women used their incomes from weaving to support their husbands' businesses. Cheng Shenbao from Shanheli of Qimen in the Ming was so poor that "[he] usually lived on picking up and collecting goods." His wife, "née Li, helped him [with incomes from] silk weaving and [contributed] his ornaments and clothes, amounting to thirty [ounces of silver in total]. [Cheng] traded in Xiajiang."[8] Wu Ruiyu, a native of Huangnan of She County in the Qing, "was so poor that he engaged in an uxorilocal marriage with Ms. Yao. [Yao] wove day in and day out. Later, Ruiyu traded in Taizhou."[9]

*Mutual supports by relatives to form commercial networks*

After the Chenghua and Hongzhi reigns, commercial competitions intensified. "[Businesses] demised and rose [so quickly] that [they] were like ebbs and flows."[10] Huizhou merchants consolidated their cooperation. The bond of their cooperation was the marriages between clans. Intermarriage led to the intersections of blood relationship of different clans so that the cooperative network was expanded. To take salt traders in Yangzhou as an example. According to *She County Gazetteer*, "Those from our county who gained matchless reputations in the country by serving as the leaders of salt traders were Huang initially and then Wang and Wu, all of whom possessed [a wealth] of hundreds of thousands or millions [of ounces of silver]."*Jiangdu xianzhi* (*Gazetteer of Jiangdu County*) printed in Jiaqing and *Five-color Stone Ester* authored by Chen Qubing, a writer of the modern times added Cheng, Fang, Jiang, Hong, Pan, Zheng, and Xu besides Huang, Wang, and Wu. Meanwhile, they claimed "The prosperity of Yangzhou influential families maintained a habit of living as individual clans. It was stated in *A Record of Painted Pleasure Boat in Yangzhou* "The Wu's was an influential Huizhou family, whose members lived in villages such as Xixinan, Changqiao, Beian, and Yanzhen. Those who sojourned in Yangzhou lived separately along the line of their home villages." Huizhou merchants placed a great emphasis on building ancestral halls and worshipping ancestors. "Xu" (Preface) to *Wangshi pucheng* (*Genealogy of the Wang Clan*) stated that the clansmen who lived in Yangzhou "could not return to the native place annually. In order to perform rituals of worshipping the ancestors, therefore, they built a public shrine." In *Anthology of Taihan*, Wang Daokun pointed out that the Wang family intermarried with the Wu family in Nanxi, who "lived in the west of She County and prospered because of their engagement in trade. The most wealthy and powerful ones were called three Wu's." The Wang and Wu clans were both great salt traders in Ming. The great grandson of Wu Rucheng, who served as the chief of salt traders during the Zhengde and Wanli reigns, Wu Xunmei married to the eldest granddaughter of Wang Daokun. Their son, Wu Qichang, also became an influential merchant. Those clans tied by marriages mutually supported to enhance their capability of competing with other merchant groups. Some clans even formed relatively stable groups linked by marriage. "Haoshe lei" (The Category of Luxury) of *Anthology of Petty Matters in Qing* claimed that in Qingjiangpu, the distributing center for salt merchants in Huaibei, "the family of Wang Jishan, a Huizhou person, sojourned here for two centuries. The family accumulated a wealth of one million [ounces of silver] by running pawn shops and stores, commonly known as the great gates of the Wang family. [The Wang family] did not intermarry with local people, but with the Cheng family, salt traders in Huaibei, only."

There were many cases that relatives by marriage cooperated with each other to trade. Hong Tingmei, a timber merchant from Wuyuan, "traded timber with his relatives by marriage in distant places in Fujian, Zhejiang, Hunan, Hubei, and Sichuan. He carried his heart upon his sleeve and was cooperative without being harsh."[11] Eventually, he made a fortune. The Wang family from Xin'an "set up a store named Yimei at the Chang Gate of Suzhou." Because he "was good at hoarding and speculating," "[he] became the richest merchant after ten years, and his fabrics were sold everywhere in the country." "Later, Wang secured an official position and therefore asked Cheng, his relative, [to take over the business]. Afterwards, Chen gave the business back to Wang." The relatives ran the business alternately. "In two centuries, [people in] southern Yunnan and north of

Gobi viewed [goods sold by] Yimei as the finest."[12] Jin Sheng of the Ming pointed out, "Because people in two counties (She County and Xiuning) engaged in trade, they brought their relatives and friends to work with them." Relatives by marriage shared interests in common and went through the thick and thin together.

### Resorting to feudal political forces

Intermarrying with officials was an important avenue for Huizhou merchants to enlist support from feudal regimes. In "Han shilang bi zuo furen" (Assistant Minister Han's Maidservant Becoming Madam) of *Slapping the Table in Amazement II*, it was said, "Huizhou people had a proclivity toward black gauze caps (officialdom) and red embroidered shoes (women). Throughout their lives, they did not spare silver for those two things, but were stingy with everything else." Huizhou merchants valued black gauze caps for the sake of trade. They "did not spare silver" for black gauze caps in order to pursue more silver. In the novel, a Huizhou salt trader married his foster daughter, Jiang Ainiang, to assistant minister Han as a concubine "without demanding properties, but gave out the dowry. [He] felt satisfied with getting along with an official." Later, assistant minister Han's principal wife died, and Jiang Ainiang became the legal wife. "That Huizhou merchant was acknowledged as his foster father, and they maintained a close relationship." The relationship by marriage between the Huizhou merchant and assistant minister Han enabled the merchant to have backstage of political power. On the one hand, "noblemen who borrowed money from merchants showed favoritism to merchants."[13] On the other hand, merchants were able to obtain the status as official-bureaucrats to retain a hereditary monopoly of salt trade. There were a vast amount of descriptions in this respect. In volume 2, "Zhuoshou yisong" (Washing Hands and Leaning against the Pine), of *Jianhu jiuji* (*Anthology of Hard Calabash, No. 9*),

> A certain Mr. Wu, a Huizhou merchant, lived in Banxiang in southern Hangzhou. The merchant had only one daughter who came of age. [He] made arrangements, but did not feel satisfied. On the fifteenth day of the eighth money of the *yiyou* year of the Wanli reign, he dreamed of a dragon playing claws in the water. On the next day, Xu Yingdeng from Yaojiang finished his exam as a Confucian scholar and visited the merchant with his friend. The friend told Xu, "This family boasts of a wealth of tens of thousands [of ounces of silver]. It has a young woman available for marrying to a gifted scholar, regardless of his financial situation. You haven't passed the exams, but you go to school to study. Aren't you a gifted scholar? I personally know that person. So, please allow me to make a match. Please wait a minute." Then, he stepped in to talk to the merchant. The merchant made a verbal consent but harbored no real intention. The friend said, "The gentleman is standing outside. Please take a look." As they walked toward the door, Xu happened to be washing his hands in the jar. The merchant felt it resemble to [what he saw] in the dream and gave his consent [to the marriage]. Then,

he asked the friend as the matchmaker. The friend passed on a message to Xu. Xu wanted return to home before he could pay the bride price, but the merchant loaned him the money [for him to propose]. Later, the result of the exam was announced, and [Xu] was ranked the eleventh in the provincial exam. In 1601, he earned the *jingshi* degree.

"A young woman available for marrying to a gifted scholar, regardless of his financial situation" was a commonly held value of marriage among Huizhou merchants. Such marriages were two-way. When Huizhou people secured positions as officials, they were happy to intermarry with great merchants. "Wu Muan wushi xu" (Biographic Note on Wu Muan's Fiftieth Birthday) of *Gazetteer of Fengnan* recorded, "Xu Guo's father was originally a merchant and had built hidden virtue. Therefore, Xu was willing to intermarry with ultra-wealthy merchants. For example, his daughter married to Cheng Juzi from Yu Village of Xiuning, who possessed millions of [ounces of silver]." The confluence of merchants and Confucian scholars, on the one hand, destabilized the classification of people into four categories. On the other hand, it was a recipe for success of Huizhou merchants. The cooperation between merchants and Confucians was a main avenue.

*Keeping house to relieve merchants from worries from family*

*Xiuning Shuaidong Chengshi jiapu* (*Genealogy of the Cheng Family from Shuaidong, Xiuning*) had an account of the life of Sun Qinxing, a merchant's wife:

> After [she] married to Mr. [Cheng Weizong], [she] was diligent, respectful, and meticulous. [Her] knowledge was superior. As Mr. Cheng was kept away from home to engage in trade, [she] managed household duties. [She] did not get her own peace, but [she] did not make mistakes in her acts. [She] suffered predicaments and troubles repeatedly, but [she] remained composed. [Her] neighbors praised her for being a virtuous [wife].

In the scroll entitled "Shou Siyuan Chenggong liushi xu" (Biographic Note on Mr. Cheng Siyuan's Sixtieth Birthday), Xu Guo wrote that the Huizhou merchant Cheng Siyuan "prospered in his career as [he] multiplied his properties by tenfold. All [that happened] because of Child Nurturess Lai's assistance at home." How did merchants' wives manage household affairs and play a role as good wives? First of all, they helped their husbands start their businesses. Women who were born from merchants' families usually had a higher consciousness of commodity. When they married into their husbands' families, they often persuaded their husbands to engage in trade to improve their families' financial situations. For example, Wang Daokun's grandmother

> once seized a chance to tell his grandfather, "Your family adheres to [moral codes such as] filial devotion and fraternity and has been engaged into farming for generations. My father is a businessman. I heard from him that being

a merchant could usually be prosperous. If you follow my father to trade, I would like to sponsor you." My grandfather replied, "Great [idea]." Since my grandfather did business, the financial situations improved.[14]

Ms. Zhu, a merchant's daughter, married to the Wang family in Ximen of Xiuning.

> In Wang Tianfu's family, people did not engage in trade. Thus, as Child Nurturess Zhu married into the family, she was in poverty. Hence, [she] persuaded Mr. Wang to gather surplus money to trade in Jingzhou and Xiang-yang. [She] said, "You just go. I'll serve [your parents] for you. I'll under-take your responsibility of taking care of your parents. You don't flinch."[The reason why] Mr. Wang prospered by doing business was because of Child Nurturess's assistance.[15]

It had been a widely accepted custom in villages of merchants that men engaged in trade elsewhere and women managed the household affairs. "Customs" of *Gaz-etteer of the Xiuning County* described women's fulfillment of household duties:

> Women could endure hardship and work hard. In middle-class families, women abstained from fish and meat, but weave hemps day in and day out. Goods like hats, belts, shoes, and socks were usually made manually. Those who were diligent could feed two or three people. Because their husbands usually traveled elsewhere to trade for years, women fed themselves or even their children. Merchants' ability to save money was enhanced because of [women's] assistance at home.

"Customs" of *Gazetteer of She County* featured the similar descriptions: "Women were particularly diligent and stingy. It usually happened that a husband engaged in trade somewhere else, but the income was meager. A family of several people relied on the wife to exempt from cold and hunger." The merchant's wife man-aged to make both ends meet with her hands and free merchants from worries of the family. Huizhou merchants' wealth was accumulated and reinvested in pro-duction because of their wives' frugality. "*Fuxi Fangmu Xu ruren muzhiming*" (Epitaph of Child Nurturess Xu, mother of Fang Xicheng from Fuxi) written by Xiong Xi was included in *She Chun Fangshi hui zongtong pu* (*General Geneal-ogy of the Whole Fang's Clan in She County and Chun'an*). This epitaph gave a detailed account on how Child Nurturess Xu supported Fang Xicheng, a Huizhou merchant, to start his business:

> [Fang] Xicheng traveled around to do business and did not return to home in several years. When [he] returned, [he] stayed for several months before packing up things to leave without any concerns over fam-ily affairs. Child Nurturess [Xu] was [accompanied by] only one lamp and stayed alone but without displaying the slightest unhappiness. [He] sewed luggage and [prepared] what was needed during the trips. [Fang]

felt handy [with his trips], but Child Nurturess [Xu] did not tell him [what she had done for him].

When the Three Feudatories revolted,

> Yunnan and Fujian were in chaos. Rebellious people from the mountains occupied villages and cities and recklessly pillaged. Then, Fang Xicheng stayed in Jiangxi. His house was in the thoroughfare. When bandits suddenly came, family members could barely survive. They escaped to and hid themselves in the mountain. All of them relied on Child Nurturess [Xu] for food. Child Nurturess [Xu] diligently did sewing works and prepared food for her in-laws as well as servants. Yet, [she] felt content with crude clothing and poor food.

Child Nurturess Xu's hometown was Yangzhou, where her family traded salt. "When there was surplus money each year, Child Nurturess [Xu] was always eager to [use the money] to help her own family." Thus, Fang Xicheng could engaged in trade elsewhere with easiness.

Next, women helped their husbands retain their businesses. After Huizhou merchants became rich, their wives remained frugal to manage the family affairs to retain businesses. For example, Jiang Zhongmu, a merchant from She County "engaged in trade in the North, such as Shandong and Henan. His business later prospered and then returned to engage in salt trade in Hangzhou." "Although he was rich, he wife remained frugal like before."[16] Bao Zhidao, the merchant leader of Huainan and Huaibei, "possessed a wealth of tens of thousands [ounces of silver], but his wives and children diligently worked on housewifery."[17] His wife, née Wang, did not lead a luxurious life but donated money to the home village. For example, she "purchased hundreds of *mu* of lands to collect rents for clanswomen in the village." "[She] had roads such as Damue, Qixingdune, and Tianshuixiqiao reconstructed. Until today, people in the village mention [those things]."[18] Such charitable activities helped enhance Bao Zhidao's credibility and reputation so that the Bao family enjoyed lasting prosperity. His eldest son, Bao Shufang, also served as the merchant leader. His second son, Bao Xunmao, Secretary in the Grand Secretariat and Probationary Grand Minister of State. According to "Huang ruren zhuang" (Biography of Child Nurturess Huang) of *Gazetteer of Fengnan*, Wuchang Changjun, a Huizhou merchant, "stayed in Tianjin to do business" and "returned home every ten years." "Initially, the family was poor. When it prospered, Child Nurturess [Huang] continued to haggle over every ounce and refused to use costly goods." Thus, she "became more diligent particularly at home." Wu Jihu praised Child Nurturess Huang: "[She] makes one exclaim with admiration that you become even richer." Merchants' wives assisted their husbands not only to "make [them] even richer," but also to save and resume the family line. Cheng Yue from Shuaidong of Xiuning "traveled to the Huai and Yangzi Rivers for business and died during a trip in the year of *wuyin* of the Zhengde reign." His wife, Child Nurturess Wu, managed the household when

Cheng was alive so that "Mr. Cheng was not concerned over the family." After Cheng Yue passed away, she paid off debts for him. "[She] used up her dowry to help to pay off [debts]." She told her son, Cheng Suo, "A person's duty is to serve the rulers and parents and to nurture the young. The scholarly honor or official rank are not an inherent part of the human being. How can [we] prioritize irrelevant things over body and life and give up on your ancestor's business?" Cheng Suo, who "used to study Confucian classics," complied with his mother's instruction to "follow his father's steps to be a merchant and thereby accumulate an enormous wealth."[19] Xu Yongqin, Zheng Changniang's husband, "considered reviving the family" by going out and engage in trade. Before he left, [he] asked Child Nurturess, 'I am about to stay out [of family] for a long time and won't have time to return. Can you take all the responsibilities?' Child Nurturess said, 'Yes.'" Xu "traveled faraway and stayed outside for a decade before he died there." Child Nurturess Zheng, who did not have a child of her own, raised the third son of her sister-in-law and "treated him as her own [son]. After [he] grew up, he was talented and quick-witted. Child Nurturess [Zheng] thought he could succeed to the family business. Thus, she contributed her own properties and asked him to do business elsewhere. [He] started his business in Ruxu and made a fortune to revive the family business."[20]

### Directly engaging in commercial activities

There were a lot of talented merchants' wives, who could directly engage in commercial activities. For example, Child Nurturess Wang was born in "her residence in Hangzhou." She grew up in her father's store. As she was edified by what she saw, she was good at calculating and planning. After Child Nurturess Wang, whose natal family "possessed the vastest wealth in the county," married to Wu Cigong, whose "family was as rich as princes," she actively participated in decision making. "Child Nurturess [Wang] praised or criticized those who worked with Cigong, and her comments would later be corroborated."[21] Ms. Hu, daughter of a great salt trader, married to Mr. Zhang. "Ms. Hu was so virtuous that [she] devised plans for salt trade from [her] inner chamber. [She] worked hard and made a fortune. Her two sons engaged in the same business and enjoyed high revenues, too."[22] Ms. Dai, wife of the salt trader Jin He, "used to learn bookkeeping. [She] made arrangements both inside and outside. All revenues were manually kept. The family prospered because the wife offered a lot of help."[23] Wu and Huang, who sojourned in Yangzhou, were both "influential families of She County." After Ms. Wu from Xi'nan got married into the Huang family from Songtang, "[she] calculated turnovers of money by memory without resorting to bookkeeping. After a long while, [she] did not make a mistake." "Since Mr. Huang married to Child Nurturess, [he] no longer worried about his family and focused on taking advantage the timing [to do business]. He [ended up] earning tens of thousands [of ounces of silver]."[24] The most prominent one among merchants' wives was Mrs. Wang, whose husband, Wang Shigong, was one of the eight greatest salt traders in Huainan and Huaibei. After her husband passed away, "the widow managed

affairs both at home and in the business. Therefore, people called her Mrs. Wang."
During Emperor Qianlong's southern tour, Mrs. Wang

> and salt traders in Huai selected a waste land with a size of several hundred
> *mu* north to the city to build pavilions, platforms, gardens, and waterside
> pavilions modeled after those in the scenic West Lake of Hangzhou for the
> emperor to view. However, the place was short of a pond. Mrs. [Wang] spent
> tens of thousands of [silver] by herself in gathering the craftsmen at night to
> race to build the Three Immortals Pond. The pond was completed at night,
> and the emperor arrived on the next day. Emperor Qianlong sang high praise
> [of the pond] and bestowed [to Mrs. Wang] precious things. Hence, Mrs.
> [Wang] became more famous.[25]

Mr. Wang was lauded by the highest feudal ruler, which was naturally beneficial
to her commercial activities. According to a folktale in Yangzhou, Mrs. Wang
once served as one of chiefs of the eight trades.[26]

In sum, merchants' wives were a contributing factor of the rise of Huizhou
merchants, while the thriving commodified economy effected changes in social
customs in Huizhou. The change of social customs started with altering wom-
en's attire. As the saying has it, the great transformation starts with insignificant
changes. "A Study on Customs and Confucian Ethics in She County" indicated,

> Hats, clothing, and ornaments across the country follow the customs of the
> day. No one dares to deviate [from the customs]. Women's attire in the six
> counties differs. Generally speaking, She is close to Huai and Yang, Xiuning
> to Suzhou, Wuyuan, Yi, and Qimen to Jiangxi, and Jixi to Ningguo. [People
> in] She and Xiuning are prone to the luxurious [attire]. Decades ago, even
> women from rich families rarely wore fur coats. Now, however, [fur coats]
> prevail. Meanwhile, luxurious ornaments such as pearls and jades [are also
> commonly seen]. [The luxurious lifestyle] was initiated by those traded in
> Yangzhou and Suzhou.[27]

She and Xiuning women's luxurious attire was correspondent with the two counties' commercial prosperity. During the Jiajing and Wanli reigns, a large number
of materials indicated the changes "gradually brought about by merchants." Here,
I take changes in Fengnan Village as an example to explore it in detail. *Gazetteer of Fengnan* stated, "It is at present (during the Wanli reign) that our clan
(Wu) prospers the most," which was symbolized by "women's comparisons with
each other for their wealth and their gorgeous attire." "Dandies purchased hairpins
and earrings for their newly wed wives and decorated their carriages to show off
to their fellow townspeople." The reason behind the change of customs was the
highly developed commerce, with which "grains were sold all over the country."

The change of social customs led to the transformation of Huizhou people's
values. "As a part of the Huizhou customs, a merchant returned home every several years. His wives, children, and clansmen judged him as virtuous or unworthy

based on how much he earned."[28] Those who earned more were viewed as virtuous and likable, whereas those who earned less unworthy and despicable. The change of values dealt a blow to traditional concepts and order in the feudal times, which was beneficial to the liberation of women.

The enhanced status of Huizhou women was reflected in Xie Zhaozhe's *Five Miscellanies*:

> It is hard to meet with beautiful girls, whereas jealous women are numerous. The same could be said for the fact that there are few gentlemen but more petty men. This is particularly true to Xin'an of the Yangzi Delta and Pucheng in Fujian. Their households have been accustomed to them.

The heightened status of women meant the collapse of feudal morality that fettered women. It was no wonder that they were called "jealous women." Pucheng was situated at the border area among Fujian, Zheijiang, and Jiangxi, with rich resources and convenient traffic conditions. Therefore, it was a place where merchants got together. Quite a lot of Huizhou merchants migrated to this place. Volume 24, "Jiazhuan" (Family History) of *Xiguan Zhangshi zupu* (*Genealogy of the Zhang Clan from Xiguan*) of Jixi stated that the Huizhou merchant Zhang Bitai "engaged in trade and traveled between Jiangsu and Zhejiang." "When he visited his clansmen and solicited genealogies, he met in Suzhou a certain [Zhang] Han, who belonged to the same clan, from Pucheng. They discussed reconstructing the ancestral hall. Therefore, they distributed notices to notify clansmen everywhere." "Later, [he] visited Pucheng and discovered that the genealogy for the whole clan and that of Xiguan were of no difference." The Zhang clan in Pucheng possessed a genealogy for the whole clan, revealing its large population. The perceived large of number of "jealous women" in Xin'an and Pucheng corresponded with a developed commodified economy and a higher status that merchants' wives enjoyed. Xie Zhaozhe gave three reasons why husbands were henpecked. Among the three, two were relevant to economic conditions. One was that "[wives and husbands] had lived poor and lowly lives and experienced hardships. Once getting rich, [the men] could not control [the women]." The other one was that "[the men and women] had wide disparity in their statuses, and money dictated. Therefore, [the men] surrendered their power to [the women], and could not issue their orders." Xie's analysis could be aptly compared with the aforementioned account of merchants' wives' impact on Huizhou commerce. Therefore, we can see that merchants' wives changed Huizhou society and thereby changed their own statuses with their unique social functions.

## 2 The fates of merchants' wives

How did Huizhou society impact on merchants' wives? It was true that the development of commodified economy contributed to women's liberation. In the meantime, however, it consolidated the most antiquated patriarchal clan system in Huizhou.

First, strengthening the patriarchal clan system was indispensable for controlling fellow clansmen who engaged in trade (please see Section One of Chapter 3). Second, it served the needs of stabilizing families when merchants were away.

"*Fengtu*" (Customs) of *She County Gazetteer* indicated, "The customs in this county valued the merchant. The merchant has to go to distant places and return every several years. There are also merchants who sojourn elsewhere and never come back. It is a common practice that the newlyweds part ways." Huizhou merchants' "sojourning elsewhere and never coming back" because of hardships in commerce could found frequent mentions in gazetteers and genealogies. For example, the father of Wu Kun, a Xiuning merchant in Ming,

> stayed away to engage in trade. [He] lost contact because of losing money in business. [Wu] Kun worked hard in the home village and fed his mother by selling wine. Yet, he missed his father. . . . Later, [he] went to the mountains in Kai County in Sichuan and found [his father's] body. [He] carried it and returned.[29]

"Several months after" Zhan Wenxi, a merchant from Wuyuan, "was born, his father went away and never returned. When he was seventeen *sui*, he vowed to look for his father. He traveled to Hunan, Hubei, Sichuan, and Yunnan, but could not find him after years. [His] wail of grief rose to the sky."[30] The father of Shu Bingji, a Yi County merchant, "traveled to Hunan and Hubei and did not return in over a decade."[31] "Sojourning [in other places] and never returning" and losing communications made merchants' wives feel it hard to sustain and posed a threat to the stability of merchants' families. There was a case recorded in volume 7 of *Gazetteer of Yi County* printed in the Jiaqing times.

> A certain Mr. Wang went out to trade and lost contact, and his wife was about to remarry. [Su] Yuan wrote a letter and sent money to her family. The woman's began to feel settled. Three years later, Wang returned home.

Without the righteous action of the understanding and sympathetic Su Yuan, also a Yi County merchant, the Wang family would be undoubtedly dissolved. However, relying on merchants' individual forces was not enough to reverse the trend of the destabilized families. Therefore, they invoked the talisman of the patriarchal clan system.

*An Investigation of Customs and Morality in She* claimed, "Those who did evil things would be supervised collectively by fellow clansmen. [Therefore,] tricks and schemes would not prevail. This was not because people were all good, but because people lived as a clan and the public opinion disallowed [evil actions]." Iterant merchants resorted to their fellow clansmen's to supervise and the public opinion of clansmen who "lived together as a clan" to prevent women from "doing evil things" and devising "tricks and schemes" – namely, remarrying. Such a "public opinion" was nothing but the Confucian Three Principles and Five Virtues, "upholding the heavenly principle and annihilating human desires," and "dying of starvation is a lesser misfortune than losing one's chastity" proposed by

Neo-Confucians. That was also family rules and regulations specified in the clan lineages that Huizhou merchants expended huge amounts of money to compile. Take the clan rule recorded in *Qimen Fangshi zupu* (*Genealogy of the Fang Clan of Qimen*) compiled in 1874 as an example. This rule featured 32 provisions, touching upon all aspects of social life. Among them, 13 provisions were specific or related to women. They were "For Parents," "Being Friendly to Brothers," "Hierarchizing Spouses," "Being Strict to Concubines," "Admonishing the Woman," "Disciplining the Boudoir," "Valuing the Marriage," "Serving In-laws," "Being Harmonious with Brothers' Wives," "Cultivating Chastity," "Being Cautious of Step-children and Children of Concubines," "Upholding Frugality," and "Economizing on Weddings," constituting 40% of all the provisions of the clan rule. Those provisions imposed strict norms on women's behaviors throughout their lives. The most crucial part was an emphasis on the man's guiding of the woman. In "For Parents," parents were required "not to be credulous of words of women and bondservants lest troubles would arise in the households. In "Hierarchizing Spouses," it was stressed,

> the husband should cultivate himself and regulate the family, without letting hens to cackle in the morning (the woman's usurping of the man's power). The wife should submit herself to follow the husband and is not allowed to be shrewish and make a scene without controlling her temper.

In "Disciplining the Boudoir," it was ordered, "women should focus on weaving and spinning to work on textile works and fulfil their duties. When the mind is not distracted, wicked ideas would not arise." In "Cultivating Chastity," it was emphasized that "public opinions" were invoked to force women to preserve chastity after the death of their husbands:

> Women's preservation of their chastity is the most difficult thing. Those in the clan who are unfortunately widowed should be subsidized by their close relatives. After they fulfil their duties of preserving chastity, they should be publicly praised to encourage the good morality.

On the other hand, for those "who intend to remarry," Huizhou clans were not tolerant but resorted to "public opinions" to suppress them. In "Fanli" (Guidance) of *Guilin Fangshi zongpu* (*Genealogy of the Guilin Fang Clan*), it was specified, "A woman who intends to remarry will not have her name left [on the genealogy], even if she has sons. This is because she loses chastity." "Guidance" of *Shangshu Fangshi zongpu* (*Genealogy of Minister Fang's Clan*) claimed, "A woman's marrying to an influential clan is called *shi*. If she remarries, she would be ousted [from the genealogy] without leaving a record." "[The name of a woman who] remarries would be expelled from [the entry of] her husband to display the termination of their conjugal relationship." All such clan rules and family regulations were like shackles that tightly fettered merchants' wives in order to maintain stability of merchants' families. The power of "public opinions" was not insignificant. Patriarchal clans praised "talented scholars who entered politics, graduates of the civil service exam, outstanding women, and female paragons" for "being valued by the state and glorifying the clans." Therefore, virtually all clans inserted in their genealogies, "records of graduates of the civil service exam and biographies of chaste women to praise [the people] in the past and to encourage [the people] in the future."[32] Biographies of virtuous women and moralities of women in the boudoir performed the function to guide public opinions, clamp down on women's thoughts, and impose restrictions on women's actions.

The massive production of genealogies of clans led to the prosperity of the publishing industry in Huizhou. *Five Miscellanies* claimed,

> In the Song, Hangzhou-made block-printed books were superior, those from Sichuan were second, and those from Fujian the inferior. Today, those printed in Hangzhou do not deserve mentioning. Those printed in three places, Jinling, Xin'an, and Wuxing, are finely carved and are of the same quality as those of the Song edition. Books printed in Hunan, Hubei, and Sichuan are not spectacular.

Huizhou merchants invested in not only the finely carved genealogies but also Confucian classics, *Zhuzi jiali* (*Master Zhu's Family Rites*), *Nüer jing* (*Scripture for Girls*), and *Guifan tushuo* (*Illustrated Note on Women's Norm*) in order to tighten the control over women's morality. *She County Gazetteer* published in the Republican times included an account of a maidservant's suicide for her husband, revealing how "public opinions" had enormous impact on women psychologically and dictated their choice of values. Here is the account:

> Yin Chun married to Zhang. Yin Chun (of the late Ming), a Tandu native, was Huang Shiyao's (a Huizhou merchant) servant. Zhang had been a maidservant from Huang Shiyao's mother's natal family. Ms. Cheng, Huang Shiyao's wife, was familiar with Confucian classics and history. Her mother-in-law used to ask her to tell stories about virtuous women to the whole family. Zhang served and liked to listen to [the stories] without feeling tired. Years later, Yin Chun passed away. Zhang wept and bade farewell to the master with an intention to commit suicide. Wang cried and saw her off by asking, "Do you also want to hand down a good reputation?" Zhang [returned and] closed the door to hang herself. Her family rushed to save her. On the next day, she went to the market to buy arsenic. The trader gave her something else, and therefore she did not die. She thus purchased a coffin and slept inside it. Wang advised, "You can serve me in the rest of your life without hurting your chastity. Why do you rush to die?" Zhang wept and said, "My will could not bend. I have made my decision when I listened to biographies of virtuous women." She thus kept sleeping [in the coffin] and refused to eat until her death.

When "public opinions" were internalized into personal integrity of individuals whose "wills could not bend," Huizhou merchants' families remained stable even though they "sojourned elsewhere for a long time and did not return." In the *Lyrics of Bamboo Shoots of Xin'an*, Fang Shituo, a Huizhou merchant, stated, "The vigorous woman managed the household and I sojourned elsewhere. [I left home when] my hair was black, but [returned when] my hair turned white. Sons and grandsons grew up but did not recognize me. [They] asked where the old guy came from." The customs portrayed in this lyric demonstrated the stability of most Huizhou merchants' families. Restricted by "public opinions," merchants' families stayed stable and sustainable even though they left home and did not return or even died on the foreign soil. Xu Guo once wrote a bibliographic note for Ms. Fang, a virtuous woman, whose husband left hometown forever and died in Guichi only four years after they got married. When her husband passed away, Fang, the virtuous woman, was only 23*sui* with one daughter and one posthumous son. Fang, the virtuous woman, experienced hardships in order to sustain the blood of the Fang family. In the beginning, "her clansmen intended to force her to remarry in order to annex her properties. She brought the posthumous son to hide in her mother house and asked her brother to file a lawsuit to preserve the properties." Later, Fang, the virtuous woman "wove hemp fabrics, raised chicken and pigs, and farmed in the vegetable garden to support herself." She raised up the children and arranged marriages for them. She gathered commercial capital for his son, Fang Shun, to engage in trade. Xu Guo sang high praise of Fang, the virtuous woman:

> Preserving an orphan [who was born] six months [after the father died] and keeping the family running. External troubles hit just like the assault of wind and rain. Though [she was] physically weak and her hair turned white, [she] did not lose what she defended. Alas, how difficult it could be.[33]

From this we can see, Huizhou merchants' activism in compiling genealogies, constructing ancestral halls, and tightening blood ties did not spring from their love of ancestors but due to the realistic necessities.

Third, it was because of the feudal rulers' advocate. The consolidation of the patriarchal clan system gained support from the feudal rulers. Ming and Qing rulers' emphasis on human relations and ethics of the three cardinal guides and the five constant virtues was out of the necessity of strengthening the imperial power. Three cardinal guides was a system. The rationality of "the monarch being the guide to the subject" was built on the rationality of "the father being the guide to the son" and "the husband being the guide to the wife." The suzerainty was an extension to patriarchy. The feudal patriarchal clan system materialized authorities of the father and husband, which became the foundation of the monarchical power. The monarchical power entailed the power of the clan to maintain the rule in local places, while the power of the clan depended on the monarchical power to strengthen the control over clansmen and women. In Huizhou genealogies of the Ming and Qing, there were a large amount of materials regarding the feudal regimes' support of the power of the clan. For example, *Zhushi cizhi* (*Chronicle of the Zhu Clan's Ancestral Hall*) compiled in the Ming included "Xianji gaoshi"

(Announcement Conferred by the County Magistrate). The head of the Zhu clan, Zhu Mingjing and the chief of 21 towns and five *tu* (formerly *li*, an administrative unit with 110 rural households) in She County, Zhu Wenmo, jointly petitioned to ask the county magistrate, "to permit the rules of the ancestral hall to be publicized, the seal to be granted, the official notice to be bestowed, horizontal plaques to be made and hung as a warn against others." On September 18, 1598, the magistrate of She County posted a public notice as follows,

> This notice is for the people of the whole Zhu clan to know. Please observe family regulations. Those who violate the convention and do not observe it will be charged by the local chiefs and heads of the clan to be punished for not being filial. No forgiveness will be given.

The notice was stamped with the seal of the county magistrate. The first chapter of *General Genealogy of the Whole Fang's Clan in She County and Chun'an* was "Xianji yindie" (The Seal and Certificate Bestowed by the Authorities). In order to enhance the authoritativeness of the clan, the Fang clan requested the Huizhou Prefect to "bestow the seal to glorify [the clan] perennially and guard it in all generations." "Every genealogy is granted one seal, which will be respectfully kept and passed down endlessly." The Huizhou Prefect answered the petition and stamped the seal of the government on the genealogy.

The feudal rulers' advocate also took the form of law to transform certain clan regulations and family rules into established institutions. *Jingbiao zhi* (the system of honoring and praising) was one of the examples. Immediately after the founding of the Ming, Zhu Yuanzhang issued an edict,

> In society, a woman who becomes a widow to preserve her chastity for her deceased husband before she is thirty and refuses to lose her chastity after she turns fifty will be bestowed laudatory banners and notices and have them installed in the house. Corvée of her household is exempted.[34]

Qing rulers further stipulated that a widow who preserved her chastity for over six years and then died, an unmarried virtuous woman who stayed in her fiancé's household to preserve chastity and then died of illness, and a woman who struggled against a rapist and committed suicide were all bestowed laudatory banners and had memorial archways installed. Everyone would be given 30 ounces of silver.[35] The practicing of such regulations was found mention in genealogies. For example, volume 6, "Guiwei shude" (Ethical Virtues of Women in the Boudoir), of *Genealogy of the Fang Clan of Qimen* stated,

> [Fang] Dehuang married to Ms. Hu. Child Nurturess became a child bride when she was seven *sui*, and her fiancé died when she was nine. She was famous for her chastity and serving her unmarried in-laws with filial devotion. Her mother-in-law considered that her eldest son died prematurely.

Therefore, she discussed fostering Deqi, a nephew by the male line. Elderly gentlemen were invited to present [the petition] to the official to give [the woman] food so that the chaste woman was settled.

This was a prime example where an unmarried woman who preserved chastity was given accommodations. The confirmation given by the state law to family rules and the monarchical power's support of the clan power, after all, were intended to rationalize the autocratic imperial power.

Women helped promote the development of commodified economy, but the rise of the Huizhou merchant did not afford more opportunities to liberate women. Merchants' needs in their commercial activities and the necessity to stabilize the family when they went out prompted them to provide the consolidation of the patriarchal clan system with more material foundations. The confluence of merchants' needs and the Ming and Qing courts' needs to strengthen the autocratic imperial power coalesced into a patriarchal clan system that oppressed the woman, which was beyond merchants' wives' expectation. Huizhou society was defined by the contradictory mixture of the flourishing of commodified economy and the strengthening of the patriarchal clan system. Under the influence of Huizhou society, what were merchants' wives' fates?

*The mixture of "jealous women being numerous" and "there being the most virtuous and chaste women in Xin'an"*

"Jealous women being numerous," "particularly in Xin'an" hinted at a tendency of women's liberation, as noted earlier. Yet, Zhao Jishi noted, "There were the most virtuous and chaste women in Xin'an, whose number was as large as half of other provinces."[36] This was not an overstatement, either. Let me illustrate the point by using numbers. According to my statistics, "Renwu zhi" (People) of *She County Gazetteer* published in the Republican times contains nine volumes, in which merited officials, loyal Confucians with integrity, talented military men and filial and friendly people, righteous activities, and anecdotes of scholars made up five volumes, while biographies of virtuous women constituted four, almost half of the whole book. The total number of virtuous women far surpassed the number of other figures. The numbers of virtuous women who received official honors are: 2 in the Tang, 5 in the Song, 21 in the Yuan, 710 in the Ming, and 7,098 in the Qing. According to Xu Chengyao, a county gazetteer compiler,

In old gazetteers, as a rule, all honored [virtuous women] were mentioned without any omission. Yet, during the wars in the Xianfeng years, people in She County suffered from terrible calamities. The war flame reduced the communities to rubble. [People] could not find a place to escape in the remote creeks and deep mountains. The whole county lost seventy or eighty percent of the population. Women who unyieldingly preserved their chastity and would rather die than being dishonored were innumerable. Based on

*Liangjiang zhongyi lu* (*Records of the Loyal and Righteous in Jiangsu and Anhui*) and brief information obtained during the interview, [I] keep records to give a generalized account of all other [situations].

During the Xianfeng reign, virtuous women who were honored or not amounted to 7,896. During the Ming and Qing (up to the Xianfeng times), the total number was 8,606. Dong Jiazun once authored *Lidai jielief funü de tongji* (A Statistics of Virtuous and Chaste Women in History)[37] based on *Gujin tushu jicheng* (*The Compendium of Works of Past and Present*). The number of virtuous and chaste women nationwide in the Ming and Qing (up to the late Kangxi years) amounted to 11,529.[38] The number in Dong Jiazun's statistics was not complete. My statistics shows that the number of virtuous and chaste women soared sharply after the Kangxi reign. Let me take the statistics from *She County Gazetteer* to illustrate the variation curve. If the average number of virtuous women who were honored was 1 during the Kangxi reign, the number rose to 3.61 during the Yongzheng reign, 4.16 during the Qianlong reign, and 2.93 during the Jiaqing reign. The number of virtuous women across the country who received honor will be much bigger if the number of women after the Kangxi reign is added. Despite this, the fact that She County alone boasted 8,606 virtuous women is really stunning. In reality, the number in the statistics of Huizhou's virtuous women is still incomplete. The number of virtuous women recorded in various genealogies of clans is more accurate. Among those women, there were women who did not receive honor from the court but only gained recognition from their respective clans. Those who were honored in genealogies had their deeds recorded in chronicles of prefectures or counties. If we make analyses of a great number of biographies of virtuous women, we can clearly see that virtuous women did not enjoy fair and equal chances of receiving honor. Their husbands' power and wealth played a significant role. Ironically, merchants' wives had advantages. They constituted 70% or 80% of virtuous women whose biographies were included in county gazetteers.

*The confluence of the merchant's overflowing lust*
*and the Neo-Confucian's sanctimoniousness*

During the Ming and Qing, Huizhou was called "the hometown of Master Cheng and Master Zhu," "Zoulu (Lands of Confucius and Mencius) in the Southeast," and "the country of rites, music, and ceremony." Neo-Confucianism initiated by Cheng Yi and Zhu Xi permeated in every aspect of social life. Xu Chengyao indicated in his preface to the biography of virtuous women of *She County Gazetteer*, "She County is a mountainous area, [where people] value Neo-Confucianism and adhere to Cheng's and Zhu's theories. Women have gradually been trained. Being upright and chaste, advocating virtues, and promoting good morality become an idiosyncratic custom."[39] The large number of virtuous women in Huizhou resulted from "training" by the Cheng-Zhu Neo-Confucianism. The Cheng-Zhu Neo-Confucianism was also the ideological weaponry to maintain rules of the patriarchal clan. *Family Rites* compiled by Zhu Xi served as the blueprint to "family decrees and regulations" or "clan rules" of various clans in Huizhou. "Xuyan" (Preface) to *Mingzhou Wushi jiadian* (*Family Decrees and Regulations of the Wu Clan in Mingzhou*) compiled in the Yongzheng reign pointed out that the Wu clan's rules "originated from Zhu Xi's family rites and renamed it as family decrees and regulations." In the meantime, the clansmen were required to "read Master Zhu's books, accept Master Zhu's teachings, practice Master Zhu's rites, behave ourselves in ways of Confucius and Mencius, and pass down ways of Confucius and Mencius to the offspring." Huizhou merchants promoted Neo-Confucianism and donated money to set up academies in their native places to serve certain purposes. On the one hand, it fulfilled the merchants' aforementioned two needs. On the other hand, it helped merchants seek refuge with the feudal regime. It merits mentioning that *li* (principle) and *yu* (desire) were opposite to each other in the Cheng-Zhu Neo-Confucianism. Zhu Xi said,

> Humans have the heavenly principle and carnal desires. If one (the heavenly principle) advances, the other (carnal desires) retreats, and vice versa. It is unlikely that the two are in a stalemate with no one advancing nor retreating. If a human being does not advance, he goes back.[40]

Therefore, if one intended to "preserve the heavenly principle," it was necessary to "annihilate human desires." For Huizhou merchants, the opposition of the principle and desires turned into a mutually supportive unity. They applied the "principle" to merchants' wives, clerks, and bondservants, while they preserved "human desires." Therefore, on the one hand, Huizhou boasted "the gathering of abundant talented scholars who achieved magnificent accomplishments and out-of-office Neo-Confucianists who excelled at Confucian classics."[41]"In the land of Zhu Xi's Neo-Confucianism, [people] resist the temptation not to commit mistakes. [That is because] Zhu Xi's teachings have profound impact on people."[42] On the other hand, merchants lavished their desires. In *Five Miscellanies*, it was noted that people from Xin'an "spared no money only in taking concubines, patronizing prostitutes, and engaging in lawsuits." In *Sheshi xiantan* (*Casual Chats about Things in She County*), Wu Tianxing, a Huizhou merchant in the Jiajing reign, "had over one hundred women in his harem." "His contemporaries called [Wu] Tianxing as the master of one hundred concubines." In Yangzhou, because Huizhou merchants patronized prostitutes, the city became "the number one [place] under the heaven for beautiful women."[43] I will not enumerate so many materials in this respect.

*Merchants' wives who were "willing to relocate"*
*and "evil-minded and arrogant"*

There were numerous talented merchants' wives who were good at trading. The aforementioned Mrs. Wang, who once served as the chief of salt traders in Yangzhou, was the exemplary one. Among those women, there were quick-witted young women. For example, Xichi, Wang Daokun's grandson, "married into the

Wu family. [She] authored *Caizaoxuan gao* (*Drafts of Caizaoxuan*). Please refer to Wang Shilu's *Gongwei shiji yiwen kaolue* (*A Brief Examination of Women's Arts and Literary Works*)." Cheng Qiong, whose style name was Feixian and alias Zhuanhua and Wuya jushi, the wife of Wu Zhengsheng from a salt trader's family in Fengxi, "studied poetry. When she was young, she saw Dong Qichang's paintings and calligraphy and was able to understand them quickly. After she grew up, she excelled at calligraphy, painting, and calculating. [Her] comments were insightful, unique, and extraordinary." Talented women recorded in *She County Gazetteer* exemplified by Wang Xichi and Cheng Qiong amounted to 37. The actual number was much larger than this. It merits mentioning that the majority of those women who had displayed their wisdom and talents had left Huizhou and migrated to places for their commercial activities. Keeping themselves away from the stern ancestral halls and the stifling atmosphere of Neo-Confucianism and relocating to commercial metropolises and towns was conducive to the liberation of women and the unleashing of their wisdom and talents. Such a transformation demonstrated commodified economy's impact on Huizhou people's values. Cheng Qieshuo addressed Huizhou customs in *Ruoan ji* (*Anthology of Ruoan*): "Men valued integrity and women admired virtues. Even they died of poverty, they were unwilling to leave their hometowns." This book was written in 1718. In the late Ming and early Qing, Huizhou merchants who traveled across the country did not change their registry. *Jiangdu xian xuzhi* (*Sequel to Gazetteer of Jiangdu County*) compiled in the Jiaqing years pointed that until early Qing, salt traders in Yangzhou, "such as those from the Cheng, Wang, Fang, and Wu families from She County, who sojourned in Yangzhou for generations, but adhered to their original registry, were countless." *Five-color Stone Ester* authored by Chen Qubing, a writer of the modern times, demonstrated the change of Huizhou people's concept of "being unwilling to leave their hometowns" in late Qing. He pointed out, "Yangzhou was a colony of Huizhou merchants. Therefore, [members of] great families such as Wang, Cheng, Jiang, Hong, Pan, Zheng, Huang, and Xu prevailed in Yangzhou probably because they sojourned there and gained registry locally." *She wen* (*Questions on the She County*) written by Hong Yutu asked,

> In the past, [only] merchants [themselves] stayed away from their native places, but nowadays, they bring their wives and sons and leave; In the past, merchants returned home once in several years, but nowadays, they abandon their ancestors' graves and leave; If there are no incentives, why would [merchants] emigrate?

The Japanese scholar Usui Sachiko points out in her essay, "*Huishang jiqi wangluo*" (Huizhou Merchants and Their Network), that Huizhou merchants' "willingness to relocate" was intimately related to the change of market in mid-Qing. Because of the localization of regional market, Huizhou merchants' profit rates in long-distance trade lowered. Consequently, they crowded into the Yangzi Delta and Hankou, where commodified economy fully developed, to settle down.[44] This was the main reason of merchants' "willingness to relocation." However, merchants' wives' will was also a factor that we may not neglect. When they migrated to other places, the stability of Huizhou merchants' families was out of question. The intermarriage between descendants of Huizhou merchants in local places complicated the elements of merchants' wives, which was beneficial to merchants' wives' breaking away from the fetter of the Huizhou tradition. *Five Miscellanies* portrayed behaviors of women from wealthy merchants' households when they married into their husbands' families: "[They] appeared to be so evil-minded and arrogant that they frequently laughed at the poverty of their husbands' households." "[They] never engaged in [activities] to honor parents-in-law, harmonize with sisters-in-law, respect teachers and friends, and show kindness to servants." That showed the instability of feudal morality. Of course, it is inappropriate to overestimate that.

However, in Huizhou until the late Qing, the number of sternly erected chastity archways continued to grow. Huizhou women and most merchants still viewed chastity as the highest values. Wu Pei, a She County merchant,

> prospered by engaging in trade. [He] oftentimes told [her wife] Wang, "My younger brothers are senior licentiates in the imperial academy. In the future, they will bring glory to our family. Yet, I am engaging in trivial businesses. How can I uphold [the family honor] for my ancestors? I am willing to earn profits to contribute to the establishment of the ancestral hall. I will have to complete it." Wang respectfully consented. After a while, the gentleman [Wu Pei] died in Daliang. After conducting a funeral for the gentleman, Wang returned home. [She] pointed at the earth and cried, "You have died. It is not difficult for me to die with you. [However,] you have leave a will behind, but you don't have a son. If I died, how would your [wish] be fulfilled?" Thus, [she] consigned her husband's funds to talented people to ship grains. After several years, [she] accumulated hundreds of [ounces of silver]. Thus, she proceeded to measure the land and check timber in preparation for building the ancestral hall. . . . [When she] used up the hundreds [of ounces of silver], which was not enough, [she] took hairpins, earrings, and suitcases [in exchange for cash] to make it up. It was still not enough. [She] then borrowed money to finish [the project]. [She] boiled and scoured hemp threats and wove fabrics to pay off debts. It took many years before the [ancestral hall] was completed.[45]

The tragedy of Wang, wife of a merchant, was her willingness to carry on her deceased husband's will and try her best to finish something against women's interest. The establishment of the ancestral hall contributed to reinforcing the feudal morality and intensifying the oppression of women. Ms. Wang was so blind that she viewed the toil she experienced as an avenue to realize chastity and therefore never felt bored with it. Some merchants' wives went so far to hurt or mutilate themselves in order to materialize chastity. For example, after Fang Dazhang died in Jiahe when he was apprenticed to a businessman, Ms. Wu, his young wife,

> appeared abnormally sad as the obituary arrived. [She] tried to kill herself for four times, and refused to drink water. [Her] mother-in-law went to persuade

her [to eat] and gave her a spoon. When the mother-in-law returned, [she] threw it on the ground. . . . Then, it was the cold winter. [She] only wore two single-layered clothes and slept on a mat on the ground. No one could stand that. [But she] felt tranquil and settled. . . . [She] stitched a knot in a rope with her husband's hair and said, "this is my husband's remains. If I can be buried with it, my wish is fulfilled." At that time, [she] refused to eat for ten full days, she felt so thirsty that her mouth was filled with [foul] gas. As someone asked her to drink a little water in order to cleanse her stomach, she consoled [her] by saying, "My heart is so clean. How could my breath [be unclean]?"On the fifth day of the month, [she] died as she was sitting. [She] had requested to have her body be clothed in hemp to show that [she was] mourning [her husband].[46]

The genealogy of the Fang clan hailed Ms. Wu as "dying a righteous death calmly." The hypocrisy and cruelty of the feudal Neo-Confucianism were fully illustrated in this comment.

The development of commodified economy presupposed the collapse of natural economy. In Europe, commodified economy tolled the death knell for the medieval times and heralded a new historical age of the liberation of individuals. In China, as soon as the pendulum of commodified economy swung toward the liberation of women, the gravity of history forced it to swing to the opposite direction in order to create a new equilibrium.

## Section two: the merchant, family, and patriarchal clan system

Huizhou communities and its patriarchal clan system in the modern times took shape in a specific geographical and cultural environment in Huizhou. In the process, Huizhou merchants played a significant role. After the structure came into existence, it acted on Huizhou merchants and whole Huizhou society with its particular functions.

### 1 Family and patriarchal clan structures of modern communities

Family is the smallest unit in society, within the limit of organizations of people who live together, share wealth, and eat together. In Ming and Qing Huizhou, different modes of family structure coexisted under the patriarchal clan system. There were largely four types. The first was the "family with the same ancestor" where people lived together for generations. Directed by grandparents, such a family featured several generations under one roof. It congregated many small families in one house, whose members could amount to several hundred. For example, "Longqing sinian xuwen" (Preface Written in 1570) to *Wangshi tongzong shipu* (*General Genealogy of the Whole Wang's Clan*) of Wukou, Wuyuan stated, "People of four generations lived together. Its members amounted to over 320. People began to eat following the drumbeat. This was the peak [of the family]."

According to "Fengchenyuan qing Wangjun shishi" (Account of Mr. Wang, Chief Minister of Imperial Parks Administration) of *Wangshi pucheng* (Genealogy of the Wang Clan) in Qing, Wang Tingzhang, a great salt trader, "had [people of] five generations share the kitchen and no disputes arose." There were two cases in *She County Gazetteer*. Wang Tongbao in Ming, "had men and women of five generations amounting to over one hundred under one roof." In the Qing, Fang Tonglai's "five generations lived together." The "family with the same grandparents" was regarded as complying with the Confucian ethics the most and therefore as the most ideal mode of family. To maintain 100 or even hundreds of family members to live and eat together entailed a solid material base. Only influential officials and great merchants could accomplish it. The aforementioned Mr. Wang had a dual identity of a merchant and an official. He was not only the wealthiest one in Huainan and Huaibei but also possessed a title of Chief Minister of Imperial Parks Administration. The "family with the same ancestor" could rarely be found in Ming and Qing historical materials. The second was the "direct-line family," in which families of the same paternal grandfather merged into one larger family with three generations under the same roof. Sons and grandsons shared registry, living spaces, and wealth. The "direct-line family" featured few variations of generations and was smaller in size compared with the "family with the same ancestor." Therefore, it was easier to maintain. Volume 8, "Yian Xugong xingzhuang" (Biography of Mr. Xu Wencai), of *Xin'an Shebei Xushi dongzhi shipu* (*Genealogy of the East Branch of the Xu Clan in Xin'an and Northern She County*) claimed that Xu Wencai, a Huizhou merchant, "was diligently engaged in business and succeeded to his father. He was more and more assiduous and therefore accumulated an enormous wealth. He shared kitchen with his brother, "[Xu] Chang, without privately taking possession of one penny." Later, because his mother was getting old, "[he] thus returned and built a house in the native place to quit business but focus exclusively on caring his mother." Volume 8, "Renwu – xiaoyou" (People – the Filial and Friendly), of *She County Gazetteer* wrote that Huang Yuanjian, a Huizhou merchant, "did not possess a private wealth, but raised up two brothers, [Huang] Yuanyi and [Huang] Yuanxin, without dividing up the properties." Volume 9, "Biography of Jiang Nanneng, a Ming Gentleman", of *Jiyang Jiangshi zupu* (*Genealogy of the Jiang Clan of Jiyang*) of She County stated that Jiang Nanneng, who traded salt in Huainan, "accumulated a wealth of tens of thousands of ounces of silver. He and his brothers lived together, unwilling to divide up properties." If the number of brothers of the second generation in a "direct-line family" was large, its scale would be vast. For example, Wang Zhide, a Xiuning merchant in the Ming, "led his brothers, and the family had hundreds of members. Peacefully and happily, the family was not troubled by disputes. Therefore, the family became even more prosperous."[47]To maintain a "direct-line family" also required strong financial capability. The aforementioned families all depended on the merchant's capital – for example, "accumulating tens of thousands [ounces of silver]," "accumulating an enormous wealth," and "family becoming even more prosperous" – as the basis of their survival. The third one was the "main-stem family," in which direct relatives constituted the mainstay and its members included a pair of spouses, their parents, and junior or unmarried children, among others. A "main-stem family" differed from a "direct-line family" in whether the second-generation brothers divided up properties and lived separately. Properties that were divided up came from three sources. The first one was those passed down from ancestors. The second one was those established by first-generation members prior to the division of properties. The third one was those established by second-generation members before they lived apart. For example, in 1654, Wang Zhengke, a Xiuning merchant, established *Wangshi jiushu* (*The Wang Family's Agreement of Dividing Up Properties*)[48] to break up the family's properties into five. Such properties included both the legacy he inherited – "lands passed down from the ancestor" – and those he personally earned – "from stores he ran in Jian'ou and Jingdezhen to trade silk." Among the five, one was left for himself "for elderly care." He also made it clear that this one would "be equally divided into three for the three sons." One was for the eldest grandson from the legal wife. The remaining three would be divided up for the three sons. Hence, Wang Zhengke's "direct-line family" split into four core families. If Wang Zhengke and his wives would live with his eldest son, one "main-stem family" and two core families came into being. Volume 6, "Xiangshan Shigong zan" (Eulogy to Mr. Shi, a Charitable Person in Village), of *Xiuning Ximen Wangshi zongpu* (*Genealogy of the Wang Family from Ximen, Xiuning*) noted that Wang Shi, a great salt merchant from Xiuning,

> began to manage household affairs when he was still a boy. [He] traded in Huaihai and made a fortune. [He] shared all the wealth with her brothers without appearing condescending. His mother, née Jin, said, "Ever since the younger brother was a baby until the present day, every penny could be attributed to the eldest brother. [The younger brother] was supposed to give [Wang Shi] one thousand [ounces of silver] before he is given deeds." The gentleman [Wang Shi] insistently rejected [the offer] and eventually divided up the properties. His mother was really old so that the gentleman lived in the chamber for the sons and quit all businesses, but built a study in his chamber.

Wang Shi and his younger brother divided up properties, but "every penny could be attributed to the eldest brother." That is, all properties were earned by Wang Shi through his commercial activities. After breaking up properties and living apart from his brother, Wang Shi and his mother formed a "main-stem family," while his brother claimed independence by living in a core family. The fourth one was the "core family," which included a pair of spouses and their junior or unmarried children or without any children. The "core family" was the smallest unit for relatives sharing wealth and living spaces and the basis of all other types of family.

Judging from the number of all types of family mentioned in documents and literatures, the "main-stem family" and "core family" constituted the majority of families in Huizhou in the Ming and Qing. However, what was their percentage among all types of families? Inside those families, what was the situation of their members' ages, ages of marriage, ages of childbearing, and the composition of generations? To answer those questions, it is not enough to count on ordinary narratives in documents and literatures. It is necessary to make a scientific quantitative analysis of the historical family population to have a firm grip on quantitative characteristics and quantitative relations of the historical family population. A vast number of genealogies were compiled during the Ming and Qing times in Huizhou, in which reliable statistics of the historical population was supplied to offer a premise of a quantitative analysis. Because of the limited manpower, it is impossible to conduct a full-scale statistics for the voluminous genealogies. I adopt an approach of sample survey. To make the statistics more reasonable, I choose several branches of one clan (Fang) in various counties as the object of my investigation. Here are the reasons of my choice. First, to explore the family structure under the patriarch clan system, it is imperative to select the most representative clan in Huizhou. "Xu" (Preface) to *Fangshi zupu* (*Genealogy of the Fang Clan*) printed in 1700 claimed,

> Clans in Xin'an have their members live together. All respectable families and influential clans originated from the Han and the Tang. Ancestors' tombs still exist. [Although] descendants multiply, the offshoots and braches are knowable with investigations. [Our] clan is the most time-honored and influential one across the country.

The first immigratory ancestor of the Fang clan, Fang Hong, served as Defender-in-chief and Aide in the late Han. In order to escape from Wang Mang's usurpation, he relocated from Henan to Dongxiang of She County (it was partitioned to be Chun'an in Sui). Fang Hong's grandson, Fang Chu, was peerless across the country during the Emperor Hedi's reign in the Eastern Han dynasty because of his virtue, integrity, and political discourses. He was posthumously conferred the titles as the Director of the Imperial Secretariat and Marquis of Yi. Therefore, "Xu" (Preface) to *Fangshi zhipu* (*Genealogy of the Sub-clan of Fang*) (printed in 1746) claimed, "Ninety percent of the decedents of our clan originated from Mr. [Fang] Chu, particularly those in Chun'an and She County." *Xin'an dazu zhi* (*Chronicle of Influential Clans in Xin'an*) (printed in 1316) and *Xin'an Xiuning mingzu zhi* (*Chronicle of Famous Clans in Xin'an and Xiuning*) (printed in 1626) both ranked the Fang clan as the second most famous clan in Xin'an. Until the Ming and Qing times, the Fang clan, whose members were scattered in Huizhou and Chun'an, continued to prosper. Second, to make the sample data more inclusionary, I do not select the Fang sub-clan in the narrow Tunxi Basin but other Fang sub-clans whose members lived in vast territories with more mountains than arable lands. Third, lineages and dates of birth and death of hosts of genealogies were complete. The Fang clan featured many sub-clans and genealogies. Not all genealogies are able to supply detailed data of ages.

I select three genealogies of the Fang clan: *Genealogy of Minister Fang's Clan* (Wuyuan, printed in 1905), *Fangshi zongpu* (*Genealogy of the Fang Clan*) (Qimen, printed in 1874), and *Genealogy of the Guilin Fang Clan* (Chun'an, printed in 1906). Wuyuan is situated in southern Huizhou. Qimen is in the west of

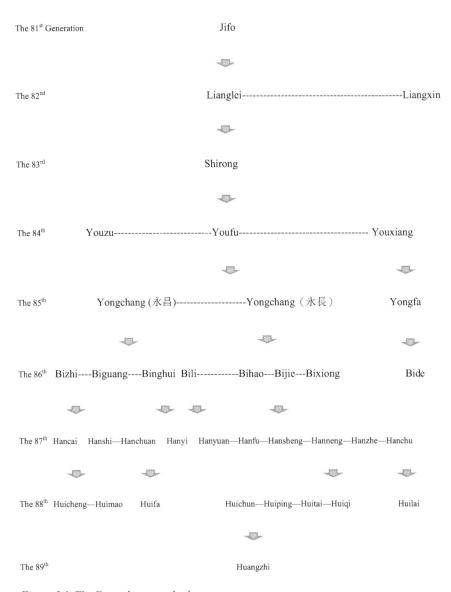

The 81st Generation                        Jifo

The 82nd                    Lianglei-------------------------------------------Liangxin

The 83rd                    Shirong

The 84th      Youzu-------------------------Youfu------------------------------------ Youxiang

The 85th      Yongchang (永昌)--------------------Yongchang（永長）      Yongfa

The 86th  Bizhi----Biguang----Binghui Bili------------Bihao---Bijie---Bixiong      Bide

The 87th  Hancai   Hanshi—Hanchuan   Hanyi   Hanyuan—Hanfu—Hansheng—Hanneng—Hanzhe—Hanchu

The 88th  Huicheng—Huimao   Huifa      Huichun—Huiping—Huitai—Huiqi      Huilai

The 89th                    Huangzhi

*Figure 5.1* The Fang clan genealogies

Huizhou. Chun'an borders on eastern Huizhou. All those three places are mountainous with few arable lands. The three were compiled quite recently. Therefore, all the three contain clear lineages and complete formats. Hosts of genealogies between late Ming and late Qing are given detailed dates of birth and death, which enables to conduct statistics over an extended time span.

The data of the family structure includes the following: population of men and women and the total population, average ages and ages of childbearing of men and women, and the composition of generations. Here take the nine-generation chart of lineage of Fang Jifo, the eighty-first generation of the Fang clan in Wuyuan, as an example (see the attached chart) to illustrate my approach of conducting statistics. The time span between 1635 when Fang Jifo was born and 1905 when Fang Huangzhi, Fang's eighty-ninth generation, was born, was 270 years. Because the ninth generation was just born, this 270 years covered the eight whole generations, with 33 years per generation on average. The total population of the nine generation was 81. If the number of women who married off is deducted, it should be 55 (with 37 men and 18 women). Since the genealogy specifies the dates of their birth and death, I can calculate their ages. Seventeen men had their years of birth and death marked. Their average age was 47.35. Twelve women had their years of birth and death specified. Their average age was 54.16. Women's life span was 6.81 years longer than that of men. Twelve husbands and two wives were older than their spouses, while one pair of spouses were of the same age. On average, husbands were 5.64 years older than wives. The genealogy does not show specific time of wedding, but this could be calculated based on their childbearing ages – the dates of the birth of the eldest sons or daughters minus the dates of the parents' dates of birth. Men's average childbearing age was 34.7, while women's was 27.06, with a difference of 7.7 years. Among 17men under the survey, four gave birth to their first child between ages 20 and 29, nine between ages 30 and 39, and four over age40. Among 15women, one gave birth to their first child between ages 15 and 19, ten between ages 20 and 29, two between ages 30 and 39, and two over age 40. Among all families in those nine generations, 12 people could constitute families with three generations under one roof. High childbearing ages decreased the percentage of three-generation families. Among the 12 families, only three families had three generations under the same roof, two of which had both paternal grandparents and one had only paternal grandfather. They lived with their grandchildren for 9.3 years on average, which was quite short. Based on ages of people of different generations, it was unlikely that a family with four generations could exist in those nine generations. Core families constituted 75%, while main-stem families 25%.

Hereunder, I shall briefly introduce other three lineages and offer a table to illustrate the data. The first one is the lineage Fang Xueliang, the ninth generation of the Qianyuan sub-clan of the Fang clan in Qimen. The lineage included six generations with 27 men. The time span was 157 years between 1705 and 1862. Eight men and seven women had complete records of the dates of their birth and death. Eight families could possibly be three-generation ones. The second one is the lineage of Fang Wenlu, the tenth generation of the Qianyuan sub-clan of the Fang clan in Qimen. The lineage included seven generations with 44 people. As Fang Wenlu's birth and death years are unknown, the statistics starts with the eleventh generation. The timespan was 159 years between 1713 and 1872. Ten men and eight women had complete records of the dates of their birth and death. Seventeen families could possibly be three-generation ones. I select two lineages of the Fang clan in Qimen to conduct statistics for the purpose of verifying the accuracy of the statistical data. The third one is the lineage of Fang Lianggui, the twenty-fifth generation of the Guiling Fang clan in Chun'an. The lineage included 31 people in six generations. The time span was 263 years between 1612 and 1875. Twenty-three men and 12 women had complete records of the dates of their birth and death. Ten families could possibly be three-generation ones. Here, I draw a table of demographic statistics of the four Fang sub-clans as follows:

Based on the quantitative characteristics of the aforementioned family popu-lation, we can make a further analysis of the quantitative relations. To make a more meticulous investigation, I classify the main-stem family into single-core and dual-core types. The single-core family referred to a family of three genera-tions with only one a complete core family in the second generation. The dual-core family referred to a family of three generations, in which two core families in the first and second generations respectively shared wealth and lived together. The average age and age of childbearing in the table show that in Huizhou with more mountainous areas than arable lands, it was difficult to form the "family with the same ancestor." The development of commodified economy also made the "direct-line family" hard to sustain. Although it is hard to differentiate the direct-line and main-stem families in the table of lineage, the percentage of the core family (65.1%) unfailingly indicated that Huizhou's direct line families were undergoing constant fission and in an extremely unstable condition. Under the patriarchal clan system in Huizhou in the Ming and Qing, the main form of the family structure was the core family, with the main-stem one being the secondary. In sum, the family-clan structure tended to be the big clan and small family.

## 2 The merchant's role in the making of the modern communal structure

The family-clan structure in modern Huizhou was a derivative of that in history. Huizhou is an area rife with mountains and hills. "In the chaotic times, the natural barriers of caves, valleys, creeks, and mountains were good to protect people."[49] In late the Han and Eastern Jin, the Southern Dynasties, and the late Tang, a num-ber of influential families and great clans migrated from the Central Plains to Huizhou to escape from wars. They settled down in gentle slopes in the moun-tains and continued to preserve their patriarchal clan organizations. In the closed environment in the mountainous areas, it was not only possible but also necessary to preserve patriarchal clan organizations. In Huizhou, where there were more mountains and fewer lands, only by relying on the collective force of patriarchal clans, could it be possible to strive for and then retain the much needed living space. Therefore, as aristocratic clans stepped down from the stage of history in the late Tang, Huizhou's patriarchal clan organizations were perpetuated. Until the Qing times, it remained the case that "not a handful of earth was removed from a millennium-old grave; a clan with thousands of members did not live apart; and a genealogy of thousands of lineages appeared in a perfect order."[50] However, the family-clan structure in Huizhou was not immutable. After centuries, the size

Table 5.1 Demographic statistics of the four Fang sub-clans

| Lineage | Average Age | | Age Difference between Spouses | Average Age of Childbearing | | The Core Family (%) | The Main-stem Family (%) | The Main-stem Family with Dual Cores (%) |
|---|---|---|---|---|---|---|---|---|
| | m | f | | m | f | | | |
| Fang Jifo of Wuyuan | 47.35 | 54.16 | Men > Women by 5.64 | 34.76 | 27.08 | 74.95 | 8.35 | 16.7 |
| Fang Xueliang of Qimen | 60 | 55.8 | Men > Women by 7.67 | 36.82 | 26.22 | 55.6 | 33.3 | 11.1 |
| Fang Wenlu of Qimen | 54 | 52 | Men > Women by 7 | 30.26 | 24.69 | 80 | 15 | 5 |
| Fang Lianggui of Chun'an | 52.74 | 58 | Men > Women by 11.28 | 36.31 | 24.7 | 50 | 30 | 20 |
| Average Values | 53.5 | 55 | Men > Women by 7.9 | 34.5 | 25.67 | 65.1 | 21.7 | 13.2 |

of patriarchal clans and kinship groups kept growing, while that of the family continuously shrank. The expansion of patriarchal clans was consistent with the natural growth of population. With the growth and migration of population, large clans multiplied into small ones, while small ones were parent clans for the even smaller ones derived from small ones. Clans diffused outward like concentric water waves. The dwindling of family size was a necessary outgrowth of the contradiction of population and land.

Geographical environment was an important factor to restrict the family structure. Volume 2, "Shihuo" (Commerce), of *Gazetteer of Huizhou Prefecture* printed during the Hongzhi reign pointed out, "This prefecture is situated in the mountains, to which boats and carriages could not gain access. Lands are few and population is large." According to a statistics, the average acreage of arable lands per person was 2.2 *mu* in the Wanli years in Ming, 1.9 *mu* in the Kangxi years in Qing, and 1.5 *mu* in the Daoguang times.[51] Based on productivity of the day, an average acreage of 4 *mu* per person was enough for subsistence.[52] Gu Yanwu once indicated that in Huizhou, "the yearly production of [grains] amounted to only ten percent of the food needed."[53] Xu Chengyao also pointed out,

> Our prefecture is situated in mountains. Grains produced yearly could support only one month. Ninety percent [of grains] are shipped from elsewhere, such as Jiangxi and Guangdong, which are thousands of *li* away, and Suzhou and Songjiang, which are hundreds of *li* away. The taxes and brokerage fees paid and transportation costs are equal to the goods shipped. Therefore, the rice price is the highest in Huizhou across the Yangzi Delta.[54]

As the land could not be expanded and the population grew, the family with the same ancestor was unsustainable. In Han, Wei, Jin, Tang, the family structure under the patriarchal clan system mainly took the form of the family with the same ancestor. Some influential families and noble clans existed in the form of the family with the same ancestor. For example, the Bao clan of She County during the Southern Dynasties, "was the richest in the village with their lands in six counties. Ten brothers and over 300 members shared the kitchen. People of the day admired it and called the residence as the Hall of Ten Peace."[55] After the times of the Five Dynasties, with the intensification of the contradiction of population and land, the family with the same ancestor could not be sustained. The rulers' polices was another factor to restrict the family structure. *Tanglü* (the *Tang Law Code*) stipulated, "When grandparents and parents are alive, sons or grandsons are not permitted to live separately and divide up the properties." The Song, Yuan, Ming and Qing dynasties followed the old ruts of the *Tang Law Code* by expressly prohibiting holding registry in non-native places and dividing up properties. After the Five Dynasties, therefore, families under Huizhou clans were usually direct-line and main-stem ones.

In the early modern times (after the sixteenth century), Huizhou's family-clan structure underwent a major transformation, for which Huizhou merchants played a pivotal role.

*Huishang bianlan* (*Guidebook to the Huizhou Merchant*) pointed out,

> Our Huizhou is situated in mountains. The hills are rugged and peaks of mountains set off one another. There are more mountains and fewer lands. . . . Because of the population growth, food produced in Huizhou could not support the population living in the Huizhou area. Therefore, commerce prospers. [Merchants] drive carriages and oxen to engage in trade in distant places. Nowadays, Huizhou merchants have left their footprints across the whole country.[56]

The contradiction between population and land prompted Huizhou people to engage in trade. Trade not only alleviated the contradiction of population and land but also played a significant role in Huizhou society. In terms of its role in affecting Huizhou's family-clan structure, there were mainly three.

### Dispersing population and restraining population growth

In the Ming and Qing, Huizhou people "mostly replaced farming with trade." "In Xindu, seventy or eighty percent of people engaged in trade."[57]"Even in a gentry family, [its members] traveled around to trade."[58] Merchants not only were numerous but also reached a wide range of places. Volume 1, "Fengtu" (Customs), of *She County Gazetteer* stated that Huizhou merchants

> went to places [as far away as] Yunnan, Guizhou, Fujian, Guangdong, Shaanxi, Hebei, Shanxi, and Henan to do business. Huainan, Huaibei, Zhejiang, Hunan, Hubei, and Hankou were nearby places [for Huizhou merchants]. In areas along the Yangzi River, there was a saying: "Without Huizhou merchants, it did not make a town."

"Fengsu" (Customs) of *Xiuning xianzhi* (*Xiuning County Gazetteer*) also said,

> [They] carried money to travel to all metropolises. They transacted goods to make up for what the specific places lacked and observed the harvests to calculate losses and profits. They reached sea islands secretly and went to the desert where people rarely arrived. They left their footprints to half of the country.

Those itinerant Huizhou traders "usually stayed [in other places] and did not return"[59] and became sojourners of areas of their commercial activities. "Customs" of *Gazetteer of Huizhou Prefecture* printed during the Kangxi reign pointed out,

> Rich people from Huizhou relocated their whole families to and settled down in Yizheng, Yangzhou, Suzhou, Songjiang, Huaian, Wuhu, and Hangzhou. Places like Nanchang of Jiangxi, Hankou of Huguang, and Beijing were all

places to which [Huizhou merchants] brought their families. [They] even buried the remains of their grandfathers in other places without feeling regretted.

When a Huizhou person engaged in trade in a certain city, town, market, or fair
and settle down, a large number of his clansmen and townspeople would be
attracted to this place to do business. For example, the Sun clan of Caoshi, Xiuning relocated the whole clan to Wuxing to engage in trade. Volume 50, "Ming
gu Libu rushi Sunchangjun muzhiming" (Epitaph of Sun Changjun, a Confucian
Scholar of the former Ministry of Rites of Ming), of *Anthology of Taihan* noted,

> Caoshi was in the east of Haiyang and bordered on She County. Clansmen
> lived close to each other, with the west being the most prosperous. . . . The
> whole clan was brought to Wuxing to engage in trade. Thus, a great wealth
> was accumulated.

The Wang clan, "an influential clan in Hongcun" of Yi County, "had a lot of
members trading in Hangzhou and Shaoxing of Zhejiang."[60] Thus, we understand
that Huizhou merchants' commercial activities were not an action of individuals or individual families. The linkage of townspeople and clansmen enabled the
snowballing of businessmen, leading to an ever increase of Huizhou people living
away from their native places. "Ninety percent of registered people in Linqing,
Shandong were Huizhou people."[61] In Huangpi, Hubei, "half of the population
in town were Huizhou people."[62] Quanzhou of Fujian "was full of Huizhou people."[63] Thus, a monopoly of local commerce was established. Meanwhile, an
immense portion of Huizhou population was dispersed to alleviate the contradiction between population and land.

Engaging in trade also helped to restrain population growth. The statistics
shown here demonstrates that the age of childbearing in most areas of Huizhou
was relatively high so that the birth rate lowered considerably. High childbearing
ages and the composition of generations in families were intimately associated
with each other. Maintaining high childbearing ages contributed to eliminating
the three-generation family or at the least keeping it in a relatively short time
span. Fang Lianggui's lineage in *Genealogy of the Guilin Fang Clan* included
five dual-core main-stem and single-core main-stem families. Yet, the time spans
of the three generations living together were all very short. In one family, the first
and third generations lived together for only five months. The longest time span
was seven years. Most families were core families. What was the relationship
between merchants and high childbearing age in the Huizhou area? In the Ming
and Qing times, Huizhou people did not necessarily get married late. *Guangzhi yi*
(*Interpretation to the Travel of the Broad Territory*) noted,

> The custom in Sichuan was to arrange marriages for the boys to marry older
> women. A boy could get married when he was twelve or thirteen *sui*. The
> custom in Huizhou was similar. Yet, Huizhou people engaged in trade. After

the weddings, they traveled across the country. It was hard to understand the custom in Sichuan.

It is fair to say that Huizhou people did not have the custom of marrying older brides. The statistics shows that between Huizhou spouses, the husband was 7.9 years older than the wife on average. However, Huizhou people did get married early. Generally speaking, men had already been engaged or married before they went out to do business. "The Huizhou custom was that a man went out to engage in trade when he was sixteen *sui*."[64] In reality, only a minority of people were mature enough to be able to give birth to children before 16. Once Huizhou merchants went out to do business, it would be extremely difficult for them to return to home and visit their kin. The author of *Guidebook to the Huizhou Merchant* bemoaned,

> There was an old practice for Huizhou merchants to return home once in three years. People residing in a place far away from home depended on this practice [to go back home regularly]. However, our Huizhou [is troubled by] inaccessible roads and inconvenient transportations. . . . It is never an easy matter to travel [between home and other places]. [Although there was a rule] of returning to home once in every three years as noted above, there were merchants who failed to return after three years.

Wei Xi of the Qing also pointed out,

> Huizhou is the richest place in the Yangzi Delta area. However, it has a large population and small lands. Therefore, half of the people travel across the country to engage in trade. Huizhou natives could get married and then leave home without having a chance to return in ten, twenty, or thirty years. When they return, their grandson has been married or their sons do not know them.[65]

Even worse, there were cases that after spouses got married, they would never meet again. Wang Yuding remarked in *Xin'an nüshi zheng* (Biographies of Talented Women in Xin'an),

> In my village, there was a man who traveled to a distant place to engage in trade three months after he got married. His wife lived on embroidery. Each year, she exchanged profits for a pearl to mark the time and called it a "pearl of tears." When the husband returned, the wife died three years before. When [the husband] opened the case, [the wife] had gathered over twenty pearls.

Why did Huizhou merchants find it hard to go back home? Aside from aforementioned factors such as inaccessible roads, a more serious problem was the hardship in trade. Wang Daokun said, "Seventy percent of families in our native place (She County) engaged in trade, [but only] thirty percent could make profits."[66]This was an objective observation. Forty percent of merchants – or the majority – failed in their businesses. The fate of losers was miserable. The Huizhou merchants Cheng Zaishi brothers "carried an enormous wealth to Liaoyang to conduct business. Several years later, their investments failed, and [they] bounced around for several years before their money was exhausted."

> As the Cheng brothers' [businesses] sank, [they] felt extremely ashamed and embarrassed and lost hope of returning to their hometown. Thus, [they] were hired by other merchants as clerks to make a living. Their houses were next to each other. Greatly depressed and indignant, [they] could hardly live.[67]

Such losers "who lost hope of returning to their hometown" were numerous. Wu Gang, a Xiuning merchant during the Longqing times, "parted ways with his wife to trade paper in western Hunan and Hubei," "before he was transferred to Jiangxi." "[He] later engaged in trade in Guanzhong. Losing money in most of the time, he lost communications with [his family]."[68] Volume 8, "Biographies: Filial Sons and Loyal Friends," of *She County Gazetteer* contained a number of cases about filial sons trudging thousands of miles to look for their fathers, who had failed in their businesses and long lost communications with their families. Some could only "find remains." Countless people "parted ways with their newly wed wives" to go out to do business, did not have children, and eventually died in a place far away from their hometowns. In places where Huizhou merchants got together, there were usually charitable cemeteries. For example, Zhu Changxiao of Wuyuan

> set up native banks in Deshan, Hunan, which was the only way which Huizhou timber merchants and thousands of rafters passed. Some died there, but had to have their corpses wrapped with straw mats to be buried in rented places. Some bodies were even abandoned in the wild. [Zhu Chang]xiao tabled a proposal by donating money to buy Shanyiju as the charitable cemetery, in which a hall called "Duyi" (Profound Comradeship) was constructed. Stones were erected to mark, in great detail, the coffins with names, awaiting the transportation of the bodies back to the hometown for burial. People who maintained the cemetery were also appointed for tomb sweeping in Qingming.[69]

Jin Zhao of Wuyuan, "who trade timber in Jinling, used to donate money to set up a charitable cemetery to pacify his traveling townspeople."[70] By contrast, there were a large number of entries of people in genealogies with neither birth nor death years or with birth years but no death years. For example, in five generations of Fang Xueliang lineage of the Qianyuan sub-clan of the Fang clan, 46.7% of the people did not carry neither birth nor death years or only carried birth years but not death years. The percentage in the Fang Wenlu's lineage was also as high as 41.46%. Various clans placed a great emphasis on compiling genealogies, which they believed to be comparable with "writing history for a nation." "Guide" to *Genealogy of the Fang Clan* included an entry of "Xiang shengzu" (Detailed Account on Birth and Death Time):

> Birthdays of grandparents should be recorded in great detail for their grand-children to know and fulfill their filial duty by offering sacrifice. If the dates are unknown, they could be made up after investigations. If they could not be investigated, "Unknown" will be directly marked.

A mistaken record of the people's birth and death years was a total disrespect to the ancestors. Therefore, marking "Unknown" was better than making up the time. *Genealogy of the Fang Clan* was compiled in 1874 with most of the figures being people of the modern times. The fact that the years of their birth and death remained unknown indicated that they left their hometown and disappeared. Even though I do not have adequate materials to explain their reasons of leaving the hometown, in Huizhou, where 70%or 80% of the people went out and traded, it is only reasonable to surmise that many were unsuccessful merchants. Interestingly enough, the percentage of those whose birth and death years were unclear and those whose birth years were known, but death years unknown was similar to that of merchants who failed in their businesses – namely, 40% – as Wang Daokun had pointed out.

In sum, the reasons of Huizhou merchants' high ages of childbearing included going out and engaging in trade early, a custom of returning to family once in three years, and being too ashamed to return to the hometown because of failed businesses or even death in places other than the hometown.

### *The development of commerce that effected changes to the family*

In 调和 mid-Ming, with the development of commodified economy, social customs in Huizhou underwent dramatic changes. *She County Gazetteer* printed in Wanli stated, "Prior to Chenghua and Hongzhi reigns, people were simple, in no need of extravagancy, preferred a retiring lifestyle, valued their hometowns, diligently engaged in farming, were honest and unwilling to strive for profits, and placed an emphasis on frugality." Such a scene of pastoral life in the middle ages "became a little bit different" in the late Zhengde and early Jiajing times. During the Wanli reign, things "became entirely different." In eight decades between the 1520s and the late sixteenth century, the relations of commodities and currencies demised the traditional interpersonal relations and big-family structure, leading to "the lack of equilibrium between the high and the low, [people's] struggling for money, [people's] predating on each other, and [people's] falling into a flut-ter." "[People] disputed over trade in relentless pursuit of profits. Vicious-minded tyrannies transformed and messed up [society], and the extremely sly people appropriated wealth." "The gold commander ruled the heaven and the money god administered the earth. [People] were extremely greedy and engaged in fratricidal fighting." The phenomena of rampant mutual predation and fratricidal fighting could not be found in genealogies whose authors usually avoided mentioning people's wrongdoings to show respect to seniors. Yet, some messages were delivered in exhortations for the clansmen. "Guide" to *Genealogy of the Fang Clan* included two entries, "Being friendly to siblings" and "Fulfilling father's duties":

> Brothers are like arms and legs. Please don't damage the relationship to unsettle your parents. Conflicts among brothers spring from two factors: believing in wives or relentlessly pursuing money. As the idea of struggling for money arises, it can lead to total failure. If only wives' opinions are adopted, brothers will be alienated. This is the unluckiest thing in a family. Now, brothers of our clan should value fraternity and emulate saints in the ancient times to surrender dates and pears to [brothers] not to provoke disputes and become a laughingstock of other people.
>
> Those who undertake fathers' duties to manage the family affair can be either the eldest sons of the legal wives or sons of concubines, as long as they are virtuous and talented. Each day, [they] should be selfless and cautious about incomings and outgoings of money and grains. When keeping accounts, [they] should avoid being selfish and not fake entries of additions and deductions in the account books to cheat fathers and brothers. It is particularly disallowed to use inconsistent measuring apparatuses to [deceive others and] hurt the hidden virtue. A violator, once revealed, would involve his whole family in penalty. Even if the misconduct is not revealed, how could the heaven, the earth, ghosts, and deities be duped?

The statement in the "Guide" demonstrated that under commodified economy, fratricidal fighting was universal, and the righteous conduct of surrendering dates and pears to brothers in the ancient times became rare. "Scrambling for properties leading to disputes" among brothers and "all being attentive to personal gains" made it hard to maintain the direct-line family whose members lived together and shared wealth. The family structure underwent constant fission.

It is true that there were a large number of rich and influential merchants with enormous wealth in Huizhou in the Ming and Qing. They were capable of maintaining a family with the same ancestor. With a pervasive ethos of "being extremely avaricious and brothers cruelly injuring each other," it was unavoidable that some members of great families "indulged themselves in the pursuit of wealth" and "harbored an intention to scramble for properties" to bring "disasters of fall and demise [of the family]." Yu Yue told of Mr. Xu's dividing up his properties and distributing them in his *Youtai xianguan biji* (*Notes of Youtai xianguan*), which was precisely about the fall of an influential family. Mr. Xu was the household head of four families of the Shangyi Hall of the Xu clan in She County. "In the past, his family was extremely rich with over forty pawn shops in Jiangsu and Zhejiang. It was still the case in Mr. Xu's times."

> Among the family members, there were a few of them who were happy with their luxurious lives. [They] drank wine and ate meat better than those

consumed by princes and dukes. Hundreds of servants were hired, and scores of horses were raised. . . . They showed off [their luxurious lives] in the countryside. One day, an official document from the prefectural government was suddenly delivered. The prefect intended to arrest and interrogate them for their overbearing behaviors. [The family] began to feel afraid and bribed [officials] to avoid punishment. The cost was so high that [the government] no longer intervened in [the family]. Those family members traveled to Jiangsu and Zhejiang. [They were willing] to go to shops run by their families, no matter how far they were. Each day, [they] delivered pieces of paper to the shops in exchange for money and never felt satiated. If shop managers came to stop them [from taking money], [they] would angrily said, "It belongs to our family. It's none of your business."[Some] brought their favorite prostitutes to the shops to take whatever they liked.

Mr. Xu considered that he was unable to control those family members. Therefore, he decided to shut down all shops and paid dismissal wages for 2,000 or 3,000 clerks. As a result, "Mr. Xu exhausted his wealth. The accumulated wealth of more than ten generations worth millions of [ounces of silver] evaporated overnight, which was really stunning." Because of this, Huizhou merchants tended to divide up properties and live apart as soon as brothers grew up or the population of a family increased. There were a lot of records about brother's dividing up properties. For example, Wang Yingheng, a great salt trader, "prioritized his brothers over himself when his father ordered to divide up properties."[71] Wang Fangxi of Wuyuan"engaged in trading salt in Zhejiang. When his father was old and brothers too young, he traded for a decade and thereby accumulated an enormous wealth. [He] divided up wealth with his brothers without possessing his private wealth."[72] Lawsuits arose because of disputes over brother's dividing up properties. During the Wanli reign, for example, the great salt traders Wu Yangchun brothers filed a lawsuit fighting for 2,400 *mu* of lands in Huangshan when they divided up properties. During the Tianqi reign, Wu Zhongxian capitalized on the old Huangshan case to make multiple arrests and extorted huge amounts of money to finance his own projects. Wu Yangchun, his father, and his brother all died in prison.[73] Unfairly dividing up properties could lead to lawsuits. From this we can see that it was hard for brothers who lived together to "avoid being selfish and not [to] fake entries of additions and deductions [in the account books] to cheat fathers and brothers."

Dividing up properties and living apart contributed to not only reducing intrafamily conflicts but also improving business administration. After dividing up properties and living separately, brothers engaged in trade independently so that they could be maximally motivated. There were cases where brothers, after dividing up properties, chose to engage in trade jointly. Dong Kuizhao from Wuyuan, for example, "divided up properties and lived separately with his brother. Then, he and his brother invested in a joint-capital timber firm in Suzhou."[74] The Gao Yingpeng brothers from She County "gathered thousands [of ounces of silver] to engage in trade."[75] As brothers became cooperative shareholders, they clarified rights and obligations and took their respective responsibilities. For example, Wang Fuxian, a Xiuning native,

> traded salt in the Yangzi and Huai Rivers with thousands of ships. [He] led his clansmen to travel around to do business as if [he] walked upon flat ground. [He] always made right decisions in choosing right personnel and timing. His wealth reached tens of thousands [ounces of silver]. . . . Those who knew him said that [he] understood the way of becoming rich.[76]

Here, "choosing right personnel and timing" should be pivotal to Wang Fuxian's way of becoming prosperous. In reality, the ways of becoming rich adopted by Dong Kuizhao and Wang Fuxian were essentially the same – namely, converting the relationships between brothers or among family members into a commercial partnership or the relationship between owners and clerks – to avoid conflicts arisen from unequal labor inputs and distribution of benefits in big families. Hence, the shrinkage of the family size was a necessary outcome of the development of commodified economy.

### Enlarge and consolidate kinship groups

The Huizhou merchant's capital, on the one hand, demised the big-family structure. On the other hand, it consolidated and enlarged kinship groups tied by blood. Huizhou merchants' commercial activities were closely related to the patriarchal clan forces. The rise of Huizhou merchants could be attributed to the patriarchal clan forces, while Huizhou merchants' further development in commercial competitions particularly depended on the patriarchal clan forces. They counted on patriarchal clan forces to establish commercial monopoly to participate in commercial competitions, control commercial partners and clerks, seek refuge with the feudal regimes, found Huizhou *huiguan*, and so forth. When patriarchal clan forces promoted the development of Huizhou merchants, Huizhou merchants in turn reinforced patriarchal clan organizations. Apart from investing in the construction of ancestral halls, purchasing fields for sacrifice, and compiling genealogies to spiritually strengthen the kinship tie within the clan through respecting the ancestors, merchants expended enormous amounts of money to buy properties for the clan to provide a material base for clan to live together. Lands purchased by Huizhou merchants were categorized as public properties of the clan, whose land rents were used to benefit the whole clan and relieve the needy. For example, *Tangyue Baoshi Xuanzhong zhipu* (*Genealogy of the Xuanzhong Hall Sub-clan of the Bao Clan in Tangyue*) of She County recorded, Bao Zhidao and his son, Bao Shufang, both serving as the chief of salt merchants in Huainan and Huaibei during the Qianlong and Jiaqing reigns, and other salt merchants sojourning in Yangzhou collectively bought over 2,000 *mu* of lands for the clan, from which a rent of over 30,000 *dou* of grains could be received. The income was used to "help widowers and widows, raise up orphans, relieve the poor, and make up for whoever was in need" within the clan. Such records of "buying righteous lands," "donating properties for ancestral halls," "establishing family shrines" were numerous in gazetteers and genealogies in Huizhou during the Ming and Qing times. Huizhou merchant's capital was continuously and steadily injected to patriarchal clans to not only strengthen but also enlarge the kinship groups. For example, the Fang clan living in Wuyuan could be traced back to Fang Qi, the clan's immigratory ancestor who migrated Wuyuan in Tang. Fang Qi graduated from the Civil Service Exam by passing the test of Confucian classics. He was at first appointed as the minister and later switched to be the prefect of Wuyuan so that he settled down in Qinghua of Wuyuan. Afterwards, his descendants "moved out and scattered like stars." After a long while, a number of minor clans, sub-clans, and family systems were derived in the times after Emperor Taizong's reign in the Tang. As they "emigrated [, they] usually lost communications with each other." It was not until the sixth month of 1560 that representatives of those minor clans, sub-clans, and families received sponsorship of Huizhou merchants to convene in Qinghua, where their immigratory ancestor had lived, and to compile genealogies of all minor clans and sub-clans. "Preface" to *Genealogy of Minister Fang's Clan* therefore stated emotionally, "After six centuries [when all clansmen were] lonely, the present day witnesses the great event of recompiling genealogies together." Later, also because of Huizhou merchants' investment, *Genealogy of Minister Fang's Clan* was recompiled for three times in 1744, 1812, and 1905. In this manner, the Fang clan, who had migrated to Wuyuan, was linked under the memorial tablet of their ancestor. The patriarchal clan expanded and consolidated.

Certainly, the strengthening and expansion of the patriarchal clan were enabled because of not only Huizhou merchants' sponsorship but also other factors such as governmental policies. Before Ming and Qing, sacrifice was offered to up to the great-great-grandfather. Therefore, the kinship relationship was limited to within four generations. In mid-Ming, the government permitted the people to worship their immigratory ancestors to pave the way for the enlargement of kinship groups. In addition, as the "Zou and Lu in the Southeast," Huizhou boasted a deep-rooted tradition of Confucian culture and Neo-Confucianism established in Song and Ming, which provided the strengthening of the patriarchal clan with a moral basis.

In sum, Huizhou merchants played a significant role in the making of the family-clan structure in Huizhou in the Ming and Qing.

## 3 The counteraction of the communal structure

Huizhou families in the Ming and Qing were principally core and main-stem families. Generally speaking, the core family would lead to the liberation of the woman, the liberalization of the youth, the alienation of the kinship, and the decline of Confucian morality. However, those did not happen in Huizhou, because of the existence of a big clan above the small family. How did the family-clan structure counteract on Huizhou's society and economy? First, it made Huizhou's social structure more resilient and mobile. The family-clan structure stratified social properties into two layers: properties of the clan and properties of the family. Properties of the clan referred to private properties whose ownership was all members of the clan. Properties of the family were private properties whose ownership was all members of the family. As properties of the clan were properties collectively owned by clansmen, family properties were private properties owned by individual families. From the perspective of family members, family properties were collectively owned by the family sharing wealth and living spaces. The family's collectively owned properties were infinitely divided because of brothers' dividing up properties and living separately, whereas collectively owned properties of the clan transcended the infinitely split families and kept enlarging. The infinite split of family properties reduced conflicts among family members, while the enlargement of the clan properties minimized clashes among clansmen caused by the polarization between the rich and the poor inside the clan. Righteous lands were set up so that the poor would not die of starvation in the wild because of the patronage of Huizhou merchants. Such a resilient structure enhanced Huizhou society's stability. Huizhou's family-clan structure was also mobile. The contradiction between population and lands compelled small families that were under big clans to keep migrating. Small families' migration was conducted in lineages and was supported by big clans. As soon as they arrived in a new place, they rebuilt new patriarchal clan organizations modeled after big clans and maintained contacts with original clans. In the Ming and Qing, Huizhou population moved continually from river valleys and basins, where the population density was high, to sparsely populated hills and mountains, which was an indication of such mobility. The mobility of the family-clan structure also manifested itself in the dispersal of population through the channel of merchants' going out and engaging in trade under the auspice of their clans. Hu Shi once pointed out that in his hometown, Shangzhuang of Jixi, there were "eight hundred [members of the Hu clan] at home and four hundred staying outside. The total number was over 1,200." One third of the whole population went out to trade. Hu Shi further noted, "The total [agricultural] production of the whole clan amounted to over 5,000 ounces of silver, but the expenditure on opium was 7,200 ounces."[77] Since revenues from farming could not match the expenditure on opium, the whole clan depended on merchants' commercial profits to provide for families. In this sense, mobility reinforced the stability of Huizhou society.

Second, as the first section and Chapter 3 shows, it was beneficial to Huizhou merchants' commercial activities.

Third, it led to the thriving of Confucian teachings. The family-clan structure was intimately related to Confucianism. First of all, the Confucian morality was the basis on which the family-clan stratum was maintained. Clan rules and household regulations stressed such Confucian teachings as respecting the ancestors, valuing rituals, serving parents with filial devotion, differentiating hierarchy based on age, harmonizing brothers, educating young generations, hierarchizing husbands and wives, promoting frugality, and advocating chastity as a way of disciplining clansmen's behaviors. Second, upholding Confucian culture was a vital means of prospering the family-clan. *Family Code of the Wu Clan from Mingzhou* claimed,

> Young people from the clan with unusual deportment and deep wisdom but incapable of receiving education should be recruited and taught. They could be either taught in the clan's school or given subsidies. If one talent or two are cultivated, they could be the paragons of the future [generations]. This is the hope of our clan and the glory of the ancestors, which is of great relevance.

Clansmen who graduated from the Civil Service Exam could "widen the gate of [the clan]," "elevate [the status] of ancestors," and glorify the clan to heighten the standing of the family-clan in Huizhou. Clansmen's earning degrees through the Civil Service Exam also benefited Huizhou merchants' cooperation with the feudal regimes by enjoying the privilege as official-merchants. Therefore, they did not spare money to promote education and culture. The flourishing of Confucianism, the high status of influential families and great clan, and the property of Huizhou merchants constituted a causal chain.

Fourth, the Huizhou family-clan structure intensified the oppression of servants and women. It had been a common practice in Huizhou to discriminate against and prosecute servants. "Customs" of *Gazetteer of Huizhou Prefecture* noted, "The differentiation of the master and the servant is particularly strict. Even though a servant accumulates an enormous wealth, he is still despised in the clan and village." The Kangxi edition of the gazetteer added an annotation: "It is still a custom nowadays. If the differentiation of the master and the servant is slightly confused, everyone, every family, every clan, and even the nation strive for clarifying it, until it is corrected." The opposition between clans and servants concealed the polarization of the wealthy and the poor and the class conflict among small families within clans. Therefore, Huizhou was troubled more by servants' resistance than peasants' uprisings in the Ming and Qing. As for the oppression of women, please see the first section of this chapter. In a sense, the family-clan structure in Huizhou was built at the cost of lives of women and servants.

In comparison, the family structure in Huizhou society in the Ming and Qing bore resemblance to that in West Europe and Central Europe. Because of the contradiction of lands and population, "in large regions of Western and Central Europe families of three generations were avoided, or at least restricted to a relatively short phase."[78] The core family dominated. The difference between the two areas was that small families in West Europe and Central Europe were independent, whereas in Huizhou, above small families there were big clans. Such a difference resulted in different social functions performed by those small families. The intensification of the family structure in West Europe and Central Europe was consistent with the modernization of European society, whereas the Huizhou family-clan structure contributed to reinforcing the traditional political order with its resilience and inclusiveness.

## Section three: the merchant and the expansion of the living space of communities

"Customs" of *Gazetteer of Huizhou Prefecture* printed in the Hongzhi times claimed, "Our prefecture is situated in the mountains, inaccessible by boats and carriages."

Therefore, in the early sixteenth century, the Huizhou community was faced with a glaring contradiction of "few lands and a large population." According to a statistic, in 272 years between 1579 and 1850, the population in this area grew from 1.2 million to 2 million with a net increase of 800,000, with an annual increase of 2,941 people or 0.19%. The contradiction of population and lands ran through the whole process of modern society. Quite a few researchers have pointed out that between the sixteenth and nineteenth centuries, "as Huizhou merchants gained a national reputation, they massively emigrated to other places."[79] Such emigration alleviated the tension of population and lands in Huizhou. However, this was just one side of the issue. The other side was: how did the surplus 800,000 people expand their living space? What roles did Huizhou merchants play in expanding the living space for their hometowns? This is no easy question, as it is related to historical geography and historical demography. Huizhou was a rural community. The main places of gathering for local residents are villages. The indicators of the expanded living space of the Huizhou community were chiefly the increase of the number of villages and some related activities such as intra-community migration and the development of mountainous areas. We adopt sociological approaches to carry out a microscopic exploration of the historical geography and historical demography of the Huizhou community[80] in order to further investigate the inherent relationship between the merchant and the expansion of living space for the survival of the community.

### 1 The merchant and the transformation of villages and communities

It merits mentioning that we select three counties, She, Xiuning, and Jixi, within the Huizhou community as the subject of study, for the convenience of our statistics. The three counties constituted a relatively independent eco-geographical zone. The Xin'an River system linked them to Zhejiang Province. The other three counties were more closely related to Jiangxi Province for geographical reasons.

Villages in the three Huizhou counties underwent drastic changes in the modern times. Because of the turmoil in the Ming-Qing transition and other political, economic, war factors, only a few villages were able retain their prosperity, while a vast number of them were reduced to rubble. Certainly, new villages emerged. The total number of those villages was enormous. In about 400 years between 1551 (during the Ming times) and 1937 (the Republican times), 1,134 villages emerged. The numbers of villages emerged in Xiuning and Jixi between the Ming and late Qing were 524 and 439, respectively. It is difficult to trace the origins of those villages and ascertain their geographical locations. I take *du* (district) as the unit to investigate all villages in the three counties. My research is based on the information from *Chronicle of Influential Clans in Xin'an* of Ming (1551), *Gazetteer of Huizhou Prefecture* printed during the Kangxi reign (1699), *Gazetteer of Huizhou Prefecture* printed during the Daoguang reign (1827), and *She County Gazetteer* of the Republican times (1937). I choose villages recorded in *Chronicle of Influential Clans in Xin'an* because places where influential clans gathered together were relatively stable. They lasted for several generations until the Qing times. Therefore, it is easy to look them up. *Chronicle of Influential Clans in Xin'an* enumerated 151 villages in She County in Ming, among which 94 (62%) still existed during the Kangxi times. The percentages of villages in Xiuning and Jixi recorded in *Chronicle of Influential Clans in Xin'an* still existing during the Kangxi reign also reached 60 and 82 respectively.

There were 37 *du* in She County, 33 in Xiuning, and 15 in Jixi, making a total number of 85. When we investigate names of villages under individual *du*, we make the "Table of Studying Names of Villages in Various *Du* in the Past Four Centuries." When studying names of villages under those *du*, it is necessary to give some notes as follows: (1) The administrative zones of *du* changed historically. Some villages, which had belonged to certain *du* could be assigned to other *du* later. (2) Some villages disappeared from the map. In She County in the past 400 years, 1,134 village names appeared. In 1937, there were 873 villages, and 261 disappeared at certain points of history, constituting 23% of the total number. (3) Names could change. Generally speaking, there were five types of change: first, homonym such as Chengcun (程村)/Chengcun (呈村), Yeqi (葉祈)/Yeqi (葉圻), Tingzishan (亭子山)/Tengzishen (藤子山)/Tengzishan (騰子山), and Zikeng (紫坑)/Zikeng (子坑)/Zikeng (梓坑); second, adding or deducting characters such as Aitou (堨頭)/Fengaitou (豐堨頭), Zhuwu (竹塢)/Zhuxiangwu (竹祥塢), Zhangjiatan (張家潭)/Zhangtan (張潭), Huangsi (黃寺)/Huangkengsi (黃坑寺), and Zhuguo (鑄鍋)/Zhuguo huangcun (鑄鍋黃村); third, combining or taking apart villages such as Fenghuang (鳳凰)/Eastern Fenghuang and Western Fenghuang, Paitou (牌頭)/Upper Paitou, Central Paitou, and Lower Paitou, and Daxi (大溪) and Xiaoxi (小溪)/Daxi (大溪); fourth, change of meaning such as Niwo (泥窩)/Yinwo (銀窩) and Shihuikeng (石灰坑)/ Huikeng (暉坑); fifth, irregular change such as Maojiatan (毛家坦)/Mugangtan (木岡坦), Hongtang (洪塘)/Hengtang (橫塘), Jinguoling (金鍋嶺)/Lengtangling (棱唐嶺), and Yunwuchuan (雲霧川)/Wumengkeng (烏蒙坑). (4) There were erroneous village names recorded in various genealogies. In some cases, both the name of a village and names of places under the village were listed as village names. In other cases, the name of a *xiang*, a *li*, a bridge, a temple, or a pond was confused with the name of the village. We try our best to correct those errors.

To study ten types of transformation among 1,134 villages under 37 *du* in She County in the past 400 years, 524 villages under 33 *du* in Xiuning County in the past three centuries, and 439 villages under 15 *du* in Jixi County in the past 300 years, I make the following table. "–" is used to indicate that the villages had disappeared, while "✓ a checkmark to indicate their existence. "Total" means the total number of villages in each time period (see Table 5.2).

*Table 5.2* The transformation of villages in the three Huizhou counties in the modern times

| Category | Year | 1551 | 1699 | 1827 | 1937 | |
|---|---|---|---|---|---|---|
| 1 | | 57 | – | – | – | She County |
| 2 | | 5 | ✓ | – | – | |
| 3 | | 10 | ✓ | ✓ | – | |
| 4 | | 79 | ✓ | ✓ | ✓ | |
| 5 | | – | 20 | – | – | |
| 6 | | – | 23 | ✓ | – | |
| 7 | | – | 142 | ✓ | ✓ | |
| 8 | | – | – | 146 | – | |
| 9 | | – | – | 231 | ✓ | |
| 10 | | – | – | – | 421 | |
| total | | 151 | 279 | 631 | 873 | |
| 1 | | 61 | – | – | | Xiuning |
| 2 | | 90 | ✓ | ✓ | | |
| 3 | | – | 2 | – | | |
| 4 | | – | 130 | ✓ | | |
| 5 | | – | – | 241 | | |
| total | | 151 | 222 | 463 | | |
| 1 | | 5 | – | – | | Jixi |
| 2 | | 1 | ✓ | – | | |
| 3 | | 22 | ✓ | ✓ | | |
| 4 | | – | 72 | – | | |
| 5 | | – | 138 | ✓ | | |
| 6 | | – | – | 201 | | |
| Total | | 28 | 210 | 361 | | |

The table gives an overview of the transformation of villages in Huizhou Prefecture. Synthesizing the data of the transformation of villages of the three counties and making comparisons and analyses of it as a whole help us examine different trajectories of social development of the three counties in the Ming and Qing times.

The data of statistics in the table at least illustrate two points: first, the starting points of the three counties' development were different in the mid- and late Ming. *Chronicle of Influential Clans in Xin'an* included 216 entries of influential clans in She County, who lived together in 164 places, among which 17 were towns and 151 were villages. There were 237 entries about Xiuning, whose influential clans lived in 168 places with 17 towns and 151 villages. There were 52 entries about Jixi, whose influential clans lived in 45 places, among which 17 were towns and 28 were villages. Influential clans referred to strong clans with power and wealth. Their members either took high positions in the government or excelled at trading, or both. She County and Xiuning had similar numbers of influential clans who lived in the countryside, indicating a similar situation of the two counties in terms of social economic development in the mid- and late Ming. The number of villages in which influential clans inhabited was only 18.54% of that of She County or Xiuning, showing an obvious backwardness in its social economy. Second, the speeds of development in the three counties were different. Take the number of villages in 1551 as the base number. In 1669, the number of villages in the She County was 1.85, while the number in Xiuning was 1.47. In 1827, the number in She County rose to 4.18, while the number in Xiuning was merely 3.07. The data indicated that She County developed faster than Xiuning in Qing. This was related to the influx of the Huizhou merchant's capital. She merchants engaged mostly in salt trade, while their Xiuning counterparts pawn-broking. Relying on the feudal privileges, salt trade was much more lucrative than pawn-broking. Therefore, salt traders became the mainstay of the Huizhou merchant. The backflow of commercial profits gave rise to economic prosperity and population growth so that the existing living space became inadequate. Therefore, some branches of big clans migrated to look for new living spaces. Commercial profits were the material base for immigratory ancestors to establish new villages, which was the reason why the number villages in She County increased considerably. The wealth of Xiuning pawnbrokers, who took control of finance, should not be underestimated. The speed of development in Xiuning was just slightly lower than that in She County. The development of villages in Jixi also synchronized with the development of its social economy. Jixi people went out to engage in trade later than their counterparts in She County and Xiuning. "Fengsu" (Customs) in *Jixi xianzhi* (*Gazetteer of Jix County*) printed during the Qianlong reign continued to state, "Only in Jixi were there few people who carried money to go out and engage in trade." Later, it became a common practice that people traveled around to do business. Because of the extremely small base number in 1551, the ratios jumped to 7.5 and 12.9 in the next two periods, but the absolute numbers remained small. The small number of villages in Jixi also resulted from the restraint of its geographical conditions. In the aforementioned material, it was indicated, "Jixi bordered on She, but suffered from numerous mountains." "Pressured by the mountains and flushed by the rivers, it was hard to find arable lands across Jixi County." Given the fact that geographical conditions remained the same in the Ming and Qing, the transformations of villages were indicative of the trajectory of development of the county's social economy.

In order to further illustrate the characteristics of the transformations of villages in the three counties, Table 5.3 shows the retention rates of villages of the three counties in different historical periods to conduct a survey on the retention rates of villages listed in *Chronicle of Influential Clans in Xin'an* in 1699, 1872, and 1937.

We understand that Xiuning commanded the highest retention rate of villages in the Ming and Qing; 99.1% of villages listed in *Gazetteer of the Huizhou Prefecture* printed in the Kangxi times continued to exist during the Daoguang reign. Only 117 new names of villages emerged during the Daoguang reign, constituting only 25.27% of all names listed in *Gazetteer of the Huizhou Prefecture* printed in the Daoguang years. There were 74.73% of villages existing ever since 1551 or 1669. The data indicated that villages in Xiuning developed steadily in a relatively stable condition. The base number of She County in 1551 was close to Xiuning, but the retention rates were lower. 231 new village names emerged during the Daoguang reign, constituting 36.6% of the total number of villages (631). Only

*Table 5.3* The retention rates of villages in three Huizhou counties in the modern times

| She County | Year 1551 | | |
|---|---|---|---|
| Year 1699 | 62.25% | Year 1699 | |
| Year 1827 | 58.94% | 91.04% | Year 1827 |
| Year 1937 | 52.32% | 79.21% | 71.63% |
| Xiuning | Year 1551 | | |
| Year 1699 | 59.6% | Year 1699 | |
| Year 1827 | 59.6% | 99.1% | |
| Jixi | Year 1551 | | |
| Year 1699 | 82.14% | Year 1699 | |
| Year 1827 | 78.57% | 76.19% | |

63.4% of villages were existing one passing down from previous generations. It demonstrates that the development of villages in She County was less stable than that in Xiuning but in a faster pace (during the Daoguang reign, She County had 168 villages more than Xiuning did). On the one hand, a large number of new villages were established. On the other hand, many villages disappeared. Such instability was an indication of the fact that She County was more dynamic than Xiuning. The retention rate of villages between 1551 and 1669 was also relatively high, which resulted from its low absolute numbers. The retention rate (76.19%) between 1699 and 1827 was lower than those of She County and Xiuning. Two hundred and one new village names emerged during the Daoguang reign, constituting 55.68% of the total number of villages (361). Only 44.32% of villages were existing ones passing down from previous generations. The data shows that this county was the least stable in the transformations of villages. Although the absolute number of villages in Jixi was smaller than that of She County and Xiuning, the ratio of newly established villages was the highest, revealing that Jixi made a substantial progress in a timespan of one century between the Qianlong and Daoguang times. The different situations of the transformations of villages in the three counties reflect different characters of their social economic development and demonstrate that merchants had immense impact on the communal life.

## 2  The merchant and population density

Huizhou is a mountainous area, whose landform consists of basins sunken from river valleys, low hills, and high hills or mountains. The expansion of the living space referred to people's migration from areas of low hills to those of high hills. Thus, it requires us to take villages as the point of departure of our study to survey population density and explain the changes of population density.

To explore population density, the first task is to ascertain the villages' spatial positions, restore the administrative units in the Ming and Qing, and draw maps based on individual *du*. With a reference to "The Table of Investigating Village Names in Individual *Du* in the Past Four Centuries," We look for villages that still exist to this day in the present-day maps of various counties. Maps we have obtained – the map of She County (printed in 1979 with a scale of 1:110,000), map of Xiuning (1977, 1:100,000), and map of Jixi (1980, 1:65,000) – mark all natural villages today. As we attempt to mark all villages that exist between the Ming and Qing times and today, the locations of various *du* could be made clear. The boundaries among *du* are more clear-cut in places with numerous villages. Adjacent villages that belonged to different *du* are used to determine borderlines. It is far more difficult to draw borderlines in remote mountainous areas. The following are our principles of determining borderlines in places with few villages: (1) The sparseness of villages did not mean that the place was a blank. In the modern times when population grew and productivity rose, more villages were built in mountainous areas. Those villages were certainly not recorded in "The Table of Investigating Village Names in Individual *Du* in the Past Four Centuries." Those villages must keep economic, cultural, and political connections with their neighboring villages which we have known. Such connections should be maintained through water or land transportations. A blank zone could border with two or more *du*. We can make a judgment of a village and the subordinate areas surrounding it by examining the rationality of traffic lines. Finally, we can draw borderlines along the trends of mountains and rivers. (2) The borderlines at present are usually the continuity of those in history. Sparsely populated areas underwent little transformation that densely populated areas. The borderline among districts and *xiang* could be referred to determine boundaries among *du* in history. Boundaries of *du* drawn with such an approach are more reasonable and dependable. Thus, we make maps of *du* in She County, Xiuning, and Jixi in the Ming and Qing times (omitted here).

The drawing of the maps of *du* in Huizhou lays a foundation of our further study of population density in *du* of Huizhou. Population density in a *du* was a ratio between the population of the residents and the area of the *du*. In order to calculate population density of a *du*, it is necessary to obtain the area and population of the *du*. How to get the two numbers? Here, please allow me to briefly show our approach.

The area of each *du* is calculated in the following way. We copy the maps of *du* on a fine drawing paper with evenly distributed weight. All *du* are cut off along their boundaries and are weighed on an extremely accurate analytical chemical balance to obtain their weights (accurate to 0.0001 gram) and the total weight of each county. The ratio between the weight of each *du* (g′) and the total weight of a county with all *du* (−g) is the ratio between the area of each *du* (S′) and the total area (S). Based on the formula,

$$S' = S \times \dfrac{g'}{-g}$$

the area of each *du* could be calculated. Although the approach lacks precision, it is enough to make an analysis of population density.

The sizes of the three counties could be acquired from *Anhui shengqing* (*Information of the Anhui Province*, 1986). Considering that boundaries among different counties kept changing in Ming and Qing, we adjust the area of each county accordingly. The total areas of the three counties and individual *du* are all projective areas. Would that affect the analysis of population density? In plain areas, projective area is equal to actual area. Therefore, the calculation of population density would not cause errors. In mountains and hills, the actual area is larger than projective area. Therefore, the calculated population density is slightly higher. That is to say, the actual population density in mountains and hills is lower than the one shown in statistics, and its contrast with high population density in plain areas would be more obvious. However, that would not affect our analysis. If any, the even lower population density in mountains and hills would be in favor of our analysis and conclusion.

The data of population is even harder to obtain. Historically, there was no such survey of population with individual *du* as a unit. Gazetteers of different historical periods usually took county as the unit to survey households. We notice that in "Yudi zhi" (Geography) of *Gazetteer of Huizhou Prefecture* printed in the Kangxi and Daoguang times and *She County Gazetteer* printed in the Republican times, numbers of *li* and *tu* of each county were recorded. In the Ming's local administrative system, *lijia* and "fish-scale registry maps" (*tu*) were consistent with each other. The consistency between *li* and *tu* contains two connotations. First, they were correspondent with each other as administrative units. *Li* was a fundamental administrate unit at the local level with 110 households making a *li*. In drawing "fish-scale registry maps," a *tu* also consisted of 110 households. Second, they were consistent with each other geographically. Initially, *tu* meant arable lands possessed by *li*. Later, it meant the geographic scope of the area of the *li*, which therefore became an administrative unit under *du*. *Li* and *tu* were used to indicate the same administrative and geographic unit from different angles (household registry and lands). In official documents, deeds, and works, it was universal to use *li* and *tu* interchangeably. Were the numbers of *li* and *tu* in a given county the same? Our answer is yes. "Geography" of *Gazetteer of Huizhou Prefecture* printed in the Kangxi times recorded that She County used to have 228 *li*. "In forty-first year of the Jiajing reign, three *tu* were separated out and five *tu* were established in Dongguan, making the total number of *li* 230." As two *tu* was added, two *li* was added accordingly. Another record showed that Jixi had 35 *li*, namely 35 *tu*, in 1596. Thus, we understand the total numbers of *tu* under individual *du* were precisely the total numbers of *li* under the counties. *Li* and *tu* were interchangeable not only as units of administration and geography but also as units of households. In light of this, we use *tu* as the household index to relative population density of *du*. Here, I use "relative population density" because, first of all, households in a *li* (*tu*) were not a set number. Beyond 110 households, there were various *jiling* (odd) households supervised by *li*. Second, in late Ming, the system of the "Yellow Registry" and "fish-scale registry maps" was in decline. Although in early Qing, some work was done to restore the "Yellow Registry" and "fish-scale registry maps," the contents were different from those in Ming. Thus, could we use the data about the number of *tu* in individual *du* contained in *Gazetteer of Huizhou Prefecture* printed in Kangxi? We argue that we still can. In the early Qing, with the restoration and development of social economy, population grew gradually. During the Kangxi reign, the total numbers of *li* in three Huizhou counties increased 34%–40% compared with those in Ming. The numbers of *tu* rose accordingly. The total numbers of *li* and *tu* were basically equal to each other. (She County: 278 *li* and 281 *tu* or three more *tu* than *li*; Xiuning: 221 *li* and 217 *tu* with four *li* than *tu*. The differences could be errors resulting from changes of boundaries of counties.) It was clear that in early Qing, *tu* and *li* corresponded with each other in Huizhou. Therefore, the data was dependable. In 1712, when the government proposed, "No taxes would be imposed on newly increased population," the target of tax levying switched from both lands and population to lands only. Thus, *li* and *tu* lost their meaningfulness as before. In 128 years between the printing of the gazetteer in the Kangxi times and that in the Daoguan times, population grew sharply. Yet, the numbers of *li* and *tu* of the three counties recorded in the Daoguang version of the gazetteer did not increase at all. Thus, the numbers of *li* and *tu* after the Kangxi times lost their values as the reference.

Since we have obtained the data of areas of various *du* and determined that *tu* was the unit as the index to households, we can calculate the relative population density of various *du*. The formula is: the relative population density of a *du*= the number of *tu*/the area of a *du* (km²). Based on areas and population density of various *du*, we make "The Table of Statistics of Areas and Population Density of *Du* in the Three Counties of Huizhou Prefecture" (omitted). We also input the data of the table into the computer and draw "The Diagram of Relative Population Density in Three Counties in Huizhou Prefecture) (omitted) with the assistance of the computer. The diagram consists of five levels. In the first level, the relative population density was 0–0.04 *tu* per km²; the second level: 0.04–0.1; the third level: 0.1–0.25; the fourth level: 0.25–0.4; the fifth level: ≥ 0.4. The distribution of relative population density in three Huizhou counties constituted three clear, hierarchal spheres of survival: the core sphere with the largest population density – namely, the fifth level of relative population density; the transitional circular sphere with secondary highest population density – the fourth and third levels; and the marginal circular sphere – the second and first levels. The three spheres of survival corresponded with the natural geographical patterns of the three counties. The core sphere with the largest population density was a continuous area from the northeastern part of She County's Huicheng (county seat) in the east, which included Yanzhen and Tunxi, to Xiuning's Haiyang Town (county seat) in the west. This core sphere overlapped with Huizhou's largest plain – the Tunxi Basin. The circular area along the peripheries of the three counties was the place with the lowest population density. This sphere of survival featured mountains and hills (including the Huangshan Mountain). The entire territory of Jixi was situated in this sphere. Between the core sphere and the peripheral sphere was the circular sphere transitioning from high to low population density. Its landform was low hills. The distribution of population density corresponded with the natural environments, which were key to human being's survival. However, we can only see the cross section of population density in the Ming and Qing but fail to examine a complete picture of the distribution of population density over the history. Limited by the lack of historical materials, we are unable to draw a diagram of the distribution of population density in various stages of the Ming and Qing history. The only thing to make it up is that we have obtained the data of the change of numbers of villages in the Ming, Qing, and even Republican times. The density of villages and population density are intimately related to each other. The former indirectly reflects the trajectory of vertical changes of the distribution of population density.

Between the late seventeenth century and the first half of the twentieth century, the transformations of the density of villages in the three Huizhou counties followed an unvarying pattern. The increase of the density of villages advanced radially from the core sphere to the transitional and marginal circular spheres. Such advancing was completed in two stages. In the first stage between 1699 and 1827, the increase of the density of villages mainly advanced toward the transitional circular sphere. After longtime reclamation and management, the living space in the core sphere had been exhausted. Limited by productivity of the day, it was hard to further exploit the existing living space. Therefore, when large families living in the core sphere were in need of branching out because of population growth, they felt it hard to find a nearby place as their new living space. Thus, the branches of those families migrated to the transitional circular sphere to enhance the density of villages in this circular sphere. Meanwhile, the increase of the density of villages advanced radially to affect the marginal circular sphere. The latter was the place with the lowest population density in late Qing, with an extremely small number of villages. Some villages in the marginal sphere were built by people living in the huts, but some came into existence because of branches of large families moved in. In the second stage between 1827 and 1937, the increase of the density of villages occurred mainly in the marginal circular sphere. The transformation of the density of villages in this stage was characterized by the shrinkage of the core sphere, the stability of the transitional sphere, and the sharp increase of villages in the marginal sphere. In all *du* situated in the core sphere of She County, the numbers of villages in 1937 were, without an exception, smaller than those in 1827. The shrinkage of the core sphere mainly resulted from the enormous loss of population and wealth during the Taiping War. The stability of villages in the transitional sphere stemmed from the fact that this area had been fully developed in the first stage. It was in the marginal sphere in the southern and southeastern parts of She County, particularly places along the Xin'an River and bordered with Zhejiang, that had the dramatic increase of numbers of villages. The marked increase of the density of villages in the mountainous areas testifies to, first of all, human being's enhanced ability to conquer the nature and, second, an urgent need explore more new living spaces because of the drastic population growth in late Qing. It merits mentioning, however, that although areas with the lowest population density experienced the fastest growth of the density of villages, their population density remained the lowest because the scale of villages was constrained by unfavorable geographical conditions.

The transformative trajectory of the density of villages allows us to take a brief look at the vertical change of the distribution of population density. It is safe to argue that the increase of population density also underwent a process of radial advancement from the core sphere to the transitional sphere and then to the marginal sphere. Between 1699 and 1827, it was the transitional circular sphere that enjoyed the largest growth rate of population density. Between 1827 and 1937, it was the marginal circular sphere that underwent the largest growth rate of population density, while population density in the core area slightly decreased. In general, the pattern of three levels, in which population density decreased progressively from the core sphere to the marginal circular sphere, did not alter.

What was the relationship between the Huizhou merchant and the distribution and transformation of population density? We understand that influential clans in modern Huizhou had their members either take position in the government or engage in trade as great merchants. Because Huizhou merchants' enormous wealth, the scale of their clans was usually bigger than that of clans of ordinary people. Therefore, the pattern of the distribution of influential clans and their migration were directly related to Huizhou merchants' wealth. Based on a survey of the number of all influential clans in the three Huizhou counties in 1551 provided by *Chronicle of Influential Clans in Xin'an*, we formulate the following equation, the density of influential clans = the number of influential clans in a *du*/area of the *du* (km²), in order to know the number of influential clans per square kilometers – namely, the density of influential clans. We input the data into computer, with which we draw "The Diagram of the Distribution of Influential Clans in Three Huizhou Counties" (omitted). The diagram features five layers of shadows: the first layer includes 0–0.02 influential clan per square kilometer; the second layer 0.02–0.08; the third layer 0.08–0.25; the fourth layer 0.25–0.5; and the fifth layer ≥ 0.5.

A comparison between the diagrams of the distribution of population density and the density of influential clans shows that the fifth and fourth layers of the diagram of influential clans overlap with the core sphere with the largest population density. The third layer of the diagram of influential clans generally corresponds with the transitional circular sphere. The first and second layers of the diagram of influential clans are about the same as the spatial scope of the marginal circular sphere. The core sphere with large population density – the Tunxi Basin of Huizhou – is a low land along the river valley formed through alluviation by the Xin'an River and its tributaries. Its terrain slopes gently, and its soil is deep and thick, beneficial to farming. Its area is over 100 square kilometers. This was a highly commercialized area with a large number of towns. Centering on the Tunxi Town, the Tunxi Basin was 12 kilometers away from Yansi Town in the north by east, which was 11 kilometers away from Huicheng in the northeast, and 13 kilometers (straight-line distance) away from Haiyang Town in the northwest. Between the four great towns, there were numerous small villages and towns connected by the water system of the Xin'an River. Peasants could spend only a whole day to buy or sell produces or other commodities in those towns. The pattern of towns here was similar to those in the Suzhou, Songjiang, Hangzhou, Jiaxing, and Huzhou area but in a much smaller scale. This was also a place congregating a large number of influential clans. Take She County as an example, Yansi Town, the core area of the county, got together 15 influential clans. The nineteenth *du* under Yansi Town featured 22 influential clans. The number 34*du* in the marginal circular sphere had no influential clan, while the four *du* (number 30to number 33) had only three influential clans.

Because influential clans possessed enormous political and economic powers, their multiplication, division, and migration exerted direct influence on the distribution of population density. It was a trend that the divided and migrating influential clans moved toward the core sphere, which was opposite to the radial advancement of population density. In order to elaborate on this point, I take a big name from *Chronicle of Influential Clans in Xin'an* as an example for further study.

The Wu clan was one of the three clans (the Wang, Cheng, and Wu clans) of Huizhou Prefecture and also one of great salt traders in Yangzhou. Over 40influential Wu clans in the three counties were mentioned in *Chronicle of Influential Clans in Xin'an*. The Wu families cited here are limited to those whose immigratory ancestors and places of residence could be determined. They could be divided into two major branches. First, the immigratory ancestor was Wu Shaowei, the *jinshi* degree holder and Investigating Censor in the early Tang, who migrated to the core sphere – the western suburb of Haiyang Town of Xiuning – in the early eighth century. Many of his descendants were *jinshi* degree holders and were "superior in the hometown because of their wealth." Between the eighth and the fifteenth centuries, the Wu clan multiplied into many branches. For example, in the tenth century, one branch migrated to the Number Fifteen *du* (in the core sphere) and later multiplied into six sub-branches, all of whom settled down in the core sphere with fine social economic conditions. Our statistics shows that among 20 branches with Wu Shaowei being the immigratory ancestors, 13 were living in the core sphere. Two were living in the county seat of Jixi. However, five moved out of the core sphere. Second, the immigratory ancestor was Wu Xuan, a commoner in late Tang, who migrated from Fuliang, Jiangxi to Jiangtan, the marginal sphere of Xiuning, to evade the turmoil of war. In the following five centuries, two thirds of Wu's branches moved to the remote marginal sphere of Xiuning County. Only a small number relocated to the core sphere.

The aforementioned situation indicates that Wu families with Wu Shaowei as the ancestor were more powerful and wealthy. Their descendants could rely on the network of blood to bolster each other and strive for new living spaces in the most affluent places. Those had no ties to Wu Shaowei and arrived late could not find a place for survival in the core sphere. They used the marginal circular sphere as the base area for further development. Because of their endeavor for several centuries, some of their descendants, though in a small number, accomplished the goal of settling down in the core sphere.

The division and migration of the Wu clan present a typical case to demonstrate a trend that branches of influential clans advanced toward the core sphere. The competition between influential clans and ordinary clans in the core sphere scrambling for living spaces was intense. Such a competition, on the one hand, led to the intensification of population in the core sphere. On the other hand, it forced branches of influential clans and ordinary clans to migrate toward transitional and marginal spheres. This was the inner dynamic of the expansion of population density from the core sphere to transitional and marginal spheres. In the process of expansion, Huizhou merchants' wealth, mediated by patriarchal clans, helped to explore incessantly new living spaces for communities so that the contradiction of population and lands was eased.

## Section four: the interaction between the merchant and the community

In sum, merchants, on the one hand, initiated the liberation of women so that "jealous women were numerous." On the other hand, they consolidated the feudal morality so that "[t]here were the most virtuous and chaste women in Xin'an, whose number was as large as half of other provinces." On the one hand, the fission of the family led to its intensification and modernization. On the other hand, merchants strengthened the ties to the patriarchal clan system and expanded the sphere of the clan. On the one hand, they explored new living spaces. On the other hand, they annexed lands and therefore elevated Huizhou's land price to top the whole country. Thus the already limited living apace became even smaller. Therefore, the merchant played a dual role in the community.

The Huizhou merchant's role in the Huizhou community was, first of all, to reinforce its feudal nature. The sociocultural structure in modern Huizhou, like that in China's vast countryside, was a landlord economic structure, in which landlords, landholding peasants, and tenant peasants were linked by the blood relationship. Through the veil of the patriarchal clan, we can see the clear class distinction. There were a lot of descriptions, such as "fields connecting to each other," "building houses and purchasing lands," and "[owning] the largest amounts of lands and estates in the village" in Huizhou people's genealogies. There was even a case that a merchant-landlord once "purchased thousands of *mu* of lands in Xiuning and She County with over 370 tenant households."[81] However, more clansmen were "poor people who could not survive by themselves." Once hit by natural disasters, "starving people who filled the land were wailing in despair." They "found nowhere to borrow grains." As a result, "people were [so weak] that they could not carry the rotten coffins."[82] In the Ming and Qing, nevertheless, such confrontation between classes did not damage the base of communities of clans. The reason behind it was the fact that Huizhou merchants continually provided for patriarchal clans. Apart from spiritually strengthening the blood tie of patriarchal clans by means of worshipping the ancestors, for which purpose ancestral halls were built, lands for sacrifice were purchased, and genealogies were compiled, merchants afforded the material basis of communities of clans by expending huge amounts of money in buying properties of clans. As Huizhou merchants purchased lands as public properties of their clans, whose rents were used to bring benefits to clansmen and relieve the poor. For example, Hu Tianlu, a Qimen native, "engaged in trade and made a fortune." He "donated three hundred *mu* of lands as righteous lands, whose incomes were used for events in the clan such as sacrifice, weddings, and funerals and as the money for the poor and helpless."[83] She Wenyi, a native of Yan Town in Ming,

> engaged in trade. . . . [He] purchased two hundred *mu* of lands and selected a clansman as the manager of the revenues [from the lands]. Everyone was given one *sheng* of grains each day, and the amount for widowers, widows, the disabled, and the sick doubled. In years of good harvest, the surplus [grains] were distributed. In the end of each year, clothes and fabrics were donated. In addition, he measured twenty-five *mu* of lands to establish the Wuyin Cemetery along the Yanxi Creek to bury the deceased clansmen.[84]

Huizhou lacked lands so that some people bought righteous lands in other prefectures. For example, Wu Xizu, a merchant from She County, and others

> collectively donated tens of thousands [of ounces of silver] to buy thousands of *mu* of lands. In the third and tenth month of every year, the yearly revenues [from the lands] were given to the poor and helpless and used to help to conduct funerals and bury [the deceased]. The rule was set in the Fanshi Coffin Home. This happened in the third year of the Qianlong reign, and the lands were bought in Zhishui of Xuancheng.[85]

Huizhou merchants donated money in different aspects, ranging from food, clothing, lodging, wedding, funeral, education to participating in the Civil Service Exam. The Huizhou merchant Wu Zongrong "sojourned in Suzhou, but donated huge amounts of money each year to his clan."[86] The Huizhou merchant Wang Jinghuang "gave grains to the poor in the clan each month. Every year, [he] spent one hundred and fifty or sixty thousand."

> For those who did not have winter clothing, [he] gave them clothing [for the winter], for which he spent about fifty thousand (each year). For the sick people who could not afford to buy medicine, [he] gave medicine. For the poor people who could not [afford to] hire tutors, [he] established a righteous school, for which he spent twenty thousand a year. For those who died without coffins, [he] gave them coffins. [He] did this every year. When [he] was ninety *sui*, he had spent over ten thousand [ounces of silver] and given two thousand coffins.[87]

The Huizhou merchant Wang Guangxun

> prepared timber and purchased stones to build a great building in the western part of the neighborhood to accommodate clansmen. [The size of the building] was 360 *bu* (footsteps). There were three chambers facing the south and six east-west ones. A hall was in the middle and a sizable space was in the front to face the Yingxi Creek.[88]

Some paid taxes to the governments for their clansmen. The Huizhou merchant Wang Jiashu "paid overdue [taxes] in his *tu*."[89] Huizhou merchant Wu Yongheng "was in charge of carrying commissariat by canal in the year of Wuyin of the Qianlong reign. The clan was short of able-bodied men, and everyone lost money. [He] thus paid the tax by himself."[90] Those extremely wealthy merchants donated some parts of their profits to give alms to their clansmen to ease the stratification of petty peasants inside their clans to some extent so that social reproduction could perpetuate. Such small favors did not reach servants who were not categorized as clansmen. It had been a custom to discriminate against and prosecute servants. The confrontation between clans and servants concealed the polarization of the poor and the rich and the class antagonism inside the clans. Accounts such as "thousands of clansmen deeply attached to each other living together like one family"[91] were nothing but fictive and embellished words. Under the aegis of wealthy merchants, poor members of clans could not fundamentally change their class statuses, although they did not die of starvation in the wild.

Second, as the Huizhou merchant wealth helped to reinforce the feudal nature, it played a role in disintegrating Huizhou's feudal society. For the sake of trade, part of commercial profits in Huizhou were invested in constructing highways to strengthen connections among different communities. For example, Zha Jie, a merchant from Xiuning, "paved stone roads in Gushu and constructed a highway of one hundred *li* in Nanling."[92] Fang Ruqi, a merchant from She County, "paved a stone road in Jinling to connect Wuhu."[93] The Qimen merchant Zheng Jiao,

> who engaged in trade in Guazhu, saw that the Grand Canal was a significant waterway for both officials and the people. When grains were being shipped, merchants' [ships] were stopped. [He] thus donated money to dredge up another river so that governments' ships would not be blocked and commercial ones would not be stopped. [The river] is still in use.[94]

The Wuyuan merchant Zhan Wenxi

> went to Sichuan under his father's orders. When [he] arrived in Chongqing, [he found] a dangerous road in Fuhe named "Beach of Startled by the Dream," which was hanged on the cliff. There was no path for [boat-trackers] to drag boats. [He] kept [the place] in mind. After several years, [he] accumulated a wealth and passed by this place. [He] donated thousands of [ounces of] silver to tunnel through the mountain and open up paths. [Thus] both land and water transportations were available. In order to praise his acts, officials carved a stone [to name the mountain] as "Ridge of Merchant Zhan."[95]

With stretching and unobstructed commercial ways, Huizhou merchants opened up new markets and involved more communities in the realm of commodified economy to inflict damage upon local natural economy and patriarchal clan organizations. Meanwhile, the closed state of Huizhou locked up in the mountains was also in demise. For example, "the Ruoling [path] was the border between Xuancheng and She County. It was the way of strategic significance [to connect] She, Xiuning, Taiping, and Jingde. It was twenty *li* high and meandered double the length." After the Huizhou merchant Cheng Guoguang

> made a fortune, [he] made the decision to stretch the road to hundreds of *li* by cutting wild grass, chiseling stones, shaving mountain peaks, filling groves, flattening precipitous places, and widening the narrow areas. Because stones produced in She was full of cracks and rocks from this mountain was not enough for use, [he] had Zhejiang-produced blue and white stones shipped back to make it up.[96]

In another case, "the Xinling [Mountain] in the northern part of the prefecture was so steep that travelers felt it hard to go through." The Huizhou merchant Jiang Yan "donated tens of thousands of [ounces of] silver to open up a new, forty *li* long road for travelers."[97] Another example was "the Dahongling [Mountain] between Qimen and Shitai, a key path between Huizhou and the rest of Anhui." The Yi County merchant Shi Shichun "proposed to repair [the road] by making an advance and donating thousands of [ounces of] silver."[98] Along the newly opened roads, the merchant's commercialism of valuing profits made inroads into this closed area to ruthlessly assault the traditional pastoral life style and erode the economic base of clan communities. However, the Huizhou merchant's capital's role in conforming to the historical trend at the best created a historical precondition for capitalism. By comparison, Huizhou merchants played a more important part in cementing the feudal nature of their communities.

The community was also of dual significance to merchants. On the one hand, the patriarchal forces and the Huizhou merchant closely tied to each other and mutually supported to enhance the latter's competitiveness. Thus merchants were able to accumulate enormous wealth through trades that bought cheap and sold dear, and their forces "reached almost half of the country." On the other hand, the patriarchal forces inherited a heavy burden of tradition, which refrained Huizhou merchants from further development. Politically, citizens in cities confronted with feudal lords in Europe. As the citizen class grew into bourgeoisie, they damaged all traditional, patriarchal, and primitive relations and mercilessly destroyed variegated feudal fetters in all places they ruled. Yet, Huizhou merchants tightly integrated with feudal political forces. Economically, the rising bourgeoisie in West Europe conducted their primitive accumulation of capital in two ways: to seize small craftsmen's lands and to accumulate monetized wealth. The primitive accumulation of capital accelerated the historical process of transforming the feudal mode of production into the capitalistic one. Capital accumulated by the Huizhou merchant, however, was massively consumed in the form of relieving clansmen and purchasing public properties for the clan, which unwittingly strengthened small-peasant economy. In addition, enormous capital they accumulated was constantly divided. In line with the practice of inheritance under the patriarchal clan system, Huizhou merchants "evenly divided their properties with no personal gains." Issues related to inheritance mentioned in *xingzhuang* (biographies) or epitaphs were all about merchants' selflessness: "possessing an enormous wealth and divided it evenly with the younger brother";"dividing all the wealth with brothers"; "the wealth accumulated in decades being divided among brothers"; and "any slightest gains being divided evenly without possessing a penny of his own." The chiefs of the clan had the rights to intervene in inheritance. When a Huizhou merchant did not have offspring, the clansmen would be the inheritor. *Brief Information of Three Ridges* had an account: the Huizhou merchant Wang "engaged in trade and accumulated tens of thousands [of ounces of] silver."

> Wang did not have a son and was seriously sick. The clansmen strove to seize [his wealth], and [his wealth] was exhausted. Servants all grabbed the valuables and left. Wang [was so sick that he] lay in the bed without food. [He] looked around and died of indignation.[99]

The endless cycle of accumulation, division, re-accumulation, and re-division limited the capital's capacity to grow and thereby limited the Huizhou merchant's ability to participate in further competitions.

## Notes

1  Gu Yanwu (顾炎武), *Tianxia junguo libing shu* (天下郡国利病书), 1012.
2  "Libi shushing gao xu" (厘弊疏商稿序), in *Zhian ji* (止庵集).
3  "Wang Wei zoushu" (汪伟奏疏), in *Xiuning xianzhi* (休宁县志), volume 7.
4  Wu Jihu (吴吉祜), "Cunjie gong Zhuang" (存节公状), in *Fengnanzhi* (丰南志), volume 5.
5  "Ming gu shuzumu ruren Wangshi xingzhuang" (明故叔祖母孺人王氏行状), in *Xushi shipu* (许氏世谱) of She (歙) county, volume 5.
6  Xu Guo (许国), "Mu ruren shishi" (母孺人事实), in *Xu Wenmu gong ji* (许文穆公集), volume 13.
7  Wang Daokun (汪道昆), "Jinmu qishi shouxu" (金母七十寿序), in *Taihan ji* (太函集), 640.
8  Li Weizhen (李维桢), "Cheng Shenbao zhuan" (程神保传), in *Dami shanfang ji* (大泌山房集), volume 73, 265.
9  Shi Guozhu (石国柱) and Xu Chengyao (许承尧), "Renwu zhi – lienü" (人物志·烈女) in *Shexian zhi* (歙县志), volume 14.
10  Wang Daokun (汪道昆), "Chushi Wujun Chong muzhiming" (处士吴君重墓志铭), in *Taihan ji* (太函集), 215.
11  "Qinghua Xuezhai gong zhuan" (清华雪斋公传), in *Dunhuang Hongshi tongzongpu* (敦煌洪氏通宗谱) of Wuyuan (婺源), volume 58.
12  Xu Zhongyuan (许仲元), *Sanyi bitan* (三异笔谈), volume 3.
13  Wang Daokun (汪道昆), "Ming chengshilang Wangjun muzhiming" (明承事郎王君墓志铭), in *Taihan ji* (太函集), 313.
14  Wang Daokun (汪道昆), "Xian damu Zhuang" (先大母状), in *Taihan ji* (太函集), 298.
15  "Chushi Tianfu gong pei Zhu ruren jiefu xingzhuang" (处士天赋公配朱孺人节妇行状), in *Xiuning Ximen Wangshi zupu* (休宁西门汪氏族谱), volume 6.
16  "Ming zeng chengdelang Nanjing Bingbu chejia shu yuanwailang zhushi Jianggong ji anren Zhengshi hezang mubei" (明赠承德郎南京兵部车驾署员外郎主事江公暨安人郑氏合葬墓碑), in *Xi'nan Jiangshi zupu* (溪南江氏族谱).

17 Li Dou (李斗), *Yangzhou huafang lu* (扬州画舫录), volume 6.

18 Ji Yun (纪昀), *Zhongxian dafu Baogong Kenyuan ji pei Wang gongren mubiao* (中宪大夫鲍公肯园暨配汪恭人墓表).

19 "Chengmu Wu ruren zhuan" (程母吴孺人传), in *Xiuning Shuaidong Chengshi jiapu* (休宁率东程氏家谱), volume 11.

20 "Ming gu Xumu Yongzhen ruren Zhengshi xingzhuang" (明故许母永贞孺人郑氏行状), in *Xushi shipu* (许氏世谱).

21 Wu Jihu (吴吉祐), "Yigong ruren zhuang" (一恭孺人状), in *Fengnanzhi* (丰南志), volume 5.

22 Wang Daokun (汪道昆), "Shouzhang chushi xu" (寿张处士序), in *Taihan ji* (太函集), 645.

23 Wang Daokun (汪道昆), "Haiyang chushi Jin zhongweng pei Daishi hezang muzhiming" (海阳处士金仲翁配戴氏合葬墓志铭), in *Taihan ji* (太函集), 391.

24 "Huangmu Wushi ruren xingzhuang" (黄母吴氏孺人行状), in *Songtang Huangshi zongpu* (竦塘黄氏宗谱) of She (歙) county, volume 5.

25 Xu Ke (徐珂), "Haoshe lei" (豪侈类), in *Qing bailei chao* (清稗类钞).

26 Yang Dequan (杨德泉), "Qingdai qianqi liang Huai yanshang ziliao chuji" (清代前期两淮盐商资料初辑), *Jianghaixuekan* (江海学刊), No. 11 (1962).

27 Xu Chengyao (许承尧), "She fengsu lijiao kao" (歙风俗礼教考) in *Sheshi xiantan* (歙事闲谭), 606.

28 Cai Yu (蔡羽), "Liaoyang haishen zhuan" (辽阳海神传), in *Wenshi yinghua – xiaoshuo juan* (文史英华·小说卷), ed., Bai Shouyi (白寿彝), collated and annotated by Gong Zhaoji (龚兆吉) (Changsha: Hunan chubanshe, 1993).

29 Fang Chongding (方崇鼎), He Yingsong (何应松), et al., "Renwu – xiaoyou" (人物·孝友), in *Xiuning xianzhi* (休宁县志) of the Jiaqing (嘉庆) reign, volume 14, photocopied edition of the Jiaqing 20 version (Taipei: Chengwen chubanshe, 1985).

30 "Renwu – xiaoyou" (人物·孝友), in *Wuyuanxianzhi* (婺源县志) of the Guangxu (光绪) reign, volume 28.

31 "Renwu – xiaoyou" (人物·孝友), in *Yixian xuzhi* (黟县续志).

32 "Fanli" (凡例), in *She Chun Fangshi huizong tongpu* (歙淳方氏会宗统谱), volume 1, edition of Qianlong (乾隆), 18.

33 "Jiexiao zhi" (节孝志), in *She Chun Fangshi huizong tongpu* (歙淳方氏会宗统谱), volume 20.

34 *Ming huidian* (明会典).

35 *Guangxu huidian shili* (光绪会典事例).

36 Zhao Jishi (赵吉士), *Jiyuan ji suoji* (寄园寄所寄), volume 11.

37 *Xiandai shixue* (现代史学), volume 3, No. 2.

38 Cited in Cao Dawei (曹大为), "Zhongguo lishishang zhenjie guannian de bianqian" (中国历史上贞节观念的变迁), *Zhongguo shi yanjiu* (中国史研究), No. 2 (1991).

39 Shi Guozhu (石国柱) and Xu Chengyao (许承尧), "Renwu zhi – lienü" (人物志·烈女) in *Shexian zhi* (歙县志), volume 11.

40 Li Jingde (黎靖德), *Zhuzi yule i* (朱子语类), volume 13 (Beijing: Zhonghua shuju, 1986).

41 Cheng Huaijing (程怀璟), "Chongxiu Huizhou fuzhi xu" (重修徽州府志序), in *Zhongguo difangzhi jicheng – Daoguang Huizhou fuzhi* (中国地方志集成·道光徽州府志) (Nanjing: Jiangsu guji chubanshe, 1998).

42 Xu Chengyao (许承尧), "She fengsu lijiao kao" (歙风俗礼教考) in *Sheshi xiantan* (歙事闲谭), volume 18, 607.

43 *Yangzhou guchui ci* (扬州鼓吹词).

44 Usui Sachiko (臼井佐知子), "Huishang jiqi wangluo" (徽商及其网络), originally published in *Chūgoku, shakai to bunka* (中国, 社会と文化), No. 6 (1991); translated version published in *Anhui shixue* (安徽史学), No. 1 (1992).

45 Wu Jihu (吴吉祐), "Xi'nan Wushi citang ji" (溪南吴氏祠堂记), in *Fengnan zhi* (丰南志), volume 8.

46 "Jiexiao zhi" (节孝志) in *She Chun Fangshi huizong tongpu* (歙淳方氏会宗统谱), volume 20.

47 "Xingzhuang" (行状), in *Wangshi tongzongpu* (汪氏统宗谱), volume 42.

48 *Wangshi jiushu* (汪氏阄书), collected in the library of Anhui Normal University.

49 "Chengdong Xushi chongxiu zupu xu" (城东许氏重修族谱序), in *Chongxiu gu She Dongmen Xushi zongpu* (重修古歙东门许氏宗谱), volume 9.

50 Zhao Jishi (赵吉士), *Jiyuan ji suoji* (寄园寄所寄).

51 Ye Xian'en (叶显恩), *Ming Qing Huizhou nongcun shehui yu dianpu zhi* (明清徽州农村社会与佃仆制) (Hefei: Anhui renmin chubanshe, 1983), 40.

52 Hong Liangji (洪亮吉), a Huizhou scholar during the Qianlong Reign, pointed out that at that time, "one person could survive with four *mu*, and a family with ten members needed forty *mu*." See "Yiyan – shengji" (意言·生计), in *Juanshige wen jiaji* (卷施阁文甲集), volume 1.

53 "Jiangnan" (江南), in *Tianxia junguo libing shu* (天下郡国利病书).

54 Xu Chengyao (许承尧), "Mingji xianzhong yunmi qingxing" (明季县中运米情形), in *Sheshi xiantan* (歙事闲谭), volume 6, 181.

55 Shi Guozhu (石国柱) and Xu Chengyao (许承尧), "Renwu – yixing" (人物·义行) in *Shexian zhi* (歙县志), volume 9.

56 Wu Rifa (吴日法), "Yuanqi" (缘起), in *Huishang bianlan* (徽商便览).

57 Wang Daokun (汪道昆), *Taihan ji* (太函集), volume 6.

58 Gui Youguang (归有光), "Baian Chengweng bashi shouxu" (白庵程翁八十寿序), in *Zhenchuan xiansheng ji* (震川先生集), volume 13.

59 Chen Qubing (陈去病), *Wushizhi* (五石脂).

60 "Yiwen – Wang Wenxue zhuan" (艺文·汪文学传), in *Yixian zhi* (黟县志), volume 15.

61 Xie Zhaozhe (谢肇淛), *Wu zazu* (五杂俎), volume 14.

62 Zhao Jishi (赵吉士), "Luotashan ji" (罗他山记), in *Jiyuan ji suoji* (寄园寄所寄), volume 9.

63 He Qiaoyuan (何乔远), "Fangyu zhi" (方域志), in *Mingshu* (闽书), volume 8.

64 *Doupeng xianhua* (豆棚闲话).

65 Wei Xi (魏禧), "Jiangshi si jiefu zhuan" (江氏四节妇传), in *Wei Shuzi wenji* (魏叔子文集), volume 17.

66 Wang Daokun (汪道昆), *Taihan ji* (太函集), volume 16.

67 Cai Yu (蔡羽), "Liaoyang haishen zhuan" (辽阳海神传), 152–153.

68 Xu Zhuo (徐卓), *Xiuning suishi* (休宁碎事), volume 3, quoting *Suntang ji* (荪堂集) by Wu Wenkui (吴文奎).

69 "Renwu shi – yixing ba" (人物十·义行八), in *Wuyuan xianzhi* (婺源县志) of the Guangxu (光绪) reign, volume 35,18.

70 "Renwu shi – yixing qi" (人物十·义行七), in *Wuyuan xianzhi* (婺源县志) of the Guangxu (光绪) reign, volume 34, 2.

71 "Jingzhao Yingheng gong Jin anren hezhuan" (京兆应亨公金安人合传), in *Xiuning Ximen Wangshi zongpu* (休宁西门汪氏宗谱), volume 6.

72 Xie Yongtai (谢永泰) et al., "Renwu zhi – shangyi zhuan" (人物志·尚义传), in *Yixian sanzhi* (黟县三志), volume 7.

73 Wu Jihu (吴吉祐), *Fengnan zhi* (丰南志), book 10.

74 "Renwu shi – yixing ba" (人物十·义行八), in *Wuyuan xianzhi* (婺源县志) of the Guangxu (光绪) reign, volume 35, 10.

75 Wang Daokun (汪道昆), "Ming gu Hui shilang pan Xinzhoushi Gao Xianggong muzhiming" (明故徽仕郎判忻州事高香公墓志铭), in *Taihan ji* (太函集), 340.

76 "Gaifu dianshan Fugong ji pei Jin ruren muzhiming" (盖府典膳福公暨配金孺人墓志铭), in *Xiuning Ximen Wangshizongpu* (休宁西门汪氏宗谱), volume 6.

77 *Dunfu nianpu* (钝夫年谱) (Teipei: Yuanliu chuban gongsi, 1986).

78 Maikeer Mikeluoer and Leiyinhade Xideer, *Ouzhou jiating shi* (欧洲家庭史), translated by Zhao Shiling (赵世玲), Zhao Shiyu (赵世瑜), and Zhou Shangyi (周尚意) (Beijing: Huaxia chubanshe, 1987), 35.

79 He Jie (贺杰), "Ming Qing Huizhou de zongzu yu shehui liudong xing" (明清徽州的宗族与社会流动性), paper presented to the Symposium of Ming History of China (1985).

80 Part of the statistical work was conducted jointly by Dr. He Jie (贺杰) of Princeton University, U.S., and the author.

81 *Shuaidong Chengshi jiapu* (率东程氏家谱) of Xiuning (休宁).

82 "Renwu – xiaoyou" (人物·孝友), in *Xiuning xianzhi* (休宁县志) of the Jiaqing (嘉庆) reign, volume 14.

83 Zhao Jishi (赵吉士), *Jiyuan ji suoji* (寄园寄所寄), volume 9.

84 "Renwu zhi – yixing" (人物志·义行), in *Chongxiu Anhui tongzhi* (重修安徽通志) of the Guangxu (光绪) reign, volume 249, in *Xuxiu siku quanshu* (续修四库全书), book 654 (Shanghai: Shanghai guji chubanshe, 2002), 263.

85 Wu Jihu (吴吉祐), *Fengnan zhi* (丰南志), book 10.

86 "Renwu shi – yixing ba" (人物十·义行八), in *Wuyuan xianzhi* (婺源县志) of the Guangxu (光绪), volume 35, 6.

87 Shi Guozhu (石国柱) and Xu Chengyao (许承尧), "Renwu zhi – yixing" (人物志·义行) in *Shexian zhi* (歙县志), volume 9.

88 Ibid.

89 Ibid.

90 "Renwu – xiangshan" (人物·乡善), in *Xiuning xianzhi* (休宁县志) of the Jiaqing (嘉庆) reign, volume 15.

91 Xie Yongtai (谢永泰) et al., "Yiwenzhi – renwu zhi – shangyi zhuan" (艺文志·人物志·尚义传), in *Yixian sanzhi* (黟县三志).

92 "Renwu zhi – yixing" (人物志·义行), in *Anhuitongzhi* (安徽通志) of the Daoguang (道光) reign, volume 249, *Xuxiusikuquanshu* (续修四库全书), book 654 (Shanghai: Shanghai guji chubanshe, 2002).

93 Ibid.

94 "Renwu zhi – yixing" (人物志·义行), in *Qimen xianzhi* (祁门县志) of the Tongzhi (同治) reign, volume 30, *Zhongguofangzhi congshu* (中国方志丛书) (Taipei: Cheng-wen chubanshe, 1975).

95 "Renwu – xiaoyou" (人物·孝友), in *Wuyuan xianzhi* (婺源县志) of the Guangxu (光绪) reign, volume 28.

96 *Huizhou fuzhi* (徽州府志) of the Daoguang (道光) reign, volume 3.

97 "Renwu zhi – yixing" (人物志下·义行), in *Chengyang sanzhi* (橙阳散志), volume 3.

98 Xie Yongtai (谢永泰) et al., "Yiwenzhi – renwu zhi – shangyi zhuan" (艺文志·人物志·尚义传), in *Yixian sanzhi* (黟县三志).

99 Dong Han (董含), "Jicai yihai" (积财贻害), in *Sangang zhilue* (三冈识略), 177.

# Bibliography

## 1 Official history, unofficial history, veritable records, political documents, encyclopedia, classics

*Ershier shi zhaji* (二十二史札记, A note to the twenty-two histories).

Fu Weilin (傅维麟), *Mingshu* (明书, Book of Ming), edition of *Jifu congshu* (畿辅丛书) of Qing.

*Guangxu huidian shili* (光绪会典事例, Cases of comprehensive institutions in Qianlong).

*Guanzi* (管子).

*Guochao dianhui* (国朝典汇, Comprehensive institutions of the dynasty).

*Hanshu* (汉书, Book of Han).

He Qiaoyuan (何乔远), *Minshu* (闽书, Book of Fujian).

*Huangchao zhengdian leizuan* (皇朝政典类纂, Compilation of political classics of the imperial dynasty).

*JiuTangshu* (旧唐书, Old book of Tang).

Liu Jinzao (刘锦藻), *Qingchao xu wenxian tongkao* (清朝续文献通考, Sequel to comprehensive examination of literature of Qing) (Hangzhou: Zhejiang guji chubanshe, 2000).

*Lunyü* (论语, The Analects).

*Ming huidian* (明会典, Comprehensive institutions of the Ming).

*Ming Shenzong shilu* (明神宗实录, Veritable records of Emperor Shenzong of the Ming).

*Ming Shizong shilu* (明世宗实录, Veritable records of Emperor Shizong of the Ming).

*Ming Taizu shilu* (明太祖实录, Veritable records of Emperor Taizu of the Ming).

*Ming Wuzong shilu* (明武宗实录, Veritable records of Emperor Wuzong of the Ming).

*Ming Xianzong shilu* (明宪宗实录, Veritable records of Emperor Xianzong of the Ming).

*Minggong shi* (明宫史, History of the Ming Palace).

*Mingshi* (明史, History of Ming).

*Nan Qi shu* (南齐书, Book of southern Qi).

"Qianlong chao waiyang tongshang an – Qingfu zhe" (乾隆朝外洋通商案·庆复折), *Shiliao xunkan* (史料旬刊), No. 22 (1931).

*QingGaozong shilu* (清高宗实录, Veritable records of Emperor Gaozong of the Qing) (Beijing: Zhonghua shuju, September 1985).

*Qingshizong shilu* (清世宗实录, Veritable records of Emperor Shizong of the Qing) (Beijing: Zhonghua shuju, September 1985).

*Sanguo zhi* (三国志, Records of the three kingdoms).

*Shij i* (史记, Historical record).

Shu Hua (舒化), "Da Ming lü fuli" (大明律附例, The subsidiary legislation of the great Ming code) of "Bing lü san" (兵律三, Law of military 3), in *Da Ming lü* (大明律, The great Ming code), volume 15 carved in the Jiajing (嘉靖) reign of Ming.

*Songshi* (宋史, History of Song).

*Songshi quanwen* (宋史全文, Full text of history of Song).

*Songshu* (宋书, Book of Song).

*Tanglü shuyi* (唐律疏议, Annotation and critique on Tang dynasty law).

*Tongdian* (通典, Comprehensive institutions).

*Wenxian tongkao* (文献通考, Comprehensive examination of literature).

*Zizhi tongjian* (资治通鉴, Comprehensive mirror in aid of governance).

*Zuozhuan* (左传, Commentary of Zuo).

## 2 Gazetteer

*Anhui tongzhi* (安徽通志, Gazetteer of Anhui) of Daoguang (道光), in *Xuxiu siku quanshu* (续修四库全书, Sequel to complete library of the four treasuries), book 654 (Shanghai: Shanghai guji chubanshe, 2002).

*Changsha fuzhi* (长沙府志, Gazetteer of Changsha prefecture) of the Qianlong (乾隆) reign.

*Changsha xianzhi* (长沙县志, Gazetteer of Changsha county) of the Jiaqing (嘉庆) reign.

*Chaozhou fuzhi* (潮州府志, Gazetteer of Chaozhou prefecture) of the Qianlong (乾隆) reign.

Cheng Huaijing (程怀璟), "Chongxiu Huizhou fuzhi xu" (重修徽州府志序, Preface to reproducing the gazetteer of Huizhou prefecture), Daoguang (道光) 7, in *Zhongguo difangzhi jicheng – Daoguang Huizhou fuzhi* (中国地方志集成·道光徽州府志, Collection of gazetteer in China – gazetteer of Huizhou prefecture in Daoguang) (Nanjing: Jiangsu guji chubanshe, 1998).

Cheng Shangkuan (程尚宽), *Xin'an minzu zhi* (新安名族志, Chronicle of influential clans in Xin'an) (Hefei: Huangshan shushe, 2007).

*Chenghai xianzhi* (澄海县志, Gazetteer of Chenghai county) of the Republican times.

*Chongxiu Anhui tongzhi* (重修安徽通志, New Gazetteer of Anhui) of Guangxu (光绪), in *Xuxiu siku quanshu* (续修四库全书, Sequel to complete library of the four treasuries), book 654 (Shanghai: Shanghai guji chubanshe, 2002).

*Chongxiu Yangzhou fuzhi* (重修扬州府志, New Gazetteer of Yangzhou prefecture) of the Kangxi (康熙) reign.

*Daoguang Jining Zhili zhou zhi* (道光济宁直隶州志, Gazetteer of prefecture of Jining, Zhili of Daoguang).

*Dinghai xianzhi* (定海县志, Gazetteer of Dinghai county) of the Jiajing (嘉靖) reign.

Dong Sizhang (董斯张), *Wuxing beizhi* (吴兴备志, Gazetteer of Wuxing).

Fang Chongding (方崇鼎), He Yingsong (何应松) et al., *Xiuning xianzhi* (休宁县志, Gazetteer of Xiuning county), photocopied edition based on the Jiaqing (嘉庆) 20 copy of Qing (Taipei: Taiwan chengwen chubanshe, 1985).

Gu Yanwu (顾炎武), *Zhaoyu zhi* (肇域志, The annals of founding the territories) (Shanghai: Shanghai guji chubanshe, 2004).

Gu Yanwu (顾炎武), *Tianxia junguo libing shu* (天下郡国利病书, Merits and drawbacks of all the provinces and counties in China), collated and annotated by Huang Kun (黄坤) (Shanghai: Shanghai guji chubanshe, 2012).

Guo Pei (郭裴), *Guangdong tongzhi* (广东通志, Chorography of Guangdong), edition of Wanli (万历) 30.

*Hangzhou fuzhi* (杭州府志, Gazetteer of Hangzhou prefecture) of the Qianlong (乾隆) reign.

*Huizhou fuzhi* (徽州府志) of the Daoguang (道光) reign, in *Zhongguo fangzhi congshu* (中国方志丛书, The Chinese gazetteer series) (Taipei: Taiwan chengwen chubanshe, 1975).

*Huizhou fuzhi* (徽州府志, Gazetteer of Huizhou prefecture) of the Hongzhi (弘治) reign.

*Huizhou fuzhi* (徽州府志, Gazetteer of Huizhou prefecture) of the Kangxi (康熙) reign.

*Jiading xianzhi* (嘉定县志, Gazetteer of Jiading county) of the Wanli (万历) reign.

Jiang Dengyun (江登云) and Jiang Shaolian (江绍莲), *Chengyang sanzhi* (橙阳散志, Alternative gazetteer of Chengyang).

*Jiashan xianzhi* (嘉善县志, Gazetteer of Jiashan county) of the Jiaqing (嘉庆) reign.

*Kaixian zhi* (开县志, Gazetteer of Kai county), carved in Xianfeng (咸丰) 3.

*Liangshan xianzhi* (梁山县志, Gazetteer of Liangshan county) of the Jiaqing (嘉庆) reign.

*Longyou xianzhi* (龙游县志, Gazetteer of Longyou county) of the Republican times.

*Ningbao fuzhi* (宁波府志, Gazetteer of Ningbo prefecture) of the Yongzheng (雍正) reign.

*Pinghu xianzhi* (平湖县志, Gazetteer of Pinghu county) of the Kangxi (康熙) reign.

*Qianmentang xiang zhi* (钱门塘乡志, Gazetteer of Qianmentang town).

*Qimen xianzhi* (祁门县志, Gazetteer of Qimen county) of Tongzhi (同治), in *Zhongguo fangzhi congshu* (中国方志丛书, The Chinese gazetteer series) (Taipei: Taiwan chengwen chubanshe, 1975).

*Qimen xianzhi* (祁门县志, Gazetteer of Qimen county) of the Wanli (万历) reign.

*Quzhou fuzhi* (衢州府志, Gazetteer of Quzhou prefecture) of the Tianqi (天启) reign.

*Shanhua xianzhi* (善化县志, Gazetteer of Shanhua county) of the Guangxu (光绪) reign.

*Shezhi* (歙志, Gazetteer of She county) of the Wanli (万历) reign.

Shi Guozhu (石国柱) and Xu Chengyao (许承尧), *Shexian zhi* (歙县志, She county gazetteer), edition of 1937.

Song Minqiu (宋敏求), *Chang'an zhi* (长安志, Gazetteer of Chang'an).

*Taixing xianzhi* (泰兴县志, Gazetteer of Taixing county) of the Kangxi (康熙) reign.

*Tangqi zhi* (塘栖志, Gazetteer of Tangqi) of the Guangxu (光绪) reign.

Wang Rizhen (汪日桢), *Nanxun zhenzhi* (南浔镇志, Gazetteer of Nanxun town), edition of Tongzhi (同治) 2.

Wang Shixing (王士性), *Guangzhi yi* (广志绎, Interpretation to the travel of the broad territory) (Beijing: Zhonghua shuju, 1997).

Weng Shu (翁澍), *Juqu zhi* (具区志, Gazetteer of Juqu).

Wu Jihu (吴吉祜), *Fengnan zhi* (丰南志, Gazetteer of Fengnan).

*Wujiang xianzhi* (吴江县志, Gazetteer of Wujiang county), in "Jiangsu fuxian zhiji 20" (江苏府县志辑20, Collection of prefectural and county gazetteer of Jiangsu, 20), *Zhongguo difangzhi jicheng* (中国地方志集成, Collection of Chinese gazetteers) (Nanjing: Jiangsu guji chubanshe, 1998).

*Wuyuan xian caiji* (婺源县采辑, Comprehensive gazetteer of Wuyuan county).

*Wuyuan xianzhi* (婺源县志, Gazetteer of Wuyuan county) of the Guangxu (光绪) reign.

*Xi Huai yanfa zhi* (西淮盐法志, Records of salt in Western Huai) of Jiaqing (嘉庆).

Xia Xinming (夏辛铭), *Puyuan zhi* (濮院志, Gazetteer of Puyuan), edition of 1928.

Xie Bi (谢陛), *Shezhi* (歙志) of the Wanli (万历) reign.

Xie Yongtai (谢永泰) et al., *Yixian sanzhi* (黟县三志, Gazetteer of Yi county, third version), in *Zhongguodifangzhi congshu* (中国地方志丛书, The Chinese gazetteer series), photocopied edition of the Tongzhi (同治) 9 version (Taipei: Chengwen chubanshe, 1970).

*Xin'an Xiuning mingzu zhi* (新安休宁名族志, Chronicle of famous clans in Xin'an and Xiuning).

*Xiuning xianzhi* (休宁县志, Gazetteer of Xiuning county) of the Jiaqing (嘉庆) reign.

*Xiuning xianzhi* (休宁县志, Gazetteer of Xiuning county) of the Kangxi (康熙) reign, in*Zhongguo fangzhi congshu* (中国方志丛书, The Chinese gazetteer series) (Taipei: Taiwan chengwen chubanshe, 1975).

*Xiuning xianzhi* (休宁县志, Gazetteer of Xiuning county) of the Wanli (万历) reign.

*Xiushui xianzhi* (秀水县志, Gazetteer of Xiushui county) of Wanli (万历), reprint edition of 1925.

Xu Jishe (徐继畲), *Wutai xinzhi* (五台新志, New Gazetteer of Wutai).

Yan Congjian (严从简), *Shuyu zhouzi lu* (殊域周咨録, Records of Information from foreign territories), carved in the Wanli (万历) reign of Ming.

*Yangzhou guchui ci* (扬州鼓吹词, Gazetteer of Yangzhou).

*Yanzhen zhicao* (岩镇志草, Draft of the Yan Town Gazetteer), handwritten edition.

*Yijian zhi* (夷坚志, Records of Yijian).

*Yinxian tongzhi* (鄞县通志, Comprehensive gazetteer of Yin county) of the Republican times (Ningbo: Ningbo chubanshe, 2006, photocopied edition).

*Yixian xuzhi* (黟县续志, Gazetteer of Yi county, second version), in *Zhongguo difangzhi jicheng Anhui fuxian zhiji 56* (中国地方志集成安徽府县志辑 56, Collection of Anhui prefectural gazetteer 56 of Collection of gazetteer of China) (Nanjing: Jiangsu guji chubanshe, 1998).

*Yixian zhi* (黟县志, Gazetteer of Yi county) of the Jiaqing (嘉庆) reign.

*Yixian zhi* (黟县志, Gazetteer of Yi county) of the Kangxi (康熙) reign.

*Zhangzhou fuzhi* (漳州府志, Gazetteer of Zhangzhou prefecture), edition of Guangxu (光绪) 3.

*Zhongjiang xianzhi* (中江县志, Gazetteer of Zhongjiang county), reprinted in 1930.

## 3 Notes and fiction

Cai Yu (蔡羽), "Liaoyang haishen zhuan" (辽阳海神传, Biography of ocean god in Liaoyang), in *Wenshi yinghua – xiaoshuo juan* (文史英华·小说卷, Essence of literature and history – volume of fiction), eds., Bai Shouyi (白寿彝) and annotated by Gong Zhaoji (龚兆吉) (Changsha: Hunan chubanshe, 1993).

Chen Qubing (陈去病),*Wushizhi* (五石脂, Five-color stone ester).

Dong Han (董含), *Sangang zhilue* (三冈识略, Brief information of three ridges) (Shenyang: Liaoning jiaoyu chubanshe, 2000).

Du Bao (杜宝), *Daye zaji* (大业杂记, Miscellaneous records of Daye).

Hu Yuanjing (胡元敬), *Tangqi fengtu ji* (塘栖风土记, Records of customs in Tangqi).

Huang Junzai (黄钧宰), *Jinhu qimo* (金壶七墨, Seven inks in golden kettle) (Shanghai: Shanghai guji chubanshe, 2002).

*Huishang gongsuo zhengxin lu* (徽商公所征信录, Records for public trust of the Huizhou merchant public association) of the Xuantong (宣统) reign.

*Jianwen jixun* (见闻纪训, Records and interpretations of what was seen and heard).

Jin Youli (金友理), *Taihu beika o*(太湖备考, Remarks on Lake Tai), annotated by Xue Zhengxing (薛正兴)(Nanjing: Jiangsu guji chubanshe, 1998).

Kang Jitian (康基田), *Jinsheng weilue* (晋乘蒐略, Weird notes on Shanxi history), carved in Jiaqing (嘉庆) 16.

Letian jushi (乐天居士), *Tongshi – di shiqi zhong – Longwu yishi* (痛史·第十七种·隆武遗事, History of tragedy – book 17 – anecdotes of Longwu), edition of 1911.

Li Dou (李斗), *Yangzhou huafang lu* (扬州画舫录, A record of painted pleasure boat in Yangzhou) (Yangzhou: Guanglin shushe, 2008).

Li Shaowen (李绍文), *Yunjian zazhi* (云间杂识, Miscellaneous notes on Songjiang).

Lu Ji (陆楫), *Jianjiatang zazhu zhaichao* (蒹葭堂杂著摘抄, Excerpts from miscellaneous works of Jianjia hall) (Beijing: Zhonghua shuju, 1985).

*Puchuan suowen ji* (濮川所闻记, Notes of what was heard in Puchuan).

Qu Dajun (屈大均), *Guangdong xinyu* (广东新语, New remarks on Guangdong) (Beijing: Zhonghua shuju, 1985).

Tao Zongyi (陶宗仪), *Shuofu* (说郛, Miscellaneous talks) (Beijing: Zhongguo shudian, 1986).

Wu Jingzi (吴敬梓), *Rulin waishi* (儒林外史, The scholars) (Nanjing: Fenghuang chubanshe, 2011).

*Wufeng lu* (吴风录, Record of customs in Wu).

Xie Zhaozhe (谢肇淛), *Wu zazu* (五杂俎, Five miscellanies).

Xu Chengyao (许承尧), *Sheshi xiantan* (歙事闲谭, Casual chats on affairs in She county) (Hefei: Huangshan shushe, 2001).

Xu Ke (徐珂), *Qing bailei chao* (清稗类钞, Qing petty matters Anthology) (Beijing: Zhonghua shuju, 1986).

Xu Zhongyuan (许仲元), *Sanyi bitan* (三异笔谈, Brush talks on three oddities).

Xue Fucheng (薛福成), *Yong'an biji* (庸庵笔记, Notes of Yong'an).

Yan Zhitui (颜之推), *Yanshi jiaxun* (颜氏家训), interpreted and annotated by Tan Zuowen (檀作文) (Beijing: Zhonghua shuju, 2007).

Yinfu laoren (蟫伏老人), *Kangxi nanxun miji* (康熙南巡秘记, Secret records of emperor Kangxi's southern tour) (Shanghai: Shanghai jinbu shuju, 1910).

*Yueshi bian* (阅世编, Compilation of knowing the world).

Zhang Han (张瀚), *Songchuang mengyu* (松窗梦语, Dream words of pine windows), annotated and commented by Sheng Dongling (盛冬铃) (Beijing: Zhonghua shuju, 1985).

Zhang Siwei (张四维), *Tiaolutang ji* (条麓堂集, Anthology of Tiaolu Hall), collected in the Shanxi University library, carved by Zhang Taizheng (张泰征) in Wanli (万历) 23.

Zhang Xie (张燮), *Dongxiyang kao* (东西洋考, Investigation of the eastern and western oceans), edition of Xiyin xuan congshu (惜阴轩丛书, Xiyinxuan book series) of Qing.

Zhao Jishi (赵吉士), *Jiyuan ji suoji* (寄园寄所寄, Jiyuan's transmitted notes), carved in Kangxi (康熙) 35.

Zheng Shungong (郑舜功), *Riben yijian* (日本一鉴, Guide to Japan), photocopied edition of 1939.

Zhu Yunming (祝允明), *Zhuzi zhiguai lu* (祝子志怪录, Mr. Zhu's record of the weird).

## 4 Anthology, epitaph, and comments on poetry

Ai Nanying (艾南英), *Tianyongzi quanji* (天佣子全集, Complete works of Tianyongzi).

The Archives of Qing, *Guanli hubu shiwu Qi Guizao Xianfeng sannian zhengyue ershiliuri zouzhe*(管理户部事务祁㝹藻咸丰三年正月二十六日奏折, Memorial on the 26th day of the 1st month of Xianfeng 3 by Qi Guizao who is in charge of affairs of the department of revenue).

The Archives of Qing, *Yushi Zhang Wei Xianfeng yuannian shiyue ershiba ri zouzhe* (御史张炜咸丰元年十月二十八日奏折, Memorial on the 28th day of the 10th month of Xianfeng 1 by the censor Zhang Wei).

Bao Shichen (包世臣), *Anwu sizhong* (安吴四种, Four categories of Anwu).

Cai Xiang (蔡襄), *Cao Zhonghui gong wenji* (蔡忠惠公文集, Anthology of Lord Cai Zhonghui).

Cheng Jiasui (程嘉燧), *Songyuan ji'an ji* (松园偈庵集, Anthology of Gentleman Ji'an of the pine garden).

*Doupeng xianhua* (豆棚闲话, Chitchat in beans canopy).

Fan Shouji (范守己), *Yulongzi ji – Quweixinwen* (御龙子集·曲洧新闻, Anthology of Yulongzi – new information from Quwei).

Feng Congwu (冯从吾), "Fengshi jiasheng" (冯氏家乘, Family history of the Feng's), *Shaoxu ji* (少墟集, Anthology of Shaoxu), volume 20, *Qinding siku quanshu* (钦定四库全书, Complete library of the four treasuries made by imperial orders), section *ji*, book 1293.

*Gengshengzhai wen jiaji* (更生斋文甲集, Anthology of Gengsheng chamber, book I).

Gu Yanwu (顾炎武), *Rizhi lu* (日知录, Records of daily understanding).

Gui Youguang (归有光), *Zhenchuan xiansheng ji* (震川先生集, Anthology of Mr. Zhenchuan, in Sibu congkan (四部丛刊, Book series of four treasuries), section *ji*, book 1597 (Shanghai: Shanghai guji chubanshe, 1981).

Gui Zhuang (归庄), *Guizhuang ji* (归庄集, Anthology of Gui Zhuang) (Beijing: Zhonghua shuju, 1962).

Han Bangqi (韩邦奇), *Yuanluo ji* (苑洛集, Anthology of Yuanluo), in *Qinding sikuquanshu* (钦定四库全书, Complete library of the four treasuries made by imperial orders), section *ji*, book 1269.

Hu Zongxian (胡宗宪), *Chouhai tubian* (筹海图编, Atlas for the marine stratagem), edition of complete library of the four treasuries in Wenyuan (文渊) pavilion of Qing.

*Huang Qing zouyi* (皇清奏议, Memorials in Qing).

Huang Xingzeng (黄省曾), *Wuyue shanren ji* (五岳山人集, The Anthology of the recluse of five mountains), in *Siku quanshu cunmu congshu – jibu* (四库全书存目丛书·集部, The reserved catalog of the complete library of the four treasuries – section of collection), book 94, category of alternative *ji* (Jinan: Qilu shushe, 1997).

*Huangchao jingshi wen xubian* (皇朝经世文续编, Royal anthology of practical social management II).

*Huangchao jingshi wenbian* (皇朝经世文编, Royal anthology of practical social management).Jiangsu sheng bowuguan (江苏省博物馆) ed., *Jiangsu sheng Ming Qing yilai beike ziliao xuanji* (江苏省明清以来碑刻资料选集, Selected stele inscriptions in Jiangsu since Ming and Qing) (Beijing: Sanlian shudian, 1959).

*Jin Zhongjiegong wenji* (金忠节公文集, Anthology of Lord Jin Zhongjie).

*Jixi xianzhi caifang biao* (绩溪县志采访表, The list of interviews for the gazetteer of Jixi county).

*Juanshige wen jiaji* (卷施阁文甲集, *Anthology of Juanshi Pavilion I*).

*Junjichu lufu – Guangxidao jianchayushi Zhang Siheng zouzhe* (军机处录副·广西道监察御史章嗣衡奏折, Duplicate copy of the Grand Council – memorial from Zhang Siheng, censor overseeing the Guangxi circuit), the 13th day of the 10th month of Xianfeng (咸丰) 3.

Li Cheng (李澄), *Huaicuo beiyao* (淮鹾备要, Essential of salt in Huai).

Li Guangjin (李光缙), *Jingbi ji* (景璧集, Anthology of Jingbi) (Fuzhou: Fujian renmin chubanshe, 2012).

Li Jingde (黎靖德) ed., *Zhuzi yulei* (朱子语类, Quotations of master Zhu) (Beijing: Zhonghua shuju, 1986).

Li Sui (李燧) and Li Hongling (李宏龄), *Jinyou riji: tongzhou zhonggao – Shanxi piaoshang chengbaiji* (晋游日记·同舟忠告·山西票商成败记, Diary of the trip to Shanxi: advice from a fellow in the same vessel – the rise and fall of Shanxi native bankers), annotated and commented by Huang Jianhui (黄鉴晖) (Taiyuan: Shanxi jingji chubanshe, 2003).

Li Weizhen (李维桢), *Dami shanfang ji* (大泌山房集, Anthology of Dami shanfang), in *Siku quanshu cunmu congshu – jibu* (四库全书存目丛书•集部, The reserved catalog of the complete library of the four treasuries – section of collection), section *ji*, book 152 and 153.

Liang Fangzhong (梁方仲), *Zhongguo lidai hukou, tiandi, tianfu tongji* (中国历代户口、田地、田赋统计, Statistics of residential registry, lands, and land taxes in Chinese history) (Shanghai: Shanghai renmin chubanshe, 1980).

Lin Xichong (林西冲), *Yikuilou xuangao* (挹奎楼选稿, Selected writings of Yikui building).

Liu Kunyi (刘坤一), *Liu Kunyi zoushu* (刘坤一奏疏, Liu Kunyi's memorials) (Changsha: Yuelu shushe, 2013).

Ma Guohan (马国翰), *Zhu ruyi* (竹如意, Bamboo scepter).

*Ming jingshi wenbian* (明经世文编, Ming anthology of practical social management).

*Mingchen zouyi* (明臣奏议, Memorials of Ming officials).

*Moli Wangshi jiawei* (莫厘王氏家谓, Family code of the Wang clan from Moli).

*Shaxi jilue* (沙溪集略, Anthology of Shaxi).

Suzhou lishi bowuguan (苏州历史博物馆) ed., *Ming Qing Suzhou gongshangye beike ji* (明清苏州工商业碑刻集, Collection of stele inscriptions of industry and commerce in Suzhou in Ming and Qing) (Nanjing: Jiangsu renmin chubanshe, 1981).

*Tao Wenyi gong quanji* (陶文毅公全集, Complete works of Lord Tao Wenyi).

*Taoyuan suyu quanshi ci* (桃源俗语劝世词, Ballads of the land of peach blossoms for advising the people of the world) of Huizhou (徽州).*Tongshang geguan Huayang maoyi zongce Guangxu shiqi nian* (通商各关华洋贸易总册光绪十七年, The general volume of China-foreign trades in various customs of trading ports, Guangxu 17).

Wan Biao (万表), *Wanluting gao* (玩鹿亭稿, works of pavilion of playing with deer), *Siming congshu* (四明丛书, Siming book series), ed., Zhang Shouyong (张寿镛), book 7.

Wang Ao (王鏊), *Zhenze ji* (震泽集, Anthology of Zhenze), in *Qinding siku quanshu huiyao* (钦定四库全书荟要, Essence of the complete library of the four treasuries made by the order of the emperor), section *ji*, volume 16843.

Wang Daokun (汪道昆), *Taihan fumo* (太函副墨, Supplementary writings of Taihan).

Wang Daokun (汪道昆), *Taihan ji* (太函集, Anthology of Taihan), in *Xuxiu siku quanshu – jibu* (续修四库全书·集部, Sequel to complete library of the four treasuries), book 1347.*Wang Linchuan ji* (王临川集, Anthology of Wang Linchuan).

Wang Shizhen (王世贞), *Wozhi* (倭志, Records of Japan).

Wang Shizhen (王世贞), *Yanzhou shanren sibu gao* (弇州山人四部稿, Four-category works of the recluse of Yanzhou).

Wang Shizhen (王世贞), *Yanzhou shanren xugao beizhuan* (弇州山人续稿碑传, Sequel to anthology of recluse of Yanzhou and inscriptions), in *Mingdai zhuanji congkan* (明代传记丛刊, Book series of Ming biographies), miscellaneous category, book 55 (Taipei: Taiwan mingwen shuju, 1991).

Wang Shizhen (王世贞), *Zhanggong Juzheng zhuan* (张公居正传, Biography of lord Zhang Juzheng), see *Guochao xianzheng lu* (国朝献徵录, Records of dynastic institutions).*Wangshi jiushu* (汪氏阄书, Deeds of the Wang's).

Wei Xi (魏禧), *Wei Shuzi wenji waibian* (魏叔子文集外编, Additional works of Wei Shuzi's anthology).

Wu Rifa (吴日法), *Huishang bianlan* (徽商便览, Guide to Huizhou merchants).

Xu Fuchu (徐复初), *Chongjian xianzhi ji* (重建县治记, Notes on rebuilding the county seat).

Xu Guo (许国), *Xu Wenmu gong ji* (许文穆公集, Anthology of master Xu Wenmu), 1924 edition of Jiansutang of the Sun's in Wuxi (无锡孙氏简素堂), print in red.

Xu Zhuo (徐卓), *Xiuning suishi* (休宁碎事, Trivial matters in Xiuning), quoting WuWen-kui (吴文奎), *Suntang ji* (苏堂集, Anthology of Suntang).

Xue Lundao (薛论道), *Linshi yixing* (林石逸兴, Leisured pleasure in groves and stones) (Kunming: Yunnan daxue chubanshe, 2010).

*Yantie lun* (盐铁论, Discourses on salt and iron).

Yao Shilin (姚士麟), *Jianzhi bian* (见只编, Works of what was seen and known).

*Yongzheng zhupi yuzhi* (雍正朱批谕旨, Emperor Yongzheng's comments on memorials in red).

*Zhao Nanxing quanji* (赵南星全集, Complete works of Zhao Nanxing).

*Zhenze xiansheng wenji* (震泽先生文集, Anthology of Mr. Zhenze).

*Zhi'an ji* (止庵集, Anthology of Zhi'an).

Zhu Jiaxuan (褚稼轩), *Jianhu miji* (坚瓠秘集, Esoteric anthology of solid gourd).

## 5  Genealogy, chronicle, diary, and memoir

*Chengshi Mengsun gong zhipu* (程氏孟孙公支谱, The genealogy of master Mengsun, the Cheng sub-clan) of She (歙) county.

*Chongxiu gu She Dongmen Xushi zongpu* (重修古歙东门许氏宗谱, Newly compiled genealogy of the Xu clan of the East Gate in ancient She).

*Dunfu nianpu* (钝夫年谱, Dunfu's chronicle) (Taipei: Yuanliu chuban gongsi, 1986).

*Dunhuang Hongshi tongzong pu* (敦煌洪氏通宗谱, General genealogy of the Hong family in Dunhuang) of Wuyuan (婺源).

*Jiyang Jiangshi zupu* (济阳江氏族谱, The genealogy of the Jiang clan in Jiyang) of She (歙) county. *Lingnan Xianshi zongpu* (岭南冼氏宗谱, The genealogy of the Xian clan in Lingnan).

*Qian Xi Xushi zongpu* (迁锡许氏宗谱, The genealogy of the Xu clan who migrates to Wuxi).

*Qingjiang Xiangtian Nieshi chongxiu zupu* (清江香田聂氏重修族谱, The newly compiled genealogy of the Nie clan in Xiangtian, Qingjiang).

*Santian Lishi tongzongpu* (三田李氏统宗谱, General genealogy of the Li clan in Santian) of Wuyuan (婺源).

*Shangchuan Mingjing Hushi zongpu* (上川明经胡氏宗谱, The genealogy of the Hu family of Mingjing, Shangchuan) of Jixi (绩溪).

*She Chun Fangshi huizong tongpu* (歙淳方氏会宗统谱, General genealogy of the Fang clan in She and Chun), carved in Qianlong (乾隆) 18.

*Songtang Huangshi zongpu* (竦塘黄氏宗谱, The genealogy of the Huang clan in Song-tang) of She (歙) county.

*Tandu Huangshi zongpu* (潭渡黄氏宗谱, The genealogy of the Huang clan in Tandu) of She (歙) county.

*Tangyue Baoshi Xuanzhongtang zhipu* (棠樾鲍氏宣忠堂支谱, The genealogy of the Bao sub-clan of Xuanzhong Hall at Tangyue) of She (歙) county.

*Wangshi tongzong pu* (汪氏统宗谱, General genealogy of the whole Wang's Clan).

*Xiguan Zhangshi zongpu* (西关章氏宗谱, The genealogy of the Zhang clan in Xiguan) of Jixi (绩溪).

*Xin'an Chengshi tongzong buzheng tu zuancun* (新安程氏统宗补正图纂存, Reserved materials andcorrected illustrations of the general genealogy of the Cheng clan in Xin'an).

*Xi'nan Jiangshi zupu* (溪南江氏族谱, The genealogy of the Jiang clan in Xi'nan).

*Xin'an Shebei Xushi dongzhi shipu* (新安歙北许氏东支世谱, The genealogy of the Xu sub-clan of eastern branch of northern She, Xin'an).

*Xin'an Zhangshi xuxiu zongpu* (新安张氏续修宗谱, Newly compiled genealogy of the Zhang clan in Xin'an).

*Xinguan Baoshi zhucuntang cipu* (新馆鲍氏著存堂祠谱, The genealogy of the Bao clan of Zhucun Hall in Xinguan) of She (歙) county.

*Xiuning Gulin Huangshi chongxiu zupu* (休宁古林黄氏重修族谱, Newly compiled genealogy of the Huang clan at Gulin, Xiuning).

*Xiuning Shuaidong Chengshi jiapu* (休宁率东程氏家谱, The genealogy of the Cheng clan in Shuaidong, Xiuning).

*Xiuning Ximen Wangshi zongpu* (休宁西门汪氏宗谱, The genealogy of the Wang clan at West Gate, Xiuning).

*Xushi shipu* (许氏世谱, The genealogy of the Xu clan) of She (歙) county.

*Xushi tongzongpu* (许氏统宗谱, General genealogy of the Xu clan).

# 6 Inscriptions, archival materials, roster, and newspaper, etc.

Gugong bowuyuan (故宫博物院) ed., *Jin taishi ji* (金太史集, Anthology of Censor Jin) (Haikou: Hainan chubanshe, 2000).

Ji Yun (纪昀), *Zhongxian dafu Baogong Kenyuan ji pei Wang Gongren mubiao* (中宪大夫鲍公肯园暨配汪恭人墓表, The Epitaph for Mr. Bao Kenyuan, grand master exemplar, and Wang Gongren, his wife).

*Jiushu qidi*(阄书契底, Deeds and contracts) of Huizhou (徽州), collated in the Institute of History Studies, Chinese Academy of Social Sciences, No. 1000461

Li Hua (李华), *Ming Qing yilai Beijing gongshang huiguan beike xuanbian* (明清以来北京工商会馆碑刻选编, Selected stele inscriptions of industrial and commercial guilds in Beijing since Ming and Qing) (Beijing: Wenwu chubanshe, 1980).

Lou Zuyi (娄祖诒), *Zhongguo youyi shiliao* (中国邮驿史料, Historical materials about Chinese postal and courier system) (Beijing: Renmin youdian chubanshe, 1958).

Lugong (路工) ed., *Mingdai gequ xuan* (明代歌曲选, Selected songs of Ming) (Beijing: Gudian wenxue chubanshe, 1956).

*Minguo ribeo* (民国日报, Republican daily).

*Mingzhou Wushi jiadian* (茗洲吴氏家典, Family code of the Wu clan from Mingzhou).

Shanghai bowuguan (上海博物馆), *Shanghai beike ziliao xuanji* (上海碑刻资料选辑, Selected materials of stele inscriptions in Shanghai) (Shanghai: Shanghai renmin chubanshe, 1980).

Suzhou lishi bowuguan (苏州历史博物馆) ed., *Ming Qing Suzhou gongshangye beike ji* (明清苏州工商业碑刻集, Collection of stele inscriptions of industry and commerce in Suzhou in Ming and Qing) (Nanjing: Jiangsu renmin chubanshe, 1981).

*Xiandai shixue* (现代史学, Modern history).

Zhongguo renmin yinhang Shanghai shi fenhang (中国人民银行上海市分行编) eds., *Shanghai qianzhuang shiliao* (上海钱庄史料, Historical materials of Shanghai native banks) (Shanghai: Shanghai renmin chubanshe, 1960).

# 7 Monograph

## *Theory*

Lenin, *Eguo ziben zhuyi de fazhan* (俄国资本主义的发展, The development of capitalism in Russia) (Beijing: renmin chubanshe, 1960).

*Makesi Engesi quanji* (马克思恩格斯全集, Complete works of Marx and Engels) (Beijing: Renmin chubanshe, 2006).

*Makesi Engesi xuanji* (马克思恩格斯选集, Selected works of Marx and Engels) (Beijing: Renmin chubanshe, 1995).

*Mao Zedong xuanji* (毛泽东选集, Selected works of Mao Zedong) (Beijing: Renmin chubanshe, 1991).

Marx, Karl, *The capital* (Beijing: Renmin chubanshe, 2006).

### Academic works of Chinese scholars

Cao Dawei (曹大为), "Zhongguo lishi shang zhenjie guannian de bianqian" (中国历史上贞节观念的变迁, The transformations of conceptions of chastity in Chinese history), *Zhongguo shi yanjiu* (中国史研究, Journal of Chinese Historical Studies), No. 2 (1991).

Chen Hansheng (陈翰笙), *Guangdong nongcun shengchan guanxi yu shengchan li* (广东农村生产关系与生产力, Relations of production and productivity in rural Guangdong) (Shanghai: Shanghai zhongshan wenhua jiaoyu guan, 1934).

Dai Yixuan (戴裔煊), *Mingdai Jia Long jian de Wokou yu Zhongguo ziben zhuyi mengya* (明代嘉隆间的倭寇与中国资本主义萌芽, Japanese pirates during Jiajing and Longqing times in Ming and the sprout of capitalism in China) (Beijing: Zhongguo shehui kexue chubanshe, 1982).

Dou Jiliang (窦季良), *Tongxiang zuzhi zhi yanjiu* (同乡组织之研究, Studies on native-place organizations) (Nanjing: Zhengzhong shuju, 1946).

Fang Zhiyuan (方志远) and Huang Ruiqing (黄瑞卿), "Ming Qing Jiangyou shang dejingying guannian yu touzi fangxiang" (明清江右商的经营观念与投资方向, Business conceptions and investments of Jiangyou merchants in Ming and Qing), *Zhongguo shi yanjiu* (中国史研究, Journal of Chinese Historical Studies), No. 4 (1991).

Ge Guopei (葛国培), "Ningbo bang de xingcheng chutan" (宁波帮的形成初探, An preliminary investigation of the making of the Ningbo group), *Ningbo shifan xuebao* (宁波师范学报), No. 2 (1990).

He Bingdi (Ping-ti Ho) (何炳棣), *Zhongguo huiguan shilun* (中国会馆史论, Treatises on the history of guilds in China) (Taipei: Xuesheng shuju, 1966).

He Jie (贺杰), "Ming Qing Huizhou de zongzu yu shehui liudongxing" (明清徽州的宗族与社会流动性, Huizhou clans and social fluidity in Ming and Qing), paper presented to the Symposium of Ming History of China (1985).

Hu Shi (胡适), *Hu Shi jiashu* (胡适家书, Hu Shi's letters with family) (Beijing: Jincheng chubanshe, 2013).

Lü Zuoxie (吕作燮), "Ming Qing yilai de Dongting shangren" (明清以来的洞庭商人, Merchants from Dongting since Ming and Qing), in *Pingzhun xuekan – Zhongguo shehui jingjishi yanjiu lunji* (平准学刊 – 中国社会经济史研究论集, Pingzhun academic journal – collected works on social economic history in China), ed., Sun Yutang (孙毓棠), No. 1 (Beijing: Zhongguo shangye chubanshe, 1985).

Ming Qing Guangdong sheng shehui jingji yanjiuhui (明清广东省社会经济研究会), *Ming Qing Guangdong shehui jingji yanjiu* (明清广东社会经济研究, Studies on social economy in Guangdong in Ming and Qing) (Guangzhou: Guangdong renmin chubanshe, 1987).

Nanjing daxue lishi xi Ming Qing shi yanjiu shi (南京大学历史系明清史研究室) eds., *Zhongguo ziben zhuyi mengya wenti lunwen ji* (中国资本主义萌芽问题论文集) (Nanjing: Jiangsu renmin chubanshe, 1983).

Quan Hansheng (全汉昇), *Yapian zhanzheng qian Jiangsu de mianfangzhi ye* (鸦片战争前江苏的棉纺织业, Cotton textile industry in Jiangsu before the Opium War), in

*Zhongguo jingji shi luncong* (中国经济史论丛, Series of Chinese economic history), book 2.

Wu Chengming (吴承明), "Guanyu Zhongguo ziben zhuyi mengya de jige wenti" (关于中国资本主义萌芽的几个问题, A few questions regarding the sprout of capitalism in China), *Wen shi zhe* (文史哲), No. 5 (1981).

Yan Zhongping (严中平), "Sichou liuxiang Feilübing baiyin liuxiang Zhongguo" (丝绸流向菲律宾白银流向中国, Silk flowed to Phlippines, and silver flowed to China), *jindaishiyanjiu* (近代史研究), No. 1 (1981).

Yang Dequan (杨德泉), "Qingdai qianqi liang Huai yanshang ziliao chuji" (清代前期两淮盐商资料初辑, Materials of salt merchants in Huainan and Huaibei in early Qing, the first issue), *Jianghai xuekan* (江海学刊), No. 11 (1962).

Ye Xian'en (叶显恩), *Ming Qing Huizhou nongcun shehui yu dianpu zhi* (明清徽州农村社会与佃仆制, Rural society and serfdom in Huizhou in Ming and Qing) (Hefei: Anhui renmin chubanshe, 1983).

Zhang Shouguang (张守广), "Ming Qing shiqi Ningbo shangren jituan de chansheng he fazhan" (明清时期宁波商人集团的产生和发展, The rise and development of the Ningbo merchant group in Ming and Qing), *Nanjing shida xuebao* (南京师大学报), No. 3 (1991).

Zhang Zhengming (张正明), "Jinbang de dingsheng shiqi – Qingmo" (晋帮的鼎盛时期 – 清末, The heyday of the Shanxi merchant gang – the late Qing times), unpublished manuscript.

Zhao Lingyu (赵令瑜), "Zhongguo huiguan zhi shehuixue de fenxi" (中国会馆之社会学的分析, A sociological analysis of China's guilds), Department of Sociology, Yenching University, Bachelor's degree thesis, 1937.

### Scholarly works of non-chinese scholars

Mikeluoer, Maikeer and Leiyinhade Xideer, *Ouzhou jiating shi* (欧洲家庭史, The European family), translated by Zhao Shiling (赵世玲), Zhao Shiyu (赵世瑜), and Zhou Shangyi (周尚意) (Beijing: Huaxia chubanshe, 1987).

Tōa Dōbunkai (东亚同文会), *Shina shōbetsu zenshi* (支那省别全志, Full chronicle of Chinese provinces) (Tokyo: Tōa Dōbunkai, 1917–1920).

Usui Sachiko (臼井佐知子), "Huishang jiqi wangluo" (徽商及其网络, Huizhou merchants and their networks), originally published in *Chūgoku, shakai to bunka* (中国, 社会と文化), No. 6 (1991); translated version published in *Anhui shixue* (安徽史学), No. 1 (1992).

Weber, Max, *The Protestant Ethic and the Spirit of Capitalism*.

Yamawaki Teijirō (山脉悌二郎), *Nagasaki no Tōjin bōeki* (长崎的华人贸易, Chinese businessmen in Nagasaki) (Tōkyō: Yoshikawa Kōbunkan, 1964).

Yasuhiko Kimiya (木宫泰彦), *Ri Zhong wenhua jiaoliu shi* (日中文化交流史, History of cultural exchange between Japan and China), translated by Hu Xinian (胡锡年) (Beijing: Shangwu yinshuguan, 1980).

# Index

For Product Safety Concerns and Information please contact our EU
representative GPSR@taylorandfrancis.com
Taylor & Francis Verlag GmbH, Kaufingerstraße 24, 80331 München, Germany

www.ingramcontent.com/pod-product-compliance
Ingram Content Group UK Ltd.
Pitfield, Milton Keynes, MK11 3LW, UK
UKHW020959180425
457613UK00019B/751